INTRODUCTION TO CRIMINAL JUSTICE

INTRODUCTION TO CRIMINAL JUSTICE

FIRST EDITION

Edited by Stephanie Manzi and Sean Varano

cognella
SAN DIEGO

Bassim Hamadeh, CEO and Publisher
John Remington, Executive Editor
Gem Rabanera, Senior Project Editor
Susana Christie, Senior Developmental Editor
Celeste Paed, Associate Production Editor
Jess Estrella, Senior Graphic Designer
Kylie Bartolome, Licensing Associate
Stephanie Adams, Senior Marketing Program Manager
Natalie Piccotti, Director of Marketing
Kassie Graves, Senior Vice President, Editorial
Jamie Giganti, Director of Academic Publishing

Printed in the United States of America.

cognella® | ACADEMIC PUBLISHING
3970 Sorrento Valley Blvd., Ste. 500, San Diego, CA 92121

CONTENTS

THE LAW

EDITOR'S INTRODUCTION

The foundations of the criminal justice system are built on two things: The first is a general understanding of why society defines certain behaviors as criminal, and what we know about these "crimes." The second is the creation of and purpose behind our laws. The American criminal justice system employs over two million people and is designed to provide justice to all members of society, treat individuals as equal before the law, and protect its citizens against future crimes.

In "Crime in Society," author Joycelyn Pollock begins by asking the reader "What is crime?" to provide an understanding of the difficulty answering what appears to be a simple question. This is a difficult question to answer because sometimes a behavior that is labeled criminal by one culture is not defined as criminal in another, just as a behavior can be criminal in one jurisdiction yet not in another. An example of a cultural difference in defining behaviors as criminal is honor killing. In Pakistan, killing a woman who has cheated on her husband is not considered murder, but it is considered murder in the United States. An example of a behavior labeled as criminal in one jurisdiction but not another in the United States are the laws pertaining to the use of recreational marijuana; in some states marijuana use is legal for those of a certain age while in other states it is still illegal, regardless of the age of the user. The latter is also an example of how the definition of crime changes over time; marijuana was once illegal in every state, but over time several states have decided to either completely legalize its use or lessen the penalties for use. This foundational information prepares readers for the overarching focus of Pollock's writing, which is to highlight how a behavior becomes a crime, patterns of crime, sources of crime, and crime rates.

In "Law and Society," Pollock provides the reader with an overview of the purpose of law in general, and then discusses the specific purposes of criminal law. This general understanding of the law provides a framework within which to explore critical issues, such as the differences between criminal and civil law, challenges to created laws, the elements of a crime that need to be proven in order to convict a person of a crime, and defenses to criminal culpability.

READING 1.1

LAW AND SOCIETY

Joycelyn Pollock

[READING] PREVIEW

- What Is the Purpose of Law? What Is the Purpose of Criminal Law?
- What Is the Origin of Our Legal System?
- What Are Some Differences Between Civil and Criminal Law?
- What Are Some Constitutional Challenges to Creating Laws?
- What Are the Elements of a Crime?
- What Are Some Defenses to Criminal Culpability?
- What Are Some Recent Issues in Criminal Law?
- Focus on Data: Is Medical Marijuana Crime or Cure?
- Summary
- Critical Thinking Exercises

WE TAKE THE LAW FOR GRANTED, but it is important to continue our critical thinking stance and take a moment to think about the purpose and origins of law. There is a tendency to believe that the law is objective, neutral, and predictable; is that true? There is a belief that we all agree on what constitutes criminal behavior; is that true? Why are certain behaviors defined as crimes? Who do we excuse from criminal culpability? In this [reading], we will answer these questions and others before moving on to describe in more detail the American court system. As always, it is important to understand the fundamentals before one can discuss current issues.

[...] [M]any court cases are cited and the law is described as the outcome of a court's legal analysis of the issues, e.g., why some piece of evidence is subject to the exclusionary rule while another is not; why someone is legally culpable for their actions and another is not. Legal analysis is a specific type of critical thinking. Our "Focus on Data" sections ask questions that require empirical analysis; however, we could be asking legal questions that require legal analysis. In this form of critical thinking, the legal issue or question is addressed by exploring precedent cases, legal rules, and making determinations based on these "facts." *Objective* legal analysis doesn't decide a case and then construct an argument to support one's opinion, but, rather, looks to build and/or extend legal principles by carefully utilizing existing law.

What IS the Purpose of Law? What IS the Purpose of Criminal Law?

The law serves as a written embodiment of society's norms and morals. It regulates relationships between people in order to ensure fair dealings, e.g., between employer and employee; landlord and tenant, or parties to a contract. It makes business and personal relationships more predictable and, by doing so, creates stability in society. The purpose of criminal law is to:

- define the wrongs that are considered necessary to protect individuals
- define the method of determining guilt or innocence
- designate the type of punishment or treatment following conviction for violating the laws of society.[1]

Why are some behaviors prohibited through law? **Natural law** refers to the belief that some laws exist in the natural world and can be discovered by reason. Natural law theorists equate law with morality—what is immoral is illegal and what is illegal is immoral. In fact, St. Augustine argued that an immoral law is no law at all because law must conform to natural laws of morality. **Positivist law** theorists believe that law is entirely a man-made creation (not part of the natural world) and, thus, law can be, but is not necessarily, relevant to questions of morality. Related to the discussion of natural versus positivist views of law are the concepts of ***mala in se*** acts (wrong in themselves) which are said to be intrinsically wrong acts; as compared to ***mala prohibita*** acts that are behaviors prohibited in certain societies, but not necessarily inherently wrong. We can say, for instance, murder is a *mala in se* crime, but not paying your taxes or driving on the wrong side of the road are *mala prohibita* crimes. These acts are wrong only because the law says so, there is nothing inherently evil about the actions.

Positivists would argue that an extremely immoral law (e.g., Jim Crow laws or the Nuremberg Laws of Nazi Germany[2]) are still legitimate laws as long as they were passed according to legal procedures of the time; natural law theorists would argue that such laws are not legitimate because they offend natural laws of morality. This is not just a theoretical or philosophical argument—consider that civil disobedience is premised on the belief that the existing law is wrong and those who commit civil disobedience believe that they have moral authority to contest the law.

Recall, we discussed the **social contract** in [...], a concept originating with Thomas Hobbes and John Locke in the Age of Enlightenment. The social contract refers to the "contract" individuals make when living in civil society where certain liberties are given up in return for being protected by society. We give up the "right" to steal what we want in return for society's protection against our being victimized by others. We agree to follow the law but, in return, society should impose laws that are minimally intrusive upon our individual liberties. Law can be considered always balancing individual liberty and societal control. According to John Stuart Mill, a famous philosopher, the law should only exist if it protects against harm. There are three forms of harm that criminal law protects against:

- protection from the harm caused by others
- protection from the harm caused by ourselves
- protection of societal morals.

The most obvious protection that the criminal law provides is protection against harm caused by others. Laws against homicide, rape, theft, and arson offer obvious protections. If we are harmed, these laws ensure that the offender will be punished if caught. Some legal writers identify a second set of wrongs that are not harmful but are offensive. Laws against public indecency or public disturbance aren't exactly prohibiting *harmful* behaviors but, rather, behaviors that are offensive to the majority of the population. One might say, then, that these "harm" our sense of order rather than threaten our physical security.

The second form of protection that the law provides is protection against harm caused by ourselves. So-called **paternalistic laws** protect us against our own foolish behavior. Seat belt laws are one example of a paternalistic law. Although you may prefer to drive your car without such a restraint, you will be punished with a fine if you do so. Paternalistic laws exist with the expectation that they will deter most people from doings acts that are not in their best interest.

The third form of protection the law provides is protection of societal morals. We used to have many more laws that protected societal morals. Laws against businesses operating on Sunday, blasphemy, and adultery may all be relics of the past, but some of our current laws (gambling, pornography, prostitution) still have the major purpose of enforcing society's morals. The most controversial court cases, such as challenges to consensual sodomy laws in *Lawrence v. Texas*[3] or same-sex marriage in *Obergefell v. Hodges*,[4] involve arguments between the law's role in protecting society's morals and whether laws should exist to protect individuals' rights to private, consensual behaviors. Laws related to obscenity, pornography, gambling, prostitution, and even drugs are justified by those who support them by legal moralism. Even though legal moralism may be a legitimate justification for laws, privacy rights often conflict with the government's right to enforce morality because we live in a heterogenous society where belief systems about right and wrong conflict.

In some cases, individuals may agree that a particular action is immoral but at the same time believe that the government should not have the power to restrict an individual's choice. For

EXHIBIT 1.1.1 Jim Obergefell sued when the state of Ohio refused to recognize his marriage to John Arthur. The Supreme Court weighed the individual's right to make decisions about personal and private matters and equal protection against states' rights to utilize their police power to pass laws defining the parameters of marriage and, in that way, enforce their view of morality. The Court ultimately ruled in his favor and held that states could not ban same-sex marriages and they must recognize same-sex marriages that took place in other states.

Source: AP

instance, some who advocate decriminalization of drugs do so because of cost effectiveness or libertarian reasons, not necessarily because they approve of drug use. One other thing to think about is that sometimes the state loses its moral authority to condemn actions; for instance, states have little moral ground to justify laws against gambling when there is a state lottery. Laws that are based on the rationale of moral harm are usually the most controversial of all laws, and they have been, and continue to be, subject to shifts in public opinion and concern.

What Is the Origin of Our Legal System?

Our criminal law system in the United States is especially complex, because the criminal law is derived from English common law, statutory law, and our own case law tradition, split into 50 different state jurisdictions, the federal system, and thousands of counties and municipalities. We can trace the history of law back to very early codes, such as the Code of Hammurabi (ca. 2000 BCE), which mixed secular and religious rules of behavior. These codes also standardized punishments. However, most of our present-day crimes in the United States have their origins in the so-called **common law**. This was the law that developed in England. William the Conqueror (1066) and his son, Henry I (1100–35), are generally credited with the development of a national court system that involved judges who traveled across England and provided guidance to local magistrates. The effect was a gradual consistency in court decisions that led to the establishment of similar decisions in similar cases, which became known as the "common law." Eventually, judges decided the cases that came before them according to established principles from prior cases. In 1765, William Blackstone published *Commentaries on the Laws of England*.[5] This work was the most comprehensive written source of the common law at the time, and is still cited as a legal source.

Common law became the starting point for American law. Gradually, states passed their own criminal codes that supplanted the common law, but if a particular code was silent on an issue, many courts would fall back to common law principles. For instance, in the 1970 case of *Keeler v. Superior Court*,[6] the defendant was prosecuted for intentionally killing his wife's unborn child by kicking her in the stomach. However, because the California statute in question defined homicide as the killing of a "person," and the common-law definition of person did not include the unborn, Keeler could not be prosecuted for the death of the fetus. This led to California and other states changing their criminal code by redefining "person" to include a fetus, or creating the new crime of feticide. However, the decision in the *Keeler* case had to be made based on common-law definitions because the California Penal Code was silent on the issue.

Today, almost all crimes in all states are "statutory crimes," meaning that the state criminal code defines it as a crime. When a legislative body (federal or state) determines that certain conduct is undesirable and should be forbidden, a bill is prepared describing what conduct should be prohibited. This is introduced in the state house of representatives or the state senate, and is voted upon by the elected members of the legislative body. If both houses of the state legislature approve the bill, it then goes to the governor for consideration and approval. If the chief executive officer signs the legislation, it then becomes a law to be enforced by those involved in the justice process. Even if the chief executive officer refuses to sign (in other words, vetoes the bill), the bill may become law if enough members of the legislative body approve it, overriding the veto. The same process

To view a few selected state penal codes, go to http://www.statutes.legis.state.tx.us/Index.aspx. (Texas); http://www.legis.state.wv.us/WVcode/code.cfm?chap=61&art=1. (West Virginia); http://www.leginfo.ca.gov/cgi-bin/calawquery?codesection=pen. (California).

applies at the federal level in the creation of federal crimes. The legislature is permitted to define criminal offenses in any way it chooses, as long as the law is not arbitrary and does not violate state or federal constitutions.

States have primary **police power**, which is the authority to enact and enforce legislation to protect the health, welfare, morals, and safety of the people of the state. The 10th Amendment to the Constitution was added to make clear that the powers not delegated to the United States by the Constitution would remain in the states, respectively, and the people. The 10th Amendment states:

> The powers not delegated to the United States by the Constitution, nor prohibited by it to the States, are reserved to the States respectively, or to the people.

The federal government has no inherent police power. In the federal system, there have never been common-law crimes, because the federal government only has the power that is delegated to it by the Constitution. Certain crimes, such as treason, are federal crimes because the Constitution grants to the federal government the specific right to define and prosecute treason. Congress may also pass laws that are related to one of the express powers granted to the federal government by the Constitution. The enumerated powers granted to the federal government are found primarily in Article I, Section 8 of the Constitution. Federal crimes must be derived from these enumerated powers. For example, under the power to regulate interstate and foreign commerce, Congress has created federal crimes such as transporting stolen vehicles (interstate) and kidnapping (with interstate elements). Counterfeiting is specifically mentioned in Article I, Section 8 as a federal crime. Drug smuggling comes from the federal power to protect our borders, but other drug laws are justified under the power to regulate interstate commerce. In the last 30 years, the number of new federal laws has increased dramatically with attendant increases in the federal law enforcement, judicial, and correctional systems.

To look at the United States Criminal Code, go to http://www.law.cornell.edu/uscode/18/usc_sup_01_18.html

Cities, counties, townships, and municipal corporations also have limited authority to make and enforce rules and regulations. State legislatures have given these units of government the power to create laws as long as the regulations and ordinances do not conflict with the U.S. Constitution, the state constitution, or the laws of the state. The state may withhold, grant, or withdraw powers and privileges as it sees fit. City ordinances may vary quite a bit and are constantly being updated and revised in response to citizens' concerns.

What Are Some Differences Between Civil and Criminal Law?

Early codes of law did not differentiate between what we might call public wrongs and private wrongs. Today, we have separated criminal law (public wrongs) and civil law (private wrongs). **Criminal law** is the branch or division of law that defines crimes and provides for their punishment. In a criminal case, the state pursues justice to preserve the public peace. On the other hand, in **civil law** a person seeks a remedy against their perceived wrongdoer by bringing a civil, or *tort*, action. **Torts** are personal wrongs. Some examples of torts are assault, defamation, intentional infliction of emotional distress, and arson. *Torts* and *crimes* are not synonyms. While there is a great deal of overlap between crimes and torts, some crimes are not torts, and some torts are not crimes.

With torts, the emphasis is on adjusting the conflicting interests of individuals to achieve a desirable social result. The aggrieved party is the plaintiff and he or she must pay for the cost of the trial, although if he or she wins the court may order the defendant to reimburse the plaintiff for costs incurred. There may also be punitive damages assessed in addition to compensatory damages. For example, if Ann hits Bob, causing him bodily injury, Bob may bring an action in court for recovery of expenses and for compensation for losses incurred. The state may also initiate an action against Ann for assault and prosecute the case in criminal court. You may remember that there was a successful civil suit against O.J. Simpson for wrongful death *after* his acquittal in criminal court. It is entirely possible for a defendant to "win" in one court and "lose" in the other, partially because of the different burdens of proof in civil versus criminal court. Exhibit 1.1.2 presents some examples of torts and comparable crimes if they exist.

Victims are essentially witnesses in a criminal case, not parties in the action, as they are in a civil case. That is why criminal cases are called "*State v. Defendant* "while in civil cases, the plaintiff is a named party in the case title. It is not correct to say, however, that victims are ignored in criminal prosecutions. Prosecutors will often confer with victims before offering plea bargains and take their wishes into account in terms of charging decisions. Victim witness statements are heard in court before sentencing in most jurisdictions. There is a difference in the goal of criminal and civil justice however. In civil law, the goal is to secure one's compensation for loss or injury and, if appropriate, punitive damages, while the aim of the prosecutor is justice (whatever that might mean).

What Are Some Constitutional Challenges to Creating Laws?

The federal government, states, and municipalities have great powers, but they do not have the power to pass a law that violates one of the rights granted by the United States Constitution. [...]

EXHIBIT 1.1.2 Examples of Torts Compared to Crimes

Tort	Definition	Crime
Assault	Intentionally threatening harmful or offensive contact creating reasonable fear	Assault
Battery	Harmful or offensive contact with a person without consent	Assault (assault and battery is combined in criminal law)
False imprisonment	Confinement without legal authority against consent	False imprisonment
Intentional infliction of emotional distress	Intentional conduct that results in extreme emotional distress	n/a
Trespass	Intentional entrance onto the land of another without lawful excuse	Trespass
Conversion	Willful interference with plaintiff's possessory rights of property	Embezzlement
Defamation	Intentional false claim that may harm the reputation of plaintiff	Libel, slander
Invasion of privacy	Intrusion into the personal life of another person without just cause	n/a (although voyeurism, computer crimes, wiretapping, and other crimes address similar behavior)
Breach of confidence	Disclosure of private information conveyed in confidence to detriment of plaintiff	n/a (honest services fraud may address similar behavior)
Fraud	False representation with intention to induce harm or loss to other party	Fraud (criminal law limits to financial loss or injury)
Tortious interference	Intentionally damaging the plaintiff's contractual or other business relationships	n/a
Nuisance	Preventing owners of quiet enjoyment of real property	Public nuisance (somewhat different definition)
Breach of duty of care	Not adhering to a reasonable standard of care while performing acts that could possibly harm others	This would be an attendant circumstance to a crime that resulted in death or serious injury, e.g., involuntary manslaughter

[P]rotections protections are found in the first ten Amendments, which make up the **Bill of Rights**. We are protected against laws that are vague, punish behavior after the fact (**ex post facto laws**), or infringe upon our freedom of expression, association, religion, or right to bear arms. Furthermore, laws that treat people in a discriminatory manner or that unreasonably infringe upon individual privacy rights are prohibited. A summary of some of the rights granted in the Bill of Rights which might give rise to a challenge against a criminal law appears in Exhibit 1.1.3.

EXHIBIT 1.1.3 Bill of Rights

1st Amendment: Freedom of religion, expression, association
2nd Amendment: Right to bear arms
3rd Amendment: Right not to have soldiers quartered in people's homes
4th Amendment: Right to be free from unreasonable governmental search and seizure
5th Amendment: Right to be free from compulsory self-incrimination, federal right to grand jury, protection against double jeopardy, due process
6th Amendment: Right to an impartial jury trial that is speedy and public, with specified due process elements
7th Amendment: Right to trial in suit at common law, jury to be trier of fact
8th Amendment: Right against excessive bail, right to be free from cruel and unusual punishment
9th Amendment: States "The enumeration in the Constitution, of certain rights, shall not be construed to deny or disparage others retained by the people."
10th Amendment: Reserves all other powers not specifically delegated in the Constitution to the states

There has been a great deal of press over federal, state, and local attempts to control the sale and/or possession of firearms. This controversy has reignited after the mass killing in an Orlando nightclub in June of 2016 and we explored the research relating to the effectiveness of gun control laws [...]. As you probably know, there are legal challenges to these laws which are based on the 2nd Amendment's right to bear arms and the Supreme Court's interpretation of that right as an individual right in *D.C. v. Heller* (2008) and *McDonald v. Chicago* (2010).[7] Gun control laws range from outright bans (e.g. of some types of weapons or by some groups of people) to background checks before purchases. Each law must be subjected to scrutiny to determine if it unduly interferes with one's 2nd Amendment rights, but it is not correct to assume that a right enumerated in the Bill of Rights cannot be subject to *reasonable* restrictions. For instance, the 1st Amendment gives you freedom of speech, but you cannot defame someone with lies; the

2nd Amendment protects your right to bear arms, but no one argues against laws that prohibit children from buying firearms; even though the 4th Amendment protect your from unreasonable governmental invasion of your home or papers, government agents can still search your home with a warrant; and, in similar ways, all of the rights provided in the Bill of Rights are subject to reasonable restrictions.

Other challenges to the constitutionality of laws are based on at least one of the following arguments:

- vagueness
- ex post facto
- equal protection
- 1st Amendment rights
- right to privacy.

Vagueness. It is a fundamental principle of criminal law that the legislation must not be vague, meaning that there is some reasonable doubt as to the meaning of the law. In vagueness challenges, the law is criticized as being so unclear as to what is prohibited that reasonable people would not have proper notification that some act was wrong.

In *City of Chicago v. Morales*,[8] the Supreme Court struck down an anti-gang law passed by Chicago City Council in order to control gang activity. The law/ordinance prohibited those "believed to be criminal street gang members" from "loitering in any public place." Criticisms of this law centered on the vague nature of identifying who were street gang members and the vagueness of the terms "loitering" and "public place." The majority of the Court objected to the fact that it was solely within the police officer's discretion to define when loitering was occurring. The Supreme Court, in this case, indicated that there may be anti-gang laws that could pass the vagueness test, but they needed to be written in a way that definitely stated what actions would be defined as criminal.

Basically, the right to be free from vague and overbroad laws comes from the 5th and 14th Amendments. Both Amendments provide that an individual should receive "due process of law" before being deprived of life, liberty, or property. The 5th Amendment provision has been interpreted to provide protection against due process violations by federal actors (such as the FBI), and the 14th Amendment provision protects us from due process violations by state governmental actors (such as your municipal police). **Due process** has been defined as the procedures designed to protect against error in the governmental deprivation of life, liberty, and property. Due process includes the right to notice (to know what we are being accused of). Obviously, in order to have notice, a law must be clear and not subject to arbitrary definitions.

In *Skilling v. United States*,[9] Jeffrey Skilling, one of the executives of Enron who ended up in prison after the collapse of the huge energy company, challenged his federal conviction under what is informally called the "honest services" law. The federal law made it a crime to deprive your employer or anyone owed a **fiduciary duty** to your honest services. A fiduciary duty is the requirement to prioritize that person's interests over one's own interests—such as a stockbroker to a client. The federal law was used successfully in many corruption cases and was especially useful to prosecutors when they could not prove specific bribes or kickbacks were received or offered in return for specific acts, although they could prove a pattern of behavior that rose to a level that indicated the "honest services" of the accused were compromised by some inappropriate enrichment. The Supreme Court in June 2010 held that the law was void for vagueness, arguing that a reasonable person would not know when they violated the law. The holding spurred many public corruption defendants to file challenges to their convictions.

Ex Post Facto Laws

The U.S. Constitution and state constitutions specifically prohibit ex post facto laws. The two sections of the federal Constitution that relate to ex post facto laws are Article I, Section 9, which provides that "no bill of attainder or ex post facto law shall be passed," and Section 10, which provides that "[n]o state shall ... pass any ex post facto law."[10] These provisions were added to the Constitution of the United States and similar provisions have been added to the constitutions of the respective states to prohibit legislative bodies from punishing a person for an act that was neither a crime nor punishable when the act was committed, or from increasing the punishment after the fact. Two critical elements are necessary to establish an ex post facto claim:

- The law must be retrospective—that is, it must apply to events occurring before its enactment.
- It must disadvantage the offender affected by it.[11]

A mere procedural change in the law, not increasing punishment, or not changing the elements of the offense, does not result in a constitutional violation. A law may be invalid as ex post facto toward a particular person who committed an act before its enactment, but that does not affect its validity generally to those who commit the crime after the legislation has passed.

Even though defining an act as criminal and/or punishing an act retroactively violates ex post facto prohibitions, if the governmental action is considered administrative as opposed to punitive, there is no violation. Laws forcing sex offenders to register, even those who were already convicted of a sex crime and serving their sentence, seems as if it is imposing retroactive punishment; however, the Supreme Court decided that it was not a criminal punishment to register, but rather, a regulation or administrative action, and therefore, there was no violation of the ex post facto laws prohibition.[12] Later cases have been decided differently based on state constitutions. A new law that forced convicted sex offenders to register for longer than their original sentence entailed was ruled a violation of the ex post facto prohibition under the Oklahoma constitution.[13] Laws that allow the indefinite commitment of sexually violent predators in mental institutions have also faced ex post facto challenges and, in *Kansas v. Hendricks*,[14] the Supreme Court has ruled that such laws do not violate either ex post factor prohibitions or double jeopardy because commitment to a mental institution is not punishment.

Equal Protection Violations

The 14th Amendment to the Constitution prohibits the government from treating "similarly situated" people differently. That is, if two groups are similar, then they must be treated equally under the law unless there is a substantial governmental objective to be served in treating them differently. The 14th Amendment states:

> No State shall make or enforce any law which shall abridge the privileges or immunities of citizens of the United States, nor shall any State deprive any person of life, liberty, or property, without due process of law, *nor deny to any person within its jurisdiction the equal protection of the laws*. [emphasis added]

The government must have a very good reason for treating different racial, ethnic, or religious groups differently under the law. If a law that is neutral on its face differentially affects only one group of people, it would also be scrutinized.

In 1967, the Supreme Court struck down Virginia's **miscegenation laws**, which made it a crime to marry someone of a different race.[15] The Court held that the state did not have a reason that was sufficiently important to justify treating those who wanted to marry someone from another race and those who married within their own race differently. The holding invalidated all miscegenation laws in not only Virginia, but also the other states that had them.

In the case *In re Michael M.*,[16] a California statutory rape law was challenged. The law made statutory rape a crime that could only be committed by male perpetrators against female victims. The argument was that the law violated equal protection because it treated male and female actions differently by defining the crime in such a way that only men could be perpetrators and only girls could be victims. In this case, the Supreme Court upheld the law because the parties were *not* considered similarly situated, in that only female victims could become pregnant, and the law's imputed purpose was to prevent teenage pregnancy. Through the 1970s and 1980s, however, sexual assault laws were rewritten in most states with gender neutral language so that boys and men can be victims of sexual assault, and girls and women can be prosecuted as perpetrators.

Many laws that treat men and women differently have been struck down, such as laws that had different drinking ages (*Craig v. Boren*[17]). However, in *Rostker v. Goldberg*, [18] the Supreme Court in 1981 upheld the law that only required young men, not young women, to register for the draft. If this legal mandate was challenged today under equal protection grounds, the holding of the current Supreme Court might be different. In equal protection cases, a law that treats groups differently can be upheld if (a) the groups are not "similarly situated," or (b) if the reason for the difference passes the so-called "strict scrutiny" standard, which requires that the government have a substantial and important government purpose and the difference is narrowly tailored to meet that purpose.

1st Amendment Rights

Neither the states nor the federal government can pass a law that *unreasonably* limits 1st Amendment rights. As you know, the 1st Amendment protects our freedoms of speech, association, and religion.

> Congress shall make no law respecting an establishment of religion, or prohibiting the free exercise thereof; or abridging the freedom of speech, or of the press; or the right of the people peaceably to assemble, and to petition the government for a redress of grievances.

The government does have a right to pass laws that do not unduly interfere with these rights. Thus, for instance, if our speech creates an imminent danger to others, it can be prohibited and even punished. One does not have the right to incite a riot, utter a threat, or verbally agree to commit a crime.

When is a threat serious enough to be prosecuted as a crime? Consider the case of Justin Carter. Carter was an eighteen-year-old Texas student who, on a gaming website, was in an argument with another gamer who said that he must be crazy. Carter responded with this statement: "I'm (messed) up in the head alright, I think I'ma SHOOT UP A KINDERGARTEN ... AND WATCH THE BLOOD OF THE INNOCENT RAIN DOWN ... AND EAT THE BEATING HEART OF ONE OF THEM." A different person took a screen-shot of the exchange and sent it to police in Comal County, Texas, and Justin was arrested in 2013 for making a terroristic threat. The Texas law in question defines a criminal threat as:

> A person commits an offense if he threatens to commit any offense involving violence to any person or property with intent to: 4) cause impairment or interruption of public communications, public transportation, public water, gas, or power supply or other public services: 5) place the public or a substantial group of the public in fear of serious bodily injury.

He was jailed with adults and beaten by other jail inmates before being able to make bail. His trial is set to begin sometime in 2016.[19] Although many legal experts contend that his actions do not meet the definition of a terroristic threat, the determination to charge is within the prosecutor's discretion and it will be up to the jury to decide if he is guilty.

In *Texas v. Johnson* (1989), an individual was arrested and punished under a Texas statute that made flag burning illegal. The Supreme Court ruled that the law violated 1st Amendment rights because flag burning was defined as symbolic speech.[20] This case decision is still controversial and a large number of people believe that burning the American flag, even if done as a protest, should be criminalized. In response, Congress has considered a proposal for a constitutional amendment that would criminalize flag burning. This illustrates the dynamic nature of law—what is criminal today may not be tomorrow, or vice versa.

Other constitutional challenges may involve the 1st Amendment protections of religion, speech, or association. Generally, one has the right to speak, associate freely, and practice one's religion without state interference. However, laws can be passed if the behavior in question harms others or intrudes unduly on governmental interests in safety and order. These areas can raise interesting questions in how to balance individual freedoms and societal interests. Should worshipers, for instance, be allowed to sacrifice goats as part of their religion, or should they be bound by animal cruelty laws? Should followers of certain religions be allowed to have multiple wives, or be subject, as everyone else, to bigamy laws? These challenges to created laws are always difficult and are resolved by balancing individual interests against government interests.

Privacy Violations

The right to privacy is not identified specifically in the Constitution, but has been recognized by the Supreme Court in various case decisions. Basically, the Justices' position in these decisions has been that the framers of the Constitution meant that privacy rights should exist, based on their language in certain amendments, such as the 4th Amendment. One of the most important cases that established the protected right of privacy against governmental interference was *Griswold v. Connecticut*.[21] In that case, the Supreme Court struck down Connecticut's criminal law that punished the distribution of information regarding birth control and contraceptives to married couples. According to Justice William O. Douglas, the 1st, 3rd, 4th, 5th, 9th, and 14th Amendments can be read to construe a privacy right that restricts the government from interfering with private decisions of procreation by a married couple. *Griswold* and similar case decisions identifying a right of privacy even though it is not specifically enumerated in the Bill of Rights, were used as the precedent for the *Roe v. Wade*[22] decision which invalidated laws criminalizing all abortions.

The balance between individual liberty and governmental interest in many so-called privacy cases is typically the individual's right to make personal decisions versus protection of society's morals. Laws against drugs, pornography, gambling, and prostitution have been challenged under the privacy rationale, but generally have lost to the argument that the government's interest in societal safety and protection of societal morals justifies such laws. Laws against same-sex consensual sexual intercourse were ruled a violation of the Constitution in *Lawrence v. Texas*.[23] Many commentators believed that the decision in *Lawrence* signaled that other privacy challenges would be successful as well; however, such cases are still being litigated and there may be differences between what is legal and illegal between jurisdictions. For instance, a law in Alabama prohibits the sale of "any device designed or marketed as useful primarily for the stimulation of human genital organs" and it was similar to a law in Texas that prohibited the sale of "obscene devices," defining "with intent to sell" as having more than six devices. In challenges to these laws using *Lawrence* as precedent, the Fifth Circuit (covering Louisiana, Mississippi, and Texas) struck down the Texas law as infringing on privacy, while the Eleventh Circuit (covering Alabama, Florida, and Georgia) upheld Alabama's law.[24] The Supreme Court refused to hear an appeal from the Eleventh Circuit case so, at this point, selling sex toys is illegal in Alabama but not in Texas. Federal Circuit Court decisions are the law in that jurisdiction unless or until they are overturned by the Supreme Court and it is entirely possible to have different holdings regarding points of law, just as it is possible to have different state court decisions so that what is law in one state may not be the same in another.

What Are the Elements of a Crime?

If a law is not struck down because it violates one or more constitutional rights, it is enforceable as a crime. All crimes are classified as felonies, misdemeanors, or treason. These classifications are important not only in determining the degree of punishment, but also when determining the authority of justice personnel to take action. For example, in some states, law enforcement officers may not make misdemeanor arrests unless the offense was committed in their presence (or they had an arrest warrant).

According to most authorities, crimes punishable by death or by imprisonment in a state prison or penitentiary are **felonies**. A crime may be made a felony by reference to the punishment attached, or it may be made a felony by a statute that specifically says that it is a felony. When an offense is not designated by statute as either a felony or a misdemeanor, but a specific punishment is prescribed, then the grade, or class, of the offense is determined by the punishment. Generally, felonies are punishable by at least one year in prison.

Misdemeanors are offenses for which the punishment is other than death or imprisonment in a state prison or that have not been designated felonies by statute. A person convicted of a misdemeanor will ordinarily be incarcerated in a local jail or be required to pay a fine, but will not be sent to a state penitentiary. What is defined as a felony in one state may be a misdemeanor in another, except for the most serious crimes, such as murder, robbery, and rape, which are always felonies.

Treason is one of the only crime that is described in the Constitution. Because those who commit treason threaten the very existence of the nation, it is given a higher classification than a felony. According to the Constitution:

> Treason against the United States shall consist only in levying war against them, or in adhering to their enemies, giving them aid and comfort.[25]

Also, the Constitution provides that no person shall be convicted of treason unless on the testimony of two witnesses to the same overt act, or on confession in open court.

Each crime, as defined in a criminal code, must include a specific prohibited act (or omission), a prescribed mental state, and possibly attendant circumstances. A crime, then is composed of the parts as represented in Exhibit 1.1.4.

EXHIBIT 1.1.4 A Crime

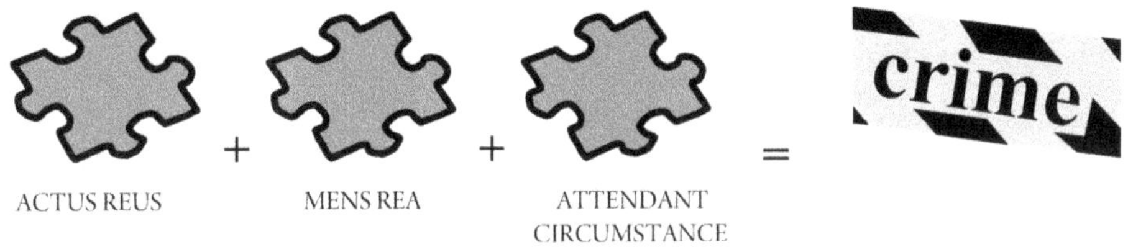

The first necessary element to a crime is referred to as the ***actus reus.*** The law does not punish mere criminal thoughts, nor does it punish a person for who he or she is. Each crime's definition includes a physical act or, in some instances, a failure to act. The physical act must be voluntary, such as pulling the trigger of a gun or breaking into a house to commit theft. There have been a few cases in criminal law in which the act was deemed to be not "volitional" or voluntary on the part of the perpetrator. Examples of acts that are not considered voluntary include actions taken during epileptic seizures or spasms, reflexive actions, or actions taken while sleepwalking or in some other form of "unconscious" state.

In some cases, the crime consists of a failure to act, such as a failure to register for the draft or failure to prepare income tax returns. An omission to act can only constitute a crime when there is also a legal duty. Legal duties are created by:

- statute
- relationship
- contract
- voluntary assumption of care.

Examples of statutory duties are, for instance, the duty to file tax returns and the duty (of convicted sex offenders) to register in sex-offender registries. Failure to perform these duties is a crime in itself.

Certain relationships also carry duties. The most obvious and common is the duty of a parent to care for a minor child. Care includes not only feeding and housing your child, but also providing medical care and ensuring that school-age children receive an education. In about twenty-eight states, **filial responsibility laws** exist. These statutes create a duty for adult children to financially provide for one's aged and infirm parents if one is able to do so. In some states, a defense can be offered that the parent abandoned the child before the age of majority. Despite the fact that these state statutes exist, they are rarely enforced; in eleven of these states, *no one* has ever been prosecuted for failing to care for their elderly and infirm parents.[26]

Contractual duties arise when one person receives something of value in exchange for a duty to care for others. If they are negligent in that duty, criminal culpability may be created. Examples of contractual duties exist between the following actors:

- lifeguards to swimmers
- child care providers to those in their care
- doctors to patients.

If a person who has no statutory, relationship, or contractual obligation to render aid chooses to begin administering assistance, then they may create a duty for themselves. For instance, unless a state has a **Good Samaritan law**, there is no statutory duty to stop and render assistance if one sees a traffic accident (unless one is involved in the accident). However, if a passerby does stop and begins to help, then they must not abandon their effort if it would leave the victim in a worse condition than before. If one sees a person in distress on the street, there is no duty to render aid; however, if the passerby helps the person in distress to a park bench or helps them to a doorway, or in any other way moves them away from where they might have received assistance from others, then the duty to continue care has been created. The rationale is that abandoning one's effort would leave the victim in a worse condition than before.

The second necessary element of every crime, in addition to the *actus reus*, is a criminal state of mind, or ***mens rea***. Under common law, each crime possessed a *mens rea*, but the language used in old English cases and early state statutes and cases in this country was not uniform; thus, for instance, the necessary intent for homicide was defined as malicious, premeditated, depraved indifference, depraved heart, or wanton disregard. The **Model Penal Code** condensed all the myriad definitions of *mens rea* into only four enumerated mental states. In all states that have adopted the Model Penal Code, statutes clearly specify that the actor must have acted *purposely, knowingly, recklessly,* or *negligently*. Further, the definitions of these terms do not vary state by state; they always mean the same thing. The definitions of these terms are as follows:

- Purposely: when the actor intends the act and intends to cause the result.

- Knowingly: when the actor is aware of the nature of his conduct and is aware of the practical certainty of the result of his conduct.
- Recklessly: when the actor knows of, but consciously disregards, an unjustifiable risk (and the action involves a gross deviation from a reasonable standard of conduct).
- Negligently: when the actor is unaware of, but should have been aware of, an unjustifiable risk (and the action involves a gross deviation from a reasonable standard of conduct).

One other concept important to criminal *mens rea* is the principle of **transferred intent**. This can be remembered as "bad aim" intent because the classic example is that if the defendant intends to kill victim A, but misses and kills victim B instead, he will be guilty of first-degree murder (for B's death) and attempted murder (for trying to kill A). The intent to kill was transferred to the actual victim.

The third element to a crime is attendant circumstances. For example, if the crime is receipt of stolen property, the attendant circumstance must be that the property is indeed stolen. Lack of consent (of the purported victim) is an attendant circumstance in many crimes. The criminal law must clearly specify all the required elements to any and all crimes.

If you examine any crime in your state's criminal code, you should be able to identify the specific *actus reus* and the *mens rea* required for criminal culpability. In Exhibit 1.1.5, several serious crimes are given with the *mens rea* and *actus reus* attached. Obviously, these represent only a small portion of the crimes in any jurisdiction. It is important to remember that these definitions may not match exactly your state's definition. Each state's penal code may define the crimes in slightly different ways. If the *mens rea* is not specifically stated, case law usually assumes the legislators meant "knowingly."

What Are Some Defenses to Criminal Culpability?

Defenses to the accusation of a crime fall into two main categories: (1) I didn't do it (e.g., alibi); and (2) I did it, but ... In the second category of legal defenses, the accused argues various reasons why they are not legally culpable for their actions. These defenses include: "infancy"; insanity or incompetence; duress or compulsion; necessity (choice of evils); self-defense; entrapment; and, ignorance or mistake. One last defense is when the prosecution occurs after the statute of limitations has run.

Infancy

Under this defense, an individual argues that they were too young to understand the consequences of their actions and, therefore, cannot form criminal *mens rea*. Infancy, in the legal sense used

EXHIBIT 1.1.5 Crimes and Mental States

Crimes	Mens Rea	Actus Reus
Homicide, first degree	Purposely	An act that resulted in the death of another (and intended the result)
Homicide, second degree	Knowingly	An act that resulted in the death of another either intentionally or with knowing it was an almost inevitable outcome
Voluntary manslaughter	Knowingly	An act that resulted in the death of another (and intended the result *but with provocation*)
Involuntary manslaughter	Recklessly	An act that resulted in the death of another by engaging in behavior where the risk was known to the defendant
Rape/sexual assault	Knowingly	Penetrated the sexual organ of another with the use or threat of force, against the consent of the victim
Robbery	Knowingly	Took something of value from another in their presence with the use or threat of force
Burglary	Purposely/ with intent	Breaking and entering with the intent to commit a felony inside
Theft	Purposely/ with intent	Taking something from another, without consent, with the intent to permanently deprive

here, means only that the child does not have the capacity to determine right and wrong. The age of infancy is set by case law or statute. We also use the term **juvenile** to refer to a child below the age of legal culpability. Under common law, anyone under seven years of age was deemed too young to be legally culpable. Today, states set their age of infancy—the age at which no criminal prosecution would commence (although the youngster would be dealt with in the juvenile court). States also have a "rebuttable" age range—this age range, e.g., seven to fourteen, is when the child is presumed to be too young to be held legally responsible, but that presumption can be rebutted by evidence of maturity. For instance, the state of Washington sets the age of infancy this way:

> Children under the age of 8 are incapable of committing crime. Children of 8 and under 12 years of age are presumed to be incapable of committing crime, but this presumption may be removed by proof that they have sufficient capacity to understand the act or neglect and to know that it was wrong.[27]

A juvenile court may "waive" jurisdiction to an adult court if the crime is serious enough and the court finds the juvenile knew the consequences of their actions. Federal and state statutes define the way legal infancy can act as a defense to criminal culpability. Supreme Court cases have also slowly expanded the parameters of this legal "excuse" for criminal culpability by addressing what punishments are considered "cruel and unusual" and a violation of the 8th Amendment when directed to juveniles. In *Roper v. Simmons* (2015), the Supreme Court held that an individual could not be executed if they committed murder before the age of eighteen.[28] In *Graham v. Florida* (2010),[29] the Supreme Court held that juveniles could not be given sentences of life without parole for non-homicide crimes; then, in *Miller v. Alabama* (2012)[30] they decided that life without parole for juveniles convicted of murder was also too harsh. Juveniles are treated differently under the law because their decision-making capabilities are not fully developed, and they have a greater possibility of rehabilitation. [...]

Mental Capacity

Mental capacity is relevant in criminal prosecution at (1) the pre-trial stage, (2) the verdict stage, and (3) the sentencing stage. First, one can be found **incompetent to stand trial** which means that there is a decision that the defendant doesn't understand what is happening and cannot assist in their own defense. If there is a determination of incompetence, criminal prosecution cannot move forward. Incompetency can be because of mental illness, mental development, or medical conditions like amnesia. The individual may be held in an institution until such time as they become competent.

The second way mental capacity is relevant is when the accused's defense is that their mental state was the reason they committed the offense. **Insanity** is a legal term, not a medical term. It refers to any mental illness that meets the legal threshold for incapacity. The most common legal test of insanity is the **M'Naghten Test**, from an early English case. If the defendant "was laboring under such a defect of reason, from disease of the mind, as not to know the nature and quality of the act he was doing, or, if he did know it, that he did not know he was doing what was wrong" then he should be acquitted. This has become known as the "right and wrong test." A person is insane if they did not know what they were doing or they did not know what they were doing was wrong. Not all jurisdictions use this test, but the majority use some version of it.

One of the difficulties in applying the test is when the mentally ill person, because of his or her delusion, believes they are saving the world or killing a demon, but they understand they are breaking the law. If they knew that killing was against the law, they could be found sane, not insane, because most jurisdictions instruct the jury that the knowledge requirement relates to *legal* or *societal* definitions, not *moral* definitions. This is a frequent issue because schizophrenics often have religious delusions that they are doing the work of God or that victims are some form of demon or an alien that need to be killed.[31]

Some people are uncomfortable with the mentally ill person being acquitted due to insanity when they have committed a horrific crime. In fact, this might result in a jury finding someone sane when evidence clearly indicates they were under some form of schizophrenic delusion during the crime. As noted before, insanity is a legal term and judges or juries have discretion to determine whether insanity was the cause of the crime. An alternative occurs when insanity is removed as a legal defense. About thirteen states now have adopted the "guilty but mentally ill" concept, which preserves the traditional insanity defense but provides an alternative to it. A jury can choose between a verdict of "not guilty by reason of insanity," which results in acquittal, or a verdict of "guilty but mentally ill," which will result in a sentence for the same term provided for a regular guilty verdict. The sentence, however, would be served in a state mental hospital.[32] In general, these changes in statutes have been upheld against constitutional challenges. For instance, an Indiana court upheld the state statute that permits the jury to find the defendant guilty but mentally ill, agreeing that the statute did not violate the equal protection clause and the statute had a rational relationship to a legitimate state interest in securing convictions and obtaining treatment for defendants who suffer from mental illness.[33] In fact, courts have held that due process does not require states to offer the insanity defense at all.[34]

In some cases, an individual is not pleading insanity, but evidence of diminished capacity may reduce the seriousness of the crime. The argument is that they could not have formed the highest level of intent. Diminished capacity defenses have included the PMS defense (that premenstrual syndrome symptoms include behavioral and emotional incapacitation to the extent that the defendant could not control her actions), PTSD (post-traumatic stress syndrome symptoms caused the individual to commit the criminal act), and the battered woman syndrome (repeated victimization was responsible for the defendant attacking the perpetrator). Alcoholism has never been successful as a defense to a crime although some states allow it to be used to prove the defendant didn't have the highest level of *mens rea*.

Recall in February of 2013, Chris Kyle, the author of the book *American Sniper* which was made into a recent movie of the same name, was shot by Eddie Ray Routh while they were target shooting at a gun range. Routh suffers from PTSD, and Kyle was helping him to recover from his condition brought on by military service in Iraq. Routh, who evidently experienced paranoia, delusions, and sleeplessness, had been under treatment with Veterans Affairs doctors who prescribed a variety of mood-disorder and anti-psychotic medications, but refused to hospitalize him even though he had threatened violence and suicide. The motive for the shooting is unknown, but Routh confessed he killed Kyle and Kyle's friend, Chad Littlefield, at the shooting range. His defense was PTSD but the jury convicted him of first degree murder and sentenced him to life in prison without parole.[35]

The third and final way one's mental state might be relevant in criminal prosecution is at the sentencing stage. Even if a defendant does not convince a jury that they were legally insane and not responsible for their actions, relevant evidence may be introduced at the sentencing stage to

EXHIBIT 1.1.6 Eddie Ray Routh was convicted of first-degree murder in the killing of Chris Kyle and Chad Littlefield. Routh argued he had diminished capacity due to PTSD after serving in Iraq, but the jury sentenced him to life without parole.

Source: Getty

affect the sentencing decision. Most state prison systems have psychiatric units (or whole facilities in larger states). In fact, it is a sad commentary that there are now more mentally ill individuals in prison than in mental hospitals.[36]

It is important to remember that mental illness and insanity are not synonyms—insanity is a legal term that denotes mental disability to the point where one cannot be held legally culpable while mental illness is a broad term that encompasses many disorders. The Diagnostic and Statistical Manual of Mental Disorders (DSM-V), the definitive guide by the American Psychiatric Association, defines a mental disorder as a behavioral or psychological syndrome or pattern that occurs in an individual that reflects an underlying psychobiological dysfunction with consequences that include clinically significant distress (e.g., a painful symptom) or disability (i.e., impairment in one or more important areas of functioning). The symptom must not be merely an expectable response to common stressors and losses (e.g., depression after the loss of a loved one), caused primarily a result of social deviance or conflicts with society.[37] It is important to remember that one can be mentally ill, but not necessarily legally insane.

Duress

Another defense is called either **duress** or compulsion. Except in the case of homicide, an act that would otherwise constitute a crime may be excused when committed under duress or compulsion that is imminent, and produces a well-grounded fear of death or serious bodily harm.[38] There must be no reasonable escape without committing the crime.[39] This defense cannot be used if the defendant has committed murder; someone holding a gun to your head threatening you does not give you a legal justification to kill an innocent party. It can excuse other crimes, however, like theft. The test as to whether the coercion was enough is reasonableness—was the threat sufficient to overcome the will of a reasonable person? The threat must be imminent—the person making the threat must intend and be prepared to carry out the threat immediately—if someone says, "rob a bank or your family will be killed next week", this does not constitute an imminent threat.

The battered spouse/woman syndrome has been described as a type of diminished capacity, but it could also be placed here under duress. Basically the defense is that the defendant experienced severe abuse that affected the ability to leave the abuser, and, ultimately, the defendant felt the only way to get away from the abuse was to kill the abuser, often not during an active abuse incident but, rather, when the abuser is incapacitated either by sleep or alcohol. Not all courts recognize this defense, however, and some have refused to allow in evidence of prior abuse, as it is not relevant to the immediate crime.

Necessity

Duress and necessity are somewhat similar defenses; however, while duress always involves fear of harm or intimidation, necessity is a broader defense that justifies criminal actions if it is to avoid greater harm. For instance, if you are trapped in a snowstorm on a mountaintop and the choice is to freeze to death or break into someone's cabin, the law allows you to break and enter (as long as there is compensation to the victim). The necessity defense, similar to duress, will not allow one to sacrifice an innocent to save oneself or one's property. The classic necessity case is *Regina v. Dudley and Stephens.*[40] In this case, Dudley and Stephens were tried for the murder of another sailor. All three had been adrift in an open boat for twenty days and were starving. They killed and ate the victim, because he was the youngest and the weakest, and were rescued four days later. The court found that they would have most probably died if they had not committed the act and that the boy would have died before them; however, they were convicted because necessity was not recognized as a defense to murder. They were sentenced to death but the Crown commuted their sentence to six months' imprisonment.[41]

Examples of successful and unsuccessful uses of the necessity defense include: a convicted felon who was legally prohibited from possessing weapons and who grabbed one to defend himself used the defense successfully when charged with "Felon in Possession of a Firearm";[42] a person who stole food argued economic necessity unsuccessfully;[43] and a defendant who kidnapped another to save them from a religious cult was unsuccessful in the use of the necessity defense.[44] Recently, some defendants have tried to use the necessity defense when they have been prosecuted for marijuana possession in the states that do not have medical marijuana legislation, arguing that marijuana is a necessary treatment to an illness or condition. They have not been successful.[45]

Self-defense

Self-defense is as old as common law. The law allows you to protect yourself and others with violence if necessary, but there are certain elements that must be present in order for self-defense to be successful. Other elements vary from state to state. The basic elements of self-defense are: (1) fear of serious harm; (2) the fear is reasonable; (3) the harm is imminent; (4) the defense is proportional; and (5) the defendant did not create the threat. In some jurisdictions (but not all), there is a (6) duty to retreat (but not in one's own home).

The reasonableness of the fear is determined by an objective test; the question asked is not if the defendant was in fear, but whether a reasonable person would have been in fear given the same set of circumstances. The danger must be immediate, and the response must be proportional (in caselaw this is not a very consistent requirement, however, and is quite subjective). For instance, self-defense can be used when someone attacks you, but your response has to be reasonable to the level of the threat. Another element that some states have as a necessary element for self-defense is "clean hands," the idea that you couldn't have started the fight or set up the situation which created the need to use violence to defend yourself. Some states also have the duty to retreat—this means that before using violence to defend oneself you must try and escape the threat. Even in those states that have a duty to retreat element to self-defense, the requirement does not apply when one is at home. You have no duty to retreat in your own home. Other states have no duty to retreat at all.

In some states, **"stand your ground" laws** have expanded the legal right to use lethal force. Florida became the first state to pass such a law in 2005 and now over a dozen states have similar laws. Statistics showed a sharp increase in justifiable homicides after 2005, when Florida and sixteen other states passed the laws. Overall homicide rates in those states stayed relatively flat, however the average number of justifiable homicide cases per year increased by more than 50 percent in the decade's latter half.[46] In Texas and Georgia, such cases nearly doubled, and in Florida, they nearly tripled. Meanwhile, in states that saw no new "stand your ground" laws, justifiable homicides reported to the FBI stayed nearly flat after a slight uptick in the middle of the decade.

In 2012, Florida's law was the center of controversy in the shooting of Trayvon Martin, a teenager shot by a neighborhood watch volunteer who followed him as he was walking through the neighborhood and ended up shooting him when he engaged the youth and a fight ensued. His release without charges set up a national outcry.[47] The Florida statute allows an individual to use force up to lethal force when he or she has a reasonable fear of being harmed. There is no duty to retreat.[48] Another recent analysis of homicides comparing states without "stand your ground" laws to those with such laws[49] found that rates of homicides ruled justifiable were generally significantly higher in states with "stand your ground" laws. The only exception was that there was no difference in the rate of homicides ruled justifiable between a Black perpetrator and White victim in states with "stand your ground" laws and those without. In states without the laws, only 1.13 percent of Black-on-White homicides were ruled justifiable and 1.4 percent of homicides in states with the laws were ruled justifiable—not a significant difference. On the other hand, for White-on-Black shootings, justifiable rulings increased from 9.51 percent of all to 16.85 percent of all homicides in states with "stand your ground" laws. Black-on-Black and White-on-White homicides showed less dramatic increases. There is no way to interpret these findings with only the numbers available. It is possible, perhaps, that they represent victims who are defending themselves during a criminal event; or, alternatively, they represent a negative outcome of the "stand your ground" law which may allow too much latitude in defining what is a reasonable use of deadly force.

Generally, violent actions have been justified by self-defense only to prevent serious bodily harm. **"Make My Day" statutes** in some states expanded self-defense by allowing individuals to use deadly force against a home intruder in situations where there is no immediate threat from the person who made the unlawful entry, as long as there is a reasonable belief that a crime is intended. Colorado's law, for instance, states that:

> any occupant of a dwelling is justified in using any degree of physical force, including deadly physical force, against another person when that person has made an unlawful entry into the dwelling, and when the occupant has a reasonable belief that such other person has committed a crime in the dwelling in addition to the uninvited entry, or is committing or intends to commit a crime against a person or property in addition to the uninvited entry, and when the occupant reasonably believes that such other person might use any physical force, no matter how slight, against any occupant.[50]

What the Colorado law and similar laws in other states do is expand self-defense from defending oneself or others against physical harm to defending one's property. Not all states have such laws for the public policy reason that property should not be prioritized above life.

If all the required elements of self-defense are proven, the defendant should be found not guilty of a crime, either by a judge as a matter of law or by a jury decision. In some situations, however, not all the elements are proven leading to the "imperfect defense" of self-defense. Generally the effect of an imperfect defense is to reduce the level of *mens rea* and severity of the crime. For instance, if the defendant is in a fight with the victim and he kills him, he may argue self-defense. However, if there is a finding that he started the fight or used disproportional force; in this case, the self-defense facts may go toward reducing the crime from a first or second degree murder to a voluntary manslaughter. Similarly, if an objective test of reasonableness is used and the defendant mistakenly and unreasonably believed he was in danger and used unlawful force, then his defense is imperfect and the use of force will not be justified, although he might be found to have a lesser *mens rea*.

Entrapment

Entrapment did not exist as a defense under common law. It was first recognized in a federal case in the 1930s. In this defense, the defendant is saying, "Yes, I did it, but the police made me do it." The argument is that law enforcement creates the crime by providing too much of a temptation for a person who has no predisposition to crime. Entrapment tends to be used most often in drug cases, although recently it has been used when individuals have plotted to commit terrorist acts with undercover federal agents. Police engage in a wide variety of situations where they provide the opportunity to commit a crime. They may pretend to be:

- individuals offering public officials a bribe in return for special treatment
- drug sellers (or buyers)
- prostitutes (or "johns")
- children in Internet chat rooms offering to meet a predator for sex
- fences encouraging the theft of certain types of automobiles
- hit men who are willing to kill for money
- someone who can provide cable service for free
- a drunk on the street with money sticking out of his pocket.

Generally, the guideline for which of these situations constitutes entrapment is whether the person who succumbs to the temptation had a "predisposition" to commit the crime, basically asking the question: "Would a person with no predisposition to commit that type of crime be tempted by governmental actions to do so?"[51] The test was developed by the federal courts in a federal case, but many states have adopted it as well. For instance, Colorado's statute is as follows:

Colo. Rev. Stat. § 18-1-709

The commission of acts which would otherwise constitute an offense is not criminal if the defendant engaged in the proscribed conduct because he was induced to do so by a law enforcement official or other person acting under his direction, seeking to obtain that evidence for the purpose of prosecution, and the methods used to obtain that evidence were such as to create a substantial risk that the acts would be committed by a person who, but for such inducement, would not have conceived or engaged in conduct of the sort induced. Merely affording a person an opportunity to commit an offense is not entrapment even though representations or inducements calculated to overcome the offender's fear of detection are used.

Merely offering the opportunity to commit a crime is not sufficient for an entrapment defense to be successful. Especially for drug offenders, any past criminal history will probably mean that there will be a presumption the defendant had a predisposition to commit the crime. In a federal case, the Ninth Circuit Court stated that for a defendant to prove the defense of entrapment, he must point to undisputed evidence making it patently clear that an otherwise innocent person was induced to commit the illegal act by trickery, persuasion, or fraud of a government agent.[52]

Ignorance or Mistake

You have probably heard the phrase "ignorance of the law is no excuse," and that is generally true; however, sometimes ignorance of a law is an excuse if the law itself is obscure or a reasonable person would not be presumed to know of it. Also, a mistake about a crime may be a defense. There are two types of mistakes—mistakes about the legality of an action ("I made a mistake thinking that my action was legal") and mistakes about an essential fact ("I made a mistake in that I believed the goods were not stolen"). Mistakes of law are rarely successful defenses; mistakes of fact (if honest and reasonable) may excuse criminal culpability if the mistake is about an element of the offense. The classic example of a mistake of fact defense is when someone mistakenly takes another person's coat from a restaurant thinking it was his or hers. Taking possession of the property of another is ordinarily theft, but since the *mens rea* of theft is *intentionally* taking the property of another, the mistake of fact (thinking it was your coat) means that the *mens rea* requirement of theft is not present. Another example would be when you accept a gift from someone thinking they bought it for you, only to find out from police that it was stolen. You would have a valid defense if you were charged with receipt of stolen property because the *mens rea* for that crime is *knowing* the property is stolen and *intending* to receive stolen goods.

Drug smuggling cases have posed a thorny problem for criminal law when the smuggler is mistaken as to the substance. For instance, if Jack buys white powder in Mexico that he thinks is cocaine and smuggles it across the border by hiding it in a secret compartment of his luggage, has he committed a crime if it turns out to be talcum powder? Before changes in the law, some judges decided that no crime was committed because it is not illegal to smuggle talcum powder. However, federal law and many state statutes are now written in such a way that a mistake as to the actual substance does not change criminal culpability—if one intends to smuggle or sell a controlled substance and acts to do so, then they are still culpable even if the substance turns out not to be a controlled substance.[53]

Statute of Limitations

One last defense is when the time limitation (Statute of Limitations) for prosecution has expired. The rationale for the time limitations is that the defendant should have some substantial safeguards against an erroneous conviction because of the staleness of the evidence and because the defendant is entitled to a speedy trial. Therefore, when the defendant claims that the statutory period has expired, the guilt or innocence of the defendant is not an issue. If the statutory period has expired, the defendant is entitled to an acquittal as a matter of right. As a general rule, the time begins to run when the crime is committed and runs until the prosecution is commenced. Depending upon the provisions of the statute, the running of the time is stopped by the filing of an indictment or information or at the time a complaint is laid before a magistrate and a warrant of arrest is issued.[54] If the defendant leaves the jurisdiction or otherwise prevents prosecution, then the Statute of Limitations does not run during that time period.

What Are Some Recent Issues in Criminal Law?

As noted above, cases concerning privacy and equal protection continue to be controversial. The reason why confirmation hearings of Supreme Court Justices are so contested is that the law is not a simple math equation and the interpretation of the law, and constitutional rights in particular, are fraught with political influence. For instance, even though *Roe v. Wade*[55] was decided in 1973, it is by no means a settled area of law and cases continue to be heard as states refine and restrict the "right" to abortion. The most recent case continued to utilize the test of "undue burden." In *Whole Woman's Health v. Hellerstedt*, decided in June 2016, the Supreme Court decided that a new law requiring abortion clinics to meet high standards of surgical centers with doctors required to have privileges at local hospitals posed an undue burden to women's right to access abortion services. At this point, it appears the Supreme Court is following the precedent set; however, it is

> To listen to the arguments in this case, go to http://www.scotusblog.com/case-files/cases/whole-womans-healthv-cole/

entirely possible that one day the *Roe* decision will be overturned if the composition of Justices shifts to a majority that believed it was wrongly decided.

Even though the Supreme Court decided *Obergell v. Hodges*[56] in June of 2015 affirming that the right to marry someone of the same sex was a fundamental right that could not be infringed upon by state laws, this area of law is clearly not settled either. A recent legal controversy is whether "faith-based" statutes could give business owners the right to refuse services to same-sex couples or transgenders based on their religious objections to such individuals. Ultimately, the question becomes: do the laws violate either group's constitutional rights (either of equal protection, privacy, or some other right embedded in the Bill of Rights).

One need only look in the newspaper to see current legal controversies. Should hate crimes be extended to gender? Should concealed firearms be allowed on college campuses? Should there be a crime that holds owners of dogs that maul victims criminally culpable? Should federal drug laws override state medical marijuana laws? Should marijuana be legalized for recreational use? Should teenagers be prosecuted for pornography for "**sexting**"? The point is that the law affects you every day and it is a dynamic entity. It constantly changes in response to current events and political and social influences. Our focus on data for this [reading] discusses one current controversy—whether medical marijuana should be a crime.

Focus on Data: Is Medical Marijuana Crime or Cure?

Marijuana is a crime under federal law and the law of most states; however, four states have legalized marijuana for recreational purposes, and 23 states have legalized medical use of marijuana.[57] Recent news indicates that perhaps five states will be voting on legalizing small amounts of marijuana for recreational use in the next election cycle. This is a very interesting legal issue because any possession or sale of marijuana is still illegal under federal law. The federal government has created a "schedule" of controlled substances, which categorizes substances by potential for addiction and whether there are legitimate medical uses. Marijuana was placed in "Schedule 1" along with cocaine, heroin, methamphetamine, and other highly addictive drugs that have no legitimate medical uses.

The Federal Bureau of Investigation reports that there were an estimated 1,663,582 arrests for drug abuse violations in 2009 and 1,120,133 in 2014. In 2014, only about 17 percent of arrests were for sales or distribution, the majority (83 percent) were for possession. Of the possession arrests, 39.7 percent were for marijuana (down from 45 percent in 2009); thus, the majority of drug arrests in this country are for possessing marijuana.[58] The Gallup poll shows that in 2015, 58 percent of Americans were in favor of legalizing marijuana,[59] and an even greater number favor legalizing marijuana for medical use (89 percent).[60]

In some cases, defendants have attempted to use the necessity defense to a marijuana prosecution arguing that medical necessity created the need to violate drug laws.[61] As of this point, medical necessity has not been recognized as a defense by the courts. Some argue that with the increased number of states that have passed medical marijuana laws, the medical necessity defense should be re-examined in those states without medical marijuana laws. However, the Supreme Court as of 2016 has not ruled that those states' laws (utilizing medical necessity or any other legal argument) can usurp or overcome the 1970 Controlled Substances Act; therefore a person may conform to state law in their possession of medical marijuana, but still be in violation of federal drug laws.[62] Proponents argue that the sole Supreme Court case involved distribution, not possession, and that it is possible the Court would be more sympathetic to a case of a seriously ill individual who possessed marijuana for their medical needs. Under the Obama administration, the Department of Justice has shifted its enforcement to de-emphasize marijuana prosecutions in the states that have decriminalized marijuana; however, those individuals could still be prosecuted under federal law.

Proponents argue the time has come to recognize that marijuana (cannabis) presents some health benefits for individuals who cannot ingest other forms of pain medicine. Opponents to such laws argue that there are other safer methods, and that medical marijuana dispensaries are nothing more than legalized drug shops, and they bring an undesirable element to the community and serve as a gateway to other drugs. What are the facts concerning marijuana as a medical treatment?

A growing number of people argue that marijuana is the only effective treatment for symptoms of medical conditions such as glaucoma, cancer (nausea), multiple sclerosis (pain), and AIDS (pain). A barrier to good research has been that mere possession of marijuana has been illegal in all states until fairly recently, thus there has been little scientific research as to marijuana (cannabis) benefits. Scientists do know that the chemicals in cannabis prompt a response in the brain that affects many of the body's functions, such as in the heart, digestive, endocrine, immune, nervous, and reproductive systems. Cannabis has been proven to help manage pain and reduce muscle spasms in patients with multiple sclerosis.[63]

Thus far the medical community has not spoken with one voice in support of whether marijuana poses more risks than benefits in the treatment of certain ailments. As with other issues discussed throughout the book, advocacy and interest groups are not necessarily objective purveyers of facts. The issue has been hampered by the lack of ability to run stringent experimentation on the effects of cannabis in scientific settings. No doubt in the years to come, more data will be available, although it seems clear that the public support for legalization, at least for medical use, continues to grow. At this point the legal position of those who either distribute or possess medical marijuana is precarious since until the federal government changes federal laws, they can still be prosecuted. This is true as well, of course, for those in the few states that have passed laws decriminalizing marijuana for recreational use.

Summary

What Is the Purpose of Law? What Is the Purpose of Criminal Law?

Society has law in order to regulate and guide personal and public interactions. Criminal law is the branch or the division of law that defines crimes, their elements, and provides for their punishment. The protections of law fall into three areas: protection from harm from others, protection from harm from oneself, and protection of society's morals.

What Is the Origin of Our Legal System?

Most present-day crimes in the various states had their origins in the common law of England. This was the law developed in early English court decisions and was modified by English legislative bodies. Common law became the starting point for our criminal law, but has now largely been supplanted by statutory law as found in state and federal criminal codes.

What Are Some Differences between Civil and Criminal Law?

Civil law is concerned with private wrongs (torts). The plaintiff brings the case instead of the state. Crimes can also be torts and a civil action can take place along with a criminal prosecution. Civil law is much broader than criminal law and deals with property law, contract, tax, estate, and other branches of law.

What Are Some Constitutional Challenges to Creating Laws?

Constitutional challenges fall into the areas of vagueness or ex post facto violations; or, the law violates the rights recognized in the 1st, 2nd, or 14th Amendments, or violates privacy rights.

What Are the Elements of a Crime?

Crimes are also classified as felonies, misdemeanors, and treason. Each crime's definition includes a prohibited action (the *actus reus*), the requisite state of mind (*mens rea*), and possibly specified attendant circumstances.

What Are Some Defenses to Criminal Culpability?

Defenses include: "infancy"; insanity or incompetence; duress or compulsion; necessity (choice of evils); self-defense; entrapment; ignorance or mistake; and Statute of Limitations.

What Are Some Recent Issues in Criminal Law?

Law is dynamic and it changes depending on public opinion and shifting public morals. On any given day, one could identify numerous legal issues in the daily newspaper or from an analysis of current events. Today, issues of religious freedom, LGBT rights, gun control, marijuana legalization, and euthanasia all appear in news stories frequently.

Critical Thinking Exercises

1. Find the penal code for your state; you should be able to find a copy online. Find out whether your state uses the Model Penal Code's *mens rea* definitions (purposeful, knowing, reckless, and negligent). Look up specific crimes to see if you can identify the *mens rea*—is the language clear or does it leave room for argument as to the mental state required?
2. Read a newspaper and identify any and/or all legal issues that appear that day. Can you identify natural law positions versus positivist positions in the proponents and opponents of the issue?

Notes

1. J. Pollock, *Criminal Law*. New York, NY: Routledge, Taylor & Francis, 2015, p. 3.
2. Read about anti-semitic legislation of Nazi Germany at https://www.ushmm.org/outreach/en/article.php?ModuleId=10007695
3. *Lawrence v. Texas*, 539 U.S. 558, 2003.
4. *Obergefell v. Hodges*, 76 U.S.____, 2015.
5. W. Blackstone, *Commentaries*, vol. 4, 1769.
6. *Keeler v. Superior Court*, 470 P.2d 617 (Cal. 1970).
7. *D.C. v. Heller* (554 U.S. 570, 2008); *McDonald v. Chicago* (561 U.S. 742, 2010).
8. *City of Chicago v. Morales*, 119 S. Ct. 1849, 1999.
9. *Skilling v. United States*, 561 U.S. 358, 2010
10. U.S. Const. Art. I, §§ 9 and 10, Cl. 1.
11. *United States v. Abbington*, 144 F.3d 1003 (6th Cir. 1998); *Myers v. Ridge*, 712 A.2d 791 (Pa. 1998).
12. *Smith v. Doe*, 538 U.S. 84, 2003.
13. *Starkey v. Oklahoma Department of Corrections*, 2013 OK 43, 2013.
14. *Kansas v. Hendricks*, 521 U.S. 346, 1997.
15. *Loving v. Virginia*, 388 U.S. 1, 1967.
16. *In re Michael M.*, 450 U.S. 464, 1981.
17. *Craig v. Boren*, 429 U.S. 190, 1976.
18. *Rostker v. Goldberg*, 453 U.S. 57, 1981.
19. Various news articles, e.g., http://www.expressnews.com/news/local/article/Facebook-threat-case-back-on-track-for-trial-6485258.php.
20. *Texas v. Johnson*, 491 U.S. 397, 1989.
21. *Griswold v. Connecticut*, 381 U.S. 479, 1965.
22. *Roe v. Wade*, 410 U.S. 113, 1973.
23. *Lawrence v. Texas*, 539 U.S. 558, 2003

24. *Williams v. Morgan*, 478 F.3d 1316 (11th Cir. 2007); *Reliable Consultants v. Earle*, 517 F.3d 738 (5th Cir. 2008).
25. U.S. Const. Art III, Sec. 3.
26. See "Caring for our parents in an aging world: Sharing public and private responsibility for the elderly." *N.Y.U. Journal of Legislation and Public Policy* 5 (2001): 563–595.
27. Rev. Code Wash. § 9A.04.050.
28. *Roper v. Simmons*, 543 U.S. 551, 2005
29. *Graham v. Florida*, 130 S. CT. 2011, 2010.
30. *Miller v. Alabama*,132 S. CT. 2455, 2012
31. *State v. Crenshaw*, 659 P.2d 488 (Wash. 1983).
32. 730 Ill. Comp. Stat. § 515–2 (1999); Mich. Comp. Laws § 768.36 (1999).
33. *Gambill v. State*, 675 N.E.2d 668 (Ind. 1997).
34. *Ake v. Oklahoma*, 470 U.S. 68, 1985; *State v. Searcy*, 789 P.2d 914 (Idaho 1990).
35. News articles, e.g., http://www.theguardian.com/film/2015/feb/25/american-sniper-trial-eddie-ray-routh-found-guilty-andsentenced-to-life-in-prison-without-parole
36. http://www.thejha.org/node/54
37. APA, *Diagnostic and Statistical Manual of Mental Disorders-5*. Available at https://www.psychiatry.org/psychiatrists/practice/dsm
38. *United States v. Anthony*, 145 F. Supp. 323 (M.D. Pa. 1956); *Jackson v. State*, 558 S.W.2d 816 (Mo. Ct. App. 1977).
39. *State v. St. Clair*, 262 S.W.2d 25 (Mo. 1953); *Jackson v. State*, 504 S.W.2d 488 (Tex. Crim. App. 1974).
40. 14 Q.B.D. 273 (1884).
41. A similar American case was *United States v. Holmes*, 26 F. Cas. 360 (C.C.E.D. Pa. 1842).
42. *United States v. Paolello*, 951 F.2d 537 (3d Cir. 1991).
43. *State v. Moe*, 24 P.2d 638 (Wash. 1933).
44. *People v. Brandyberry*, 812 P.2d 674 (Colo. Ct. App. 1991).
45. *Jenks v. State*, 582 So.2d 676 (Fla. Dist. Ct. App. 1991); *State v. Hanson*, 468 N.W.2d 77 (Minn. Ct. App. 1991), *State v. Ownbey*, 996 P.2d 510 (Ore. App. 2000), *State v. Poling*, 531 S.E.2d 678 (W. Va. 2000), *United States v. Randall*, 104 Daily Wash. L. Rptr. 2249 (D.C. Super. Ct. 1976). For review, see J. Pollock, *Criminal Law*, 11th ed. New York, NY: Routledge, Taylor & Francis, 2016.
46. J. Palazzolo and R. Barry, "More killings called self defense." *Washington Post*, April 2, 2012. Retrieved from http://www.wsj.com/articles/SB10001424052702303404704577311873214574462
47. Various news stories, e.g. http://www.outsidethebeltway.com/federal-civil-rights-charges-against-george-zimmerman-said-tobe-off-the-table/
48. Fla. Stat. 776.012.

49. J. Roman, "Race, justifiable homicicide, and stand your ground laws: Analysis of FBI Supplementary Homicide Data." Washing-ton, DC: Urban Institute, 2013.
50. Colo. Rev. Stat. §18–1–704.
51. 411 U.S. 423, 1973.
52. *United States v. Mendoza-Prado*, 314 F.3d 1099 (9th Cir. 2002). See also *Matteo v. Superintendent*, SCI Albion, 171 F.3d 877 (3d Cir. 1999).
53. J. Pollock, *Criminal Law*. New York, NY: Routlege, Taylor & Francis, 2016.
54. *Jarrett v. State*, 49 Okla. Crim. 162, 292 P. 888 (1930).
55. *Roe v. Wade*, 410 U.S. 113, 1973.
56. *Obergefell v. Hodges*, 576 U.S.____, 2015,
57. See http://medicalmarijuana.procon.org/view.resource.php?resourceID=000881
58. FBI, Uniform Crime Reports, Arrest Tables, 2009, 2014. Retrieved 6/15/2016 from https://www.fbi.gov/about-us/cjis/ucr/crime-in-the-u.s/2014/crime-in-the-u.s.-2014/persons-arrested/main
59. J. Jones, "In U.S., 58% back legal marijuana use". Gallup.com, October 21, 2015, http://www.gallup.com/poll/186260/back-legal-marijuana.aspx
60. Quinnipiac University Poll, retrieved 6/17/2016 from http://www.pollingreport.com/drugs.htm
61. *Jenks v. State*, 582 So.2d 676 (Fla. Dist. Ct. App. 1991); *State v. Hanson*, 468 N.W.2d 77 (Minn. Ct. App. 1991), *State v. Ownbey*, 996 P.2d 510 (Ore. App. 2000), *State v. Poling*, 531 S.E.2d 678 (W. Va. 2000), *United States v. Randall*, 104 Daily Wash. L. Rptr. 2249 (D.C. Super. Ct. 1976).
62. *United States v. Oakland Cannabis Buyer's Cooperative*, 532 U.S. 483 (2001).
63. WebMD.com, retrieved 6/17/2016 from http://www.webmd.com/news/breaking-news/marijuana-on-main-street/medical-marijuana-research-web?page=2

READING 1.2

CRIME IN SOCIETY

Joycelyn Pollock

[READING] PREVIEW

- What Is Crime?
- What Is the Role of Legislators, Victims, Police, and Prosecutors in Defining Crimes?
- What Sources Do We Use to Find Out About the Patterns of Crime?
- What Crimes Are People Most Frequently Arrested for?
- What Do We Know About Homicide?
- What Has Been the Pattern of Crime Over the Years? Has It Declined?
- Does The Public Have an Accurate Perception About the Prevalence of Crime?
- How Do the Crime Rates of the United States Compare to Other Countries?
- Focus On Data: Is There a Ferguson Effect? Is There a Current Crime Wave?
- Summary
- Critical Thinking Exercises

What Is Crime?

What is crime? This seems like an easy question, and it is, in a way. However, the answer is not necessarily murder, robbery, or rape. Those may be examples of crime, but the definition of **crime** is simply "an action that is prohibited by law." For instance, the definition of simple **assault** in one state is as follows:

1. Intentionally, knowingly, or recklessly causes bodily injury to another, including the person's spouse.
2. Intentionally or knowingly threatens another with imminent bodily injury, including the person's spouse.
3. Intentionally or knowingly causes physical contact with another when the person knows or should reasonably believe that the other will regard the contact as offensive or provocative.[1]

So, if you pushed or even hugged someone who you knew would consider it to be provocative or offensive, you have committed simple assault. This is a Class A misdemeanor unless some other conditions are met; therefore, it is not a very "serious" crime. Most simple assaults are not brought to the attention of the criminal justice system. However, many other, more serious crimes are also never reported. This creates what is known as the **dark figure of crime**, which is crime that does not find its way into official numbers. Crimes such as domestic violence, acquaintance rape, and even theft, are more likely than other crimes to be part of this dark figure of crime.

Because the dark figure of crime is so high, it makes theorizing about who commits crime difficult. We do not know if the offenders who never come to the attention of authorities are similar to those who do. We do not know if these unknown offenders have similar motivations and patterns of criminal offending. Studies that are based only on known offenders may be faulty in that they are not able to present findings on all offenders—only those we know about. It is important to ask relevant questions about crime, e.g. has homicide increased or not; but, it is also important to note the weaknesses of our data sources when trying to understand crime patterns.

What Is the Role of Legislators, Victims, Police, and Prosecutors in Defining Crime?

Crime is called a "constructed reality" because it is created by the definitions and perceptions of the legislators, perpetrators, observers, victims, and formal system actors (such as police and prosecutors). Take for instance, the following scenario: Person A shoves Person B. Is it a crime? It might be simple assault if Person A did it intentionally, believing it to be offensive to Person B. Is it prosecutable? It might be, only if Person B reports it to police or perhaps if a police officer happened to be close enough to see it and chose to arrest. Will it be prosecuted? A variety of factors affect the decision to prosecute, including the wishes of the victim, the resources of the prosecutor's office, the nature of the evidence and, some would say, perhaps the race and ethnicity of the offender and/or victim.

EXHIBIT 1.2.1 Crime: A "Constructed Reality."

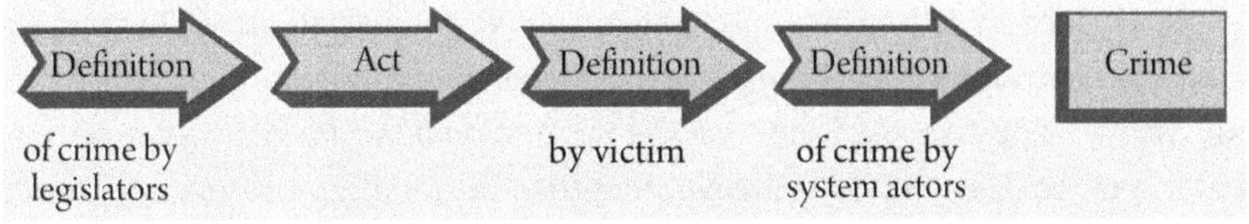

Before we can punish any act as a crime, a law has to be created by legislation. [...] [M]ost of our laws come from common law; however, state and federal legislators are constantly fine-tuning our criminal codes and adding new laws or changing existing laws. Recent changes in some states have legalized possession of small amounts of marijuana, and the carrying of guns on college campuses. Other changes in some states' laws have criminalized talking on your cellphone while driving, and posting nude pictures of someone on social media sites without their permission. [...] [S]tates are free to create new crimes as long as they do not violate individuals' federal constitutional rights. It is not at all unusual to have one state legislature pass a new law that criminalizes behavior that is still legal in other states or vice versa.

Before a crime can be counted by officials, it must be reported by the victim. Why might someone *not* report a crime to authorities? The most common reason is that they believe police can't do anything about it, but they might also interpret the event as a private matter and not a crime. Domestic violence victims sometimes do not want the involvement of the police, even though they are obviously victims of assault. Rape victims also may not report their own victimization, sometimes because they do not want formal intervention, but sometimes because they do not interpret the event as a crime. Studies have shown that female victims who are raped in "date-rape" scenarios by someone they know in circumstances where the lack of consent may be somewhat ambiguous sometimes do not define what occurred as a crime. If the victim does not perceive the event as a crime, or does not want formal system intervention, then the event is never reported to police and does not appear in our crime statistics.[2] In 2007, only 40 percent of all criminal victimizations were reported to police. Robberies with injury and auto theft were reported by 85 percent of victims, but only a quarter of some other types of crimes were reported to police.[3] In Exhibit 1.2.2, we display 2013 figures, but also show those for 2004. We see that the percentage of individuals who report their victimization to the police has decreased in many crime categories since 2004, but has increased in some crime categories.

> To find the most current statistics regarding victim reporting, go to the website of the Bureau of Justice Statistics. The 2014 report can be found at: http://www.bjs.gov/content/pub/pdf/cv14.pdf.

Even if the victim calls police, there may not be an arrest. Police do not arrest in a large percentage of cases where an arrest is legally justified; perhaps in as many as half of all cases. Although arrests are usually made in serious felony cases, or in situations in which victims demand an arrest, even assaults may be dealt with informally rather than by initiating a formal report or arrest.[4] Obviously, arrest statistics represent only the cases in which police officers receive a report and

EXHIBIT 1.2.2 Percent of Victimizations Reported to Police, by Type of Crime, 2004 and 2013*

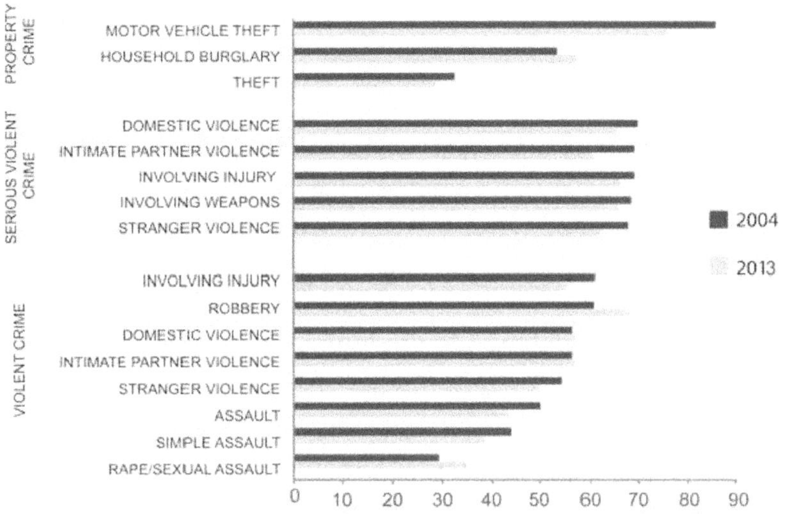

*Important footnotes regarding methodology omitted. See source.

Source: J. Truman and L. Langton, 2014. Criminal Victimization, 2013. *Washington, DC: Bureau of Justice Statistics, DOJ. Retrieved from: http://www.bjs.gov/content/pub/pdf/cv13.pdf*

decide to make an arrest. These numbers represent only a small portion of the total number of criminal incidents.

Before we can ask [the] question "Why do people commit crime?" we need to become familiar with the patterns and characteristics of crime. We use a number of sources that provide crime data. These are not perfect and each has inherent weaknesses, but they are the source of everything we think we know about crime in this country.

What Sources Do We Use to Find Out About the Patterns of Crime?

The two most common sources of crime data are the Uniform Crime Reports (which includes both reports to police and arrests) and the National Crime Victimization Survey. It is important to note that everything that we think we know about crime is derived primarily from these sources; thus, if there is some bias (inaccuracy) in the way these sources present the patterns of crime, then what we think we know is not necessarily accurate. It is important to know when you are looking at crime statistics whether the numbers reflect "reports to police," "arrests," or respondents reporting in a victimization survey. Each reflects slightly different realities of crime.

The Uniform Crime Reports

The most well-known and used source of crime statistics in this country is the **Uniform Crime Reports.** This collection of local crime reports and arrest data began in 1929 and is now produced by the Federal Bureau of Investigation. The numbers come either directly from local law enforcement agencies or from a state agency that collects the data from local agencies and delivers it in a centralized format. About 98 percent of law enforcement agencies submit crime data to the FBI.[5]

You can find the UCR at https://www.fbi.gov/about-us/cjis/ucr/ucr

The Uniform Crime Reports present crime reports in terms of **rates** as well as raw numbers. The rates you will see in the Uniform Crime Reports are the number of crimes divided by the population and then multiplied to display by a standard number. You can compute a rate (per 100,000) using the following mathematical formula. The rate tells you how many crimes took place for each 100,000 people.

$$\text{Rate} = (\text{Number of Crimes} \div \text{Population}) \times 100{,}000$$

The advantage of a rate is that it allows us to compare patterns of crime in very different populations. For instance, with rates, we can compare the same city in two different periods, even if the city's population has dramatically changed. We can also compare two different cities, even if one is very large and the other very small. Knowing, for instance, the raw number of burglaries in New York City; Portland, Oregon; Austin, Texas; and Los Angeles, California, tells us something, but it doesn't tell us the relative risk of victimization in these cities because they do not have similar populations. The only way to compare the crime of two different populations is to compute the rate of each city, then compare the rates. In 2013, the *numbers* of reported burglaries and the *rates* for these cities looked like this:[6]

City	Population	Number of Burglaries	Rate
New York City	8,396,126	16,606	197
Portland	609,136	4,128	678
Austin	859,180	6,550	752
Los Angeles	3,878,725	15,728	405

Who would have thought that there were more burglaries per 100,000 people in Portland, Austin, and Los Angeles than in New York City? Compare other big cities which also show quite different rates for burglary.

City	Population	Number of Burglaries	Rate
Houston	2,180,606	23,733	1088
Chicago	2,720,554	17,775	653

The FBI cautions against anyone using these numbers to compare the crime risk between cities because there are so many variables that go into them, including police departments' recording practices, urban density, victim reporting practices, and so on. If city limits extend out into the suburbs, the crime rate will be lower because crime occurs less often in suburban than in urban areas. Any or all of these factors may help to explain why New York's burglary rates are so much lower than other cities. New York City also may have a low rate of burglaries because of a higher percentage of buildings with security, a lower percentage of occupied dwellings than other metropolitan areas, or a number of other factors that affects the number of burglaries in that geographic area. Even though we want to be cautious when comparing rates across cities, an examination of these rates do tell us that just because New Yorkers report over 16,000 burglaries and citizens of Austin report only about 6,500 does not mean necessarily that an individual has a greater risk of being burgled in New York City.

It is very important to have an accurate population base for rates to mean anything. If the population base is inaccurate, then so too will be the rate. If, for instance, the population base is out of date and the actual population has grown considerably, then the crimes (which inevitably would increase with a larger population) will be divided by an artificially small population indicating that the rate of crime in that locale (the amount of crime per person) is higher than what it actually is. In contrast, if the population used is inaccurate in the other direction and shows a much larger population than what actually exists (perhaps because people have been moving away from that area), and the crime rate is computed using this inaccurately high population, then the crime rate will appear to be lower than it actually is. Usually, the FBI uses the most recent census numbers for the area, but these numbers may be vulnerable to rapid fluctuations in population/migration.

Crime reports are gathered from law enforcement agencies via a standard reporting form so that, for instance, larceny means the same thing in all states whether or not state laws differ in defining the dollar amount that would change larceny from a misdemeanor to a felony. Because these are standard definitions, they may or may not conform to the state's definition for that particular crime.

The UCR provides the total number of reported crimes for the eight **index crimes**: murder and non-negligent manslaughter, forcible rape, robbery, aggravated assault, burglary, larceny-theft, motor vehicle theft, and arson. Violent crimes include the first four crimes and property crimes include the last four crimes. These index crimes are also presented as rates per 100,000. In Exhibit 1.2.3a and b,

EXHIBIT 1.2.3a and 1.2.3b, Uniform Crime Reports—Violent Crime and Property Crime, 1986–2014

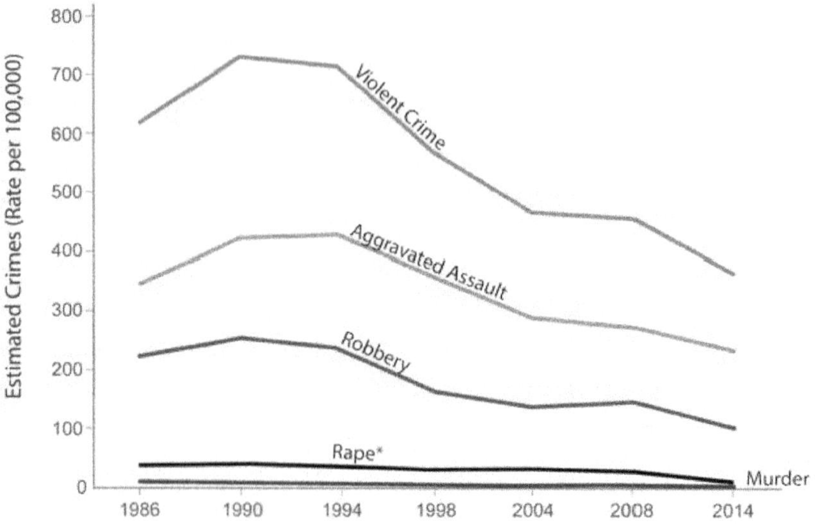

*The definition of rape changed for reporting purposes and the 2014 report included both the "legacy" rape rates (with the word forcible included) as shown here, but also a rate of 36.6 for the new definition: The revised UCR definition of rape is: "penetration, no matter how slight, of the vagina or anus with any body part or object, or oral penetration by a sex organ of another person, without the consent of the victim."

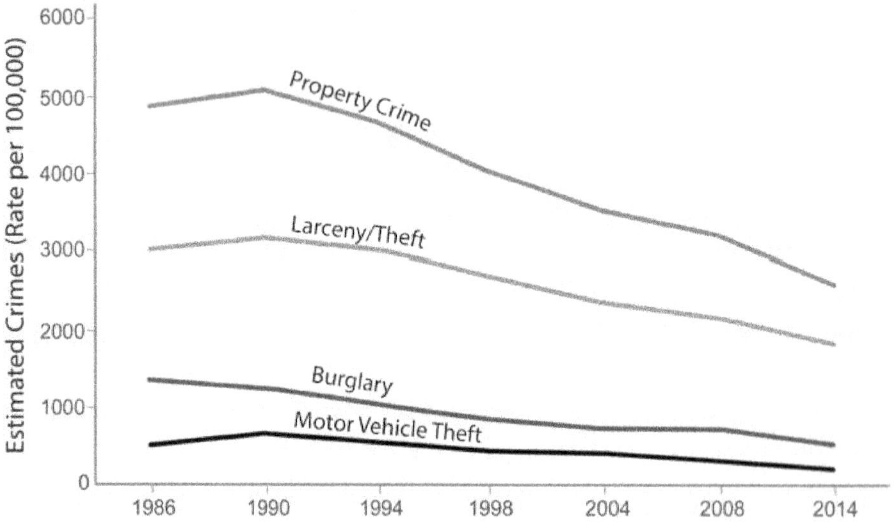

Source: UCR, Table 1, Crime in the United States, Table 1. By Volume and Rate, 1986–2005. Retrieved from www.fbi.gov/ucr/05cius/data/table/_01/html. Crime in the United States, 2008, Table 1. By Volume and Rate, 1989–2008. Retrieved from www.fbi.gov/ucr/cius2008/data/table_01.html. Crime in the United States, 2014. Table 1. By Volume and Rate. Retrieved from https://www.fbi.gov/about-us/cjis/ucr/crime-in-the-u.s/2014/crime-in-the-u.s.-2014/tables/table-1.

we see the UCR rates for violent and property crimes across several decades. Note that all crime categories show dramatic declines in the crimes reported to the police.

One of the most oft-cited criticisms of the UCR is that it represents only reported crimes. If someone does not report a criminal victimization to the police, it does not get counted as a crime. Consequently, there is a "dark" figure of crime that never appears in the UCR. The amount of unreported crime varies by the type of crime. We saw in Exhibit 1.2.2 that less than half of violent crime victimizations and a little over a third of property crime victimizations are reported to police and, thus, are represented in the UCR. This presents a distinct problem if one uses the UCR as a measure of crime. In fact, it is not a measure of crime, but only a measure of *reported* crime. Another problem is that crimes such as identity theft, cybercrimes, and domestic violence are not easily identified in the traditional UCR because the reporting system is not set up to identify them.

One more potential problem is that some police departments have been exposed as "cooking" their numbers, meaning that they systematically downgrade citizens' reports of crimes in official reports. Scandals in New York City,[7] Chicago, and other cities[8] are troubling reminders that what we think we know about crime is dependent on accurate crime counts. When police departments categorize deaths as "undetermined" despite clear indications of homicide, they are not counted; when they record a robbery as theft instead of robbery, the true nature of the crime is hidden. These troubling incidents potentially make it unwise to utilize the UCR as the only source of understanding crime patterns—at least in specific cities.

The FBI also presents statistics on arrests. Arrest data is presented for 21 crime categories. In addition to the eight index crimes, arrests are also reported for other assaults, forgery, fraud, prostitution, and even curfew violations. The numbers of arrests are by no means a measure of crime, because they capture only the crimes in which a suspect was identified and a decision to arrest was made. Arrest data are presented for 21 crime categories in Exhibit 1.2.4, arranged in order of frequency. The graph shows that arrests for most crimes decreased. For some crimes, such as prostitution, changes over time are likely due to changes in decisions to arrest; for other crimes, such as homicide, arrest decisions are less likely to change because of discretionary enforcement. We must always remember that fluctuations in arrest rates may be real differences in such behavior, differences in perception and/or enforcement of the behavior, or differences in counting crimes. In this graph, the last several crimes are displayed separately since they show up as almost non-existent when in the same display as more frequent crimes.

Many crimes go unsolved or are not cleared. Crimes are considered cleared when an arrest is made for an offense. The FBI reports on the number of crimes cleared by arrest with a statistic called the **clearance rate**. The clearance rates vary greatly by crime. In 2004, murder and non-negligent homicide had the highest clearance rate (62.6 percent), while burglary had the lowest clearance rate (12.9 percent).[9] In 2009, the clearance rate for murder and non-negligent homicide increased to 66.6 percent, while motor vehicle theft and burglary declined to 12.4 percent and

EXHIBIT 1.2.4 Uniform Crime Report Arrests, 2014.

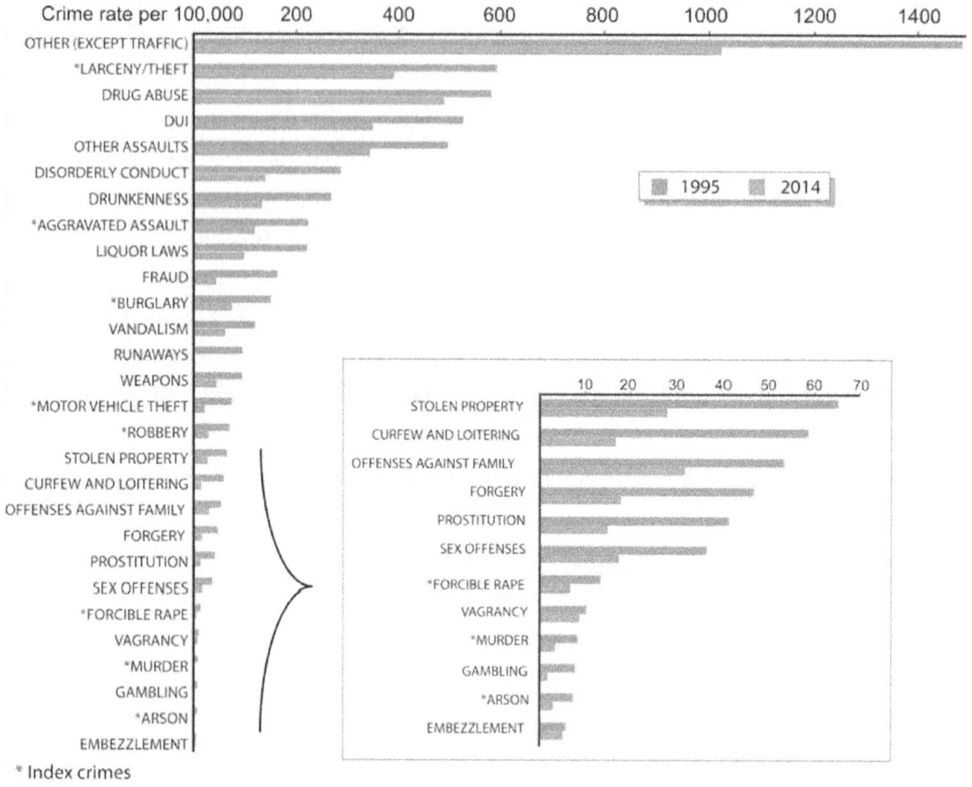

Source: FBI, Crimes in the United States, 2014, Arrest Rates. *https://www.fbi.gov/about-us/cjis/ucr/crime-in-the-u.s/2014/crime-in-the-u.s.-2014/tables/table-30*

Note: Murder includes murder and non-negligent manslaughter.

12.5 percent, respectively.[10] In 2014, the clearance rate for murder and non-negligent manslaughter slipped to 64.5 percent. The clearance rate for motor vehicle theft and burglary was 12.8 percent and 13.6 percent, respectively.[11]

To see clearance rates, go to http://www.fbi.gov/ucr/cius_04/offenses_cleared/index.html

The FBI has also been collecting crime statistics in a different format to address other recognized problems. The National Incident-Based Reporting System (**NIBRS**) gathers much more detailed information about each criminal incident. While the UCR reporting format is hierarchical, meaning that only the most serious crime is counted, NIBRS requires information to be submitted on each crime within a criminal transaction. Instead of reporting crimes via the eight index offenses, NIBRS will display information on Group A offense categories (22 different crimes) and Group B offenses (11 different crimes). More information is obtained about each offense, including information about the victim and offender. For 22 offense categories, the following information is being collected and will be reported in NIBRS reports, also available on the FBI website:

- Victim, offender, and arrestee data
- Location and time of day of incidents
- Weapon data for select offenses
- Drug, alcohol, and gang involvement in offenses
- Attempted versus completed offenses
- Clearances by incidents
- Relationship of victims to offenders.

NIBRS reports are not comparable to the UCR because the way crimes are counted is different. For instance, a robbery, rape, and murder would only be reported as a murder in the UCR, but as three separate crimes under NIBRS. Law enforcement agencies have been slow to adopt the NIBRS reporting procedures, probably because it is much more detailed, requiring more effort to enter the data. There is also the concern that NIBRS will make it appear that there is an increase in crime because it would report each separate criminal incident instead of the hierarchical reporting system of the UCR. In 2012, about 30 percent of the nation's population was represented by crime statistics reported under NIBRS.[12] Currently only fifteen U.S. states have complete NIBRS agency participation, with an additional 18 states that submit both summary UCR and NIBRS data.[13]

Victimization Studies

Another source of crime statistics comes from victimization surveys. The Bureau of Justice Statistics presents findings from the **National Crime Victimization Survey** (NCVS). Begun in 1973 as the National Crime Survey, the U.S. Bureau of the Census has been interviewing household members in a nationally representative sample. In 1992–93, the survey was redesigned and relabeled as the National Crime Victimization Survey. The redesign effort was intended to obtain more information and include less serious crimes. The items in the survey capture more information than what is available through the UCR. For instance, one question asks the respondent whether the crime was reported to the police. This is the source for our information in Exhibit 2.2, about how much crime goes unreported. Findings from the National Crime Victimization Survey can be accessed most easily through the Bureau of Justice Statistics, an agency that also presents other statistics about corrections, police, and specific crimes.

For more information, go to http://bjs.gov/

These two sources of crime data may be compared, but it is important to note their differences. The NCVS excludes homicide, arson, commercial crimes, and crimes against children under age twelve (the UCR includes these crimes). The NCVS also does not include any information on victimless crimes such as drug crimes, gambling, or prostitution. The UCR only collects arrest data on simple assault and sexual assaults other than rape, not reported crimes. Further, the NCVS calculates rates on the basis of 1000 *households,* while the UCR calculates rates based on 100,000 *persons*. Thus, it would be a mistake to treat findings from the two sources as comparable statistically. In general, the UCR gives us a broad picture of crime patterns (as reported to police) in the United States, while the NCVS gives us more information about the characteristics of victimizations in certain selected crime categories and reporting trends by victims.

Because the NCVS is based on a random sample of the population and does not collect reports of all victimizations, it is subject to all the potential problems of sampling and survey weaknesses. If any principles of **random sampling** are violated, then the applicability to the general population is in doubt. The sample size of the NCVS has been decreasing over the years, and some observers have begun to worry that the smaller sample size has begun to affect the representativeness of the sample.[14]

The advantage of having both the UCR (reports to police) and the NCVS (survey respondents' reports of victimization) is that, even if not completely comparable, we can note whether the general crime patterns are similar, thus being more confident in the accuracy of either source. Recall that the UCR shows a dramatic decline in crime reports across the last several decades. We can be more confident that the UCR is accurately representing a crime decline because the NCVS also shows dramatic declines in the number of people reporting victimization (whether or not they reported the victimization to the police). We will explore these patterns more closely when we answer the question about crime patterns below.

Self-Report Studies

Another source of crime data is simply to ask the offender. Self-report studies ask individuals to report the crimes they have committed. Obviously, there are problems inherent in such an approach, such as whether the individual is answering honestly or not. Self-reports are generally only obtained from targeted groups, specifically juveniles (who are still in school) and offenders (who are incarcerated). We do not administer self-report surveys door-to-door to samples of citizens. Self-report studies provide interesting information, but the findings must be considered in light of the characteristics of the sample. For instance, self-report studies of juveniles often use measures of behavior that stretch the definition of "crime" to the breaking point by including minor deviances, such as truancy and other forms of juvenile misbehavior. The definitions of wrongdoing are expanded in such studies because the vast majority of students have not committed any criminal acts. Therefore, in order to get sufficient numbers for statistical analysis, the definition of "offender" is expanded. It should be kept in mind when reading these studies that these "offenders" are not necessarily who we think of as criminals.

Part of the reason that student self-report studies have difficulty obtaining sufficient numbers of offenders for statistical analysis when testing crime theories is that by the time they are administered in junior or senior years, many high-risk juveniles have already dropped out or are not in school the day the study is administered. Therefore, the young people most likely to have committed crimes are likely to be absent from the study, and the reports of criminal activity are likely to under-represent the true nature of juvenile crime.

Like school samples, prisoner samples are relatively easy to obtain, but non-representative. Prisoners do not represent all offenders (only those who are caught and sentenced to prison). They also may not admit or may exaggerate their criminal activities. In addition, these surveys are subject to the potential inaccuracies of all surveys in that respondents may forget or misremember when events occurred. Self-report studies are typically used to understand behavior differences between offenders; for instance, the finding that a small percentage of offenders are responsible for a disproportional number of crimes came from offender self-report studies.

Cohort Studies

One other source of crime data is the **cohort study**, which follows a group of subjects over a long period. For instance, one cohort study followed all males born in Philadelphia in 1948.[15] Another longitudinal study conducted by the Harvard Program on Human Development and Criminal Behavior collected data on a cohort sample.[16] Typically, the follow-up period extends throughout childhood and into adulthood. A large number of factors have been identified as influencing criminality, including family factors, genetic factors, school and neighborhood factors, and peer factors. Proponents of longitudinal research argue that this method of data collection can illuminate how causal factors work at various times in one's life.

What Crimes Are People Most Frequently Arrested For?

When people think of crime, they probably think of robbery, murder, or violent assault. These crimes fill our newspapers and prime-time television, either as drama or reality television. It is important to note, however, that the most common crimes are fairly mundane. Looking again at Exhibit 1.2.4, we see that, in reality, the picture of crime is much different than what is reflected in the popular media. Murder, rape, and even robbery arrests are extremely rare. In contrast, the most common arrests are for a wide variety of minor misbehavior ("other"), drug violations (possession and distribution combined), and theft.

Since one of the most frequent types of arrest is for a drug offense, this category bears further scrutiny. In Exhibit 1.2.5, we see that over 80 percent of all drug arrests are for possession, and the most common drug for those arrests is marijuana. In fact, about 40 percent of all drug violation arrests are for marijuana possession.[17]

EXHIBIT 1.2.5 Arrests for Drug Abuse Violations

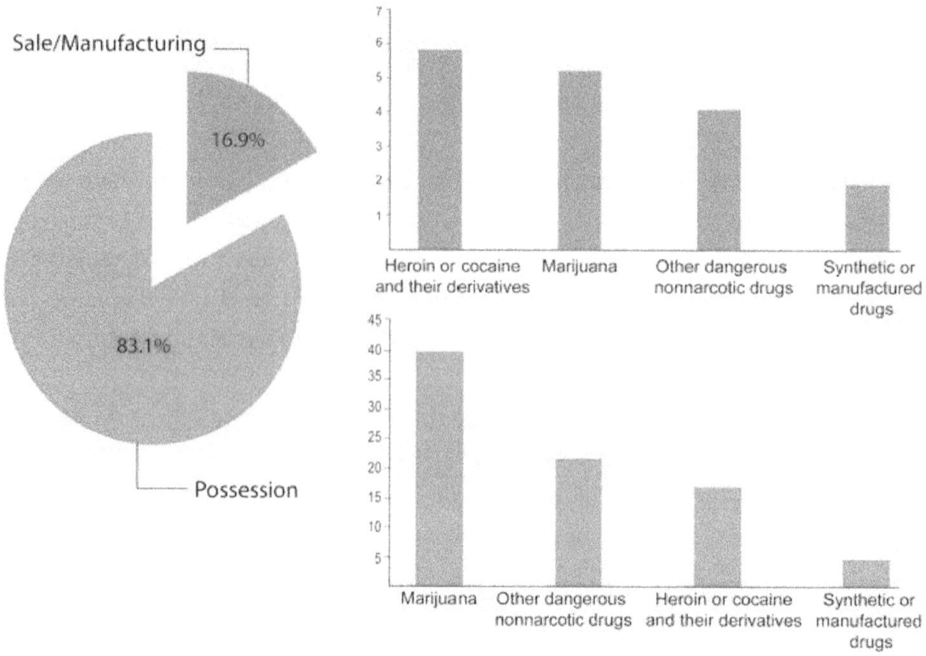

Source: FBI, Crimes in the United States, 2014. Arrests, *main page. Retrieved 12/9/2015 from https://www.fbi.gov/about-us/cjis/ucr/crime-in-the-u.s/2014/crime-in-the-u.s.-2014/persons-arrested/main*

As we noted before, it is important to remember that arrests are not a true reflection of crimes committed; they only represent who is arrested. Reports to police would provide more information about frequency of crimes, but the UCR only offers information on the eight index crimes. Exhibit 1.2.6 below presents these reports for 2014. We see that the most frequent crime reports are of larceny/theft, and following far behind are reports of burglaries. Recall, however, that most people report only a fraction of all crimes to police, thus, this picture of crime is also an inaccurate representation of crime.

Victimization surveys are closer to approximating the true prevalence of crime, but they are not comparable to the crime categories of the UCR or arrest tables. Recall that the most frequent

EXHIBIT 1.2.6 Crime Reports Rate, 2014

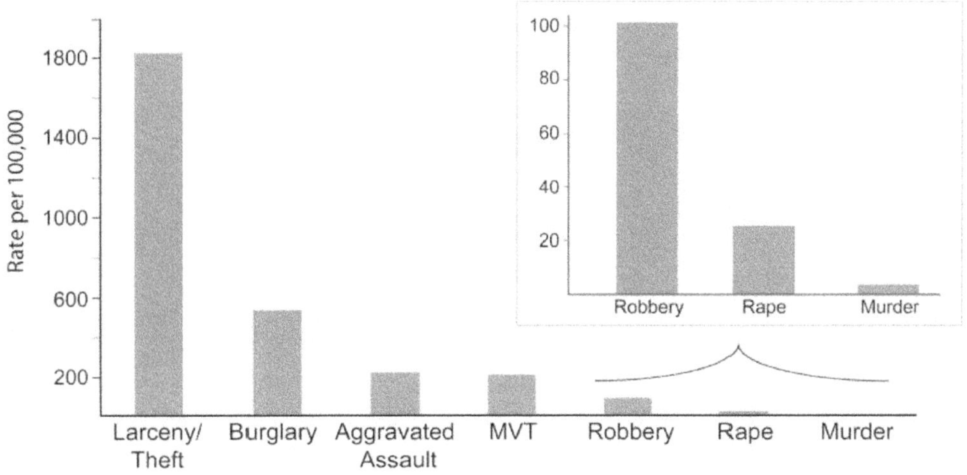

Source: FBI, Crime in the United States, *2014. https://www.fbi.gov/about-us/cjis/ucr/crime-in-the-u.s/2014/crime-in-the-u.s.-2014/tables/table-1*

arrests are for drug violations, but that crime category is not represented at all in the victimization reports. In the latest NCVS report, the most frequently reported victimization was theft (at 6.41 reports per 1,000), followed by burglary (at 1.67 reports per 1,000). Thus, these two crimes appear as the most frequent crimes in both reports to the police (UCR) and reports in the NCVS. In contrast, the least frequently reported victimization was serious intimate partner violence (at 0.05 reports per 1,000), which does not have a crime category parallel in the UCR, and rape/sexual assault (at 0.06 reports per 1,000).[18]

To summarize, our crime sources give us fragmented information about the true prevalence of crime. The most frequent arrests in 2014 were for drug offenses, and the most frequent victim-harming crimes seem to be larceny/theft and burglary, as reported to police and in victimization reports. The constant media focus on violent crimes is highly disproportionate to the true prevalence of crime categories.

What Do We Know About Homicide?

Even though homicide is a very rare occurrence, people are quite rightly more fearful of homicide, rape, aggravated assault, and robbery than property crimes. The rate of homicide has been declining for decades—the murder rate fell by more than half nationally from its peak in 1980, as seen in Exhibit 1.2.7. It is also true, however, that some cities have experienced increases in some years.

EXHIBIT 1.2.7 Homicide Rates Over Time

Source: C. Bialik, "Scare headlines exaggerated the US crime wave." Fivethirtyeight.com. Retrieved 12/12/2015 from https://fivethirtyeight.com/features/scare-headlines-exaggerated-the-u-s-crime-wave/

We can obtain more detailed information about homicides from the supplemental homicide reports of the FBI. Exhibit 1.2.8 shows that the most recent report indicates that homicides are most likely to be single victim and single offender.

> You can explore the statistics on homicide by going to a data analysis tool offered by the Office of Juvenile Justice and Delinquency: http://www.ojjdp.gov/ojstatbb/ezashr/asp/off_selection.asp

Exhibit 1.2.9 displays information from the FBI's supplemental information on homicides. We see that, in 2012, information was known about the relationship between victim and offender in only slightly more than half of all cases. Of those cases, the most common relationship between victim and offender was acquaintance. The family members most likely to be killed by another family member were wives. Only 12 percent of the victims where the relationship between victim and offender was known were killed by strangers. However, because that information seems to be

EXHIBIT 1.2.8 Murder: Victim/Offender Situation

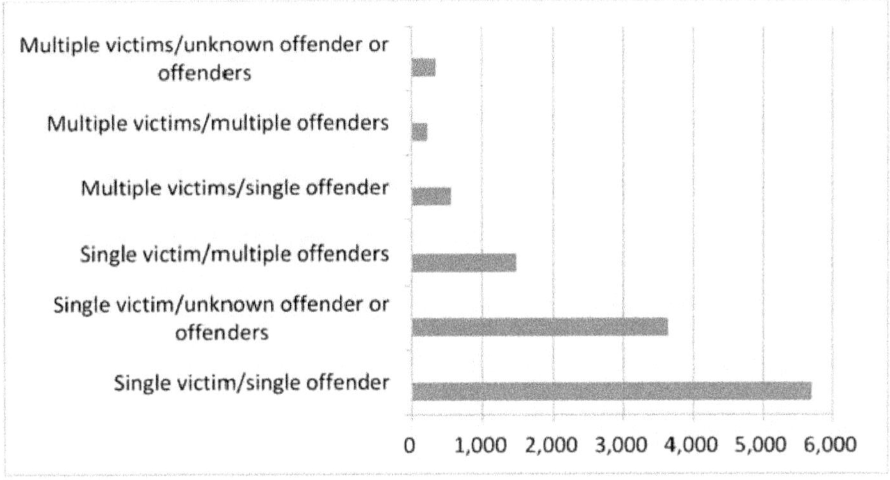

Source: Crime in the U.S., 2014, Table 4.

EXHIBIT 1.2.9 Relationship between Homicide Victims and Offenders

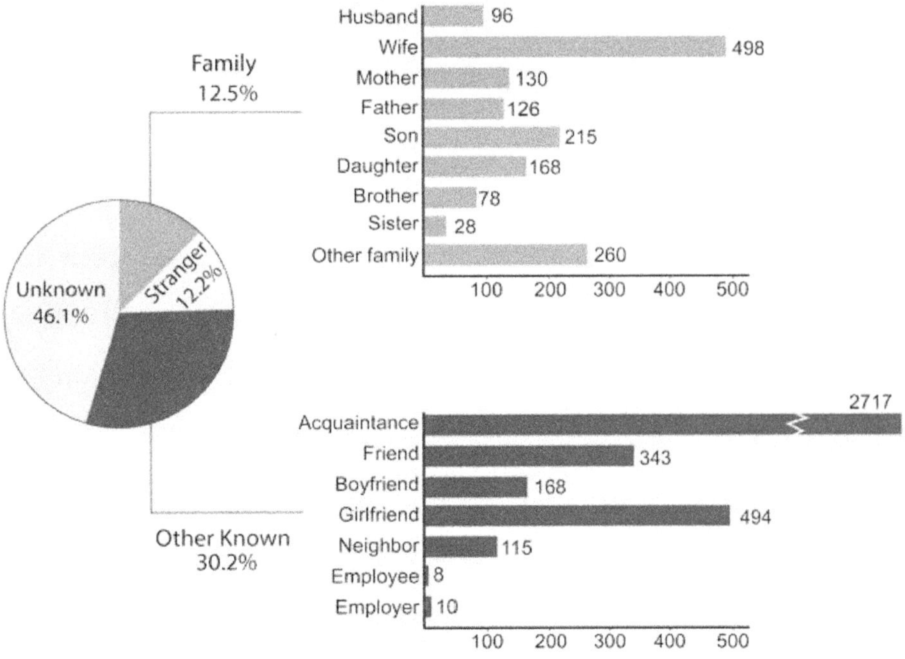

Source: FBI. Retrieved 1/4/2016 from https://www.fbi.gov/about-us/cjis/ucr/crime-in-the-u.s/2012/crime-in-the-u.s.-2012/offenses-known-to-law-enforcement/expanded-homicide/expandhomicidemain

missing from almost half of all homicides, we must be cautious about assuming anything about the relationship between victim and offender from those cases where we do have the information.

Using 2013 data, it is clear that homicide offenders *and* victims are likely to be male and disproportionately African American (Exhibit 1.2.10).

It is important to note that these percentages are of total homicide numbers. Rates (per 100,000) would look much different since African Americans comprise only about 13 percent of the total population; thus, the fact that 44 percent of all murder victims are African American is a truly astounding figure. Data analysis from the time period of the most dramatic decline in homicide illustrated the fact that between the mid-1990s and late 2000s, the most dramatic declines in homicide also took place with African American men (see Exhibit 1.2.11).[19]

EXHIBIT 1.2.10 Homicide Offenders/Victims

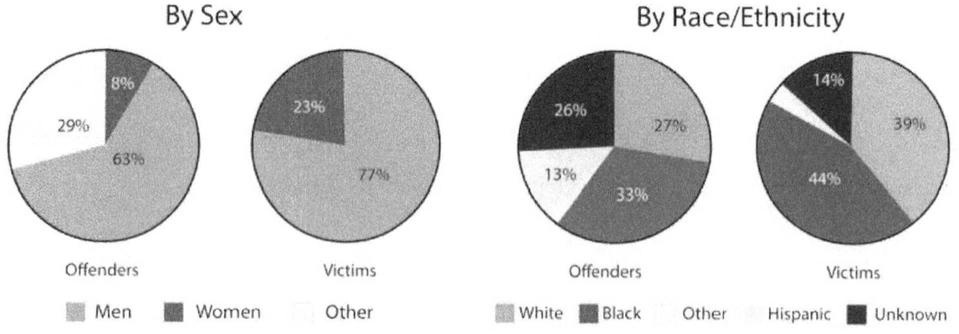

*Not all departments report ethnicity so Hispanic victims and offenders may be included in other categories.

Source: Crime in the United States, *2014, Table 3; 4; Table 6*

EXHIBIT 1.2.11 Homicide Declines by Race, 1985–2012

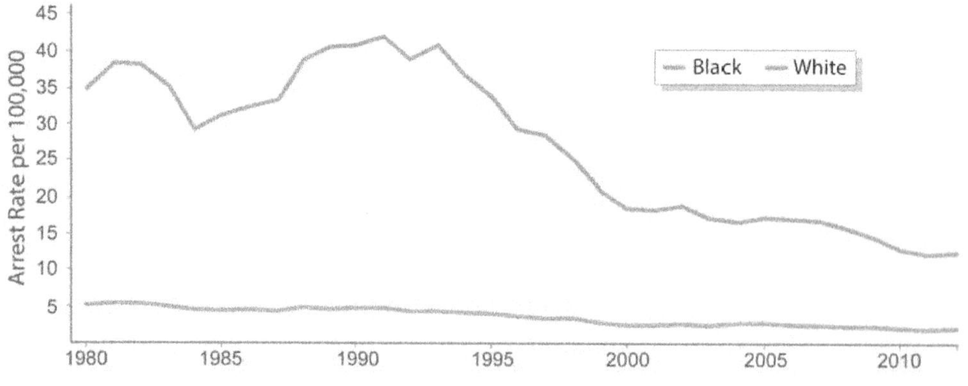

Source: Crime in the United States, *2014, Table 3; 4; Table 6*

It is important to note that when there are changes in the number of homicides, not all racial/ethnic and gender groups are equally at risk. Homicides have increased in some urban areas, but, similar to past patterns, not everyone is equally vulnerable.

What Has Been the Pattern of Crime Over the Years? Has It Declined?

Recall from the above discussion that the UCR has recorded dramatic declines in all crime categories in the last twenty years. This could be due to a true decrease in criminal activity, or it could be due to less people reporting their victimization. The way to know for sure is to compare victimization reports to crime reports. [...] [T]riangulating data utilizes different sources to compare facts. We can be more confident that we have truly experienced a decline in crime because the UCR, the National Crime Victimization Survey, and arrest tables all show a steady overall decline since the early 1990s. Exhibit 1.2.12 illustrates this consensus. Although there was a bit of an increase in 2012, the decline continued afterwards.

EXHIBIT 1.2.12 Composite View of Decline in Crime, 1990–2014

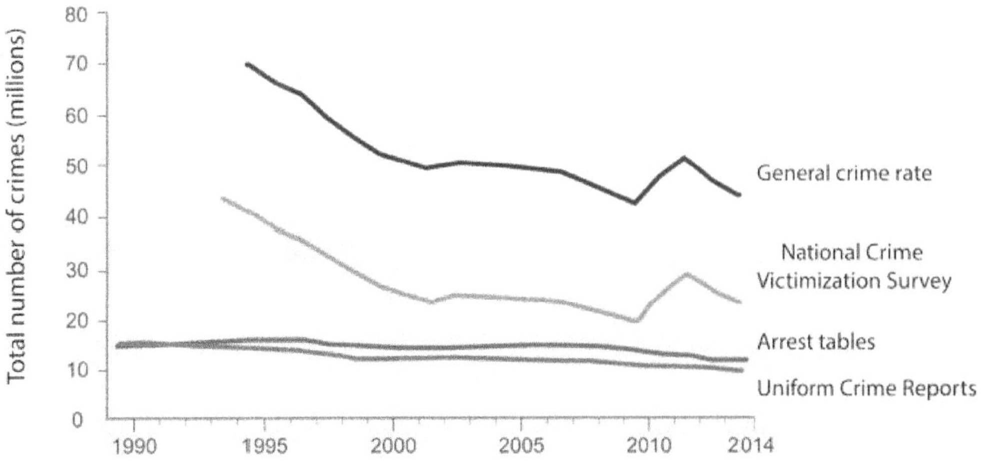

Source: Bureau of Justice Statistics, Criminal Victimization Survey, *1994–2014. Online Sourcebook of Criminal Justice Statistics, Table 3, Estimated number and rate of offenses known to police, 1990–2014. UCR, Crime in the United States, 1995–2014.*

Does the Public Have an Accurate Perception About the Prevalence of Crime?

There is no doubt that our crime rates are about as low as they have been since the 1970s, but does the public know that? The short answer is no. A Gallup poll indicates that about 70 percent of Americans think there is more crime in the U.S. now than there was a year ago. In fact, in most years, the majority of Americans think crime was higher than the year before, but they have been wrong. The only year the minority of citizens (41 percent) thought crime had declined was in 2001.

It is also interesting to note that women are more likely to think crime has risen. Conservatives (80 percent) are more likely than liberals (57 percent), and those in rural towns are more likely than urban residents to think crime has risen. Exhibit 1.2.13 shows these differences. In 2015, nearly six in ten Americans (59 percent) said U.S. crime is an "extremely" or "very" serious problem—up slightly from 55 percent in 2014.[20]

EXHIBIT 1.2.13 Public Perceptions of Crime in the U.S., 1989–2015

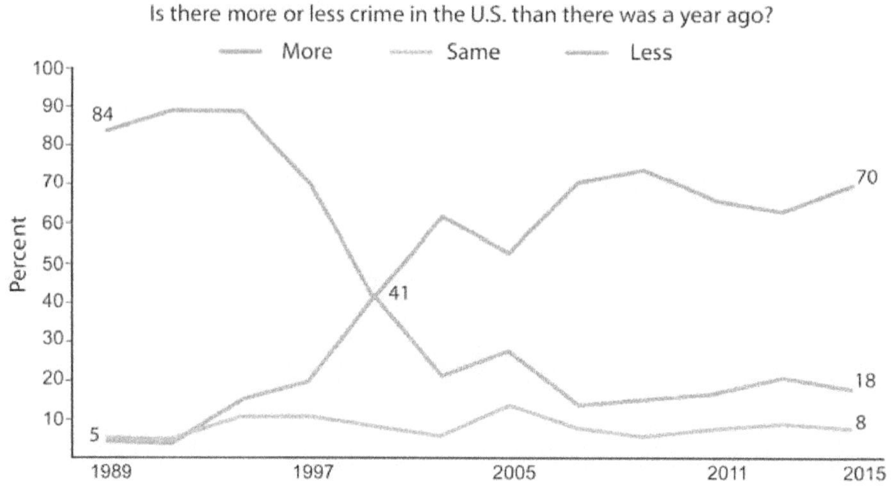

Source: Gallup Poll. Retrieved 1/4/2015 from http://www.gallup.com/poll/186308/americans-say-crime-rising.aspx?utm_source=alert&utm_medium=email&utm_content=morelink&utm_campaign=syndication

How Do the Crime Rates of the United States Compare to Other Countries?

There is a widespread perception that one of the reasons the United States leads the world in incarceration rates is because there is more crime here than in similar Western countries such as the

United Kingdom, France, or Canada. This is true only for homicide. Property crime rates in the United States are roughly comparable to those of other countries. It should be pointed out that comparing crimes cross-culturally is difficult because definitions and reporting practices that affect crime statistics vary. The United Nations Office of Drugs and Crime, however, has collected and makes available crime rates as reported by member nations in order to make some tentative comparisons. In the latest report available, about 138 countries are represented. In Exhibit 1.2.14 below, certain selected countries and crimes are displayed.

Homicide is perhaps the most consistently reported crime and offers the most reliable comparison. The homicide rate per 100,000 of the United States is about 3.8. That is down from previous years, but still higher than many European countries, Canada, and Australia. On the other hand,

EXHIBIT 1.2.14 Selected Crimes in Selected Countries: Homicide, Robbery, Burglary

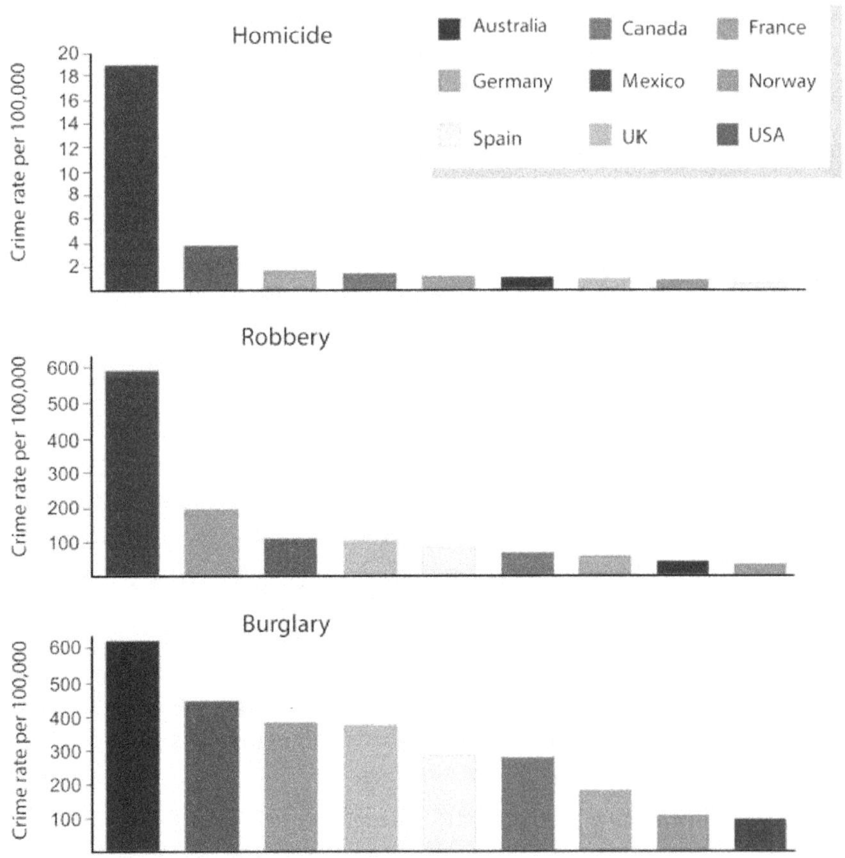

Source: United Nations Office of Drugs and Crimes, Crime Data tool, retrieved 12/9/2015 from https://data.unodc.org/#state:14

the rate of homicide in the U.S. is much lower than Mexico's or other countries in South America and Africa. Mexico's robbery rate is extremely high compared to other countries. France has a higher robbery rate than the U.S. and Australia has a higher burglary rate. While we must be careful with these statistics because it is unknown how accurate or consistent reporting is across all the countries, it does indicate that the crime rate in the U.S. is not wildly disproportionate to other Western, industrialized countries, except for the homicide rate.

> To explore for yourself some of these statistics, go to https://data.unodc.org/#state:14

Before we leave this [reading] on crime statistics, we will offer a discussion that illustrates how important accurate data and reasonable data interpretation can be when discussing current events. A current controversy playing out in newspapers and other public arenas today is whether there has been a "**Ferguson Effect**" on American policing that has resulted in "**de-policing**" which, in turn, has led to a spike in homicides and violent crimes in major cities. The Focus on Data section below examines this question.

Focus on Data: Is There a Ferguson Effect? Is There a Current Crime Wave?

In the summer and fall of 2014, the shooting of young Black men by police officers led to a number of violent protests in several American cities, most notably in Ferguson, Missouri and Baltimore, Maryland. Some argued that the public scrutiny and criticism of police led to a change in police behavior, dubbed the "Ferguson Effect," which referred to police officers choosing not to engage with citizens for fear of being labeled racist or violent. This "de-policing," as it was also called, then, arguably, led to a spike in homicide.

Beginning in 2015, major news outlets began reporting on big-city crime spikes. Eventually the *Washington Post*, *New York Times*, NPR, CNN, BBC, *USA Today*, Reuters, *Time*, and other major news outlets had "crime spike" stories. In August of 2015, the Major Cities Chiefs Association (MCCA) reported increased homicides as a problem. In contrast, others (*New York Daily News*, Brennan Center, Marshall Project) argued that there was no evidence yet to indicate alarm was warranted. Let's look at the facts.

Heather MacDonald's much publicized article in the *Wall Street Journal* reported that gun violence was up 60 percent in Baltimore with May 2015 as the most violent month the city had seen in fifteen years. A list of cities with percentage increases were offered, including Milwaukee (180 percent by May 17 over the same period the previous year), St. Louis (25 percent), Atlanta (32 percent),

EXHIBIT 1.2.15 Demonstrators marking the one-year anniversary of the shooting of Michael Brown confront police during a protest in Ferguson, Missouri. Some have argued that criticism of police, both in the media and through protests, has led to the "Ferguson Effect."

Source: Getty

Chicago (17 percent), and New York (13 percent). Then she argued that city-wide statistics masked much larger neighborhood increases such as 500 percent in one East Harlem neighborhood. Because the first six months of 2014 continued a twenty-year pattern of decline, her argument was that the increases in the first six months of 2015 were due to a surge of lawlessness because of people's agitation against police departments and media focus on the events. MacDonald noted the "Ferguson Effect" (a term evidently coined by St. Louis police chief Sam Dotson) was the phenomenon of police officers disengaging from discretionary enforcement activity, with a resulting feeling of empowerment by criminals. She pointed to the fact that arrests in St. Louis city and county had dropped a third since the shooting of Michael Brown in August, while homicides surged 47 percent and robberies were up 82 percent through November 2014. Other cities also showed a decline in arrests; for instance, she reported that Baltimore had 56 percent fewer arrests by May 2015 compared to 2014. In New York City, stop-and-frisk policies led to a lawsuit and intense media scrutiny; consequently, stops dropped 95 percent from the 2011 high according to MacDonald. She further argued that aggressive policing has led to urban reclamation and saved thousands of Black lives and warned that continued criticism of police would lead to losing the gains in crime reduction that had been achieved in the last twenty years.[21] There are [three] arguments to this position:

1. Homicides and other crimes in American cities are increasing.
2. Police officers are not policing in the way they have in previous years, meaning they are less likely to engage in "pro-active" policing such as stop-and-frisks and arrests for minor crimes due to the public and media scrutiny and criticism that has arisen since the summer of 2014.
3. The reduction in pro-active policing, if it exists, caused the increase in homicides and other crime, if the increase exists.

1. Are Homicides and Other Crimes in American Cities Increasing?

Unfortunately, the UCR and the FBIs Supplemental Homicide Report are not as current as we would need to answer this question. It usually takes six months to a year before crime reports are available for public consumption. The latest FBI data (UCR) for 2014 indicate that there was a 2 percent decrease in homicide rates per 100,000 nationwide, however, the pattern was different between cities and suburban and rural areas. In the largest cities (over 1 million), there was a 2.2 percent *increase* in homicides per 100,000, but a 16 percent *decrease* in non-metropolitan counties. Thus, contrary to MacDonald's proposition that the first months of 2015 were an aberration due to changing circumstances after the Michael Brown shooting, homicides had already begun to increase in cities (as opposed to suburban and rural areas) in 2014.

Recent analyses of 2015 homicides for the largest American cities showed that there was probably about a 17 percent increase in homicides in the first six months of 2015 compared to the first six months of 2014—a dramatic increase, but this increase seems to be confined to only some cities.[22] In fact, the pattern is highly skewed: ten cities account for two-thirds of the increase. These cities are characterized by: higher poverty, a falling population, and high unemployment.[23] The National Institute of Justice published an analysis of the increase (using data collected by the *New York Times* and *Washington Post*) and showed that from 2014 to 2015, 127 more people were killed in Baltimore (a 59 percent increase); 61 more people were killed in Milwaukee from the year before (a 73 percent increase); 57 more people killed in Cleveland (a 91 percent increase) and 34 more people killed in Nashville (an 83 percent increase).[24]

Note that, even with over 200 murders in 2015, that number is dramatically lower than the high in 1993 when New York City recorded 1,946 murders.[25] UCR trend data shows that homicide and violent crime has been declining for the last twenty years.

News headlines that refer to large percentage increases in murder rates in specific cities usually neglect to mention that large percentage increases happen more easily with small base numbers. A 50 percent increase in murders sounds ominous, but a 50 percent increase of twelve is six additional homicides. Homicide numbers, because they have been quite small in the last decade, can be influenced by such things as an intra-familial multiple murder, or police recording practices,

EXHIBIT 1.2.16 Rising Murder Rates in Big Cities, 2014–2015

City	Absolute Increase	% Increase	Cumulative % of Total Increase
Baltimore	127	58.5	15.5
Chicago	61	15.0	22.9
Houston	61	25.2	30.3
Milwaukee	61	72.6	37.8
Cleveland	57	90.5	44.7
Washington DC	57	54.3	51.6
Nashville	34	82.9	55.8
Philadelphia	32	12.9	59.7
Kansas City	29	37.2	63.2
St. Louis	29	18.2	66.7

Source: City police departments, reported in M. Davey and M. Smith. "Murder Rates Rising Sharply in Many Cities." New York Times *(September 1, 2015), p. A1.*

such as reclassifying cases from undetermined to homicide, or other reporting changes. In fact, several journalists, in articles analyzing crime increases in certain cities such as Chicago, New York, and Los Angeles, have suggested that at least part of the increase might be due to changes in reporting practices after major scandals that exposed police departments as not recording crime reports accurately. For instance, Domanick reported that violent crime in Los Angeles rose more than 20 percent during the first half of 2015, with felony assaults up 26 percent and robberies up 19 percent and suggested that the increase might be due, in part, to a *Los Angeles Times* investigation of the department's crime numbers for the first half of 2014, which discovered the misclassification of 1,200 violent felony assaults as misdemeanors, thus making it appear that serious violent crime was going down when, in fact, it went up by 14 percent.[26] A similar article describing Chicago's crime reporting described how, by categorizing a death as "undetermined," despite clear indices of murder, the number of homicides were artificially reduced.[27] While some amount of misrepresenting the seriousness of crimes probably would not significantly influence percentage increase numbers of burglary because the base numbers are so large, such practices could definitely result in significant increases or decreases in crime categories that involve smaller numbers such as homicide and robbery.

While the MacDonald article presented data from cities that had increased homicides, others have noted that the pattern is not uniform across American cities. An analysis by FiveThirtyEight.com utilized city data, news reports, and other sources to construct a table with 60 cities and homicide numbers for 2015 compared to the same time period in 2014.[28] In 26 cities, homicides were up by 20 percent or more from a year ago, but the number of homicides was down in nineteen other cities.

More generally, crime analysts will warn against year to year comparisons of homicide, or any crime, because year-to-year rates fluctuate. The better way to understand data is by looking

EXHIBIT 1.2.17 Homicide Patterns in Selected Cities: Los Angeles, New York, Chicago

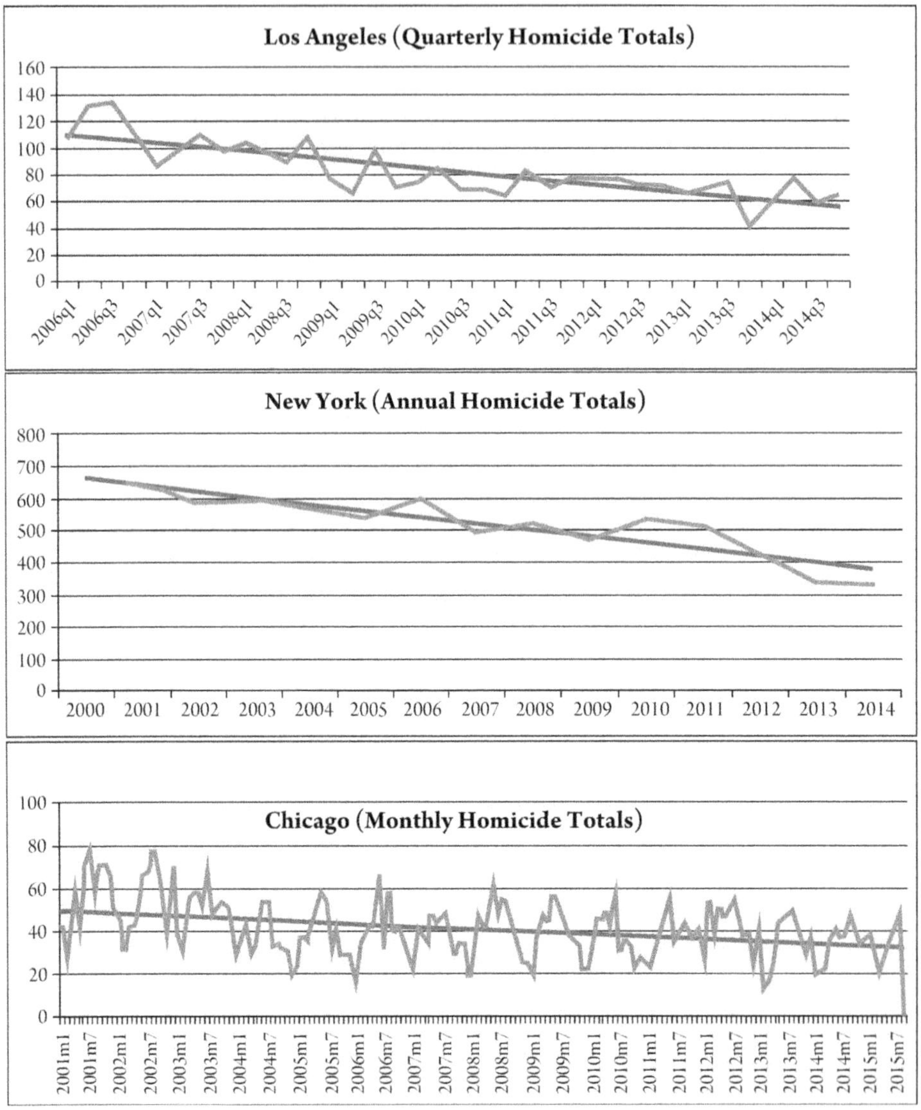

Source: M. Friedman. "Just facts: America's non-existent 'spike in crime.'" Brennan Center for Justice (August 10, 2015). Retrieved 12/12/2015 from https://www.brennancenter.org/blog/americas-non-existent-spike-crime.

at longer periods of time. When we examine murder trends we see that, although there may be year-to-year increases, the general trend has been downward, in this set of tables from a report produced by the Brennan Center.[29]

Moving from homicide to all violent crime, the UCR reported that nationwide violent crime reports to police were down by 0.2 percent and property crime declined by 4.3 percent in 2014.[30] The latest National Crime Victimization Survey, released in August 2015, reported no significant change in violent crime victimization, and property crime victimization fell from 131.4 per 1,000 to 118.1 per 1,000 in 2014.[31]

In summary, many American cities, but not all, have seen recent increases in homicides. Further, it may be that the increases are occurring in large cities, not in smaller towns and suburban areas. The FBI had reported a small increase in large metropolitan areas in 2014 so this increase began at least as early as 2014. Further, analysts point to trend data to show that year-to-year fluctuations have occurred continuously even throughout the twenty-year decline in homicide and other violent crimes.

2. Are Police Officers Not Policing in the Way They Have in Previous Years? If So, Is This Due to the Public and Media Scrutiny and Criticism That Have Arisen Since the Summer of 2014?

MacDonald reported fairly dramatic declines in arrests in some cities, arguing this was evidence of "de-policing." Interestingly, fewer arrests can be presented as a decline in crime or a decline in policing, depending on one's perspective. While MacDonald reported dramatic declines, criminologists have pointed to other cities that have not shown declines in arrests.[32] Misdemeanor arrests, traffic tickets, and investigative stops are subject to more discretionary decision making by officers than felony arrests, therefore, all three should be considered to determine if "de-policing" is occurring.

New York City has definitely seen a dramatic drop in the number of stop-and-frisks undertaken by New York City police officers, but the decline had begun earlier than the summer and fall of 2014 when the protests in Ferguson, Missouri and Baltimore, Maryland occurred. A report by the John Jay College of Criminal Justice indicated that between 2011 and 2014 the total number of arrests for felonies and misdemeanors, criminal summonses, and stop-and-frisks fell by more than 800,000, or 31 percent. Street stops declined from a high of 685,000 in 2011 to under 46,000 in 2014, a 93 percent decline in only three years. The declines were mostly in poorer and minority neighborhoods where they had grown the fastest over the previous decade. The decline in stops occurred because of a court ruling in 2013 that found such stops unconstitutional as well as a growing public outcry that the stops were unfairly targeting minority and poor residents who had the misfortune to live in certain areas of the city. Despite the multi-year decline in such stops, crime reports continued to decline as well. In 2014, rates of both violent and nonviolent crime in New York City were lower than the year before, and were almost 90 percent lower than they were in 1980.[33]

Another city that saw arrests and investigative stops decline was Seattle. In May of 2014 it was reported that police enforcement of lower-level crimes, traffic offenses and infractions dropped dramatically, including a 49 percent decline in misdemeanor criminal arrests between 2005 and 2013. While service calls had increased by 9 percent between the first quarter of 2010 and first quarter of 2014, independent officer-initiated activity had dropped by 44 percent, from 15 percent of their time in 2011 to only 8 percent of their time in the same quarter in 2014. Officer checks of suspicious people and suspicious vehicles dropped by 80 percent. Bookings into the jail fell by 51 percent between 2006 and 2013. Between 2007 and 2013, infractions filed in Seattle Municipal Court fell 71 percent, covering unlawful activity such as liquor violations, public urination, and noise problems. Because the Seattle Police Department was investigated by the Department of Justice and entered into a consent decree that required substantial changes in policies and practices to address alleged racism and use of force abuses, the dramatic decline was attributed to "de-policing."[34] Others pointed to alternative explanations such as programs of diversion. Recall, also, that Washington legalized small amounts of marijuana effective December 2012, which must have had a significant effect on the number of police investigative stops and misdemeanor arrests. More importantly, however, there has not yet been a connection shown between decreased police actions and UCR index crimes or victimization reports. Unfortunately, the time lag that occurs in our ability to access this information will prevent any immediate analysis.

We can count arrests, stops, and traffic tickets, and we can document whether or not totals are higher, lower, or the same as the year before, but we can't say for certain why such police actions have declined because we have no way of knowing whether or not the number of underlying acts have changed, other factors have affected the decision (e.g. charging practices of the prosecutor's office or changes in the law), or the officers have changed their policing practices (e.g. less likely to arrest or stop-and-frisk). As noted above, court orders requiring the NYPD to change their stop-and-frisk practices and Washing-ton's legalization of marijuana possession have probably more to do with the observed changes than police officers changing their decision-making practices on patrol in these cities than "de-policing."

Anecdotal evidence has been offered (e.g., quotes from individual officers or police administrators) that police officers felt scrutinized and unfairly criticized after the public protests in 2014 and 2015 and reacted by "de-policing." One small study that surveyed officers in a small police department found that officers reported a decline in motivation to do their job and work with the community because of public criticism, but that they did not change their decisions. Further the decline in motivation evidently was also influenced by administrative and managerial practices of the police department, not simply the "Ferguson Effect."[35]

3. Is the Reduction in Pro-Active Policing (If It Exists), the Cause of the Increase in Homicides and Other Crime (If There Is Significant Increase)?

Proposed explanations for the increase in violent crime, including homicides, in some cities have included (in addition to the Ferguson Effect) a rise in heroin use; increased gang violence; entrenched poverty and hopelessness; release of career criminals from prison (who have served their 25–30-year sentences from the high-crime years of the 1980s); more guns, especially automatic weapons like the AK-47; and, as noted before, simply yearly fluctuations in a two-decade decline. What we do know about these homicides is that they are often gang-related and occur most often in poverty-stricken areas of the city. The only academic study thus far that has addressed this question specifically looked at violent crimes in 81 cities in the year before and the year after the Michael Brown shooting in Ferguson and concluded that the only crime that showed a significant change in direction (from decease to increase) in the second time period was robbery. The study's authors cautioned that even documenting the increase could not "prove" that the increase was due to de-policing because there might be many other factors that affect the increase in robbery.[36] Also, as noted earlier, there have been previous upticks in homicide and violent crime in some cities periodically in the last several decades, even within a general trend of decreasing homicide rates over those years.

A recent study paper from the National Institute of Justice also offered the hypotheses of the growth of heroin markets, an increase in the number of parolees in the community, and a loss of "legitimacy" in Black communities as explanations for the increase in homicide in some American cities.[37] There is no doubt that heroin/opiate deaths have increased, but part of the well-known heroin epidemic is legally obtained opiates through prescriptions so there is no data as yet to prove that illegal heroin markets are fueling the homicide increase. Also, there has been no increase in the number of drug arrests. An increase in the number of parolees contributing to the homicide increase would require a knowledge of whether or not perpetrators were on parole—data we do not have yet for 2015, even for those arrested (and recall that a certain portion of homicides are not ever solved). As for the hypothesis that a legitimacy crisis in the minority community toward the police is causing an increase in homicide, Rosenfeld, in the NIJ analysis referred to above, pointed out that the cities with the largest homicide increases also had higher percentages of Blacks, and public opinion polls show that Blacks have historically low confidence in policing today. He argued that it is a difficult methodolgical problem to determine to what extent a rise is homicides is due to a loss of legitimacy of police and the justice system and suggested ethnographic research.[38] Another possibility is to look at the motivations for killings since part of the loss of legitimacy argument is that people who do not trust the justice system engage in retaliatory behavior. A good question to ask might be: what portion of homicides in these cities are due to retaliation? Also, is the proportion of retaliatory homicides correlated with a decrease in trust in police? We don't have motivation data yet for 2015 (although it will eventually be available in Suppmental Homicide Reports from the FBI).

To conclude, there is no evidence of a trend of increasing homicides at this point. We don't know if the recent increase in some cities will continue nor do we know whether it will spread to more cities. An increase in 2006 spurred similar concern, which proved to be unnecessary since the increase evaporated and the decline in homicides and other violent crimes continued their multi-decade decline after a couple of years.[39] As for "de-policing," there is some quantitative evidence that police discretionary actions (investigative detentions, traffic tickets, and misdemeanor arrests) have declined in some cities, but not the cities that have experienced the most dramatic increase in homicides.

The proposed explanations for the increase in homicides in some American cities offered instead of a "Ferguson Effect" include: growing heroin markets, an increase in parolees returning from prison, and a loss of legitimacy of police and the justice system in the Black community leading to retaliatory and vigilante justice. Absence of current data make any study of these hypotheses difficult.

Summary

What Is Crime? What Is the Role of Legislators, Victims, Police, and Prosecutors in Defining Crimes?

Crime is a "constructed reality" created by legislators who define acts as crimes, acts of the perpetrator, the perceptions of the victim and decision to report to authorities, and decisions by system actors (e.g., the decision to arrest). Only a portion of all crimes find their way into official statistics.

What Sources Do We Use to Find Out About the Patterns of Crime?

The Uniform Crime Reports present data on eight index crimes that are reported to police. They can be accessed from the FBI's website, which also has data on arrests on a larger number of crime categories. Problems with the UCR include the fact that many people do not report crimes to the police and arrests are not necessarily an accurate representation of crimes committed. We also have the National Crime Victimization Survey, which is a random survey of the population to discover the number of people who have been victimized and some characteristics of their victimization. We also use self-report studies and cohort studies in our study of crime.

What Crimes Are People Most Frequently Arrested for?

The largest category of arrests in 2014 was for drug crimes and possession was the most frequent of these arrests. Larceny/theft is the next most frequent arrest category, along with DUI and non-aggravated assault. The crimes the media focuses on (murder, rape, robbery) are extremely rare.

What Do We Know About Homicide?

Homicide, as most crime, has been on the decline since the mid-1990s. It is important to remember that the relative risk of being a homicide offender or a homicide victim is dramatically dependent on population group. Young Black males are much more likely than other population groups to be both homicide victim and offender.

What Has Been the Pattern of Crime Over the Years? Has It Declined?

All measures of crime (UCR, arrests, and victimization reports) show dramatic declines over the last two decades so that today's crime rates—for both violent and property crimes—are about the same as they were in the 1970s.

Does the Public Have an Accurate Perception About the Prevalence of Crime?

The public seems incredibly unaware of the dramatic declines in crime that have taken place in the last decades. A majority of the public thinks that crime is increasing despite all measures showing declines. It is possible that recent upticks in homicides and violent crimes in cities may be a sign that crime rates may be poised to begin an upward trend.

How Do the Crime Rates of the United States Compare to Other Countries?

While the U.S. has higher murder rates than European countries, other crimes do not show any consistent pattern. In general, property crimes in the U.S. are not higher than many other countries.

Critical Thinking Exercises

1. Go to the FBI website for the UCR which is reported in *Crime in the United States*. The 2015 crime statistics have just recently been released at: **https://ucr.fbi.gov/crime-in-theu.s/2015/crime-in-the-u.s.-2015**. See if homicide and/or violent crime rates are higher than they were in 2014. Write an update to the Focus on Crime section—is there more information available regarding any of the questions raised in the section?
2. Go to the United Nations Office of Drugs and Crime website: **https://data.unodc.org/#state:4**. Look up the crime rates (not raw numbers) for other crimes to see how the United States compares to other countries. Why do you suppose the homicide rates are so much higher here? How would you test your hypothesis?

Notes

1. Texas Penal Code. Retrieved 4/10/2007 from http://tlo2.tlc.state.tx.us/statutes/docs/PE/content/htm/pe.005.00.000022.00.htm#22.01.00.
2. See H. Cleveland, M. Koss and J. Lyons, "Rape tactics from the survivor's perspective." *Journal of Interpersonal Violence* 14 (5) (1999): 532–548.
3. *Sourcebook of Criminal Justice Statistics 2010*. Retrieved 9/9/2010 from http://www.albany.edu/sourcebook/pdf/13332007.pdf.
4. See C. Mendias and E. Kobe, "Engagement of policing ideals and the relationship to the exercise of discretionary powers." *Criminal Justice and Behavior* 33 (2006): 70–77.
5. N. James, *How Crime in the United States Is Measured*. Washington, DC: Congressional Research Service (CRS), 2008.
6. Federal Bureau of Investigation, *Crime in the United States, 2013*, Table 6, Crime in the United States by State, by City, 2013. Retrieved 9/12/2007 from https://www.fbi.gov/about-us/cjis/ucr/crime-in-the-u.s/2013/crime-in-the-u.s.-2013/tables/6tabledatadecpdf/table-6.
7. J. Eterno and E. Silverman, "The trouble with Compstat: Pressure on NYPD commanders endangered the integrity of crime stats." *New York Daily News*, February 15, 2010. Retrieved 9/15/2010 from http://www.nydailynews.com/opinions/2010/02/15/2010-02-15_the_trouble_with_compstat.html; J. Eterno, A. Verma, E. Silverman, "Police manipulations of crime reporting: Insiders' revelations." *Justice Quarterly*, 2014. Accessed from: doi.org/10.1080/07418825.2014. 980838.
8. D. Bernstein and N. Isackson, "The truth about Chicago's crime rates, Part I and II." *Chicago Magazine* (May, June, 2014) Retrieved 12/9/2015 from http://www.chicagomag.com/Chicago-Magazine/June-2014/Chicago-crime-statistics/.
9. Federal Bureau of Investigation, *Crime in the United States, 2004*. Retrieved 8/1/2006 from http://www.fbi.gov/ucr/cius_04/offenses_cleared/index.html.
10. Federal Bureau of Investigation, *Crime in the United States, 2009*. Retrieved 9/15/2010 from http://www.fbi.gov/ucr/cius2009/offenses/data/table_25.html.
11. Federal Bureau of Investigation, *Crime in the United States, 2014*. Retrieved 12/5/2015 from https://www.fbi.gov/about-us/cjis/ucr/crime-in-the-u.s/2014/crime-in-the-u.s.-2014/tables/table-25.
12. Bureau of Justice Statistics, NIBRS. Retrieved 12/5/2015 from BJS website, note on methodology on NIBRS. http://www.bjs.gov/index.cfm?ty=dcdetail&iid=301#_ftnref3.
13. D. Roberts, "Why participating in NIBRS is a good idea." *Police Chief Magazine*, December 2015. Retrieved 12/5/2015 from http://www.policechiefmagazine.org/magazine/index.cfm?fuseaction=display&issue_id=92014&category_ID=4.
14. S. Ansari and N. He, "Convergence revisited: A multi-definition, multi-method analysis of the UCR and the NCVS crime series." *Justice Quarterly*, 32 (2012): 1–31.

15. M. Wolfgang, R. Figlio and T. Sellin, *Delinquency in a Birth Cohort*. Chicago: University of Chicago Press, 1978.
16. M. Tonry, L. Ohlin and D. Farrington, *Human Development and Criminal Behavior: New Ways of Advancing Knowledge*. New York: Springer-Verlag, 1991.
17. Federal Bureau of Investigation, *Crime in the United States, 2014*. Retrieved from https://www.fbi.gov/about-us/cjis/ucr/crime-in-the-u.s/2014/crime-in-the-u.s.-2014/persons-arrested/main.
18. J. Truman and L. Langton, *Criminal Victimization, 2014*. Table 4. Retrieved from http://www.bjs.gov/content/pub/pdf/cv14.pdf.
19. See, for instance, J. Cancino and J. Pollock, "Gender, race, and ethnicity: An analysis of homicide rates and trends in San Antonio, 1990–2004." Paper presented at the American Society of Criminology Meeting, Los Angeles, CA (2006, November).
20. Gallup poll. Retrieved from: http://www.gallup.com/poll/186308/americans-say-crime-rising.aspx?utm_source=alert&utm_medium=email&utm_content=morelink&utm_campaign=syndication.
21. H. MacDonald, "The new nationwide crime wave." *The Wall Street Journal*, May 29, 2015. Retrieved 12/12/2015 from http://www.wsj.com/articles/the-new-nationwide-crime-wave-1432938425.
22. R. Rosenfeld, *Documenting and Explaining the 2015 Homicide Rise: Research Directions*. Washington, DC: NIJ, OJP, June 2016, p. 6.
23. J. Gravwert and J. Cullen, *Crime in 2015: A Final Analysis*. Washington, DC: Brennan Center, April 2016.
24. R. Rosenfeld, *Documenting and Explaining the 2015 Homicide Rise: Research Directions*. Washington, DC: NIJ, OJP, June 2016, p. 8.
25. D. Hamill, "Keeping a running score of New York's homicide rate seems a bit ridiculous." *New York Daily News*, June 28, 2015. Retrieved 12/15/2015 from http://www.nydailynews.com/new-york/murder-statistics-don-show-return-bad-old-daysarticle-1.2273859.
26. J. Domanick, "Why L.A.'s crime rise is no surprise." *Los Angeles Times* (August 27, 2015). Retrieved 12/12/2015 from http://www.latimes.com/opinion/op-ed/la-oe-domanick-los-angeles-rising-crime-20150827-story.html.
27. D. Bernstein and N. Isackson, "The truth about Chicago's crime rates, Part I and II." *Chicago Magazine* (May, June) Retrieved 12/9/2015 from http://www.chicagomag.com/Chicago-Magazine/June-2014/Chicago-crime-statistics/.
28. C. Bialik, "Scare headlines exaggerated the US crime wave." Fivethirtyeight.com. Retrieved 12/12/2015 from https://fivethir tyeight.com/features/scare-headlines-exaggerated-the-u-s-crime-wave/.
29. M. Friedman, "Just facts: America's non-existent 'spike in crime'." Brennan Center for Justice (August 10, 2015). Retrieved 12/12/2015 from https://www.brennancenter.org/blog/americas-non-existent-spike-crime.

30. Federal Bureau of Investigation, *Crime in the United States, 2014*. Tables 12. Retrieved 12/12/2015 from https://www.fbi.gov/about-us/cjis/ucr/crime-in-the-u.s/2014/crime-in-the-u.s.-2014.
31. Bureau of Justice Statistics, *Criminal Victimization, 2014*. Office of Justice Programs. Retrieved 12/12/2015 from http://www.bjs.gov/content/pub/pdf/cv14.pdf.
32. L. Bui, A. Phillip and W. Lowery, "Around St. Louis, bloodshed rises in year since Michael Brown was killed." *Washington Post*, August 11, 2015. Retrieved from http://www.washingtonpost.com/national/around-st-louis-bloodshed-rises-in-year-sincemichael-brown-was-killed/2015/08/11/b0ea430c-405c-11e5-bfe3-ff1d8549bfd2_story.html?hpid=z7
33. New York Times Editorial Board, "New York policing, by the numbers." *New York Times*, December 28, 2015, p. A18.
34. S. Miletich, "Report cites plunge in SPD enforcement of low-level crime." *Seattle Times*, May 24, 2014. Retrieved 1/3/2016 from http://www.seattletimes.com/seattle-news/report-cites-plunge-in-spd-enforcement-of-low-level-crime/.
35. Scott E. Wolfe and Justin Nix, "The alleged 'Ferguson Effect' and police willingness to engage in community partnership." *Law and Human Behavior*, 2015; DOI: 10.1037/lhb0000164.
36. D. Pyrooz, S. Decker, S. Wolfe and J. Shjarback, "Was there a Ferguson Effect on crime rates in large US cities?" *Journal of Criminal Justice* 46 (2016): 1–16.
37. R. Rosenfeld, *Documenting and Explaining the 2015 Homicide Rise: Research Directions*. Washington, DC: NIJ, OJP, June 2016.
38. R. Rosenfeld, *Documenting and Explaining the 2015 Homicide Rise: Research Directions*. Washington, DC: NIJ, OJP, June 2016.
39. R. Rosenfeld, *Documenting and Explaining the 2015 Homicide Rise: Research Directions*. Washington, DC: NIJ, OJP, June 2016.

DISCUSSION QUESTIONS

1. Compare and contrast the Uniform Crime Report and the National Crime Victimization Survey. Are crime rates expected to increase or decrease over the next decade? Provide evidence to support your response.
2. Should self-report survey data be used as a source to help people understand crime data and crime trends? Discuss the major disadvantages of the collection of data through self-report surveys.
3. Define and distinguish between criminal law and civil law.
4. Describe the elements of a crime. Which element do you believe is the most important, and why?
5. Assume that you are a state legislator and that you want to create a "Stand Your Ground" law. Would you advocate for your state to be a "duty to retreat" state or one that does not require a duty to retreat? Support your response.

THE POLICE

EDITOR'S INTRODUCTION

There are two unique factors that separate the police from the public they serve: The first is the mandate that police officers enforce the laws, which dictate what behaviors are legal and illegal. The second is a police officer's ability to legally use force, and in particular, deadly force, against members of society. Each of these factors put the police in direct conflict with community members and serve to isolate them further from the public. In addition to these differences, the police have a unique role because their responsibilities come from many different sources: local, state, and federal governments; their home agency; and the community in which they work. Sometimes these responsibilities conflict with one another and lead to greater tensions among those that law enforcement agencies serve. As the gateway to the criminal justice system, police officers strive to fulfill their roles of fighting crime and order maintenance evenhandedly and without prejudice.

Pollock's "Police in America" is a foundational chapter that provides an understanding of how the policing profession has transformed over time and explores the specific roles police officers have in society, the demographic makeup of today's police officers, and the multitude of agencies that have law enforcement powers. Knowledge of the history, role, power, and face of policing gives the reader the building blocks to be able to critically analyze major issues that face policing today.

In "Police Operations," Pollock discusses how police agencies recruit, select, train, and supervise their officers. It is through these processes that (1) law enforcement agencies seek to hire people who will enforce the law fairly and without prejudice; and (2) police officers are socialized into the police role and learn to adopt the values and beliefs of their subculture. Although the majority of police officers enforce the law without issue, Pollock provides the reader with an understanding of the types and causes of police misconduct, as well as the law and controversy surrounding the use of deadly force.

Discretion, which is defined as the ability to choose between two or more actions, is a staple of the criminal justice system. Police officers can utilize their discretion to decide to whom to give a speeding ticket and, to some degree, whom to arrest. Prosecutors use their discretion to determine which, if any, charges to bring against a person. Judges have discretion when it comes to setting bail amounts and the length of a defendant's sentence. In Arthur Wiechmann's reading, "Police Discretion," he explores a multitude of factors that may impact an officer's use of discretion in the decision to make an arrest. These factors include the officer's attitude; offender variables such as race, age, and demeanor; situational variables including the seriousness of the offense and the presence of a weapon; and system variables such as peer pressure and department size.

READING 2.1

POLICE IN AMERICA

Joycelyn Pollock

[READING] PREVIEW

- What Is the Function of Policing?
- What Are the Major Issues Facing Policing Today?
- Focus On Data: Are Police Officers Under Attack?
- How Many Police Officers Are There and Who Are They?
- What Is the Difference Between Federal, State, and Local Law Enforcement?
- How Did Modern Policing Evolve?
- What Is Community Policing?
- Summary
- Critical Thinking Exercises

In this [reading] we begin our exploration of one of the "sub-systems" of the criminal justice system—law enforcement. Today, law enforcement is under intense scrutiny and weekly, it seems, there are news stories that show police officers seemingly abusing their authority and opinion pieces that allege law enforcement is practiced in a racist manner. On the other side, law enforcement officers and officials and their supporters allege politicians, the media, and some law enforcement leaders are responsible for lowering the morale of all police officers by unfairly sensationalizing a few egregious cases. Many believe that by endorsing the idea that law enforcement officers are abusing the rights of citizens, it makes the job of an officer more difficult and dangerous. Obviously, people have strong opinions in both directions. What we want to do in this text is apply a critical thinking approach to uncover facts, taking care not to allow assumptions or bias affect our understanding of the issues. Before we can explore the current issues of policing today, we need to take several steps back to see where policing has been, and provide some general facts to understand the issues relevant to policing. [...] [W]e will cover such topics as: What is the function of policing? How did modern policing evolve?

Who are the police officers in this country? Is there a subculture of policing? And, what are the legal parameters of police power?

What Is the Function of Policing?

What is the function of police? You probably said crime control, but that is not a complete answer. Police officers are dispatched to many different types of calls and crime calls form only a portion of their workload. According to researchers, the majority of police work is divided among patrol, service calls, and paperwork. Further, only 13 percent of their time is taken up with potentially criminal matters, according to these authors.[1]

It is common to identify crime control and **order maintenance** as the two major functions of law enforcement. Crime control includes all the tasks associated with preventing crime and enforcing the law. Patrolling neighborhoods or downtown business districts, responding to dispatched calls, investigating crimes, engaging in sting operations, arresting suspects, testifying in court, and all the other tasks associated with either preventing crime or catching criminals is included in the crime-control function. Order-maintenance tasks, sometimes called "community caretaking," include everything else police do. It is community caretaking when police respond to a car accident and control traffic and see that the victims get medical treatment. Police may be called to perform a "public welfare check" by a worried mother to check on her college-age daughter because she hasn't answered her phone in three days, respond to lost elderly calls, try to mediate neighbor disputes, and counsel recalcitrant teenagers. Increasingly, they are called when a person on a street, in a business, or with family members show signs of mental illness. Police are present when there are medical emergencies, water rescues, traffic problems, public disturbances and organized protests, weather-related and other natural disasters, and civil defense.

Order-maintenance and crime-control functions may overlap and even merge. Police officers may be performing crime control on a domestic disturbance call if someone has been injured, or order maintenance if no criminal charges are warranted. When police are called to a neighbor dispute, this is order maintenance; but if they are unsuccessful in resolving the problem, it may turn into a crime when one neighbor decides to settle the argument with a criminal assault. A mentally ill person may complain to police that their brain is being scanned by an alien, which is obviously not a crime-control issue; however, if they do not respond in an effective manner to this complaint, the delusional person may commit a crime. When neighbors call police because there is a large group of "suspicious-looking" people in a park late at night, not responding may result in nothing happening, or it may result in a series of vehicle burglaries or other crimes. On the other hand, if the park is open and the "suspicious-looking" people are not committing a crime, there is little the officers can do legally despite the neighbors' unease—they are constantly called upon to resolve issues when there is no clear legal answer.

We consider our police to be the 24-hour one-stop shop for problem solving. Whenever we are in trouble, our first thought is probably to call 911. Police officers, then, have a day that may begin with a person suffering from Alzheimer's who has forgotten where they live or even what their name is, and end with an alligator in someone's backyard pool that has just eaten the family's Chihuahua. Crime calls happen too, but car chases and catching burglars is not the day-to-day routine of most police officers. In fact, one might say that there is no such thing as a day-to-day routine.

What Are the Major Issues Facing Policing Today?

In 2015 policing came to dominate public discourse and even enter into the presidential campaign platforms. Deaths of Black men while in the custody or at the hands of police officers in Ferguson, Missouri (Michael Brown), Staten Island, New York (Eric Garner), Cleveland, Ohio (Tamir Rice), North Charleston, South Carolina (Walter Scott), Chicago, Illinois (LaQuan McDonald) and Baltimore, Maryland (Freddie Gray) spurred public attention to policing in a way that hadn't been seen since the Rodney King beating in 1991.

The events led to President Obama's creation of a panel of practitioners and experts in 2015 to report on the state of policing. Their report, *Final Report of the President's Task Force on 21st Century Policing*, called for reform in virtually all aspects of policing.[2] Then in the summer of 2016, the shooting deaths of Alton Sterling in Baton Rouge and Philando Castile in a suburb of Minneapolis reignited "Black Lives Matter" protests. In Dallas, a gunman shot and killed five officers and wounded seven others who were on duty at a "Black Lives Matter" public protest. This tragedy has seemed to be a turning point, with community members and law enforcement officials together pledging to work together to find solutions to the problem.

There is no doubt that there is a split between White and minority citizens in this country in how police are perceived. According to a Gallup poll, 59 percent of Whites have a great deal or quite a lot of confidence in the police, compared with only 37 percent of Blacks.[3] The Pew Research Center found similar disparities in how Blacks and Whites view law enforcement. Almost half of all Blacks (46 percent) had "little" or "very little" confidence that police treated Whites and Blacks similarly, compared to 20 percent of Whites.[4] After the most recent shootings in the summer of 2016, a *New York Times*/CBS telephone poll reported that 69 percent of Americans thought that race relations in America were generally bad; in fact, results were about the same as in 1991 after the Rodney King beating. The poll showed a sharp difference in how Blacks and Whites viewed law enforcement as shown in Exhibit 2.1.2 below.

EXHIBIT 2.1.1 Eric Garner, a 400-pound man who had asthma, died while being arrested by police in Staten Island.

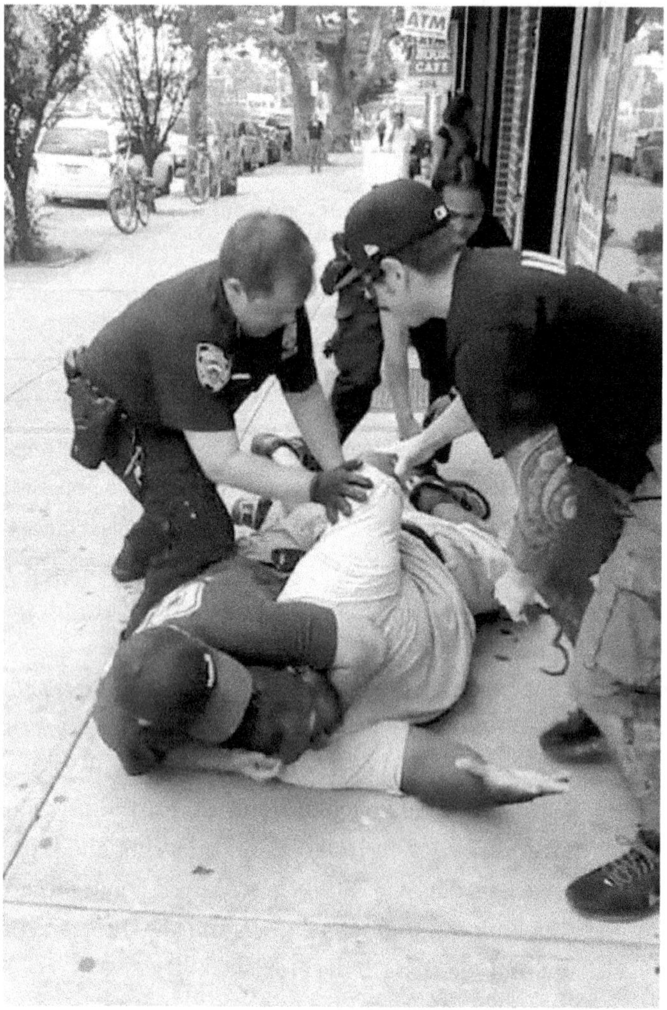

Source: Getty

The antipathy between law enforcement and minority communities is one current issue that must be considered. Another issue, related to the first, is whether police officers abuse their legal authority. Do police officers abuse their stop-and-frisk power and is it used in a discriminatory manner? Police officer use of force, including lethal force, has also been scrutinized. Is there a difference in how quickly officers resort to force when dealing with different race/ethnicity groups? Another current issue is whether police are experiencing heightened danger. This will be the subject of the Focus on Data next.

EXHIBIT 2.1.2 A Racial Divide

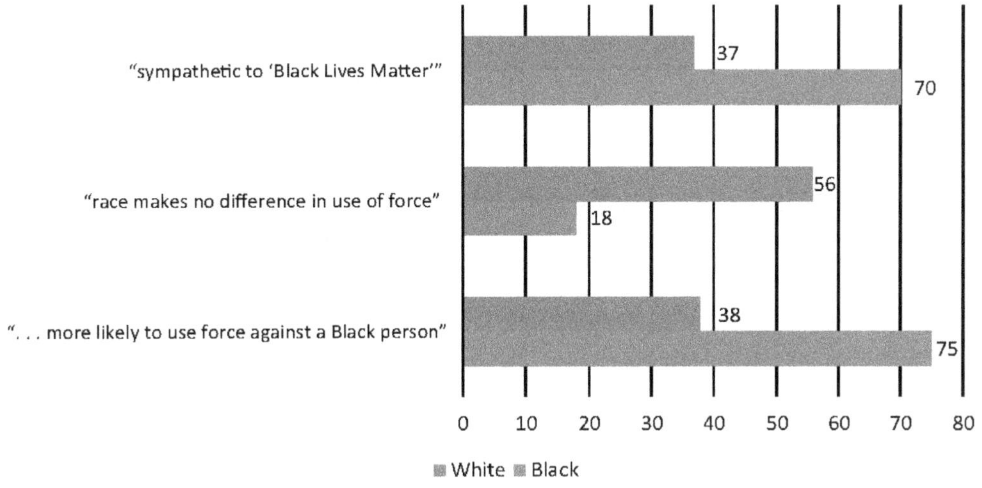

Source: Created from G. Russonello, "Race relations deemed bleak by most in U.S." New York Times, *July 14, 2016, p. A1.*

Focus on Data: Are Police Officers Under Attack?

In 2015 and 2016, numerous ambush-style killings of police officers occurred in cities across the United States. The five officers ambushed in Dallas in July 2016 while on duty at a peaceful "Black Lives Matter" protest escalated the concern that policing was under attack. Many argue that the negative media attention related to the police killings of Black men has triggered fatal attacks on police officers. As seen above, this issue threatens to undercut advances in race relations in this nation. Others have argued that policing has never been safer with fewer killings of officers than past decades. Who is right?

An annual report by the nonprofit National Law Enforcement Officers Memorial Fund found that 42 officers were killed by guns in 2015; 49 officers in 2014; 32 officers in 2013; and 50 in 2012. In 2011, 73 officers were killed in gunfire, the most in any year in the past decade. The average since 2004 is 55 police deaths annually. Note that these are deaths by gunfire only; there is about an equal number of additional deaths due to traffic accidents.

These numbers, tragic as they are, are nowhere near the highest numbers of deaths however. In 1973, 156 police officers were killed by gunfire, and the 1970s averaged about 140 officer deaths per year.[5] It is important to note that these are not rates per 1,000, so the 1973 number would have been from a much smaller total number of police officers in the country. The reduction in numbers of police officers killed is probably due to the advent of body armor and better training, now required in most departments.

What worries law enforcement officials, however, is the ambush-style killings where an officer is targeted and killed or injured without warning. Officers Wenjian Liu and Rafael Ramos were assassinated as they were sitting in their patrol car in New York City in December 2014. A man with mental health issues said he did it as a "revenge killing" for Eric Garner and Michael Brown. It has been reported that an average of ten officers per year are killed in ambush style shootings, but there had been five already by March of 2016.[6] Then, in July of 2016, five Dallas police officers—Brent Thompson, Patrick Zamarripa, Michael Krol, Michael Smith, and Lorne Ahrens—were shot and killed. Several others were wounded. The suspect was chased into a parking garage and, after negotiations broke down and officials believed he had explosives that posed a threat, he was killed by a remote-controlled robot that carried explosives.

Exhibit 2.1.3 shows that the number of officer fatalities goes up and down but has been showing generally a downward direction. Recall from above that about 55 officers on average are killed by gunfire. Exhibit 2.1.3 shows the total number of fatalities; automobile accidents account for the largest number of officer fatalities.

EXHIBIT 2.1.3 Officer Fatalities, 1965–2015

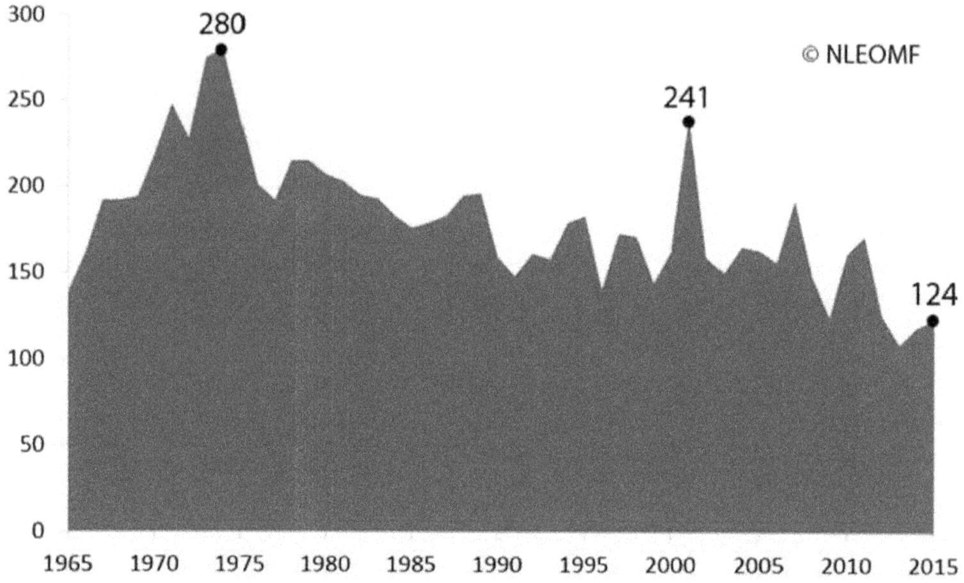

Source: http://www.nleomf.org/facts/research-bulletins/?referrer=http://www.npr.org/sections/thetwo-way/2015/12/29/461402091/number-of-police-officers-killed-by-gunfire-fell-14-percent-in-2015-study-says

Every officer in the country must experience a sense of dread when these cases arise, knowing that it could happen to them. It is true, as some point out, that, statistically, policing is safer than several other occupations when looking at on-the-job mortality rates; however, there must be some difference in how one experiences the risk of work-related deadly accidents compared to being the victim of an intentional assassination. As Exhibit 2.1.4 shows, the number of "ambush"-style killings increased dramatically in 2015. There had already been five ambush-style shooting by March of 2016 and the July 2016 killings of five law enforcement officers in Dallas was the single deadliest incident for law enforcement since 9/11. The sniper killings of police officers took place in a city that, by all accounts, had a fairly good relationship between the police force and the minority community. Following that incident, there were several others in the following days involving officers who were shot or shot at by lone assailants in ambush-style situations (e.g., calling 911 and then shooting at the officer who responded).[7]

EXHIBIT 2.1.4 Leading Circumstances of Fatal Shootings, 2014–2015

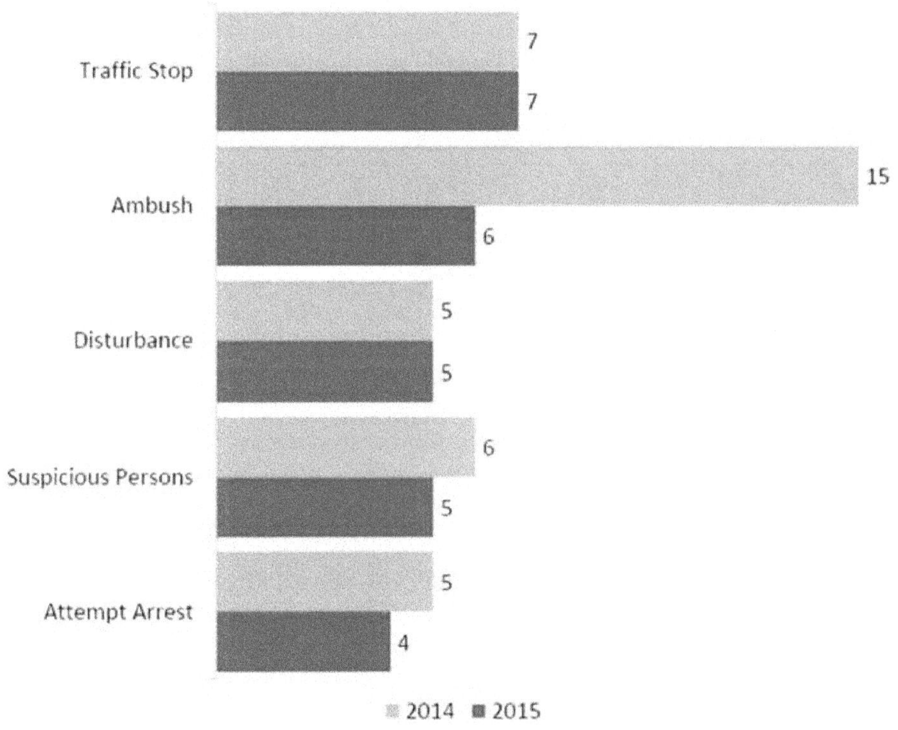

Source: http://www.nleomf.org/facts/research-bulletins/?referrer=http://www.npr.org/sections/thetwo-way/2015/12/29/461402091/number-of-police-officers-killed-by-gunfire-fell-14-percent-in-2015-study-says

Whether this is a random fluctuation in statistics or the beginning of a troubling trend remains to be seen. Thus, in answer to the question—"Are police under attack or are they more safe now than ever before?"—the answer is yes to both premises. While the number of firearm-related deaths is down dramatically from the 1970s, there has been an apparent increase in 2016 in the number of ambush-style attacks.

How Many Police Officers Are There and Who Are They?

When we read about police departments in the national news, the focus is almost always on big-city police departments such as Baltimore, New York City, and Chicago. It is important to remember that policing in America includes many very small departments with only a few officers. Most police departments are in suburban or rural areas and may employ 100 or fewer officers. These police departments are usually not the focus of academic research or receive the attention of the mass media, and their issues and concerns do not mirror those of the big-city police departments that are most often in the news.

Information about police departments is available from the Bureau of Justice Statistics. A census done in 2008 reported there 17,876 state and federal police agencies in the United States with about 1.1 million full-time state and local law enforcement personnel and 765,000 sworn personnel with another 44,000 part-time personnel. This translates to about 251 officers for every 100,000 citizens or one officer for every 400 residents.[8] A more recent survey in 2013 reported on 15,388 agencies with 1,045,360 total personnel including 724,690 full-time sworn employees. It appears this survey excluded special jurisdiction agencies.[9]

> To find numerous reports on police and policing, go to the Bureau of Justice Statistics website at http://bjs.ojp.usdoj.gov and look under the heading of "Law Enforcement."

The BJS census of police agencies in 2013 identified 12,326 local police departments, 3,012 sheriff's agencies,[10] 50 state law enforcement agencies, 1,733 "special jurisdiction" agencies, and 638 other agencies (primarily constables unique to Texas). This figure does not include federal law enforcement agencies. Most police officers work in municipal agencies (52 percent), followed by sheriff's offices (31 percent).[11]

About three-quarters of all law enforcement agencies employ less than 25 people and 48 percent employed fewer than ten officers, but about one-third of all sworn officers work in the few agencies (49) that employ 1,000 or more officers.[12] The largest police department is the New York City Police Department (NYPD) which employed over 36,000 officers in 2008 (34,454 in 2013), nearly three times the next largest department (Chicago) which employed 13,354 in 2008 (12,042 in 2013). Los Angeles (9,727 in 2008, 9,920 in 2013), Philadelphia (6,624 in 2008, 6,515 in 2013), and

Houston (5,053 in 2008, 5,295 in 2013) are the next three largest departments.[13] Some departments have increased their numbers while others have experienced a reduction in their numbers between 2008 and 2013. Exhibit 2.1.5 shows this interesting paradox that most police officers work in large agencies but most agencies are very small.

EXHIBIT 2.1.5 Number of Employees by Size of Agency

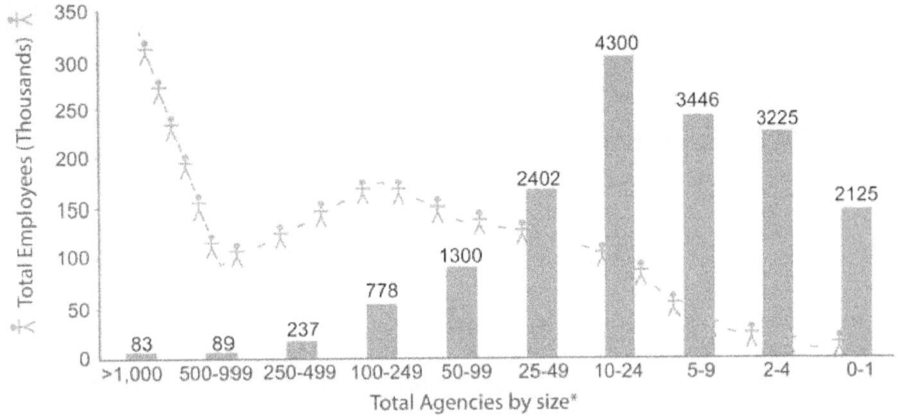

Source: Table 2 from http://www.bjs.gov/content/pub/pdf/cslleao8.pdf

Historically, most police officers were White males. Today, police departments are beginning to represent the diversity of the population they serve. All police departments require officers to be citizens, and most have age restrictions—that is, applicants must be between 21 and under 35 to 40 to be hired. Some departments now require 60 or 90 college hours. There are written, physical, and psychological tests during the selection process. The average starting salaries of new police officers range from $26,600 to $49,500, with the average salary of $44,400.[14] The median annual wage earned by police officers as of 2011 was $54,230, according to the Bureau of Labor Statistics.[15] Officers with college degrees receive higher salaries in some locations. Seniority and overtime can substantially increase the annual salary of an officer.

The first Black police officer was hired in 1861;[16] however, it wasn't until the mid-1960s that the recruitment and hiring of minority police officers began in earnest. In the most recent survey of local police departments, the BJS reports that about 27 percent of police officers are members of a racial or ethnic minority, up from about 25 percent in 1987. Exhibit 2.1.6 shows the gradual increase in minority representation in police departments.

From 2007 to 2013, the percentage of Black officers has remained the same at about 12 percent, a slight underrepresentation of their share of the general population (Blacks represent about

EXHIBIT 2.1.6 Minority Representation in Police Departments

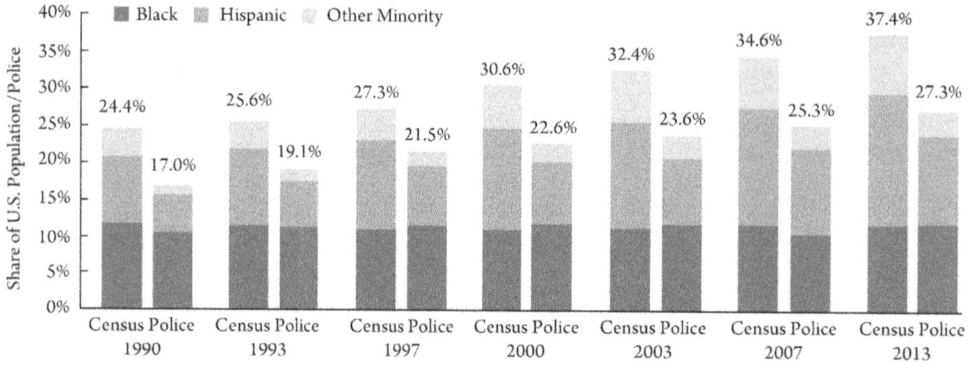

Police data represents national totals for local full-time sworn personnel not identified as non-Hispanic White.

Source: http://www.governing.com/topics/public-justice-safety/gov-police-department-diversity.html

13.2 percent of the general population[17]). In general, large cities have higher percentages of minority officers. In 2013, while minorities comprised almost 47 percent of police departments serving cities over 1 million; they comprised only about 16 percent of jurisdictions of less than 2,500.[18] Of course, it is more important to know what the representation of a particular city's police department is and whether the representation of minority officers reflects that city's population. The *New York Times* presents an interactive infographic utilizing 2007 figures from the BJS comparing the number of Black officers to the percentage of Blacks in the city's population. Some smaller incorporated areas close to large metropolitan areas have especially disparate representation with police forces that are predominately White and populations that are largely minority. For instance, in Greenbelt, Maryland, close to Washington, DC, the population is about 26 percent White, but 79 percent of its police force is White. North Charleston, South Carolina, is about 38 percent White, but 80 percent of its police force was White.[19] Although this data is somewhat outdated, it is still the case that some cities do not have a police force that represents the demographics of the residents served.

Go to the website for this infographic: http://www.nytimes.com/interactive/2014/09/03/us/the-race-gap-inamericas-police-departments.html

Another 11.6 percent of police officers are Hispanic[20] (Hispanics represent about 17.4 percent of the general population). Some cities have large percentages of Hispanic residents, but the police force does not represent them. For instance, Exhibit 2.1.7 shows the cities that seem to have disproportional representation.

EXHIBIT 2.1.7 Hispanic Representation in Law Enforcement

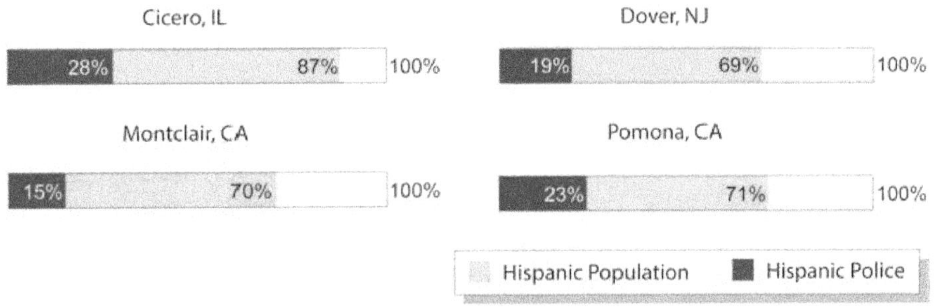

Source: http://www.nytimes.com/interactive/2014/09/03/us/the-race-gap-in-americas-police-departments.htm (accessed 2/15/2016)

It should be noted that there is little research that proves adequate representation of minority communities improves minority-police relations. A police department that represents the community it serves may be perceived as more accessible and trusted than one that does not, but there is no research that shows departments with a better representation of their community are less subject to citizen complaints or use of force lawsuits, or enjoy better relations with the community.

Although women represent about half of the general population, they comprise a small proportion of personnel in law enforcement agencies. The first female police officer was hired in 1910, but her role was restricted to dealing with children and female prisoners. Early policewomen also performed clerical tasks. Policewomen were hired under a separate job category from male police officers, with separate hiring requirements. All that changed in the 1970s, when women were integrated into the patrol ranks.[21]

By 1997, women represented 10.6 percent of all police officers. However, there has been very little increase in the percentage of women in law enforcement since the 1990s. In 2013, women still accounted for only about 12 percent of sworn officers in local police departments. Exhibit 2.1.8 shows the gradual increase in female officers.

Recently Kringen[22] examined the barriers to hiring and retaining women in a medium-size police department and discovered that certain policies (such as requiring female recruits to cut their hair) were problematic for attracting female applicants and policies such as shift work and mandatory overtime that made childcare difficult were factors that seemed to discourage women from applying or staying in policing. Unlike other professions, generally female officers cannot move to part-time status during the years when pregnancy and childrearing demand flexibility. According to at least one female law enforcement leader, departments that allowed officers to work part-time at some point in their career would probably experience no difficulty in attracting and retaining women.[23]

EXHIBIT 2.1.8 Female Police Officers in Local Departments

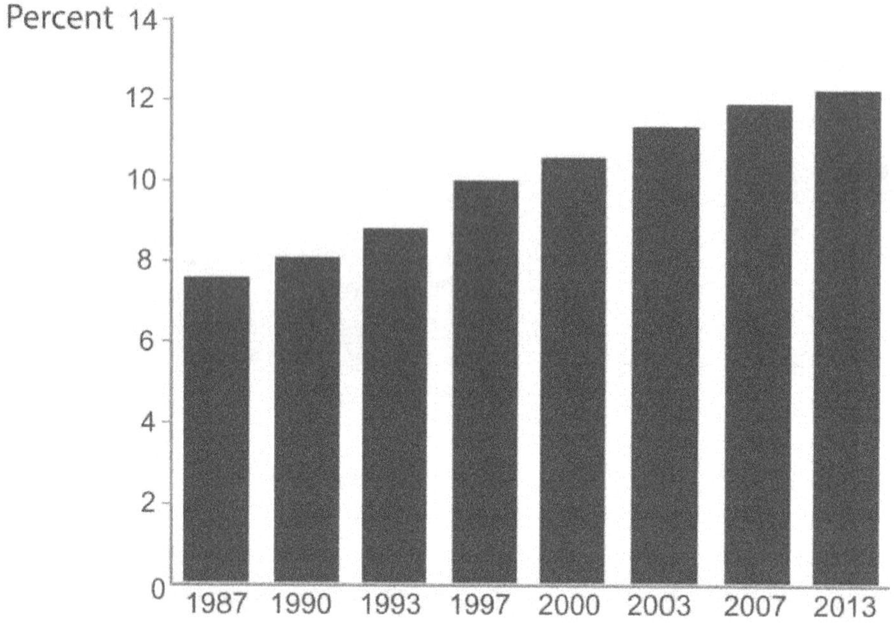

Source: http://www.bjs.gov/content/pub/pdf/lpd13ppp.pdf

Police departments that serve large cities have larger percentages of female officers (17.6 percent) than small town police departments (6.1 percent).[24] There are also large differences between cities. In an earlier study, Detroit reported 27 percent of their officers were women, compared to Las Vegas with only 9 percent. It was reported that about 15 percent of federal law enforcement personnel were women.[25]

While women represent a small percentage of all police officers, their representation in the command ranks is even smaller. In the most recent survey of police departments, it was reported that less than 10 percent of supervisory personnel in law enforcement agencies were women; and, again, the numbers were higher in big-city police departments serving 250,000 or more residents compared to small town departments. Only about 3 percent of local police chiefs were women.[26] Thus, law enforcement officers are, for the most part, White males with some college education. There are increasing numbers of minority officers, especially in large cities. The percentage of female officers has seemed to plateau at about 11–12 percent.

What Is the Difference Between Federal, State, and Local Law Enforcement?

Law enforcement in the United States is composed of a complex network of overlapping jurisdictions and agencies. There are federal, state, and local police agencies as well as special jurisdictional agencies. Some locales create private police or security forces to protect the citizenry from crime and disorder.

Federal Law Enforcement

Unlike many other countries, the United States has no national police force. Part of the reason for this is the vast area encompassed within the borders of this country, but another reason is that, since the American Revolution, there has been a cultural hostility and suspicion of centralized power. This does not mean, however, that there are no federal law enforcement officers. In fact, there are more than 120,000 federal employees who are considered law enforcement officers.[27] Prior to 2003, the Immigration and Naturalization Service (INS) employed the largest number of federal officers, followed by the Federal Bureau of Prisons, and then the U.S. Customs Service. The Department of Homeland Security (DHS) has absorbed both INS and the U.S. Customs Service, making the DHS the largest federal law enforcement agency today. In 2008, the agencies with the largest number of law enforcement personnel included the U.S. Customs and Border Protection, which employed 36,863; the Federal Bureau of Prisons 16,835; the FBI 12,760; and U.S. Immigration and Customs Enforcement 12,446.[28] Exhibit 2.1.9 shows these and other federal agencies.

The U.S. Marshals Service, for instance, is responsible for seizing and maintaining property confiscated through civil and criminal forfeiture hearings, providing security for federal courtrooms and judicial officials, transporting federal prisoners, and protecting federal witnesses (some through the Federal Witness Protection Program).

The Department of Homeland Security (DHS), created in 2002, has absorbed a number of other agencies and employs almost half (45.5 percent) of all federal law enforcement personnel. As mentioned previously, the Immigration and Naturalization Service and the U.S. Customs Service are now under DHS. The functions of these two agencies have been reorganized, and now the agency primarily responsible for border protection is called U.S. Customs and Border Protection, and the other agency, called U.S. Immigration and Customs Enforcement, enforces immigration laws within the interior of the country. Other agencies absorbed by the Department of Homeland Security include the U.S. Coast Guard and the U.S. Secret Service. The Transportation Security Administration (TSA) is charged with providing protection at airports. The same Act that created the DHS also changed the Bureau of Alcohol, Tobacco and Firearms (ATF), which is now the Bureau of Alcohol, Tobacco, Firearms and Explosives, and the law enforcement functions of the

EXHIBIT 2.1.9 Federal Agencies Employing 250+ People with Arrest and Firearm Powers

U.S. Customs and Border Protection	36,863
Federal Bureau of Prisons	16,835
Federal Bureau of Investigation	12,760
U.S. Immigration and Customs Enforcement	12,446
U.S. Secret Service	5,213
Administrative Office of the U.S. Courts*	4,696
Drug Enforcement Administration	4,308
U.S. Marshals Service	3,313
Veterans Health Administration	3,128
Internal Revenue Service, Criminal Investigation	2,636
Bureau of Alcohol, Tobacco, Firearms and Explosives	2,541
U.S. Postal Inspection Service	2,288
U.S. Capitol Police	1,637
National Park Service—Rangers	1,404
Bureau of Diplomatic Security	1,049
Pentagon Force Protection Agency	725
U.S. Forest Service	644
U.S. Fish and Wildlife Service	598
National Park Service—U.S. Park Police	547
National Nuclear Security Administration	363
U.S. Mint Police	316
Amtrak Police	305
Bureau of Indian Affairs	277
Bureau of Land Management	255

** Limited to federal probation officers employed in federal judicial districts that allow officers to carry firearms*

Source: B. Reaves, Federal Law Enforcement Officers, 2008. *Washington, DC: Bureau of Justice Statistics, 2012, p. 2. Accessed 2/1/2016: http://www.bjs.gov/content/pub/pdf/fle08.pdf*

agency have been transferred to the Justice Department while the revenue functions remain with the Department of the Treasury.[29]

Federal law enforcement agencies enforce federal laws. They share jurisdiction with state and local law enforcement agencies when an action is a violation of both federal and state law. The most common example of this is the sale of controlled substances. While smuggling drugs into the country is a federal crime, sales of controlled substances break both federal and state laws.

For more information about federal law enforcement, see http://www.bjs.gov/content/pub/pdf/fleo08.pdf

State Law Enforcement

State law enforcement agencies are typically called Highway Patrol, Department of Public Safety, or State Patrol, although their mission encompasses more than patrolling the state highways and issuing drivers' licenses. These statewide agencies usually have a state-of-the-art crime lab to assist smaller jurisdictions that have no analysis capabilities. They also provide assistance with investigation and detection to local agencies and carry out their own investigations when the criminal activity is statewide, especially if the criminal activity involves drugs or auto theft rings. The state agency may be the central repository for crime statistics, may have authority over gun registrations and investigations for licenses, and may have supervision over controlled substances registration.

There were 1,733 limited jurisdiction law enforcement agencies employing 56,968 full-time sworn personnel in 2008.[30] Examples include state law enforcement agencies that enforce alcohol and tobacco laws, fish and game agencies that enforce hunting and other laws, agencies that enforce gaming and/or racing laws, and child support enforcement agencies. State universities, state hospitals, state parks, school districts, airports, mass transit, and ports or harbors also may have their own law enforcement agencies. Each state is slightly different in the type and the number of these special jurisdiction agencies.

County Law Enforcement

Sheriffs are elected officials, but sheriff's deputies are hired through civil service selection procedures in a similar manner to municipal law enforcement officers. Usually, county sheriffs also have the responsibility of managing the county jail. In some jurisdictions, sheriff's deputies may be assigned either patrol duties or jail duties, but in other jurisdictions, the position of jailer is a different job from that of deputy. Sheriff's offices also serve warrants and civil documents, including eviction notices.

Most states, but not all, have a sheriff for each county. Texas, with 254 counties, has the largest number of sheriffs—one for each county. Alaska, Connecticut, Hawaii, and Rhode Island have no sheriffs, and Delaware has only one sheriff's office. The median number of employees for all sheriffs' offices was eighteen full-time sworn employees in 2008 although a few are extremely large. For instance, the Los Angeles County Sheriff's Office had 9,461 full-time sworn employees.[31]

While sheriffs are elected, police chiefs are hired by the city manager and/or a city council and mayor. Both, however, have notoriously short average tenures, because both positions are lightning rods for public controversy.

Municipal Law Enforcement

When we think of the police, we typically think of the municipal police department. Most towns and cities of any size have their own police department. Small towns may have a police department of only three or four officers, while big-city police forces may number in the thousands, such as New York City with over 34,000 officers. As noted above, most police *officers* work in the larger police departments, even though most police *departments* have fewer than 50 officers.

Larger police departments are typically broken into divisions, such as patrol and investigation. Under the investigation division, there may be further subdivisions, such as homicide, juvenile, and vice. Other departments exist as well, including community relations, internal affairs, training, and research and planning. Some police departments have created special domestic violence teams, police squads specially trained to respond to the mentally ill, and other specialized teams. In smaller departments, of course, patrol officers are expected to be generalists and handle a large variety of calls.

Special Jurisdiction Law Enforcement Agencies

There are also special or limited jurisdiction municipal law enforcement agencies. We've mentioned state-level special jurisdiction agencies above (e.g. state university police departments). Others occur at the municipal level. Some cities have park police and/or transit police. These agencies have the power to arrest, but their jurisdiction is limited to crimes that occur within or in relation to their specific jurisdiction.

Some Native American tribes may have their own tribal police forces that have exclusive jurisdiction on reservations. In fact, there is a completely separate justice system existing on some Indian reservations, complete with tribal police and a tribal court system. Even civil court matters are dealt with by tribal courts, and a state district court has no authority once a matter is deemed to be under the jurisdiction of these tribal courts.

> For information about one such tribal police department, go to the website for the Oneida Indian Nation police department at http://oneida-nation.net/police.

Private Law Enforcement

Private security officers are not peace officers. They are paid with private funds rather than public dollars, and their primary duty is to provide protection and investigative services to the hiring entity, which might be a company, neighborhood, or private individual. We mention private security officers here only because many people misunderstand their power and assume that they have similar powers to those of public peace officers. The other reason that we must mention them is that there may be many more private security officers than police officers. There are probably more than 1.5 million individuals employed in private security, and private security expenditures are on track to be almost double that of public expenditures.

It should also be noted that there is overlap between private and public policing because public police officers are often hired as private employees of security companies. Because police are certified peace officers who can carry a weapon and use their arrest powers even when off-duty, they carry those powers with them into the private position. Otherwise, private security officers have no greater powers of arrest or use of force than an average citizen.

The American Society for Industrial Security (now ASIS International) is the largest professional organization for security professionals. Its website states that it was founded in 1955 and has more than 35,000 members worldwide.[32]

For information about the American Society for Industrial Security, go to http://www.asisonline.org/about/history/index.xml

How Did Modern Policing Evolve?

It may surprise you to know that police agencies are a relatively recent phenomenon in the history of social order, beginning less than 300 years ago. Of course, there has always been a need to control crime and deviance, but that function was largely undertaken by the military, by private watchmen and guards, and by citizens themselves up until the 1800s.

We trace American policing back to the British "bobbie" and the "shire reeve" (sheriff). One of the earliest law enforcement officials was the **shire reeve**, who was responsible for collecting taxes for the king, and keeping the king's peace in the shires (or counties) of England. The modern-day shire reeve is the county sheriff. Another authority figure in early shires was the constable, who was responsible for the administration of shire courts and carrying out the orders of the magistrate. The constable was also responsible for keeping the **gaol** (jail) where prisoners were kept before being punished. There was no organized police force and citizens themselves participated in a watch system.

By the 1800s, this informal system of crime control had become ineffective, especially in major cities like London. Henry Fielding, a magistrate in London, created the **Bow Street Runners** in 1748, which could be considered the first type of organized police force. Their first duties were to enforce warrants from the magistrate's court, but they eventually added crime detection and investigation. Eventually, their reach extended all over England when pursuing criminals. They also provided protection in the Bow Street area of London, especially after a mounted patrol was established by Fielding's successor.

For more information and historical pictures of the London Metropolitan Police Force, see http://www.met.police.uk/history/archives.htm.

In 1829, Robert Peel, the Home Secretary of England, convinced Parliament to pass the Metropolitan Police Act, creating the first police force as we know it today. They eventually became known as "**bobbies**," referencing Peel's role in their creation. By 1839, the Metropolitan Force had absorbed the Bow Street Runners, the Bow Street mounted patrol, and the Wapping Marine Police. The force was initially based in Scotland Yard with five more watch houses and seventeen districts. In 1831, the Special Constables Act was passed, which added more officers to the force.

In the colonies, crime prevention was the responsibility of every citizen. Watch systems existed that were similar to those found in the early English shires. Boston holds the honor of having the first police department in this country, if one uses the date of origin of 1838 (when the first "day police" were hired), and not 1854 (when the police department was created as an agency separate from the constable's office).

New York City's police department was created in 1844. By the early 1800s, New York was overwhelmed with the dual problems of poverty and rising crime. The area of the Bowery, and especially the "Five Points" neighborhood, were the center of the problems that threatened to overrun the city. The power of the immigrant Irish gangs is fancifully portrayed in the hit 2002 movie *Gangs of New York*. Although there was growing support for an organized police force, citizens were suspicious of allowing such a centralized power. Still, by 1845, the Mayor of New York had created a municipal police force with an initial staffing of 900 men.

For an interesting article that compares the *Gangs of New York* movie to the historians' descriptions of the "Five Points" area of New York City and the immigrant gangs of the period, go to http://news.nationalgeographic.com/news/2003/03/0320_030320_oscars_gangs.html

New York's police force, like other city police departments, was very much influenced by politics. Police officers received "appointments" for several years and these appointments came through political patronage. Dueling political forces fought over the police department, and in 1857 the Whigs managed to get the state legislature to pass a bill disbanding the municipal police department and creating the Metropolitan Police for the City of New York, Brooklyn, and Westchester County. This led to a brawl between the two police departments in 1857 when the Metropolitan force sought to arrest the mayor. The state militia had to step in and restore order. The police force was returned to municipal control in 1870.[33]

EXHIBIT 2.1.10 The Five Points neighborhood was the center of crime and poverty problems that plagued New York in the mid-nineteenth century. The area was the site of the infamous 1857 riot between rival gangs, the Dead Rabbits and the Bowery Boys.

Source: Alamy

For an interesting website that covers the history of the New York City Police Department, go to http://www.nycpolicemuseum.org/

One of the early police commissioners was Theodore Roosevelt. Starting in 1895, he began a series of reforms in the NYPD that included:

- hiring based on skill and aptitude rather than political patronage
- the creation of disciplinary rules and enforcement
- adopting an early form of fingerprinting
- creating a bike squad
- requiring officers to have pistol practice
- instituting physical exams for officers
- hiring the first female police matron to supervise female prisoners (Minnie Gertrude Kelly)
- eliminating the practice of homeless people sleeping in the basements of the precinct offices in horribly unsanitary conditions.[34]

City police departments were slower to emerge in the West and the marshal was often the only law enforcement officer in early Western towns. For instance, a true city police department didn't emerge in Los Angeles until almost 1870. The precursor to the Los Angeles Police Department was the "Los Angeles Rangers," a group of volunteers enlisted to help the county sheriff and marshal in the unruly times of the 1850s. Los Angeles was inundated with immigrants and others who were spurred by "gold fever" to come to the West Coast to make a fortune. The Rangers wore a white ribbon that indicated they served under the authority of the Council of Los Angeles. The "Los Angeles City Guards" succeeded the Rangers and wore the first official uniform. Vigilante justice was commonplace and early authorities were unable to keep order. Evidently, during the 1860s, a group of residents was successful in their request to the French government for protection. For some period of time, French troops were deployed in the city to guard residents![35]

> For an interesting description of the early days of the LAPD, go to the official website, http://www.lapdonline.org/history_of_the_lapd/content_basic_view/1107

In 1869, six officers were formally hired and paid out of city funds. Led by the city marshal, who also acted as dog catcher and tax collector, this early force was the beginning of the LAPD of today. The mounted patrol began in 1875 and existed until 1916. In 1876, the Board of Police Commissioners was formed and a police chief was hired after the marshal was killed by one of his own men. In 1885, the chief of police commanded eighteen men and earned $150 a month. In 1886, two Black officers were hired. In 1889, professional standards emerged with a new chief, John M. Glass, who instituted hiring standards and formalized training.[36]

As the 1800s gave way to the 1900s, cities and towns grew, and most eventually created their own police departments. That process continues today and small towns sometimes make the decision to create a municipal police force, even if it is only a chief and one or two officers, rather than depend on the county sheriff's office for police protection. Sheriff's deputies provide patrol protection and crime investigation to unincorporated areas and small towns that do not have their own police department.

Policing in the Twentieth Century

Early police departments continued to be very influenced by politics through the 1930s. Positions were awarded through political patronage, and sometimes police campaigned in uniform for politicians running for re-election. Of course, if their candidate lost, they would have lost their jobs, and so there may have been, in some situations, more than a hint of coercion and corruption in their involvement with the political process. Police were implicated in coercing votes and stuffing ballot boxes.[37]

Training was minimal, and police were paid very little. Some officers were corrupt and utilized their position for graft. While early police departments were involved in a range of community activities, such as running soup kitchens and pursuing moral reforms such as anti-alcohol campaigns, they were also involved in strike-busting and immigrant control, sometimes through extra-legal and violent means. In some cities with strong political machines, police might have been seen almost as a private security force serving only those in power. The control of the working and "immigrant classes" was not necessarily done with any degree of sensitivity or even legality.[38]

August Vollmer (1876–1955) is credited with beginning the process of professionalizing the police. He was elected marshal of Berkeley, California, in 1905 and later became its first police chief. During his long tenure with the Berkeley Police Department, he was instrumental in a large number of innovations in policing that spread across the country and led to police departments being considered more as professional crime fighters than "hired muscle" for political machines. Interestingly, he is also credited with beginning the first criminal justice department at the University of California at Berkeley, where he taught some of the emerging leaders in the field.

In effect, the "professionalization" of police resulted in a real, or at least perceived, shift of police loyalty from political bosses to the law itself. Professionalization implied objectivity, professional expertise, and specialized training. The professionalization of police probably also led to the emphasis of the crime fighter role over order maintenance in following decades. Professionalization led to more training, hiring standards, and standard operating procedures.

By the 1960s, police were seen as professional crime fighters, but certain factors had combined to drastically change their relationship with the community. They were isolated in patrol cars instead of meeting and interacting with citizens while walking beats, and they had layers of bureaucracy that reduced their discretion when handling community problems. Professionalization may have led to police officers in some cities being seen as well-trained crime fighters, but it also made them seem more like soldiers than public servants.

Then in the 1960s, police departments around the country were faced with civil protests that challenged their ability to maintain public order. When civil rights protests began in the south, police were seen on television news shows using dogs and high-pressure water hoses on peaceful demonstrators.

When race riots broke out in the cities of the north, police were seen by some as an all-White force oppressing an all-Black ghetto. The antipathy one finds between police departments and urban minority communities today has its roots as far back as the late 1800s when police were used to control the immigrant classes, but the more immediate origin is the 1960s race riots. In 1992, after the acquittal of police officers accused of beating Rodney King, Los Angeles erupted in

EXHIBIT 2.1.11 In the 1960s, police were seen responding to peaceful civil rights protests with fire hoses and dogs.

Source: Getty

a riot similar to those of the 1960s. The public disturbances in Ferguson, Missouri, and Baltimore, Maryland, and the continuing protests by "Black Lives Matter" groups make it apparent that race relations continue to be problematic for at least some police departments.

Because of the discord and conflict of the 1960s, police departments around the country sought to improve their relationships with minority communities through the recruitment and hiring of minority and female officers. They also created community relations and public information officers. Citizen advisory committees were started in some communities, and other attempts were made to make the relationship between the police department and the community it served more open and cooperative. In the 1990s, these efforts coalesced into an approach called "community policing."

What Is Community Policing?

Community policing is based on a belief that police should partner with communities to prevent and reduce crime. Around the early 1980s, James Wilson and George Kelling developed what came to be called the **"broken windows" theory** of crime. These researchers argued that signs of neighborhood disintegration and deterioration indicated to criminals that no one cared and no one would intervene in criminal acts; therefore, crime is higher in these types of neighborhoods. The more crime, the less community members invest in their neighborhoods, increasing the spiral of disorder, decay, and crime. Markers of such disintegration include abandoned homes, graffiti, loitering youth, drunks and homeless people on the street, and minor offenses like public urination. Herman Goldstein argued that the police had a role in strengthening the community, which would, in turn, increase the community's ability to prevent crime.[39]

Eventually the theory that neighborhood disintegration would lead to crime served as the foundation for community policing, order-maintenance policing, zero tolerance policing, and problem-oriented policing. Depending on the source, these various models of policing are described as the same, similar, or different.

Zero tolerance policing has been mistakenly associated with community policing, but it is conceptually distinct. Zero tolerance policing is associated with William Bratton's term as head of the New York City Transit Police and then as Commissioner of NYPD (1994–96). He also instituted his reforms as Chief of the Los Angeles Police Department (LAPD) (2002–09), and in 2013 returned as NYPD Commissioner. This type of policing, based on "broken windows," deals with all public order crimes, such as graffiti, noise violations, public urination, and aggressive panhandling, with full enforcement. The idea is that you arrest the "little" criminals and it prevents serious crime. There is no necessary partnership with the community to undertake this model of policing and, in fact, eventually the community rebels because police officers become perceived as too intrusive and oppressive as they enforce minor ordinances against everyone.

Critics contend that it is a policing approach that has the risk of biased enforcement against cultural groups that do not fit into the mainstream.[40] Street people, youth, and minorities are affected, but so, too, are "law-abiding" people who violate a city ordinance, such as parking or maintenance of property. In New York City, the zero-tolerance approach taken by the police was touted as the reason crime in the city dropped substantially through the late 1990s and 2000s, but critics contend that the crime rate dropped in other places that did not implement zero tolerance. Further, the rate of citizen complaints during the same time period increased substantially, so there is a cost in citizen–police relations with zero tolerance that may not be justified by any proven link to reduced crime.

Community policing is used as a broad term that encompasses many different types of tactics and programs, all with the goal of officers and community members developing partnerships to solve some of the neighborhood's problems. The purpose of all community policing efforts was to increase the partnership between the community and the police in crime prevention.[41] The programs loosely grouped under a community policing strategy attempted to get community members to assist in crime prevention efforts. These partnerships may have been as simple as "National Night Out," where neighborhood members were encouraged to go outside on a specified night and meet their neighbors, to more elaborate citizen–police partnerships that identified problems in the community and shared the responsibility of fixing them. Community policing efforts have included the following:

- an increase in foot and bike patrols
- storefront police stations
- bilingual crime hotlines
- prevention newsletters and watch programs
- meetings with community members
- citizen police academies

EXHIBIT 2.1.12 Community policing seeks to create a partnership between police and residents to solve a neighborhood's problems. These efforts can include increased foot (or Segway) patrols and meetings with community members.

Source: Getty

- D.A.R.E. and G.R.E.A.T. programs
- officers with greater responsibility and autonomy dedicated to the neigborhoods they are assigned.

Community policing efforts also emphasize the decentralization of policing. Neighborhood storefront police stations were given greater autonomy in prioritizing and solving the problems of that particular neighborhood. The police role expanded to include helping citizens get the city to respond to abandoned cars, broken streetlights, overgrown empty lots, and dilapidated houses. Permanent assignments rather than rotating shifts help police officers develop working relationships with citizens and encourage a feeling of responsibility for their assigned community. Exhibit 2.1.13 displays some of the strategies used in community policing.

EXHIBIT 2.1.13 Community Policing Strategies

- Direct engagement with the community with greater information about neighborhood problems.
- Freeing community police officers from responding to dispatched crime calls so they can engage in proactive crime prevention.
- More visible police operations.
- Decentralized operations that lead to greater familiarity with specific neighborhoods.
- Encouraging officers to see citizens as partners.
- Moving decision making and discretion downward to patrol officers.
- Encouraging citizens to take more initiative in preventing and solving crimes.

Source: National Institute of Justice, "Community policing in the 1990s." NIJ Research Bulletin. *Washington, DC: U.S. Department of Justice, 1992, p. 3.*

Critics of community policing programs argued that the efforts were ineffective in crime prevention for a variety of reasons. One reason was that they mistakenly assumed "community" could be defined purely geographically. That is, community policing programs might have targeted a particular neighborhood, drawing boundaries by crime rates, voting districts, or through some other means of establishing the border of the "community." However, people may be affiliated more through activity than "place." For instance, a family may not know its neighbors but be very active in a church that is three miles away.[42] More police presence in a particular geographic neighborhood may have deterred some crime, but it may not have been successful in strengthening the community sufficiently to prevent criminal decision making.

Community policing efforts in some locales may have failed because there was no "community" to join with, or because the partnership was nonexistent. The neighborhoods where crime is the highest are also marked by high mobility, low home ownership, few community leaders, and a lack of willingness or ability for volunteering. Such communities may need community policing the most, but they are also the least likely places such partnerships work.

Critics argued that some programs used the community as the "eyes and ears" of police, to gain political support, monetary assistance, and moral support; but they did not involve the community in power sharing or decision making.[43] Further, in some communities, police are seen as the enemy and the antipathy felt toward police overwhelmed any attempts to gain trust. Residents may not have liked criminals, but they liked police even less. In these neighborhoods, any partnerships needed to overcome the residual distrust and dislike before becoming workable.

Evaluations of community policing efforts have been mixed. Evaluations showed that public satisfaction increased when a police department adopted community policing programs, but whether such approaches reduced crime is difficult to say. Some researchers argue that findings indicate the central organization and service delivery of policing never changed that much anyway.[44] Ironically, one of the major hurdles of community policing efforts was that the community police officer emphasized order-maintenance tasks rather than crime-control tasks. This may have been a less desirable role for many officers who preferred to see themselves as "crime fighters," regardless of the effectiveness of community policing efforts.

Problem-oriented policing has been associated with community policing and the approach is certainly consistent with community policing, but it can be removed from the community policing model and still have legitimacy. Generally, problem-oriented policing follows the so-called **SARA model** of problem solving. SARA stands for scanning, analysis, response, and assessment. It refers to how police should approach crime problems. Instead of simply patrolling and reacting to crime calls, police should be constantly scanning for problems by using crime reports and other sources of information to target a particular problem, for instance an increase in burglaries in a particular neighborhood. Then, the analysis phase identifies potential explanations for the crime problem and ways to address the situation to reduce crime. Response involves implementation, which might be increased patrol, targeted enforcement, or some other response. Finally, assessment measures whether the response was successful.

Despite literally thousands of articles and news reports of various problem-oriented programs across the country, there are fairly few rigorous evaluations of its effectiveness, although those that have been done do indicate that problem-oriented policing is effective.[45] In at least one study that evaluated the methods used in responding to identified crime problems, it was found that situational prevention responses were more effective than simple arrest strategies, calling into question the effectiveness of the zero tolerance approach.[46]

The Demise of Community Policing

Many argued that 9/11 marked the beginning of the end of the community policing era. Arguably, it was never accepted wholeheartedly by the majority of officers since it seemingly replaced a crime fighter role with a social worker role by prioritizing community problems. The threat of terrorism spurred a return to traditional policing.[47] Community policing continued to be a term seen in official documents, and the federal government continues to fund the Office of Community Oriented Policing Services (COPS), but the promise of the community policing model was supplanted by the 1033 program where local police departments could purchase for minimal amounts surplus military hardware, the majority of which was desks and other equipment, but also included armored vehicles and even grenade launchers.[48]

It appears that the President's Task Force on 21st Century Policing has spurred a new cycle of reform with police leaders across the country debating the "warrior" versus **"guardian" model.**[49] This conceptual dichotomy recognizes that police officers at times are engaged in crime fighting, but that they should not approach their role as if they are "at war" with the community they serve. They are guardians of the citizenry, and, more importantly, guardians of the law and democracy itself. The hallmarks of the guardian role are public service, promoting relationships with the community through mutual respect, and the use of communication techniques such as de-escalation to prevent the use of force unless absolutely necessary. Others have taken issue with this promotion, arguing that emphasizing a multitude of rules, policies, and best practices that discourage the use of force will endanger police officers. Thus, once again, the debate continues between the primacy of crime fighting versus public service in the police officer role.[50]

Summary

What Is the Function of Policing?

It is common to identify crime control and order maintenance (or community caretaking) as the two major functions of law enforcement. Crime control includes all the tasks associated with preventing crime and arresting criminals. Community caretaking takes up the majority of time and includes everything else police officers do.

What Are the Major Issues Facing Policing Today?

Currently, there is a great deal of scrutiny and criticism directed toward police departments. There is a split between White and minority citizens in this country in how police are perceived, with Black and other minority citizens less likely to trust police or believe that they are accountable. Other issues include whether police officers use their legal powers appropriately. There is also a current concern that attacks on police officers have increased.

How Many Police Officers Are There and Who Are They?

A survey in 2013 reported on 15,388 agencies with 1,045,360 total personnel including 724,690 full-time sworn employees. Most police departments are small (under 100 officers), however, about one-third of all police officers work in the very largest departments (New York City, Los Angeles, Chicago, etc.). About 27 percent of police officers are members of a minority group; about 12 percent are Black and about 11.6 percent are Hispanic. The percentage of female police officers is about 12 percent and has plateaued in recent years.

What Is the Difference between Federal, State, and Local Law Enforcement?

Many federal agencies have law enforcement personnel in addition to the FBI who perform investigative and apprehension functions. State law enforcement includes the highway patrol and other state-level agencies. Municipal law enforcement is the most commonly thought-of type of law enforcement, e.g. NYPD. There are also special jurisdiction agencies (such as university police, park police, transit police and so on).

How Did Modern Policing Evolve?

Modern policing evolved from the British "bobby" and has a history in this country of being tied to politics. In the early 1900s a move toward professionalization removed policing from political patronage and increased the skills required. Policing has always swung between a crime fighter role and a public service function.

What Is Community Policing?

Begun in the 1990s, community policing was an approach that put police officers in partnership with community members to solve neighborhood problems. The idea was that by working as partners, crime could be prevented. The approach was less emphasized after 9/11 when the threat of terrorism eclipsed efforts to improve relations between police agencies and communities. More recently, a similar discussion has emerged in the contrast between the warrior versus guardian role of policing.

Critical Thinking Exercises

1. Research community policing programs in your area (if there are any). Has there been any controversy over the implementation of such programs? If so, what is the controversy, and what facts are needed to help resolve the controversy?

2. Are there any issues with policing in your city or town? Research what they might be (using a search engine for the local newspaper). Are there two sides to an issue? Are there more than two sides? Is there competing data (i.e., data that doesn't seem to be consistent with each other used by either side)? Can you reconcile the data?

Notes

1. S. Mastrofski, R. Parks, A. Reiss and R. Worden, *Policing Neighborhoods: A Report from Indianapolis*. Washington, DC: National Institute of Justice, 1999.
2. Task Force, *Final Report of the President's Task Force on 21st Century Policing*. Washington, DC: Office of Justice Programs, 2015. Available at: http://www.cops.usdoj.gov/pdf/taskforce/TaskForce_FinalReport.pdf
3. Gallup. Accessed 2/16/2016 from http://www.gallup.com/poll/175088/gallup-review-black-white-attitudes-toward-police.aspx
4. Pew Research Center, accessed 2/16/2016 from http://www.pewresearch.org/fact-tank/2015/04/28/blacks-whites-police/
5. B. Chappell, "Number of police officers killed by gunfire fell 14 percent in 2015, study says." NPR. December 29, 2015. Retrieved 4/15/2016 from http://www.npr.org/sections/thetwo-way/2015/12/29/461402091/number-of-police-officerskilled-by-gunfire-fell-14-percent-in-2015-study-says
6. T. Jackman, "About 10 police officers per year are killed in ambushes, but five already in 2016." *Washington Post*, March 14, 2016.
7. Various news stories, e.g. http://www.cbsnews.com/news/cops-tennessee-shooter-targeted-white-victims-similar-to-dallasambush/
8. B. Reaves, *Census of State and Local Law Enforcement Agencies, 2008*. Washington, DC: Bureau of Justice Statistics, 2011, p.3.
9. B. Reaves, *Local Police Departments, 2013: Personnel, Policies, and Practices*. Washington, DC: Bureau of Justice Statistics, 2015.
10. Ibid., p. 2. The 2015 Reaves report does not provide information on special jurisdiction agencies.
11. Reaves, 2011.
12. Reaves, 2015, p. 3.
13. Reaves, 2011, p. 4; Reaves, 2015, p. 14.
14. Reaves, 2015, p. 6.
15. *Houston Chronicle*, retrieved 2/16/2016 from http://work.chron.com/police-officers-starting-salary-6740.html

16. J. Kuykendall and P. Burns, "The black police officer: A historical perspective." *Journal of Contemporary Criminal Justice* 1 (1980): 103–113.
17. Accessed census from http://www.census.gov/quickfacts/table/PST045215/00
18. Reaves, 2015, p. 5.
19. Accessed 2/15/2016: http://www.nytimes.com/interactive/2014/09/03/us/the-race-gap-in-americas-police-departments.html
20. Reaves, 2015, p. 6.
21. S. Martin, *Breaking and Entering: Policewomen on Patrol.* Berkeley, CA: University of California Press, 1980; L. Langton, *Women in Law Enforcement, 1987–2008.* Washington, DC: Bureau of Justice Statistics, 2010, p. 3.
22. A. Kringen, *Understanding Barriers That Affect Recruiting and Retaining Female Police Officers: A Mixed Method Approach* (Doctoral dissertation), 2014. Retrieved from ProQuest Dissertations & Theses Global (3681033).
23. Discussion with Sue Rahr, March 2016.
24. Reaves, 2015, p. 4;
25. M. Hickman and B. Reaves, *Local Police Departments, 2000.* Washington, DC: Bureau of Justice Statistics, 2003, p. 4.
26. Reaves, 2015, p. 5.
27. B. Reaves, *Federal Law Enforcement Officers, 2008.* Washington, DC: Bureau of Justice Statistics, 2012, p. 1.
28. Ibid.
29. B. Reaves and L. Bauer, *Federal Law Enforcement Officers, 2002.* Washington, DC: Bureau of Justice Statistics, 2003, p. 5.
30. Ibid, p. 8.
31. B. Reaves, *Census of State and Local Law Enforcement Agencies, 2008.* Washington, DC: Bureau of Justice Statistics, 2011, p. 6, 18.
32. ASIS International. Retrieved 6/8/2007 from http://www.asisonline.org/about/faqs.xml
33. W. Andrews, *The Early Years: The Challenge of Public Order, from 1845 to 1870.* New York Police Department, 2007. Retrieved from http://www.ci.nyc.ny.us/html/nypd/html/3100/retro.html
34. W. Andrews, *An Era of Corruption and Reform: 1870–1900.* New York Police Department, 2007. Retrieved from http://www.ci.nyc.ny.us/html/nypd/html/3100/retro.html
35. Los Angeles Police Department. Retrieved 4/16/2016, from http://www.lapdonline.org/history_of_the_lapd/content_basic_view/1107
36. Los Angeles Police Department. Retrieved 6/1/2007, from http://www.lapdonline.org/history_of_the_lapd/content_basic_view/1107
37. J. Crank, *Understanding Police Culture.* Cincinnati, OH: Anderson Publishing, 2003.

38. V. Kappeler, R. Sluder and G. Alpert, *Forces of Deviance: Understanding the Dark Side of Policing*. Prospect Heights, IL: Wave-land Press, 1994, p. 41; S. Walker, *A Critical History of Police Reform: The Emergence of Professionalism*. Lexington, MA: Lexington Books, 1977.
39. H. Goldstein, *Problem-Oriented Policing*. New York: McGraw-Hill, 1990.
40. C. Kubrin, "Making order of disorder: A call for conceptual clarity." *Criminology and Public Policy* 7 (2) (2008): 203–214.
41. P. McCold and B. Wachtel, "Community is not a place: A new look at community justice initiatives." In J. Perry (Ed.), *Repairing Communities through Restorative Justice*. Lanham, MD: American Correctional Association, 2002, p. 47.
42. Ibid., p. 40.
43. Ibid., p. 43.
44. J. Zhao, N. He and N. Lovrich, "Community policing: Did it change the basic functions of policing in the 1990s? A national follow-up study." *Justice Quarterly* 20 (4) (2003): 697–724.
45. D. Weisburd, C. Telep, J. Hinkle and J. Eck, "Is problem-oriented policing effective in reducing crime and disorder?" *Criminology and Public Policy* 9 (1) (2010): 139–172.
46. A. Braga, "Setting a higher standard for the evaluation of problem-oriented policing initiatives." *Criminology and Public Policy* 9 (1) (2010): 173–195.
47. J. Pollock, *Ethical Dilemmas and Decisions in Criminal Justice*. Belmont, CA: Wadsworth/ Cengage. 2016.
48. Apuzzo, M, "Local police gearing up with tools of combat." *The Seattle Times*, June 9, 2014, A4.
49. Rahr, S. and S. Rice, *From Warriors to Guardians: Recommitting American Police Culture to Democratic Ideals* (New Perspectives in Policing Series). Washington, DC: U.S. Department of Justice, National Institute of Justice, 2015. NCJ 248654
50. K. Johnson, "In face of criticism, police officials preaching de-escalation strategies." *USA Today*, October 7, 2015. Retrieved 4/16/2016 from: http://www.usatoday.com/story/news/nation/2015/10/07/police-encounters-violent-baltimore-ferguson/72636622/

READING 2.2

POLICE OPERATIONS

Joycelyn Pollock

[READING] PREVIEW

- How Are Police Officers Selected and Trained?
- What Is the Difference Between Proactive and Reactive Policing?
- How Has Technology Affected Policing?
- Is Police Officer Stress a Problem and, If So, What Is the Role of Organizational Justice?
- What Is the Police Subculture?
- What Are Some Types of Police Misconduct?
- Do Police Officers Discriminate Against Minorities?
- What Is the Law and Policy Concerning Police Use of Force?
- Focus On Data: Do Police Officers Abuse Their Power to Use Lethal Force?
- What Were the Recommendations of the 21st Century President's Task Force on Policing?
- Summary
- Critical Thinking Exercises

WHAT MAKES A GOOD POLICE OFFICER? In this [reading], we will discuss how police departments select, train, and supervise their police officers. In a few cases, selection, training, and supervision fail, and police misconduct occurs. It is important to realize, however, that the vast majority of police officers perform their role, whether it be involving proactive or reactive policing, with integrity and competence. Most of the discussion in this [reading] focuses on law enforcement at the local municipal level.

How Are Police Officers Selected and Trained?

The qualifications for being hired by a police department typically include only a few absolute requirements. One major department, for instance, requires that applicants have the following qualifications:

- be 21 to 44 years old
- have put in 60 hours of college or possess an honorable discharge from the military
- be a U.S. citizen
- be height and weight proportionate
- have a valid driver's license
- have no more than two moving violations within the last eighteen months
- have no felony or class A misdemeanors
- have no class B misdemeanors within the last ten years
- have a stable credit history.

Applicants who meet these qualifications must pass a civil service test that is, to a large extent, basic reading comprehension and writing. The next steps of the hiring process include a preliminary interview, physical fitness test, polygraph test, criminal background check, interview, medical exam (including a drug test), and a psychological exam.[1]

The hiring process is described as a "screening out" process rather than a selection process.[2] In other words, all applicants are, in effect, considered as applicants and then are eliminated when factors indicate they would be inappropriate for policing. Factors that would screen out applicants include a lack of intellectual ability (failing the civil service exam), lack of responsibility (bad credit), lack of honesty (failing the polygraph test), lack of physical fitness (failing the physical test), or lack of mental stability (failing the psychological exam).

The psychological exam utilizes objective personality tests, such as the Minnesota Multiphasic Personality Inventory (MMPI), and a personal interview. The psychologist looks for personality characteristics such as aggressiveness, bias, or anxiety, which would indicate that the candidate is a poor fit for the job. On the other hand, there is no desired personality profile that all police departments use to look for candidates. Little research has been done to explore whether certain personality profiles are more or less successful in policing careers. The Inwald Personality Inventory (IPI) was developed to measure personality characteristics and behavioral patterns specific to fitness for law enforcement. The so-called Big Five personality traits (extroversion, neuroticism, agreeableness, conscientiousness, and openness) have been validated as reliable measures of personality and, of these, conscientiousness seems to predict good performance in other jobs and professions. Conscientiousness is related to the degree of organization, control, and motivation one has, and has been related to being organized, reliable, hard-working, self-governing, and persevering. There has been very little research, however, as to whether the trait accurately measures police performance success. Generally, desirable traits and characteristics for officers include higher education, varied life experiences, cognitive problem-solving skills, communication skills, empathy, and respect for others.[3]

In the past, height and weight requirements excluded women and some minorities from being hired by police departments. Stringent height and weight requirements have been struck down as discriminatory by the courts, so today you may see very short police officers. It is still necessary for applicants to be in good physical shape, however, and requirements that applicants be height and weight proportionate have generally been upheld. Applicants are also typically required to pass some form of physical fitness test. Although these vary from department to department, they usually involve some form of cardiovascular fitness (running), strength, and agility. There is some concern that physical ability tests unfairly exclude women or others who might otherwise make good police officers; however, studies have validated that such tests do measure bona fide occupational qualifications (**BFOQ**) for police officers.[4]

Many, if not most, police departments do not require officers to maintain physical standards once hired however. Some have advocated for years that physical standards be adopted by police departments, much as the military does, with gradations of fitness based on age. Arguably, departments could save money in insurance costs and lost time due to sickness and injury if officers were required to maintain height and weight ratios and cardiovascular fitness. These demands would reduce heart attacks or injuries when carrying out police duties, but most departments have not instituted such standards as mandatory.

One interesting topic that has been explored by researchers is whether there is such a thing as a "police personality" that is attracted to policing. A related question is whether the career attracts people with certain personality characteristics, or whether the career changes people so that they develop such characteristics after working in the field. The so-called police personality has been described as having the traits of cynicism, authoritarianism, and suspiciousness. Some researchers have found police officers to be generally cynical, isolated, alienated, defensive, distrustful, dogmatic, and authoritarian. However, there is conflicting research as to the prevalence of these traits in policing. Research has also not shown whether the traits exist prior to being hired, or whether the job changes officers (e.g., makes them more cynical or suspicious than the general population). Furthermore, it is not clear that any particular traits are associated with undesirable behaviors or less effective officers. These are important research questions and should be addressed.[5]

Training

Early officers had no training and were basically given a uniform and nightstick and told to go do their job. Training has expanded exponentially and today police departments require 600–700 hours or more of academy training. To be certified as a peace officer in most states, one must have graduated from a recognized academy and passed standardized tests that include academic subjects as well as skills training, such as firearms and driving. Police officers receive training in departmental or regional academies. Smaller departments may prefer to hire individuals who have already received certification through attendance at a regional academy, but larger departments have their own academies and require all applicants to attend, even those who may already have certification. Some states have centralized training whereby all or almost all law enforcement officers train at one statewide academy. Recruit training includes law, operations, mental health assessments, communication skills, domestic violence, firearms, physical combat, and driving skills, among other topics.

> Look at the website for Washington State's Training Commission at https://fortress.wa.gov/cjtc/www/

Field training officer (FTO) programs started in 1972.[6] This last portion of training pairs the new recruit with an **FTO** who supervises the trainee for a period that may range from weeks to months. FTOs are expected to help new academy graduates apply their academy training to real-life problems of the street. FTOs generally work from a checklist of sorts that requires him or her to certify the competence of the recruit in a standard list of tasks. Some FTOs and others convey the idea that what one learns in the academy is irrelevant and now they will teach the recruit the way "it really is." Generally, however, all recognize that the academy cannot possibly teach the recruit everything they need to know and FTOs serve a valuable function in bridging "classroom" and "street" learning. FTOs should be, and usually are, chosen for their ability to teach recruits good practices that will prevent citizen complaints and lawsuits against the department. FTOs submit evaluations of the new recruit that determine whether he or she passes the probationary period.

In-service training hours are required for all police officers to maintain their certification. This in-service training usually has content that is mandated by the state, and also optional training segments that can be selected by the department or individual officer. In Massachusetts, for instance, 40 hours of training is required each year, and includes legal updates, eyewitness identification, defensive tactics skills training, use-of-force concepts and tactics, community interactions, Critical Incidents, firearms training and requalification, CPR recertification and first-aid training.[7]

Police management training has been criticized as non-existent; however, there is very advanced training available for police leaders. Various organizations, such as the Police Executive Research Forum (PERF), provide research and training to improve administration and management. There is also training for police managers available through the Federal Law Enforcement Training Center (FLETC), which also conducts training internationally.

> To learn more about PERF, go to http://www.policeforum.org/, and for FLETC, to http://www.fletc.gov/

What Is the Difference Between Proactive and Reactive Policing?

Patrol can be considered both **reactive policing** and **proactive policing**. Typically, patrol officers spend time responding to dispatched calls for service, which is obviously reactive policing; however, they also interact with the citizenry, develop relationships with key community members, and follow up on tips which can be considered proactive policing. The idea that simply patrolling deters crime has been called into question. One of the most famous research projects in policing was the Kansas City Preventive Patrol Study. In this study, part of Kansas City, Missouri, was divided into three different areas. One area had no patrol at all—police only responded to dispatched calls. The second area had increased patrol, roughly five to six times the normal pattern. The third area was the control group, with normal patrols scheduled. Study authors found no significant differences among the three areas in level of crime or citizen satisfaction.[8] This does not mean, of course, that police have no effect on crime; but it does call into question the effectiveness of normal patrols.

While regular patrol may not be noticed or have any effect on crime, **saturated patrols**, meaning that a certain neighborhood or area of town is targeted for frequent, perhaps even constant, patrol presence, has been found to be effective. The "hot spot" is identified through crime reports and the saturated patrol continues for a set period or until the crime reports are reduced to an acceptable level. Research has indicated that saturated patrols do work in reducing crime; there is a **residual effect**, meaning reduced crime continues after the saturated patrol ends; and there does not seem to be a **displacement effect**, meaning that crime merely moves to another area of the city.[9]

Two of the most problematic calls for police officers are those that involve the mentally ill and domestic disturbances. When 911 calls are made, the patrol officers who respond have the goal to solve the immediate issue, e.g., a mentally ill person in the middle of traffic, a person threatening suicide, or a fighting couple. Some officers take a more proactive approach, however, and strive to provide more long-term solutions by referring the individuals to resources in the community that can prevent future incidents.

Some departments have special units or specially trained officers to deal with the mentally ill. The news media periodically report on incidents where police officers responding to a call about a mentally ill person resort to using violent means to subdue the individual and then encounter criticism for doing so. Crisis Intervention Training (**CIT**) helps officers identify the signs of mental illness, teaches communication techniques in how to interact with the mentally ill, and provides contact information for the resources that are available in the community to assist these individuals. More controversial are **"de-escalation" policies** that require police officers to use time, distance, and shielding to slow down interactions with the mentally ill. When officers respond to a 911 call of any person, including a mentally ill person, with a weapon, the standard response would be to secure the scene and disarm the individual as soon as possible. As long as someone is not in any immediate danger, de-escalation requires responding officers to utilize strategies to protect themselves by staying further back rather than getting close to the person and talking to them until they relinquish the weapon, sometimes for hours if that is what is necessary. Critics contend that taken to an extreme, such strategies are not feasible because police officers respond to too many calls per day and/or that there is too much danger presented in allowing the individual to control the scene. Proponents argue de-escalation is very similar to the hostage negotiation tactics that have been taught for years and even though "rushing the scene" may have a successful outcome, in some cases it has needlessly resulted in death or injury. Proponents argue that as long as officers have the time and there is no immediate threat, they should practice de-escalation.

> Read this news article for an example of a controversial de-escalation incident: http://www.nytimes.com/2016/04/26/health/police-mental-illnesscrisis-intervention.html?&moduleDetail=section-news-0&action=click&contentCollection=Health&region=Footer&module=MoreInSection&version=WhatsNext&contentID=WhatsNext&pgtype=Blogs

Some police departments also have special domestic violence units that respond to calls that involve battered women and/or abused children. These officers receive additional training. Before the 1980s, spousal violence was rarely considered a crime. If the injury was "severe," aggravated assault could be charged and the perpetrator could be arrested, but if the injury was not defined as severe, it was only misdemeanor assault and a police officer could not arrest unless the victim swore out a complaint. That changed in the 1980s when states begin passing "mandatory arrest" statutes that allowed or, in some cases, required officers to arrest without a complainant in cases of domestic violence, even if the injury did not rise to aggravated assault. Domestic violence calls comprise a substantial portion of all calls for service. Due to the heightened emotion and frequency of alcohol, these calls can be dangerous for victims and police officers alike.

In larger departments, officers are promoted to the detective ranks, but it would be incorrect to assume that patrol officers do not conduct investigations. In smaller departments officers may rotate assignments from patrol to detective and back again; and, even in departments where patrol officers are not given the title, they do conduct investigations or pick up information to pass along to investigators. Because patrol officers are the public face of the police department and interact with the community more frequently, they often receive the tips that lead to identifying suspects.

Proactive policing refers to those activities where police take the initiative in uncovering and/or preventing crime. Proactive policing includes undercover operations. In undercover operations, police officers may pretend to be drug dealers, prostitutes, or "johns." "Buy-bust" incidents are when the officer pretends to be a drug user and buys from a street dealer, and moments later an arrest is made. Similar set-ups are done to control street prostitution—policemen routinely pretend that they are "johns," and policewomen dress up as prostitutes. Ethical issues arise in undercover operations, especially when they evolve into personal relationships.[10]

In proactive investigations, the central question is: Who do police target and why? Police operations that provide opportunities for crime change the police role from discovering who has committed a crime to one of discovering who might commit a crime if given the chance. Some argue these activities create crime, but others counter by saying that the criminals would be committing such acts regardless of police involvement. In fact, that is part of the definition of entrapment and the legal test to determine if entrapment has occurred is whether the defendant had a predisposition to commit the criminal act.

How Has Technology Affected Policing?

Policing has changed dramatically in the last 40 years because of technology. The advent of computers, communication technology, and other scientific breakthroughs has provided tools for law enforcement that could only have been dreamed of in the 1960s.

Crime mapping is as old as using push-pins on a wall map, but computers have made the process much more sophisticated. One of the most publicized police management strategies has been the **CompStat program**. This approach was developed in New York City during the tenure of Chief William Bratton. Basically it uses computer-generated crime statistics and daily or weekly meetings of division heads to hold these managers responsible for the crime in their districts. Immediate feedback, in the form of crime reports, allows higher-level administrators to see who is and who is not successful in reducing crime. Some research has suggested that the format may create pressure to "doctor" crime reports. However, advocates argue that it is an efficient, modern approach to policing that is based on management principles.[11]

In addition to knowing where crimes occur, other technology has made it easier to investigate crime and catch criminals. Patrol car computers provide instant feedback to the officer about a suspect's criminal history, license plate readers provide information about car owners and whether the car has been reported stolen, and cellphones allow citizens to instantly contact officers if they have been provided a phone number. Drones have been used to provide undetected surveillance of marijuana fields, cellphone tracing technology has been instrumental in proving guilt based on a suspect's location, and thermal imaging has helped prove the presence of indoor growing operations as well as assist law enforcement in hostage situations. Officers are becoming adept at utilizing social media to investigate crime as well. Ironically, some individuals have been caught specifically because they boast about their crimes and/or post on social media.

Police departments must have the capacity to use computers because, increasingly, that's where crime occurs. **Cybercrimes** typically refer to computer hacking and the use of computers for

EXHIBIT 2.2.1 CompStat uses computer-generated crime statistics to see patterns, allocate resources, and hold managers accountable for crime in their districts. The system was developed in New York City where it is run out of this control room.

Source: AP

identity theft and fraud, but there are other crimes that either target computers or use computers to commit the crime, e.g., sexual solicitation of a minor, pornography, computer-aided voyeurism, sabotage. Now research shows by 2013, half of all state agencies and a quarter of county and municipal agencies had a cybercrimes unit or at least some police officers with primary duties related to cybercrimes. From 2007 to 2012, the FBI reported a 40 percent increase in cybercrime complaints and the number of cybercrimes units in police departments tripled from 9 percent of all agencies to 28 percent.[12]

One study of the use of technology in law enforcement reported that there were issues that prevented the value of technology from being fully utilized. Records software can be cumbersome and not particularly user-friendly and law enforcement officers reported frustration in the user interface that made them less efficient and compromised situational awareness when they spent an inordinate amount of time in their patrol car trying to input data. Further, while officers utilized technology for traditional reactive policing, e.g., finding suspects, they did not utilize technology as readily for proactive policing (e.g., using crime data to determine their patrolling patterns).[13]

Some older officers have reported that younger "millennial" officers depend too heavily on their cellphones, texting when they should be having face-to-face meetings with citizens, and showing a lack of ability to engage with citizens because they are more comfortable utilizing social media.[14]

Recently, technology in law enforcement investigations was the issue when the FBI wanted Apple to "hack" into the iPhone of the San Bernadino terrorist Syed Rizwan Farook in order to uncover information about the attack. Apple refused, and the FBI evidently located private parties who were able to do so. This controversy exposes one of the challenges and controversies over the use of technology in law enforcement. Our "surveillance" society is grappling with the situation where technology is outstripping the law and ethics to control it. We live in an age where government can read our texts or emails, facial recognition programs can identify us on the street through a multitude of cameras placed in public places, and real-time satellite images can reach places where cameras don't exist.[15]

Of course, local police don't have access to the most sophisticated equipment available but there is a great deal of overlap between what has been developed and used for international counter-terrorism and local police investigations of garden variety crimes. For instance, the stingray device that "tricks" cellphones into using it as a cellphone tower thereby compromising the user's privacy has been provided to and used by local law enforcement and has led to criminal convictions. The public has only a dim understanding of its presence. Surveillance experts worry about the encroachment of government watchers into our private lives, but even police officers are not immune and are increasingly being filmed themselves by their patrol car dashcams, by body cameras, and by bystanders' ubiquitous cellphone cameras. Research on body cameras so far indicates that their use results in fewer citizen complaints and better behavior by citizens.[16] However, no good answers have emerged over such questions as: Should individual police officers have the discretion to turn the camera off? Should private citizens have the authority to make footage of themselves private; alternatively, should all footage be subject to open records requests? Who should store the unimaginable amount of video footage collected in large cities, and for how long? These questions are only a sample of the many issues with body cameras, and other technology creates similar types of concerns.

Is Police Officer Stress a Problem and, If So, What Is the Role of Organizational Justice?

Some researchers have concluded that police officers do not experience more stress than those in other occupations, although findings are mixed.[17] One can say with certainty, however, that policing has a few unique stressors not shared by most other occupations—that is, using or being a target of lethal force is not present in most occupations. Research has found that police officers' heart rates increase dramatically when they are going to a serious call. Although heart rates go down after the call, they don't return to normal resting rates immediately. If the officer then receives another call, this raises the heart rate again, without a return to normal resting levels, and so on, so that if an officer is responding to several serious calls during the day, his or her heart rate is constantly elevated.[18]

Interestingly, in some studies officers have reported more stress comes from the organization than from what they experience on the street. Research indicates that officers experience more stress from management over such things as being "second guessed," being punished for minor infractions, and not being rewarded than they do from the "operational" elements of policing (dealing with suspects and danger). In one study on police stress, it was found that officers experienced "organizational stress" (which included perceptions of supervisors being too rigid and oppressive with a corresponding lack of discretion) and that this stress reduced their performance.[19]

Organizational justice refers to the perception that the organization is fair, decisions are made in an equitable manner, and employees are treated with respect. It is related to **procedural justice**, which refers to the idea that individuals may have positive views of what happens to them, even if they don't like the outcome, if the process is deemed as fair.[20] Studies of "organizational justice" indicate that officers have more organizational commitment and are less inclined to commit negative acts when they trust their supervisors and believe the organization is fair.[21] Perceptions of organizational justice by officers are correlated with greater job satisfaction and greater organizational citizenship behaviors (doing things above and beyond the job requirements for the betterment of the organization).

Research has also found that individuals experience the stress of policing differently, and factors such as gender, age, and ethnicity seem to affect the ability to cope with the stressors.[22] Stress is an important issue because it may lead to **burnout**, which is when officers merely "go through the motions" of their job and may be susceptible to corruption. It can also lead to turnover when officers quit or retire early because of stress.

What Is the Police Subculture?

A **subculture** exists when a group has a different set of values, beliefs, and even language from the dominant culture. In the case of the police subculture, there is research that indicates that in some departments there is a "subculture" of policing that is different from, and in conflict with, formal departmental mission statements. Researchers argue that the reason this subculture exists is the special nature of policing, including the following characteristics:

- Police typically form a homogeneous social group.
- They have a uniquely stressful work environment.

- They participate in a mostly closed social system.[23]

[...] [P]olice departments are more diverse today than in the past, but the other characteristics of the work life first described in the 1980s still hold true to a great extent. The work life of police officers is marked by shift work and special characteristics (such as dangerousness and stigma). Police officers' social lives tend to include other police officers. The subculture of policing has been described by various researchers as including certain values or themes. **Socialization** is adopting the values and beliefs of one's culture (or subculture). The police subculture has been described as including the following traits:

- stereotypical views of large numbers of citizens as troublemakers
- loyalty to colleagues over citizens or the department
- view that the use of force is acceptable even when not strictly legal
- view that police officer discretion should not be questioned
- view that the truth is relative and subject to protecting officers or crime control.[24]

Another researcher identified the three dominant characteristics of the police culture as cynicism or suspicion (of everyone); the acceptance of the use of force when their authority is threatened; and the perception that they are victims of public misunderstanding and scorn, low wages, and unfair administrators.[25]

The "**blue curtain of secrecy**," an element of the subculture, refers to the alleged tendency of police officers to cover up misconduct by other police officers. It should be noted that recent research indicates that this conspiracy of silence is breaking down.[26] There are interesting contradictions, however, because in a recent survey, while 80 percent of police officers did not think that the "code of silence" was essential for police trust and good policing, fully two-thirds reported that a "whistleblower" would suffer informal punishment from fellow officers. Further, more than half agreed that it was not unusual for police to ignore improper conduct on the part of other officers.[27]

The "blue curtain of secrecy" may not exist in some departments or may exist at varying levels in different police departments. If it does exist, it occurs for various reasons. Officers feel loyalty toward each other. They also may believe that the officer's wrongdoing is not as serious as the discipline he would receive or equal the loss of an experienced officer to the department. There may be egoistic reasons as well, because the officer may believe that he or she has also committed acts that could be disciplined. Loyalty is perhaps stronger in law enforcement than in other professions because police depend on one another, sometimes in life-or-death situations. Loyalty to one's fellows is part of the *esprit de corps* of policing and is an absolutely essential element of a healthy department, but it seems that it can also cause problems when some officers are protected from the consequences of their misconduct.

Most of the research on the police subculture is fairly old, and, although some current research seems to support the continued presence of some aspects of the subculture, it also seems to be the case that it may not be as prevalent or extreme as it once might have been. Factors contributing to the possible weakening of the subculture include: increasing diversity in race, ethnicity, and education of recruits; the formalization of grievance procedures and union advocacy (which negates the need for a subculture); and the threat of civil litigation which makes covering up for someone much more potentially costly. Also, researchers have found that there is substantial variation among officers and differences in their cultural views as well as differences between police departments and even between districts or sub-stations within police departments.[28]

What Are Some Types of Police Misconduct?

The International Association of Chiefs of Police developed the Law Enforcement Code of Ethics and the Canons of Police Ethics, and many departments have used these or adapted them to their own situations. There are at least four major themes in the International Chiefs of Police Code. Fairness is the single most dominant theme in the law enforcement code. Police officers must uphold the law regardless of the offender's identity. A second theme is that of *service*. The third theme is the *importance of the law*. Police are protectors of the Constitution and must not go beyond it or substitute rules of their own. The final theme is one of *personal conduct*. Police, at all times, must uphold a standard of behavior consistent with their public position. This involves a higher standard of behavior in their professional and personal lives than that expected from the general public.

> To read the International Chiefs of Police Law Enforcement Code, go to http://www.lib.jjay.cuny.edu/cje/html/codes/codes-usa-organizational/lece-r.html

Unfortunately, despite the code of ethics, and departmental efforts in selection, training, and supervision to minimize the occurrence of misdeeds on the part of officers, scandals do occur. Examples of widespread corruption occur periodically in the news as well as individual acts of deviance by a few officers.[29] While the vast majorities of officers are honest and perform their job honorably, it is important to understand the structural elements that allow these instances of corruption to occur. It does seem to be the case that the most extreme cases of police corruption occur in large cities. Perhaps this is because there is more anonymity in large departments and it is more difficult to supervise all officers in all divisions and squads. Further, it is harder to develop a cohesive culture of integrity and service in larger departments with thousands of officers.

Corruption can be divided into 1) economic corruption; and 2) abuse of authority. Economic corruption includes graft. **Graft** refers to any exploitation of one's role, such as accepting bribes or protection money. Graft also occurs when officers receive kickbacks from tow truck drivers, defense attorneys, or bail bondsmen for recommending them. **Gratuities** are usually prohibited by departmental policies; they are items of value received by an individual because of his or her role or position, rather than because of a personal relationship with the giver.

A different type of misconduct is abuse of authority. Police abuse of authority comes in three different areas: physical abuse (excessive force, sexual assault), psychological abuse (disrespect, harassment, intimidation), and legal abuse (unlawful searches or seizures or manufacturing evidence).[30] One type of abuse of authority is when officers extort sex from female citizens. Egregious cases in the United States include rapes by officers on duty, and by jailers in police lock-ups. One of the most recent occurred in Oklahoma City where former officer Daniel Holtzclaw was convicted and sentenced to 263 years for raping several women while on duty.[31]

The concept of "**noble cause corruption**" refers to illegal actions or rule violations perpetrated by officers for "noble" reasons, i.e., to get the criminal off the street.[32] Such practices as "**testilying**" (lying in affidavits or when giving testimony) and coercion occur because of **ends-oriented thinking**, which means that the person believes "the end justifies the means" regardless of how bad the means are. Police officers behave this way when they place a high value on crime control, even over due process. The behaviors under the noble cause category are done by those who believe they are fulfilling their oath of protecting the public. Crime lab investigators and prosecutors may also engage in shortcuts and unethical acts in order to convict the perceived guilty. Prosecutors have been known to suppress evidence and allow perjured testimony, so it is not only police officers who feel compelled to break the law in order to further the noble cause of crime control.[33]

There are individual, organizational and societal explanations for police misconduct. *Individual explanations* explain the officer was deviant when hired or became so after hire. Such explanations support better selection procedures and better supervision for reducing the possibility of corruption. *Organizational explanations* point to problems in training or supervision. The concept of organizational justice discussed above might be an organizational explanation of misconduct. Lack of supervision from front-line sergeants, and poor leadership can breed corruption.[34] *Societal explanations* of police deviance focus on the relationship between the police and the public. When societal norms encourage differential application of the law, it supports police graft. As long as the general public engages in illegal activities (like gambling, prostitution, and drug use), it is no surprise that some police officers are able to rationalize not enforcing the law. In another vein, as long as the public relays a message that crime control is more important than individual liberties and rights, then we should not be surprised when some police act on that message and violate the law.

EXHIBIT 2.2.2 Daniel Holtzclaw used his position as an Oklahoma City Police Officer to rape and sexually victimize women while on patrol.

Source: AP

A wide range of suggestions has been offered that may reduce or minimize the chance of police corruption, including those found in Exhibit 2.2.3.

Civilian review/complaint boards are increasingly being called for in communities. Citizens not connected to the police department sit on these committees, commissions, or boards to monitor how police investigate citizen complaints. There are many models for the idea of civilian review, and no one model has been reported to be more effective or better than any other.[35]

Another idea is an **early warning or audit system**. Because research shows that a small number of officers are responsible for a disproportionate share of excessive force complaints and other types of citizen complaints, the idea is to identify these officers early. Early warning systems have been used by New Orleans, Portland, and Pittsburgh. The early warning systems utilize number of complaints, use of force reports, use of weapon reports, reprimands, and other indicators to identify problem officers. Intervention may include greater supervision, additional training, and/or counseling.[36]

EXHIBIT 2.2.3 Reducing Police Corruption

- Increase the salary of police
- Eliminate unenforceable laws
- Establish civilian review boards
- Improve training, especially ethics training
- Require more education
- Improve leadership
- Set realistic goals and objectives for the department
- Provide a written code of ethics
- Provide a whistleblowing procedure that ensures fair treatment of all parties
- Create more oversight (inspectors' general offices)
- **Integrity testing**
- Perform audits (of overtime or funds paid to informants)
- Have financial disclosure rules
- Improve internal affairs departments
- Rotate staff in certain assignments, e.g., vice
- Have better evidence-handling procedures
- Use video cameras in patrol cars
- Use covert high-technology surveillance
- Decriminalize vice crimes
- Use body cameras for all patrol officers
- Employ early warning systems
- Seek formal prosecutions when appropriate

Source: J. Pollock, Ethical Dilemmas and Decisions in Criminal Justice. *Boston, MA: Cengage, 2016.*

Employee behavior is directly influenced by superiors. Even if leaders are not involved in corruption directly, encouraging or participating in the harassment and ostracism that is directed toward whistleblowers supports an organizational culture in which officers may be afraid to come forward when they know of wrongdoing. A different problem may be when certain people in the department do not receive punishment for behaviors that others would receive punishment for.

This climate destroys the trust in police leadership that is essential to ensure good communication from the rank and file.[37]

Do Police Officers Discriminate Against Minorities?

There is a longstanding, pervasive belief that police treat African Americans, and to a lesser extent, Hispanics, more harshly than Whites. In this section, we will examine the evidence, always with the recognition that one cannot discuss the 12,000 police agencies in the country as a monolithic unit, nor is it fair to assume that a half million police officers are similar on any spectrum, including discriminatory behavior.

Individual prejudices and perceptions of groups such as women, minorities, and homosexuals can influence decision making. The question is whether officers' views of the world affect the way they do their job. The point is not that police officers are more prejudiced than the rest of us; it is that their special position creates the possibility that their prejudices could cause a citizen to be treated differently than others. Essentially, when police act on prejudices while performing their jobs, discrimination takes the form of either enforcing the law differentially or withholding the protections and benefits of the law.

Recent news stories have exposed scandals where officers (e.g., in San Francisco, California; Ferguson, Missouri; Edison, New Jersey; Seattle, Washington; Baton Rouge, Louisiana; and Miami Beach and Fort Lauderdale, Florida) texted racist and homophobic messages, including death threats, calling Black citizens "monkeys," and making jokes about lynching.[38] We know that the Internet is full of racist, sexist, and homophobic rants; however, police officers do not have the same free speech rights as the rest of us to spew such hateful messages when they can be identified as police officers. Departmental policies and codes of conduct require them to meet higher standards of behavior. It is also extremely important to be aware of the power of **implicit bias**.[39] Even if officers do not feel they are treating Blacks or other minorities differently, they may be if their worldview is represented accurately by the racist statements.

> Read about implicit bias training for police officers at this website: http://www.fairimpartialpolicing.com/

Recent events indicate, perhaps, that the issue of racism is endemic. There are patterns and practices pervasive in the system of justice that seem to be evidence of unequal treatment. For instance, after the Department of Justice completed their investigation of Ferguson, Missouri, they concluded that Officer Darren Wilson used lawful force in his shooting of Michael Brown;

however, the report also documented widespread discriminatory practices directed toward the Black community. The report put into context the violent reaction of the community to the Brown shooting, explaining that there had been years of distrust and resentment because of illegal and unethical practices by the police and justice officials in the town and county. More recently, a task force was created by the Chicago mayor after the Laquan McDonald shooting video sparked widespread protests. The task force issued a scathing report concluding that racism was rampant in the Chicago Police Department based on personal testimony and an examination of police incident reports. It was criticized by the police union and other officials as being one-sided and biased, however, the mayor quickly adopted about half of its recommendations.[40]

Most studies indicate that Blacks express more distrust of police than Whites or Hispanics. [...] [A] July 2016 *NYT*/CBS poll found that 75 percent of Blacks believed police officers were more likely to use force against Blacks as compared to White residents. In a Pew Research Center public opinion report the percentage of Blacks saying they have "very little" confidence in their local police to treat Blacks and Whites equally has increased, from 34 percent five years ago to 46 percent. The group expressing the most negative views toward police was under-50, Black Democrats.[41] In Exhibit 2.2.4 below, one can see that the belief that police treat Blacks and Whites equally has decreased over the years.

In Exhibit 2.2.5, we use the Pew Research Center data to show that about 70 percent of Blacks said police forces across the country did a poor job of holding officers accountable when misconduct occurred, compared with 27 percent of Whites. About six in ten Blacks (57 percent) rated police performance as poor when it came to using the right amount of force for each situation, compared with 23 percent of Whites.[42] The *NYT*/CBS poll that was taken in July 2016 showed even worse percentages so we can assume that the next Pew Research Center poll will also show increased distrust of police by Blacks.

Hispanics also have a more negative view of police than do Whites. A nationwide poll of 1,000 Hispanics, underwritten by the W.W. Kellogg Foundation and reported in the popular press, found that two in three Hispanics fear police use of excessive force, even though 84 percent agreed that police were there to protect them. About 18 percent reported that they had friends or family members who had suffered police brutality.[43]

Academic research supports these findings. In a 33-city sample, it was found that race and age were strong correlates of distrust of police, with the level of distrust of Blacks two to five times higher than Whites across cities. What was interesting about this study was the variation across the cities. For instance, 32 percent of Blacks in New York City as opposed to 7 percent of Whites expressed distrust of police, but the differences were less pronounced in Birmingham, Alabama, with a much smaller percentage of both Whites and Blacks expressing distrust; 8.9 percent of Blacks compared to 2.08 percent of Whites expressed distrust.[44]

EXHIBIT 2.2.4 Race Differences in Perceptions of Police

Blacks Express Less Confidence than White in Local Police to Treat Blacks and Whites Equally

Confidence in local police to treat whites and blacks equally (%)

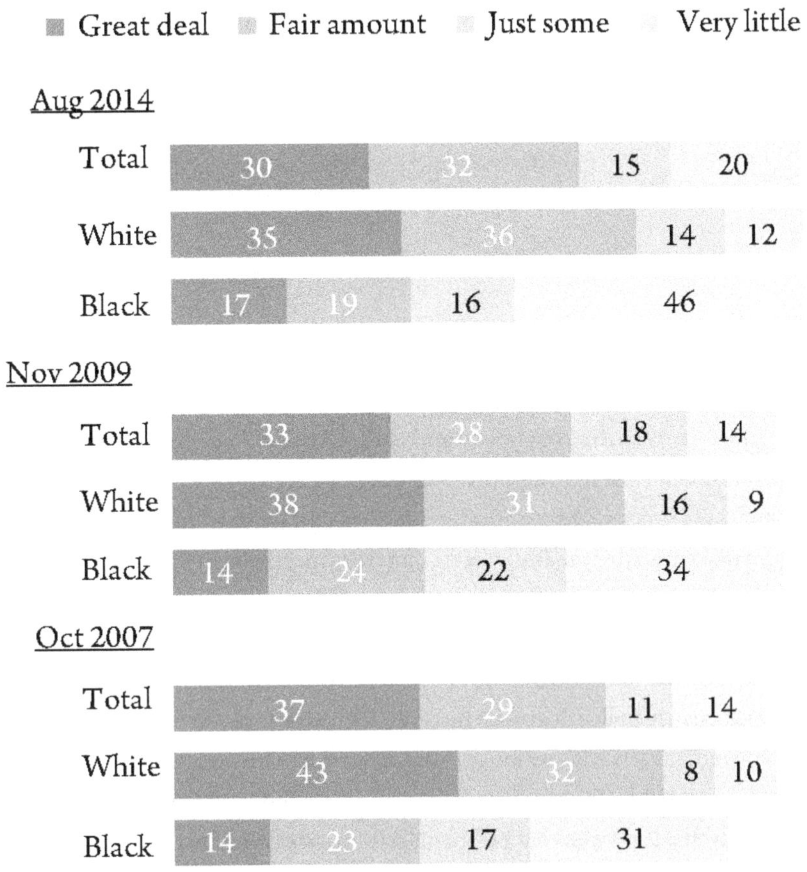

Survey conducted August 20–24, 2014. Whites and blacks include only those who are not Hispanic. "Don't know" responses not shown.

Source: Pew Research Center/USA Today

EXHIBIT 2.2.5 Public Perception of Police

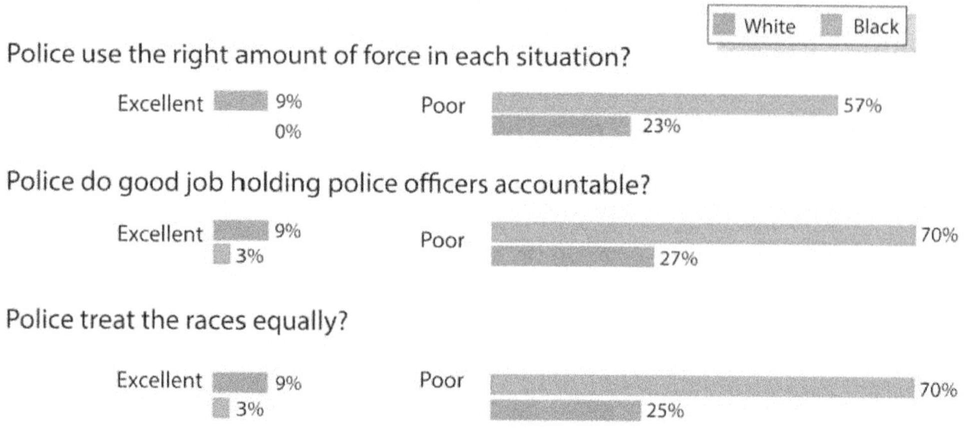

Source: Pew Research Centre/USA Today Survey, 2014

Although there is a wealth of evidence to support the idea that Blacks and, to a lesser extent, other minorities, are more likely to distrust police and believe that police officers discriminate,[45] that is not the same thing as evidence that supports a finding that police officers actually *do* discriminate based on race and/or ethnicity. Discriminatory actions can include decisions to: a) arrest, b) stop and/or search in a discriminatory manner, and c) act disrespectfully toward citizens. Unfortunately, these all pose difficult methodological problems because Blacks are more likely to live in high-crime neighborhoods where police "police" everyone who lives there more aggressively. There is no point in comparing police officer actions in a low-crime suburban neighborhood to a high-crime inner-city neighborhood because police deal with more dangerous people, they go to more calls, and they interact with more individuals with serious criminal records. The reality is that Blacks in this country are more likely than Whites to live in such neighborhoods which complicates what we observe regarding police actions. It may be that police discriminate on the basis of race or ethnicity, but it may also be that police discriminate based on the neighborhood they patrol in.

Decisions to arrest are notoriously difficult to study. Police officer discretion is such that some estimates are that officers don't arrest in about half of the cases where an arrest could be made legally. We do have some glimmer of differential arrest patterns when we look at drug use and drug arrest patterns. Overall, drug use among White and minority groups are about the same; however, Blacks are disproportionally arrested and incarcerated. Exhibit 2.2.6 below shows cocaine use figures. Whites and Blacks show only a slight difference in use patterns.

Other drugs show slightly different use patterns but the arrest figures show clearly that Blacks are arrested at rates disproportional to their use rates (about one-third of all drug arrests are of

EXHIBIT 2.2.6 Use of Cocaine by Race and Ethnicity, 2011

	Never Used Cocaine (%)	Have Used Cocaine (%)
White	82.9	17.1
Black/African American	90.1	9.9
Native American/Alaskan Native	78.7	21.3
Native Hawaiian/Other Pacific Islander	91.9	8.1
Asian	96.4	3.6
Hispanic	89.3	10.7
More than one race	84.3	15.7
Total	85.4	14.6

Source: http://www.icpsr.umich.edu/quicktables/quickoptions.do

Blacks despite comprising only 13 percent of the population). This disparity increases when one looks at prison commitment rates for drug offenses.[46] This disparity could be due to factors other than discrimination; it could be that Blacks are more likely to sell than Whites, more likely to sell in open-air markets, and/or more likely to operate in high-crime neighborhoods that fall under the scrutiny of police. However, it is hard to explain away the extent of the disparity.

Another study done in San Francisco covering the years 2010 to April 2015 showed that African Americans were cited for resisting arrest at a rate eight times higher than Whites. The study reported that of 9,633 arrests for resisting, not accompanied by a felony, Blacks (making up just 6 percent of the population) accounted for 45 percent of the arrests. Suspects can be convicted of resisting arrest, punishable by up to a year in jail and up to a $1,000 fine, even when the underlying offense is minor, such as not complying with an order to move one's car. Critics of police say the charge is used to cover up cases of police brutality.[47] Note that, without more research, we do not know if these numbers indicate resisting arrest is a charge used in a discriminatory manner, if Blacks are more likely than other groups to resist arrest, or some mixture of the two explanations.

Decisions to stop include both traffic stops and street stops or investigatory detentions based on reasonable suspicion. **Racial profiling** occurs when a police officer makes a stop based entirely on race or ethnicity. When a young Black man is seen, for instance, driving a newer-model, expensive car, police officers suspect that the vehicle is stolen and/or that the man is holding drugs. A "**pretext stop**" refers to the practice of police officers to use some minor traffic offense to stop the individual and in the course of the traffic stop look for other evidence of wrongdoing, specifically by a search, usually a consent search. The Supreme Court has upheld the legality of such stops in *Whren v. U.S.* (1996).[48]

Studies on racial profiling show that minorities may be stopped in numbers greater than their proportion of the population would indicate; however, the methodology of some racial profiling studies is problematic. Comparing stops to simply the percentage of population is not very accurate because it does not take into account the percentage of non-White drivers, the percentage of non-White drivers who engage in traffic offenses, or the percentage of minorities in the geographic area that is being targeted by heavier patrols (which would result in more stops regardless of the race/ethnicity of the driver). Most of the earlier studies used percentage-of-population figures, but other researchers are highly critical of this rough approximation of the base rate. Recently the Texas Department of Public Safety (DPS) was criticized for using percentage-of-population figures for the state to conclude that they did not engage in racial profiling because the percentage of stops that were of Black drivers was lower than their percentage of the population. Critics argued that statewide population figures are irrelevant: Blacks are more likely to be poor and not have a car, and statewide populations and counts of stops mask location-specific patterns. It was also argued that the focus should be on what happens after the stop and earlier studies of DPS statistics showed that Blacks were much more likely to be subjects of a search than Whites.[49]

There is also no clear proof that the stops are due to prejudicial views toward those stopped. Most critics blame the individual officer, but it is important to note organizational influences, especially because studies show that Black officers are just as likely as White officers to stop Blacks in disproportionate numbers.[50]

A Bureau of Justice statistics study utilizing an addendum to the National Crime Victimization Survey showed that more Black drivers than White or Hispanic (13 percent versus 10 percent) were pulled over for traffic stops, but, interestingly, no difference existed for "street stops" (individuals stopped while walking). Blacks were less likely to believe that police acted appropriately in the stops. This study also found that White drivers were searched and ticketed at a lower rate than Black drivers.[51]

Earlier studies indicated that Blacks were stopped about one and one-half times higher than their percentage of the population.[52] In a later study of what the researchers called "traffic stops" and "investigatory stops," a distinction was made between police stops that occur because the driver commits a clear violation and those where the officer is using the stop for investigatory purposes. The first stop is short and results in a ticket; the second kind of stop is longer and always includes a request for a consent search. There is little racial difference in those stopped for the traffic stop, but there is in the second type. In the study, 60 percent of all stops for Whites were for traffic safety, versus 35 percent for Blacks; however, 52 percent of all stops for Blacks (versus 34 percent for Whites) were for such minor reasons that the stop was coded as investigatory. In these types of searches, individuals are stopped for driving too slowly, broken lights, failure to signal, and other pretexts to initiate a search for drugs.[53] This second kind of stop is proactive policing for crime (mostly drug) control. It is a cost/benefit question as to whether the benefit gained is worth the cost in the antipathy it generates among those who are stopped.[54] Research seems to show that racially based stops may not be very effective anyway. The "hit rate" for finding drugs is lower for African Americans than it is for other racial groups. It is possible that when officers use race in decision making, they become less effective, not more effective, because they do not concentrate on what is important for investigation—behavior, not demographics.[55]

The Department of Justice issued new federal guidelines (mandatory for DOJ agents but only advisory for state law enforcement or other federal agencies) in December 2014. The rules added national origin, gender, gender identity, religion, and sexual orientation to characteristics for which profiling has been prohibited since 2003. Agents are prohibited from using these categories as the sole reason to investigate a target. They also eliminate the broad national security exceptions to profiling restrictions if for terrorism investigations. The new rules arguably were a compromise between the rights of targeted groups (e.g., Muslims) and national security.[56]

Disrespectful treatment by officers can be seen on YouTube videos which have examples of police officers who are rude and abusive to Black citizens. This is *not* a good representative sample of the millions of interactions that take place between police officers and citizens. Academic studies use observers to collect information on all interactions. Earlier studies indicated that residents (both Black and White) are initially disrespectful to police three times as often as police are initially disrespectful to residents (15 percent compared to 5 percent of encounters). Factors associated with being disrespectful include heightened emotion, number of bystanders, presence of intoxicants, being mentally impaired, and being in a disadvantaged neighborhood.[57]

A different methodology is to utilize surveys of citizens about their experiences. In surveys of citizens, Blacks are more than twice as likely to report disrespectful language or swearing by police officers. Minorities that live in metropolitan areas, have less education, less income, are younger, and report more bad experiences with the police, not surprisingly, perceive more police misconduct.[58] Areas of concentrated disadvantage show the least satisfaction with police, and race is still a predictor, even when controlling for neighborhood characteristics.[59] Some research has shown that race was a predictor in the use of verbal and physical coercion by officers.[60] Engel and colleagues, however, after an exhaustive review of prior studies, concluded that being a resident of a disadvantaged neighborhood was a stronger predictor of police "disrespect" to citizens than race.[61]

Thus, what may be happening is that minority citizens, probably partially because they live in high-crime poverty-stricken areas and partially because of implicit bias, are stopped more often for investigatory stops and are more likely to undergo consent searches.[62] Individuals hear of police abuse, see it via social media, or experience it themselves and those experiences may result in non-compliance and disrespect. For instance, minor traffic violation stops of young Black men to search the car for drugs while the driver and passengers are made to sit on the curb, sometimes for long periods of time, are relatively normal occurrences to police officers who probably feel they are just doing their job. However, these events, especially when they happen frequently, are embarrassing and frustrating to the car occupants and appear so to minority residents who see the stops as oppressive and abusive.[63] A pattern of this type of interaction between police officers and minority citizens builds resentment and distrust. Some minority citizens report that even if they were a victim of a crime, they would not call police. This breakdown of the social contract unfortunately may lead to more disorder as vigilantism takes the place of formal social control.

Because of prior bad experiences, minority citizens, especially men, may be non-compliant, disrespectful, and argumentative, which, in turn, triggers heavier-handed police action since police are trained and socialized that, for officer safety, control of the situation is paramount. Officers are taught that their first priority is to "secure the scene" and manage any potential threat. If individuals are arguing, not complying, and engaging in behavior that indicates opposition, then police officers will respond to that resistance as a threat to their safety. In small towns and suburban areas, police officers do not perceive the threat level as very high and so may be more patient and accommodating to non-compliant people; however, police officers in high-crime neighborhoods where violence is frequent and where there have been attacks on the police will respond much more aggressively to non-compliance. Unfortunately, this dynamic can set up a cycle whereby citizen disrespect/noncompliance leads to abuses of police power (or perceived abuses), which lead to even more distrust and hostility from the citizenry, which breeds even more distrust and antipathy between police departments and the citizenry they are sworn to protect.[64]

Hispanics also are more likely to perceive that police officers act in a discriminatory way. In 2012, Sheriff Arpaio in Maricopa County (Phoenix) lost a civil suit brought by the Department of Justice which alleged he and his deputies engaged in a pattern or practice of conduct that deprived persons of rights, privileges, or immunities secured or protected by the Constitution. In June of 2012, the Supreme Court upheld a section of an Arizona law that allowed police officers to check the immigration status of anyone they stopped for some other legal reason if they reasonably suspect the person is not a legal immigrant (*Arizona v. United States*, 2012).[65] Records showed that Hispanic drivers were four to nine times more likely to be stopped, and one-fifth of the traffic stops appeared to be unconstitutional (with no reason to stop) from a review of incident reports. Records indicated that police were dispatched when the report was only that there were "people of dark skin" or "people speaking Spanish" in an area. Findings also indicated that jail officers punished Hispanic inmates for not understanding English, refused to accept forms written in Spanish, and pressured inmates to sign forms waiving rights in English without a translation. Another finding was that there was a general culture of bias against Hispanics, including the use of excessive force against Latinos, a reduction of policing services to the Latino community, and a gender and/or national original bias by failing to adequately investigate sex crimes when the victim was Hispanic. In 2015, Arpaio admitted violating the court order that prohibited the roving patrols that targeted Hispanic-looking drivers, allowing them to continue eighteen months after the judge ordered them to cease.[66]

In cities such as Chicago and Baltimore, the relationship between the police force and the minority community seems to be broken. In other cities, police departments have also been scrutinized as engaging in racially discriminatory practices. It is a very difficult subject to study because of the high emotion on both sides: minority citizens feel they are not treated equally and police officers feel they are being unfairly criticized. Citizen complaints, arrest records, and observation studies help us understand the situation. As with many of the questions raised in this text, the best methodology would be observational studies (ride-alongs) with objective recorders, but although there are some of these studies available, they are very expensive. Body cameras may give us the best source of data for large numbers of interactions with the public and studies are underway that utilize this source.

What Is the Law and Policy Concerning Police Use of Force?

The use of force is usually perfectly legal—officers have the right to tackle a fleeing suspect, or use necessary force, including lethal force, when they are defending themselves or the suspect poses an immediate threat to the officer or others. Illegal or excessive force occurs when the officer goes beyond what is necessary to secure a lawful arrest, or has no lawful reason to use force at all. In *Graham v. Connor* (1989),[67] the Supreme Court held that officers have the right to use "reasonable" force in any interaction with the public, as determined by the facts and circumstances. They are not obligated to use the least possible force as long as the force used would be used by a reasonable officer in the same situation. It is very important to remember that force may be legal, even if the police officer's actions might have put him or her into the situation where force had to be used. "Lawful but awful" actions are those that meet the *Graham* standard of reasonableness, but perhaps violate policy because the officer did not follow proper procedures for handcuffing or performing a traffic stop, did not wait for back-up when necessary, or for some other reason helped set up the situation where force was then necessary.

Despite what we see on YouTube or the evening news, force is used very infrequently. Many police officers go through their whole career without ever drawing their weapon on the street. Some may never even experience serious physical altercations with people. In other locales, use of force incidents are more common—this is partly a function of the citizenry whose actions elicit a force response, and possibly a function of the culture of certain police departments which creates a greater likelihood that force will be utilized even when alternatives might be available. Excessive force appears to be more likely when victims challenge police authority—speeding past a patrol car, challenging police officer actions, or intervening in the arrest of another.[68]

In 1994, the Violent Crime Control and Law Enforcement Act was passed requiring the attorney general to acquire data about the use of excessive force by law enforcement officers and publish yearly reports. The annual reports required by Congress in the 1994 law were never produced. More recently, there have been calls to begin a national reporting system with some advocating that the receipt of any federal monies should come with the responsibility to collect and report use of force incidents. Estimates of the use of force come from other sources, such as the Police–Public Contact Survey and single-city studies.[69]

A number of different reports indicate that force is used very infrequently, only in 1 to 2 percent of all encounters with the public.[70] Use of force is more common in arrests, but even with arrest, only 20 percent involve some use of force, and even then it is usually just grabbing and holding.[71] However, use of force seems to vary depending on the city. Garner, Maxwell, and Heraux[72] found in their study that use of force ranged from 12.7 percent of encounters in one city to 22.9 percent of encounters in another city. In addition, a national survey of law enforcement agencies found that the rate of use-of-force events varied by region, with the highest in the South (90 incidents per 100,000), followed by the Northeast (72), the Midwest (68), and the West (50).[73] A recent study also found that use of force seems to be related to use-of-force policies. Those departments that had more stringent administrative force policies had fewer incidents where officers used force than departments where polices were less specific and/or more permissive.[74] It is also important to note that the figures above are describing use of force, not excessive force. Excessive force is estimated to occur in a miniscule portion of total encounters with the public—estimated at one-third of 1 percent.[75]

Characteristics of the target that seem to be correlated with use of force include: race, sex (male), disrespectful demeanor, emotionality, mental illness, intoxication, presence or perception of a weapon, the suspect's violent criminal record (knowledge of), suspect's use of force, gang membership, and socio-economic status.

Situational characteristics correlated with use of force include: the number of citizens present (positive association), the number of police officers present (positive association), and whether the encounter involved a car or foot pursuit.

Characteristics of the officers involved in use of force include sex (male), age (younger), and ethnicity (being Hispanic). Psychological traits of the officer have been identified as well, including lack of empathy, antisocial and paranoid tendencies, inability to learn from experience, a tendency not to take responsibility for actions, and cynicism. Officers who use force have also been found to have a stronger identification with the police subculture. Another factor in the tendency to use force was being involved in a traumatic event or prior injury (thus, use of force would be a type of post-traumatic stress behavior).[76]

It should be emphasized that these studies and the factors identified are associated with the use of force, not necessarily *excessive* force. Also, some studies have reported findings inconsistent with others. Because there is no national database, studies were obtained in various cities and using other datasets that have their own problems (e.g., victim reports, incident reports, and/or newspaper reports).

Even though use of force seems to be rare, and excessive force even rarer, that does not mean that it isn't a problem in some cities. Differences in use of force rates across cities suggest that some cities could do more to reduce use of force. Even one video of excessive force can poison the relationship between a police department and its citizenry.

Other research has shown that a small number of officers are responsible for a disproportionate percentage of the total uses of force. This may be because of their particular assignments, but it could also be because they are too quick to resort to uses of force. As mentioned previously, some studies do find an association between force and race or socio-economic status, but other factors, such as demeanor, seem to be even more influential.[77]

One problematic type of use of force is the use of conducted energy devices (CEDs), commonly known as tasers. Their use has dramatically expanded and proponents of the devices argue that they have resulted in less injury to officers and suspects alike, and officers who use them avoid having to use lethal force. Opponents, such as Amnesty International, argue that they have been responsible for an unacceptable number of deaths. Research indicates that the electricity that is conducted by the devices is not sufficient to seriously harm an individual, but there have been reports of serious injuries caused by falling and deaths occur because of pre-existing conditions. For instance, those who are under the influence of drugs may be more susceptible to injury. Also, if the taser is used multiple times on a person, there is a greater risk of injury.[78]

Some argue that news stories and YouTube videos show tasers being used inappropriately, e.g., when someone is verbally disruptive rather than physically dangerous. Arguments are that the taser should be an alternative to lethal force, not an alternative to physical control tactics. That is, the only time a taser should be used is when the alternative is to use a firearm. Generally, the courts have determined that a reasonableness standard applies to the taser as with any use of force. The officer is not obligated to use the least serious level of force, but he or she is obligated to use only that level of force (including the taser) that is reasonable given the nature of the threat. This means that the officer must feel threatened, and the taser is not appropriate for gaining compliance.

Focus on Data: Do Police Officers Abuse Their Power to Use Lethal Force?

In the summer of 2016, Alton Sterling and Philando Castile's deaths at the hands of officers reignited a wave of protest that too many Black men are killed by officers in circumstances that are not legally justified. There is a perception, especially in the Black community, that an unacceptably high number of Black citizens are killed by police officers, and that officers are not held accountable

EXHIBIT 2.2.7 Walter Scott was attempting to run away from police officer Michael Thomas Slager after a traffic stop in South Carolina when Slager shot and killed Scott. The encounter was caught on video, providing evidence for those who believe police abuse their authority.

Source: AP

when they engage in illegal uses of lethal force. The killing of Walter Scott (who is Black) by former officer Michael Slager (who is White) is the clearest example of the perception that law enforcement officers abuse their legal authority.

In that incident, a traffic stop resulted in Scott running from the officer who shot him in the back as he ran away. The former officer alleged that his shooting was legally justified because Scott had previously struggled with him and attempted to grab his gun. Slager was indicted for murder and faces trial in October 2016. The video of the incident that a bystander recorded is still available on YouTube and other websites. To some, the Walter Scott incident is an example of an endemic problem happening across the country; to others, it is an exceedingly rare event that has served to taint the entire profession unfairly. It is important to, first, ask relevant questions to be answered by data. When is lethal force legally justified? What are accurate statistics of the number of killings, but also the circumstances involved when officers shoot and kill? The second part of the question seems to be missing in many national conversations since it is not enough to simply report the percentage killed who are Black, but, also, what led to the shooting itself since no one argues that if someone is shooting at an officer or engages in conduct that is a clear threat, then the officer has a legal right to use lethal force.

In *Tennessee v. Garner* (1985),[79] the Supreme Court held that a Tennessee officer who shot and killed a teenage burglar who was scaling a fence to get away had engaged in an unconstitutional "seizure." In other words, fleeing felons could no longer be shot and potentially killed to prevent their escape. The Supreme Court held that officers did not have the right to use lethal force when there was no reason to believe that the suspect posed a serious threat. As mentioned previously, the Supreme Court has also said in *Graham v. Con-nor*, that the use of force must be reasonable, that is, reasonable police officers would have evaluated the situation and decided upon the same action. Thus, police officers have the legal right to use lethal force only if there is a reasonable belief that the target poses a serious threat to the police officer or someone else. If that belief turns out to be mistaken, for instance, if they perceive the suspect has a weapon which turns out to be a cellphone, then that mistake does not invalidate the reasonable belief and the shooting may be ruled justifiable. Further, police officers are not legally required to use lesser means of force—if someone is charging at a police officer and reasonable officers would perceive a serious threat, the police officer is not legally obligated to use a baton or taser first before his or her weapon. The legal analysis is extremely fact-specific because reasonableness is determined by many things; for instance, it is probable that it would not be ruled reasonable to perceive a seventeen-year-old girl charging at officers with only her fists as a serious threat thereby justifying shooting her; however, it might be perceived as a reasonable threat when an enraged 6' 4" 300-pound man charges an officer. Officers must treat every physical assault as weapon-involved because of the potential for their weapon to be taken from them in a fight. It is not reasonable to expect that the officer should allow himself or herself to be physically attacked if the assailant clearly means to do serious harm, and there is a possibility that the officer would be overpowered in the attack and have his or her gun taken by the assailant.

The Supplemental Homicide report of the FBI has a category of "justifiable homicides by law enforcement." These reports show that the number of justifiable homicides was in the 400s in the 1970s, dropped to the 300s in the 1980s, and rose again to averages in the 400s in the 1990s. However, it has been known for quite some time that the number reported is a woeful undercount of the true number of deaths. In 2000, the Deaths in Custody Reporting Act required law enforcement to report any deaths in custody to federal officials to be recorded. "In custody" would include shootings on the street when the individual was shot by law enforcement. The Bureau of Justice Statistics recently did an analysis of homicides from 2003 through 2009 and 2011 and found that of the total number of homicides that should have been recorded in official statistics, this reporting system captured approximately only 49 percent, while the Supplemental Homicide Reports captured only 46 percent. More than one-quarter (28 percent) were not recorded in either system.[80] So, the official number of deaths by police officers is probably less than half of the true number. Some studies now, for instance, put the true number for 2015 at around 1,000.[81] In one study comparing internal reports from the Los Angeles Police Department to FBI numbers, the 184 homicides by police provided to the FBI was 46 percent lower than the 340 uncovered in internal reports.[82] The *Washington Post*[83] and other sources are now tracking police shootings using data sources other than official reports to get more accurate counts and their numbers indicate that there were 980 killings by police officers in 2015 while the official number was 461 in 2013 (the last year available).[84] For this reason, it is probably impossible to state with any certainty whether there is a trend upward or downward in police shootings because we don't have accurate counts for previous years.

The reasons why such undercounting exists remain somewhat obscure. In one investigation of Virginia's justifiable homicide numbers, several killings went unreported because the incidents were not counted as justifiable during the investigation, and then no one went back to record the killing as a justifiable homicide after the investigation was complete. In some cases, departments simply refuse to provide the numbers because they are not legally obligated to do so. In other cases, because there is more than one jurisdiction investigating the killing, confusion results in no agency reporting it.[85]

The second part of the question was what circumstances prompted the officers' actions. Examining either the official reports or the larger set of killings collected from the *Washington Post*, it is clear that the majority of killings are of individuals who have weapons. In some earlier studies, it has been found that at least 80 percent of individuals killed had weapons.[86] In the *Washington Post* final analysis of killings in 2015, only 9 percent of the targets were unarmed. These individuals might have been trying to obtain a weapon or they may be the "mistaken weapon" type of case where an officer sees something in the target's hands, e.g., a cellphone, and misperceives it as a weapon. In three-quarters of the cases, police were actively being attacked or they were defending someone who was under attack. In one-quarter of cases, the target was fleeing. Even though the *Tennessee v. Garner* ruling established the fact that officers cannot legally shoot a fleeing suspect if there is no reason to think he or she poses a threat, if the suspect is armed and/or if there is reason to believe that he or she poses a serious danger to others (e.g., armed, fleeing bank robbers) then lethal force would be legally justified.[87]

About one-quarter of the targets of police shootings in the *Washington Post* analysis were mentally ill. This statistic has spurred efforts to provide **CIT** training to officers in the hope that de-escalation can prevent the need for lethal force. These cases are tragic in that often the police officer has been called by family members because of the erratic and/or threatening behavior of the mentally ill person. The officer arrives at the scene to help and ends up shooting the individual because of a perceived threat, e.g. the person will not relinquish a weapon or charges the officer. Then the officer is criticized for the lethal consequences.[88]

Reports also indicate that Blacks are disproportionately represented in the numbers of individuals shot and killed by police. Black men are only 6 percent of the general population, but in the *Washington Post* analysis, they comprised 40 percent of the unarmed group of those killed by police in 2015.[89] On the other hand, it is a highly misleading statistic to look at percentage of population figures because such shootings are not randomly distributed throughout the population; they are most likely in high-crime neighborhoods and when police feel threatened by the circumstances.

Implicit bias studies determine whether racial biases or stereotypes affect shooting decisions. Contrary to what many expect, researchers find that police officers were *less likely* than civilians to shoot at Black suspects in staged scenarios in laboratory settings, perhaps because they can practice what is called "cognitive control." Studies also show, however that their ability to exercise cognitive control is impeded by high cognitive load, fatigue, fear and high arousal.[90]

A very recent study utilized four different data sets to analyze police officer encounters: 1) the NYPD's records of 5 million stop-and-frisk events; 2) the Police–Public Contact Survey, a nationally representative sample of civilians; 3) event summaries from all incidents in which an officer discharges his weapon at civilians including both hits and misses from three large cities in Texas (Austin, Dallas, Houston), six large Florida counties, and Los Angeles County; and 4) a random sample of police–civilian interactions from the Houston Police Department from arrest codes in which lethal force is more likely to be justified. The study found that the race of the suspect did not influence the likelihood of fatal shootings by police. However, Blacks and Hispanics were 50 percent more likely than Whites to be the targets of all other uses of force. Police were 17 percent more likely to use their hands in encounters with Black residents; 18 percent more likely to push them into a wall, 24 percent more likely to point their weapon, and 25 percent more likely to use pepper spray or a baton against a Black citizen. Researchers said even after controlling for demographics such as age and gender, encounter characteristics such as whether individuals supplied identification or whether the interaction occurred in a high- or low-crime area, the differential treatment of Blacks was still signifi-cant.[91] The study has been criticized because much of the primary data used comes from police officer reports, with the assumption that the accuracy of the reports would favor the report writer. Since the data also provided an observed differential use of force in less than lethal situations, the supposition the reports are biased is less persuasive.

Some news reports point to the low number of indictments of police officers (only 54 officers charged between 2005 and 2015) as evidence of a system failing to hold officers accountable. This presentation is misleading, however, without noting that, as indicated above, the majority of shooting incidents show clear legal justification for the shooting. We do not know if this number represents a disproportionally low percentage of the "bad shooting" cases where there were questions about the legal justification for the decision to shoot. It also appears that indictments may be increasing with reports indicating that indictments in 2015 were three times the average of preceding years.[92] Each situation is legally evaluated through the "reasonable officer" standard, but it is what is reasonable at the time with that officer's perception of a serious threat. If that perception is reasonable, even if wrong, there is no abuse of force.

What Were the Recommendations of the 21st Century President's Task Force on Policing?

After civil unrest in Ferguson, Missouri, and Baltimore, Maryland, in the summer and fall of 2014, President Obama created the 21st Century President's Task Force on Policing to examine the issues of policing in this country, and, more specifically, the relationship between policing and minority communities. The Task Force was made up of police leaders, academics, and individuals who were affiliated with community groups that had a stake in the issue of police–community relations. They held a series of public commentary meetings where experts, community members, and criminal justice professionals testified and submitted reports about a variety of issues. Their comprehensive report was presented as Six Pillars.

Pillar 1: Building Trust and Legitimacy. The Task Force noted the research on procedural justice—a concept referring to the perception that the processes involved in an individual's interaction with the justice system are fair.[93] Perceptions of procedural justice are said to involve voice (allowing the citizen the chance to speak); neutrality (fairness in decisions); respect (using respectful language and not demeaning the citizen); and trustworthiness (the idea that the actions of the officer are for the public good).[94] Research indicates that those who perceive elements of procedural justice in their interactions with police officers are more likely to comply with orders.[95] The Task Force recommended officers be trained in procedural justice and encouraged programs to build legitimacy in the community.

Pillar 2: Policy and Oversight. The Task Force recommended that all departments work closely with the International Association of Directors of Law Enforcement Standards and Training (IADLEST), including cooperating with the National Decertification Index to remove officers who have been decertified in one state from being hired in another.

Pillar 3: Technology and Social Media. The Task Force recommended that all departments create policies concerning the use of social media and institute research and evaluations of technology.

Pillar 4: Community Policing and Crime Reduction. Community policing concepts were reinforced and recommended by the Task Force.

Pillar 5: Training and Education. The Task Force recommended training in all areas, but emphasized the need for Crisis Intervention Training (CIT) and implicit bias training.

Pillar 6: Officer Wellness and Safety. There was a strong message that the Task Force supported police officers and programs and policies to help them maintain their physical and emotional health, including evaluating shift work and overtime.

The federal COPS office has been encouraging and documenting steps taken across the country that respond to the recommendations of the Task Force's report.

> To read the entire report, go to www.cops.usdoj.gov/pdf/taskforce/taskforce_fi nalreport.pdf; to read about some of the programs that have been implemented, go to http://www.cops.usdoj.gov/policingtaskforce

Summary

How Are Police Officers Selected and Trained?

Police departments use screening tools including civil service tests, physical tests, and psychological tests. Then candidates are subjected to hundreds of hours of training in academies followed by the Field Training Officer (FTO) phase where an experienced officer accompanies the new recruit, and a probationary period. All officers receive annual in-service training.

What Is the Difference Between Proactive and Reactive Policing?

Reactive policing is responding to calls for service and investigating crimes that have already occurred. Proactive policing involves undercover investigations, hot-spot policing, "stings," and other practices where police try to prevent crime rather than respond to calls for service.

How Has Technology Affected Policing?

Computers, cellphones, computers in patrol cars, and other technology have dramatically changed policing. It has made it easier to track criminals, but some technology has had user interface problems, e.g., data software. Cybercrimes units are becoming more common in police departments, no doubt due to the increase in computer-related crimes.

Is Police Officer Stress a Problem and, If So, What Is the Role of Organizational Justice?

A long history of research on police stress shows that stress is a problem, and much of it comes from within the organization. Organizational justice is a concept that indicates officers who believe their organization is fair experience less stress and burnout.

What Is the Police Subculture?

The police subculture is said to be the informal culture in policing that encourages the "blue curtain of secrecy" whereby police officers cover up wrongdoing of fellow police officers, and "noble cause corruption," which includes testilying and other forms of misbehavior that have the goal of gaining a criminal conviction but may violate the law.

What Are Some Types of Police Misconduct?

Acts of corruption can be categorized into acts of economic corruption and abuses of power. Explanations for why some police officers engage in these practices can be categorized into individual explanations, organizational explanations, and societal explanations.

Do Police Officers Discriminate Against Minorities?

Although methodological issues complicate the answer to this question, research seems to support the premise that Black males are more likely to be stopped, searched, and perhaps arrested, at least for drug crimes, than Whites. It is important to realize, however, that much of the different treatment that minorities experience may be due to living in high-crime areas where police "police" more aggressively. There is recent research to indicate that all uses of force (except for lethal force) are more likely to be used in encounters with Blacks and Hispanics.

What Is the Law and Policy Concerning Police Use of Force?

Force, including lethal force, can be used by police officers if it is reasonable. That is, when a reasonable police officer in those circumstances would believe force was an appropriate response. Force is used rarely by officers, despite the media attention to a few instances of abuse.

What Were the Recommendations of the 21st Century Presidents' Task Force on Policing?

There were a multitude of specific recommendations that fell under six "pillars": Building Trust and Legitimacy; Policy and Oversight; Technology and Social Media; Community Policing and Crime Reduction; Training and Education; and, Officer Wellness and Safety.

Critical Thinking Exercises

1. Research and write an update to the Focus on Data section. Is there more recent data on how many people have been killed by law enforcement officers? Has there been recent research on the type of circumstances that exist in such shootings and whether there is evidence that minorities are more likely to be unjustly killed by police officers?
2. Many law enforcement officers reject the 21st Century Panel on Policing and the recommendations that came from it because of a belief that President Obama does not support law enforcement. Research this position and determine whether or not it exists. What are the points of the argument? What exactly about the Panel's recommendations are opposed and why? What evidence exists on either side?

Notes

1. Houston Police Department. Retrieved 6/1/2007 from www.houstontx.gov/police/img/hr_chart.jpg.

2. B. Sanders, "Using personality traits to predict police officer performance." *Policing: An International Journal of Police Strategies and Management* 31 (1) (2008): 129–147.
3. Ibid.; N. Claussen-Rogers and B. Arrigo, *Police Corruption and Psychological Testing*. Durham, NC: Carolina Academic Press, 2005; G. Cordner and K. Scarborough, *Police Administration*, 7th edn. Burlington, MA: Anderson, 2010, p. 159.
4. G. Anderson, D. Plecas and T. Seeger, "Police officer physical ability testing: Re-validating a selection criterion." *Policing* 24 (1) (2001): 8–32.
5. C. Johnson and G. Copus, "Law enforcement ethics: A theoretical analysis." In F. Schmalleger and R. Gustafson (Eds.), *The Social Basis of Criminal Justice: Ethical Issues for the 80s*. Washington, DC: University Press of America, 1981, pp. 39–83.
6. M. McCampbell, *Field Training for Police: State of the Art*. Washington, DC: National Institute of Justice, 1986.
7. Retrieved 4/16/2016 from http://www.mass.gov/eopss/law-enforce-and-cj/law-enforce/mptc/training-and-academies/annual-professional-development/
8. G. Kelling, T. Pate, D. Dieckman and C. Brown, *The Kansas City Preventive Patrol Experiment: A Summary Report*. Washington, DC: Police Foundation, 1974.
9. L. Sherman and D. Weisburd, "General deterrent effects of police patrol in crime 'hot spots': A randomized, controlled trial." *Justice Quarterly* 12 (4) (1995): 625–648. See also D. Weisburd and L. Green, "Policing drug hot spots: The Jersey City drug market analysis experiment." *Justice Quarterly* 12 (4) (1995): 711–735.
10. J. Pollock, *Ethical Dilemmas and Decisions in Criminal Justice*. Boston, MA: Cengage, 2017; F. Schoeman, "Privacy and police undercover work." In W. Heffernan and T. Stroup (Eds.), *Police Ethics: Hard Choices in Law Enforcement*. New York, NY: John Jay Press, 1985, pp. 133–153; G. Marx, "Police undercover work: Ethical deception or deceptive ethics?" In W. Heffernan and T. Stroup (Eds.), *Police Ethics: Hard Choices in Law Enforcement*. New York, NY: John Jay Press, pp. 83–117; T. Mieczkowksi, "Drug abuse, corruption and officer drug testing." In K. Lersch (Ed.), *Policing and Misconduct*. Upper Saddle River, NJ: Prentice-Hall, 1985, pp. 157–192; M. Baker, *Cops*. New York: Pocket Books, 1985, pp. 139–140.
11. J. Eterno, A. Verma and E. Silverman, "Police manipulations of crime reporting: Insiders' revelations." *Justice Quarterly* (2014). doi. org/10.1080/07418825.2014.980838; M. White, *Current Issues and Controversies in Policing*. Boston: Allyn and Bacon, 2007.
12. D. Willits and J. Nowacki, "The use of specialized cybercrime policing units: An organizational analysis." *Criminal Justice Studies*, 2016: http://dx.doi.org/10.1080/1478601X.2016.1170282
13. C. Koper, C. Lum, J. Willis, D. Woods and J. Hibdon, *Realizing the Potential of Technology in Policing*. Washington, DC: PERF, December 2015.
14. J. Pollock, Jan–July, 2016, unpublished, on-going research.

15. M. Lanier and A. Cooper, "From papyrus to cyber: How technology has directed law enforcement policy and practice." *Criminal Justice Studies*. Doi: http://dx.doi.org/10.1080/1478601X.2016.1170280.
16. R. Wilson, "Police accountability measures flood state legislatures after Ferguson, Staten Island." *Washington Post*, February 4, 2015, http://www.washingtonpost.com/blogs/govbeat/wp/2015/02/04/police-accountability-measures-flood-state-legislaturesafter-ferguson-staten-island/; T. Perry, "San Diego police body camera report: Fewer complaints, less use of force." *Los Angeles Times*, March 18, 2015, http://touch.latimes.com/#section/-1/article/p2p-83088560/; T. Farrar, *Self Awareness to Being Watched and Socially Desirable Behavior: A Field Experiment on the Effect of Body Worn Cameras on Police Use of Force*. Police Foundation, 2015. Available via website: http://www.policefoundation.org/content/body-worn-camera
17. J. Storch and R. Panzarella, "Police stress: State-trait anxiety in relation to occupational and personal stressors." *Journal of Criminal Justice* 24 (2) (1996): 99–103.
18. R. McCraty and M. Atkinson, *Resilience Training Program Reduces Physiological and Psychological Stress in Police Officers. Global Advances in Health and Medicine*, 2012. Available at: http://www.heartmath.com/wp-content/uploads/2014/04/police_study_GAHM.pdf; also reported on the Blue Courage website, accessed 4/28/2016 at http://bluecourage.com/
19. J. Shane, "Organizational stressors and police performance." *Journal of Criminal Justice* 38 (4) (2010): 807–818.
20. T.R. Tyler, "Procedural justice, legitimacy, and the effective rule of law." In M. Tonry (Ed.), *Crime and Justice: A Review of Research*, Vol. 30. Chicago, IL: University of Chicago Press, 2003.
21. P. Reynolds, *The Impact of Fairness, Organizational Trust, and Perceived Organizational Support on Police Officer Performance.* Doctoral dissertation, Texas State University, May 2015.
22. R. Haar and M. Morash, "Gender, race, and strategies of coping with occupational stress in policing." *Justice Quarterly* 16 (2) (1999): 303–336.
23. S. Scheingold, *The Politics of Law and Order.* New York, NY: Longman, 1984.
24. J. Van Maanen, "The asshole." In P. Manning and J. Van Maanen (Eds.), *Policing: A View from the Street*. Santa Monica, CA: Goodyear, 1978, pp. 221–240; S. Herbert, "Morality in law enforcement: Chasing 'bad guys' with the Los Angeles Police Department." *Law Society Review* 30 (4) (1996): 799–818; L. Sherman, "Learning police ethics." *Criminal Justice Ethics* 1 (1) (1982): 10–19.
25. S. Scheingold, *The Politics of Law and Order.* New York, NY: Longman, 1984, pp. 100–104.
26. T. Barker, "Ethical police behavior." In K. Lersch (Ed.), *Policing and Misconduct*. Upper Saddle River, NJ: Prentice Hall, 2002, pp. 1–25
27. D. Weiburd and R. Greenspan, *Police Attitudes toward Abuse of Authority: Findings from a National Study.* Washington, DC: National Institute of Justice, U.S. Department of Justice, 2000.

28. E. Paoline, S. Myers and R. Worden, "Police culture, individualism, and community policing: Evidence from two police departments." *Justice Quarterly* 17 (3) (2000): 575–605; also see J. Pollock, *Ethical Decisions and Dilemmas in Criminal Justice*. Boston, MA: Cengage, 2017.
29. J. Pollock, *Ethical Decisions and Dilemmas in Criminal Justice*. Boston, MA: Cengage, 2017.
30. T. Barker and D. Carter, *Police Deviance*, 3rd edn. Cincinnati, OH: Anderson Publishing, 1994.
31. P. Kraska and V. Kappeler, "To serve and pursue: Exploring police sexual violence against women." *Justice Quarterly* 12 (1) (1995): 93–142; D. McGurrin and V. Kappeler, "Media accounts of police sexual violence." In K. Lersch, *Policing and Misconduct*. Upper Saddle River, NJ: Prentice-Hall, 2002, pp. 121–142, 133.
32. J. Crank and M. Caldero, *Police Ethics: The Corruption of Noble Cause*. Cincinnati, OH: Anderson Publishing, 2000/2005.
33. J. Pollock, *Ethical Decisions and Dilemmas in Criminal Justice*. Boston, MA: Cengage, 2017.
34. J. Dorschner, "The dark side of the force." In G. Alpert (Ed.), *Critical Issues in Policing*, 2nd edn. Prospect Heights, IL: Waveland, 1989, pp. 254–274; P. Murphy and D. Caplan, "Conditions that breed corruption." In R. Dunham and G. Alpert (Eds.), *Critical Issues in Policing*. Prospect Heights, IL: Waveland Press, 1989, pp. 304–324.
35. T. Prenzler and C. Ronken, "Models of police oversight: A critique." *Policing and Society* 11 (2001): 151–180.
36. S. Walker and G. Alpert, "Early warning systems as risk management for police." In K. Lersch (Ed.), *Policing and Misconduct*. Upper Saddle River, NJ: Prentice Hall, 2002, p. 224.
37. J. Pollock, *Ethical Decisions and Dilemmas in Criminal Justice*. Boston, MA: Cengage, 2017.
38. J. Pollock, *Ethical Decisions and Dilemmas in Criminal Justice*. Boston, MA: Cengage, 2017.
39. C. Staats, K. Capatosto, R. A. Wright and D. Contractor, *State of the Science: Implicit Bias Review, 2015*. Kirwin Institute for the Study of Race and Ethnicity, 2015.
40. Accessed 4/17/2016: http://www.chicagotribune.com/news/local/breaking/ct-chicago-police-accountability-report-20160412-story.html
41. Pew Research Center/*USA Today*, "Few say police forces nationally do well in treating races equally." Author, 2014, http://www.people-press.org/2014/08/25/few-say-police-forces-nationally-do-well-in-treating-races-equally/
42. Pew Research Center/*USA Today*, "Few say police forces nationally do well in treating races equally." Author, 2014, http://www.people-press.org/2014/08/25/few-say-police-forces-nationally-do-well-in-treating-races-equally/
43. R. Planas, "Poll reveals widespread fear of police among Latinos." *Huffington Post*, November 12, 2014.
44. E. Sharp and P. Johnson, "Accounting for variations in distrust of local police." *Justice Quarterly* 26 (2009): 157–182.
45. J. De Angelis and B. Wolf, "Perceived accountability and public attitudes toward local police." *Criminal Justice Studies* (2016). http://dx.doi.org/10.1080/1478601X.2016.1158177

46. Human Rights Watch. *Decades of Disparity*, 2009. Accessed at https://www.hrw.org/sites/default/files/reports/us0309web_1.pdf; *Washington Post* infographic, accessed at https://www.washingtonpost.com/news/wonk/wp/2013/06/04/the-blackwhite-marijuana-arrest-gap-in-nine-charts; Drug Policy Alliance, 2016, fact sheet, accessed at http://www.drugpolicy.org/race-and-drug-war
47. E. Green, "African Americans cited for resisting arrest at high rate in S.F." S.F.Gate.com, April 29, 2015. http://www.sfgate.com/bayarea/article/African-Americans-cited-for-resisting-arrest-at-6229946.php
48. *Whren v. U.S.*, 517 U.S. 806, 1996.
49. E. Dexheimer and J. Schwartz, "DPS statistics showing no racial bias in stops are wrong, expert says." *Austin American Statesman*, November 22, 2015, http://www.mystatesman.com/news/news/dps-statistics-showing-no-racial-bias-in-stops-are/npSts/?mc_cid=96fc64421b&mc_eid=890ae5e127
50. M. Smith and G. Alpert, "Searching for direction: Courts, social science, and the adjudication of racial profiling claims." *Justice Quarterly* 19 (2002): 673–703; R. Engel, J. Calnon and T. Bernard. "Theory and racial profiling: Shortcomings and future directions in research." *Justice Quarterly* 19 (2002): 249–273.
51. L. Langton and M. Durose, *Police Behavior During Traffic and Street Stops, 2011.* Washington, DC: Bureau of Justice Statistics, Department of Justice, 2013.
52. S. Mastrofski, M. Reisig and D. McCluskey, "Police disrespect toward the public: An encounter based analysis." *Criminology* 40 (3) (2002): 519–551.
53. C. Epp, S. Maynard-Moody and D. Haider-Markel, *Pulled Over: How Police Stops Define Race and Citizenship*. Chicago, IL: University of Chicago Press, 2014.
54. R. Weitzer and S. Tuch, "Perceptions of racial profiling: Race, class, and personal experience." *Criminology* 40 (2) (2002): 436, 443.
55. D. Cole and J. Lamberth, "The fallacy of racial profiling." *New York Times*, May 13, 2001: A19; D. Harris, *Good Cops: The Case for Preventive Policing*. New York: The New Press, 2005.
56. M. Doyle, "U.S. adds new rules to restrict profiling." *Austin American-Statesman*, December 9, 2014, A10; M. Apuzzo, "Profiling rules said to give F.B.I. tactical leeway." *New York Times*, April 10, 2014, A1.
57. S. Mastrofski, M. Reisig and D. McCluskey, "Police disrespect toward the public: An encounter based analysis." *Criminology* 40 (3) (2002): 534; M. Reisig, J. McCluskey, S. Mastrofski and W. Terrill. "Suspect disrespect toward the police." *Justice Quarterly* 21 (2004): 241–268; W. Terrill and S. Mastrofski, "Situational and officer-based determinants of police coercion." *Justice Quarterly* 19 (2002): 216–248.
58. R. Weitzer, "Citizens' perceptions of police misconduct: Race and neighborhood context." *Justice Quarterly* 16 (4) (1999): 819–846; R. Weitzer, "Racialized policing: Residents' perceptions

in three neighborhoods." *Law Society Review* 34 (1) (2000): 129–157; R. Weitzer and S. Tuch, "Reforming the police: Racial differences in public support for change." *Criminology* 40 (2) (2000): 435–456.

59. M. Reisig and R. Parks, "Experience, quality of life, and neighborhood context: A hierarchical analysis of satisfaction with police." *Justice Quarterly* 17(3) (2000): 607–630.
60. W. Terrill, *Police Coercion: Application of the Force Continuum*. New York, NY: LFB Scholarly Publishing, 2001; W. Terrill, E. Paoline and P. Manning, "Police culture and coercion." *Criminology* 41 (2003): 1003–1034.
61. R. Engel, R. Tillyer, C., Klahm and J. Frank, "From the officer's perspective: A multilevel examination of citizens' demeanor during traffic stops." *Justice Quarterly* 29 (2011): 574–643.
62. S. Mastrofski, M. Reisig and J. McCluskey, "Police disrespect toward the public: An encounter-based analysis." *Criminology* 40 (2002): 519–551.
63. S. Whitehead, "The specter of racism: Exploring white racial anxieties in the context of policing." *Contemporary Justice Review*, 2015, DOI: 10.1080/10282580.2015.1025622
64. J. Bouie, "Black and blue: Why more diverse police departments won't put an end to police misconduct." *Slate Magazine*, October 13, 2014, http://www.slate.com/articles/news_and_politics/politics/2014/10/diversity_won_t_solve_police_misconduct_black_cops_don_t_reduce_violence.html; J. Bouie, "Broken taillight policing." *Slate Magazine*, April 8, 2015, http://www.slate.com/articles/news_and_politics/politics/2015/04/north_charleston_shooting_how_investigatory_traffic_stops_unfairly_affect.single.html
65. *Arizona v. United States*, 567 U.S., 2012
66. S. Parvini, "Sheriff Arpaio admits violating court order in profiling suit." *Los Angeles Times*, March 18, 2015. http://touch.latimes.com/#section/-1/article/p2p-83093795/
67. *Graham v. Connor*, 490 U.S. 386, 1989.
68. V. Kappeler, R. Sluder and G. Alpert, *Forces of Deviance: Understanding the Dark Side of Policing*. Prospect Heights, IL: Waveland Press, 1994, p. 159.
69. M. Doyle, "Data on police shootings is hard to find." Washington Bureau, August 20, 2014. http://www.mcclatchydc.com/2014/08/20/237137_data-on-police-shootings-is-hard.html?sp=/99/200/365/&rh=1#storylink=cpy; M. Hickman, A. Piquero and J. Garner. "Toward a national estimate of police use of nonlethal force." *Criminology & Public Policy* 7 (2008): 563–604.
70. R. Worden and S. Catlin, "The use and abuse of force by police." In K. Lersch (Ed.), *Policing and Misconduct*, Upper Saddle River, NJ: Prentice Hall, 2002, 85–120; M.Ducrose, P. Langan and E. Smith, *Contacts Between Police and the Public, 2005*. Bureau of Justice Statistics Report, April 29, 2007.
71. J. Gundy, "The complexities of use of force." *Law and Order* 51 (2003): 60–62.

72. J. Garner, C. Maxwell and C. Heraux. "Characteristics associated with the prevalence and severity of force used by the police." *Justice Quarterly* 19 (2002): 705–745.

73. W. Terrill, "Police use of force: A transactional approach." *Justice Quarterly* 22 (2005): 107–139.

74. W. Terrill and E. Paoline, "The use of less lethal force: Administrative policy matters." *Justice Quarterly*, 2016. Advance pub. http://dx.doi.org/10.1080/07418825.2016.1147593.

75. A. Micucci and I. Gomme, "American police and subcultural support for the use of excessive force." *Journal of Criminal Justice* 33 (2005): 487–500.

76. J. Garner, C. Maxwell and C. Heraux, "Characteristics associated with the prevalence and severity of force used by the police." *Justice Quarterly* 19 (2002): 705–745; G. Alpert and J. MacDonald. "Police use of force: An analysis of organizational characteristics." *Justice Quarterly* 18 (2001): 393–409; G. Alpert and R. Dunham, *Understanding Police Use of Force*. New York: Cambridge University Press, 2004; W. Terrill and S. Mastrofski, "Situational and officer-based determinants of police coercion." *Justice Quarterly* 19 (2002): 216–248; R. Worden and S. Catlin, "The use and abuse of force by police." In K. Lersch (Ed.), *Policing and Misconduct*. Upper Saddle River, NJ: Prentice Hall, 2002, pp. 85–120; W. Terrill, E. Paoline and P. Manning, "Police culture and coercion." *Criminology* 41 (2003): 1003–1034.

77. M. Ducrose, P. Langan and E. Smith, *Contacts between Police and the Public, 2005*. Bureau of Justice Statistics Report, April 29, 2007; J. Garner, C. Maxwell and C. Heraux, "Characteristics associated with the prevalence and severity of force used by the police." *Justice Quarterly* 19(4) (2007): 705–745; J. Pollock, *Ethical Dilemmas and Decisions in Criminal Justice*. Boston, MA: Cengage, 2017.

78. S. Chermak, "Conducted energy devices and criminal justice policy." *Criminology and Public Policy* 8 (4) (2009): 861–864; M. White and J. Ready, "Examining fatal and nonfatal incidents involving the TASER." *Criminology and Public Policy* 8 (4) (2009): 865–891; H. Williams, *Are the Recommendations of the Braidwood Commission on Conducted Energy Weapons Use Sound Public Policy?* Paper presented at the Academy of Criminal Justice Sciences Meeting, February 2010, San Diego, CA.

79. *Tennessee v. Garner*, 471 U.S. 1105, 1985.

80. D. Banks and M. Planty, *Assessment of Coverage in the Arrest-Related Deaths Program*. Washington, DC: Bureau of Justice Statistics, October 2015.

81. M. Hickman, A. Piquero and J. Garner, "Toward a national estimate of police use of non-lethal force." *Criminology and Public Policy* 7 (2008): 563–604; D. Klinger, "On the problems and promise of research on lethal police violence: A research note." *Homicide Studies* 16 (2012): 78–96; S. Somashekhar and S. Rich, "Final tally: Police shot and killed 986 people in 2015 with over 900 fatal U.S. police shootings in 2015, a call for retraining." *Washington Post*, January 6, 2016; M. Apuzzo and S. Cohen, "Data on use of force by police across U.S. may prove almost useless." *New York Times*, August 12, 2015, A9; M. Wines and S. Cohen, "Police killings rise slightly." *New York Times*, May 1, 2015, A1.

82. D. Klinger, "On the problems and promise of research on lethal police violence: A research note." *Homicide Studies* 16 (2012): 78–96.

83. S. Somashekhar and S. Rich, "Final tally: Police shot and killed 986 people in 2015 with over 900 fatal U.S. police shootings in 2015, a call for retraining." *Washington Post,* January 6, 2016.

84. FBI website, accessed 7/12/2016: https://www.fbi.gov/about-us/cjis/ucr/crime-in-the-u.s/2013/crime-in-the-u.s.-2013/offenses-known-to-law-enforcement/expanded-homicide

85. M. Bowes, "Untold number of police killings in Va. go unreported or uncounted." *Richmond Times-Dispatch*, February 7, 2015, http://www.richmond.com/news/article_c656c2ba-b51a-5b91-b1c7–6b6cee89b336.html

86. K. Kindy, "Fatal police shootings in 2015 appraoching 400 nationwide." *Washington Post*, May 30, 2015, http://www.washingtonpost.com/national/fatal-police-shootings-in-2015-approaching-400-nationwide/2015/05/30/d322256a-058e-11e5-a428-c984eb077d4e_story.html

87. K. Kindy and K. Elliott, *Washington Post* graphic, accessed 4/28/2016 from https://www.washingtonpost.com/graphics/national/police-shootings-year-end/

88. K. Kindy and K. Elliott, *Washington Post* graphic, accessed 4/28/2016 from https://www.washingtonpost.com/graphics/national/police-shootings-year-end/; W. Lowery, "Prosecutors will seek murder charges against Georgia officer who shot an unarmed, naked black man." *Washington Post*, January 7, 2016. Also see D. Kesic, S. Thomas and J. Ogloff, "Use of nonfatal force on and by persons with apparent mental disorder in encounters with police." *Criminal Justice and Behavior* 40 (3) (2013): 321–337.

89. S. Somashekhar and M. Walsh, "The myth of the killer-cop 'epidemic'." *New York Post*, January 2, 2016. http://nypost.com/2016/01/02/myth-of-the-cop-killing-epidemic/

90. J. Correll, S. Hudson, S. Guillermo and D. Ma, "The police officer's dilemma: A decade of research on racial bias in the decision to shoot." *Social and Personality Psychology Compass* 8 (2014): 201–213.

91. R. Fryer, *An Empirical Analysis of Racial Differences in Police Use of Force*. Cambridge, MA: National Bureau of Economic Research, July 2016. Accessed at http://www.nber.org/papers/w22399; Q. Bui and A. Cox, "Surprising new evidence shows bias in police use of force but not in shootings." *New York Times*, July 11, 2016.

92. W. Lowery, "Prosecutors will seek murder charges against Georgia officer who shot an unarmed, naked black man." *Washington Post*, January 7, 2016; K. Kindy and K. Elliott, *Washington Post* graphic, accessed 4/28/2016 from https://www.washingtonpost.com/graphics/national/police-shootings-year-end/

93. T. Jonathan-Zamir, S. Mastrofsky and S. Moyal, "Measuring procedural justice in police-citizen encounters." *Justice Quarterly* 32 (2015): 845–871.

94. T. Tyler and Y. Huo, *Trust in the Law: Encouraging Public Cooperation in the Police and Courts*. New York City: Russell Sage Foundation, 2002; T. Tyler, "Procedural justice, legitimacy, and the effective rule of law." In M. Tonry (Ed.), *Crime and Justice: A Review of Research*, Vol. 30. Chicago, IL: University of Chicago Press, 2002.

95. L. Mazerolle, S. Bennett, J. Davis, E. Sargeant and M. Manning, "Procedural justice and police legitimacy: A systematic review of research evidence." *Journal of Experimental Criminology* 9 (2013): 245–274; J. Gau. "Procedural justice and police legitimacy: A test of measurement and structure." *American Journal of Criminal Justice* 39 (2014): 187–205.

READING 2.3

POLICE DISCRETION

Arthur Wiechmann

TOPICS

- Discretion Defined
- How Discretion Varies
- Variables That Affect Discretion
- Reducing Discretion

Introduction

[…] [I]t is extremely important that police departments hire individuals as police officers who have a high ethical standard. The biggest reason for this quality is because of the *high degree of discretion* that police officers have in enforcing the law and exerting their authority.

If unethical people were hired to be police officers, the opportunities for corruption, illegal activity, and abuse of authority would be out of control. This is because police officers are out on their own, without much direct supervision because of the solitary nature of the work. This makes them true professionals—workers who subscribe to a written code of conduct, and are held accountable to it.

There is much controversy in the area of police discretion, which will be discussed in this [reading]. Most professional occupations have discretionary characteristics, but very few have such enormous arbitrary control of the personal destiny of other people. It is this distinctive difference which separates law enforcement from other occupations.

Discretion Defined

Discretion is the ability to choose two or more courses of behavior. Note that this is not the ability to choose *between* two or more courses of action, which is simply decision making. Rather, discretion is when the effective limits of a police officer's power leaves him free to make a choice among a number of possible courses of action.

> **Example:** At virtually all incidents that the police respond to, officers can take a number of different courses of action, any of which would be acceptable. For instance, the police go to a loud party. They can warn the people to be quiet, they could disperse the party, or they could arrest the people for disturbing the peace. Any of these courses of action would be appropriate; and it is up to the individual judgment of the officer to decide what he is going to do.

When involved in a job that deals with human behavior (such as law enforcement), new and unique situations always come up that require the use of discretion. Although many situations that the police encounter are similar, no two situations are ever exactly the same. Each situation involves different people, at different times, at different locations, with different problems—well, you get the picture.

So, although discretion is inherent in all professions, it is absolutely essential in law enforcement, and it is the foundation of the entire criminal justice system. No one would advocate full enforcement of all laws. First of all, it could never be done—half the population would have to be police officers—one for each citizen. Second, do we really want the police to issue tickets to people for driving two miles over the speed limit?

We expect the police to use good judgment when they enforce the law, because it is not possible to make rules for every possible situation that might arise. The point here is that jobs that require discretion also require more dependence on the individual's ethics.

Patrol officers encounter more situations that result in ethical dilemmas than any other police assignment. Probably the most significant dilemma that officers face in exerting their discretion has to do with the decision to involve the criminal justice system in an incident.

> **Example:** When a police officer makes a vehicle stop for a traffic violation, it is entirely up to the discretion of the officer whether he issues a citation or gives a warning. It is the same situation when he elects to arrest or not arrest a violator of the law. If an officer stops a drunk driver, there is no requirement that he arrest him. He can, of course, but the officer can also call a taxi for the driver, call a friend to pick him up, make him walk home, or even let him drive home.

Besides deciding what course of action to take in a variety of incidents, the police have another area of significant discretionary decision making. This is determining *what laws they will enforce and what laws they will ignore*, which extends to even which areas they will patrol in their assigned beats.

> **Example:** An officer may not feel that speeding is a big deal, so he chooses not to enforce speeding laws. Or because he was a frat boy in college, he does not think that drunk driving is a serious violation, so he does not enforce those laws either.

> **Example:** In a daily briefing session, the sergeant reads a patrol check request from an irate citizen demanding that officers patrol his street more often. The officers all laugh, because this citizen, without realizing what he has done, has effectively stopped all patrols on his street for years. No, it is not the right thing to do, but because police officers are still human beings, there is just so much they will take in the way of demands from people who have no clue about what their jobs really entail. And, because they have discretionary powers, human nature can sometimes supersede ethical responsibility, often resulting in juvenile responses to obnoxious and impertinent demands.

We hope that officers are fair and equitable (which they generally are, because the police take great pains in assuring this through the exhaustive testing process), but human nature is human nature (prolific, huh?). So, society must accept that as long as they hire human beings to do their dirty work for them, they have to buy into the whole deal; this means that from time to time these human beings are going to make their decisions and base their actions on the same imperfect and flawed reasoning as the rest of us do.

And, because society still uses human beings as police officers, these people bring into their jobs their unique personalities as well as their biases, experiences, and preferences. Only 1 percent of all police applicants ever become police officers, because only a small segment of the general population have the ethics, courage, intelligence, and disposition to do the job.

This 1 percent staves off their personal preferences in their discretionary decisions most of the time. But given the fact that they are still human, once in a while, when they have had a bad day and some idiot has pushed their buttons, the idiot will likely not get the same level of service or understanding as someone who has the intelligence to understand that you do not call a police officer an asshole when you want them to help you.

What most people do not realize is that the legal authority that officers have is not much more than that of a private citizen. About the only difference is that the police can arrest for suspicion of a felony, they can issue citations, and they can carry guns.

Other than that, much of what the police are empowered to do has more to do with accountability and responsibility rather than true power over others. They do not really have that much power over others; they just have a job that makes them exercise the power that everyone has.

Example: Because of their jobs, the police are sent to locations in which they detain and arrest people. You are not going to get a call from the police station to go handle these things. If you did, you would be detaining and arresting as many people as police officers do.

Where the real power comes in is in their day-to-day discretionary decisions to enforce or not enforce a law. It is this indiscriminate discretion that is the true power that the police have over people's lives.

Example: Would you rather be arrested by an officer who is predisposed against drunk drivers or one who is predisposed against college students? The end result is the same, but in the long run it is more equitable if the officer's decisions are made for the right reasons.

How Discretion Varies

The discretionary decisions that police officers make are affected by factors other than their personal ethics and beliefs. *The environment that these officers work in plays a large part in how they decide on a particular course of action.* Whether they realize it or not, their discretionary choices are partially controlled by their surroundings.

Discretion varies from officer to officer, from locale to locale, and from situation to situation.

Officer Variations

Police officers develop preferences through their experiences and their own lives. One officer may be strongly predisposed against drunk drivers, causing him to take a zero-tolerance approach, whereas another officer may think that drunk driving is no big deal, so he is not inclined to arrest drunk drivers.

Experiences in each of these officers' personal lives likely have caused these differences in the discretionary decisions that they make. The officer predisposed against drunk drivers may have had a friend or family member killed by a drunk driver. The officer who is more tolerant of drunk drivers may have had a history of drunk driving himself when he was younger, such as when he was a frat boy in college.

Besides their discretionary decisions being based on their personal experiences and beliefs, a police officer may target certain types of offenders because it is within his comfort zone or because it will help him to reach a goal.

Example: A police officer may target drug users because he has developed a high level of expertise that makes it easy for him to spot them. This makes his job easier; because he makes a lot of drug-related arrests, his reputation improves and his experience base expands.

Example: Another reason an officer may target drug users is that by arresting a large number of them he will get a reputation of being knowledgeable in drug enforcement, which will help him in getting assigned to the drug interdiction unit, which was a personal goal of his.

Locale Variation

Different cities have different problems, and the police officers in these different cities must deal with them differently, which affects how they make their discretionary decisions. A gang-infested city may need a more legalistic, authoritative, and strict style of policing than a quiet bedroom community that has very few serious crime problems.

Example: A city with a serious gang problem will need their police officers to be less discretionary; that is, officers will need to take much more of a zero-tolerance approach to law enforcement to solve the crime problems. This means that the officers will not give as many warnings in this type of working environment.

Example: A city that is primarily composed of upper-middle-class suburbs can afford to have its officers be more discretionary; that is, officers can be more oriented to a community policing approach, as well as be more forgiving for minor violations, as long as the serenity and harmony of the community remains intact.

The bottom line is that a doctor stopped for drunk driving in a bedroom community is more likely to be dealt with informally than a gang banger in a gang-infested neighborhood, not because of value systems or prejudice, but because some locations need more strict control and others do not.

Situational Variation

The situations that police officers find themselves in vary in the level of danger or threat that they perceive, and this affects their discretionary decisions. Some situations call for more moderation than others, depending on the ultimate goal of an incident or event.

Obviously, if a police officer is in a situation or area where he perceives a *high level of danger,* he will take on a much more law-and-order approach than if he were in a safe area. And, depending on the *goal of an incident or event*, the police may decide to be more tolerant of minor offenses, making their decisions much more discretionary.

> **Example:** If police officers at a Metallica concert were to take a zero-tolerance approach to all violations of the law, the entire audience would be in custody by the end of the night, which would bog down the courts and overfill the jails. The goal of the police presence at an event such as this would be to keep the peace and to be available for major incidents.

The enormous power that police officers have when making arrests can lead to unethical decisions. An unethical patrol officer may base his decisions on bribes or other personal interests, such as his biases and prejudices.

Variables That Affect Discretion

A variety of factors have an effect on police officers' discretionary decisions. Some of these factors simply affect the course of action that an officer takes, whereas others actually affect the officer's decision of whether or not to make an arrest, which is the most significant discretionary decision that officers make, because it has such an enormous impact on the lives of the people involved.

Variables That Determine a Course of Action

The following variables determine the officer's course of action. In essence, these are the variables that affect an officer's discretionary process:

- **Officer's attitude:** This is where the human factor comes into the equation: police officers have personal problems just like everyone else. We hope they do not take them to work with them, but that is a little too hopeful. Besides that factor, we must consider other influential factors, such as the time an officer has on the job and how seriously he takes his job, which usually go hand in hand. For example, a newer officer is pretty "gung ho" and is out to save the world and make a name for himself. And, according to police culture, he does have to prove himself. He is less likely to warn a violator or let an offender go. With time, perhaps decades, he will loosen up a little and realize that he will never save the world and that individual situations require individual judgments, which will change the way he makes discretionary decisions.

- **Citizen's attitude:** If a traffic violator denies wrongdoing, how can an officer give the driver a warning? If a driver runs a red light, then refuses to accept responsibility for it, the officer will have little choice but to issue the driver a citation, because a warning would have absolutely no value if the driver is not accepting of the fact that he made a mistake.

Additionally, if the traffic violator or criminal offender is *nonreceptive* to any warning or admonishment that the officer may give, how can a police officer just walk away? If a traffic violator is rolling his eyes as an officer tells him that his driving was dangerous, the violator may as well get on his knees and beg for a ticket, because that is what he is going to get. An officer is not going to warn a violator who is not receptive to the warning.

- **Seriousness of the offense:** Minor offenses are easily overlooked, but a serious offense begs for attention—by both the police and the criminal justice system.

Variables That Affect a Choice to Arrest

Making arrests is one of the major ways that the police solve problems. It is also discretion at its highest level, because these decisions, which involve thrusting an individual into the criminal justice system, are among the most life-changing events in a person's life.

Offender Variables

Several offender-related variables factor into a police officer's decision-making process when he is deciding whether to arrest someone. These categories of variables, developed through scientific studies, provide insight into the thought process involved when making these difficult and life-altering decisions.

- **Race:** Studies show that blacks are treated more harshly than other races, but that the area that the incident is occurring in determines the amount of force that is used. If the officer is in a dangerous area, he is more likely to use more force to maintain control of a situation. This sends a message to the gangs and other offenders that the streets belong to the police; they have to talk tough and be tough, they are not trying to make friends in dangerous areas.

  But, if the area that the police are in is not dangerous, the police are more likely to show more discretion by letting minor violations slide. This is because in some low-income or minority areas, a minor offense (such as drinking in public or playing loud music) is a lifestyle characteristic. To be hardcore about such offenses that the residents view as normal activity could result in an even more negative relationship between the police and the community, which could create a more dangerous environment for the officers.

- **Age:** Adults who complain to the police about a problem are usually taken more seriously than juveniles making the same complaints. Also, if a victim of a crime is older than the suspect, the officer is more likely to arrest the suspect. This is possibly because, in the eyes of the police, adults are more credible than juveniles. Additionally, the police probably think that an adult is more likely to expect that the police should take action than a juvenile is.
- **Demeanor:** When an offender defers to an officer, it usually results in the offender being treated more fairly. For instance, when an offender is detained by a police officer, and the officer asks the offender to step out of his vehicle, the best thing for the offender to do is to comply (defer) and do what the officer asks. To argue or to accuse the officer of violating his rights will very likely result in the officer using his discretionary power, which will result in the harshest of the available options toward the offender.

  Note that antagonistic complaints are not taken as seriously by the police. If the police respond to a call, and the informant is ranting and raving at the officer as though all this is his fault, the officer is not likely to be sympathetic with this person. Demanding, overbearing people think that this sort of behavior will get them what they want, but most of the time, especially when dealing with the police, who have discretionary power, it will backfire on them.

  When the police respond to a call, they view themselves as being in charge of the situation. If the informant tries to take that position, it will create a conflict that will likely not result in what the informant thought was going to happen. When the police are on scene, they are in charge; offenders and informants alike should defer to the officer. This will prevent conflict and a less than suitable outcome for the others involved.

  Additionally, when irate citizens call the police for service, the officer or dispatcher on the telephone is not going to be sympathetic or eager to help. And, when a citizen comes in to complain to a supervisor about an officer, if the citizen is antagonistic and angry, the supervisor is going to write it off as just another angry person who wants to get his pound of flesh as revenge against getting a ticket or being arrested.

  Lastly, and this should go without saying, *antagonistic suspects are more likely to be arrested than suspects who defer and are cooperative*. Let's face it, human nature is always going to be human nature, and while human beings are still being hired as cops, they will subtly respond as such. If a suspect acts like an asshole, he will be treated like one, each and every time, guaranteed. Police officers have as much compassion and empathy for people as anyone else, probably much, much more than others realize. But they are not going to take crap from some drunken idiot who is screaming at them and making demands.
- **Socio-economic status:** According to studies, middle- and upper-class individuals get more attention from the police and are less likely to be arrested. This information probably does

not come as a shock to most people; on the contrary, a statement this obvious is rather humorous. But we can only guess as to the reasons.

One reason is possibly *the lack of value conflict*. [...] [T]he police generally have conservative, middle-class values. When dealing with people with similar values, there is less of a chance that there will be conflict. The result of which could be a discretionary decision that would be favorable to the offender.

Another possible reason that this class of people gets more attention is that *they have contacts and political pull*. And because upper-class people are used to getting their way, when they do not, they are more likely to call and complain—directly to the chief of police, who is their golf buddy. Cops do not like problems with supervision, and if it means letting some snobby doctor slide on a ticket, it is well worth it to avoid a major headache.

Situational Variables

- **Seriousness of the offense:** The seriousness of the offense is the single most important factor that helps an officer decide if he is going to arrest someone. A police officer can more easily justify ignoring a minor offense and will be more compelled to take action when a major offense has occurred.
- **Prior record:** If the offender has a prior arrest record, and especially if he is on probation or parole, the officer is more likely to make an arrest. The mindset behind this is that if the suspect did it before, he probably did it this time also. (For every time that a person is arrested, it is estimated that he committed the same or similar offense 100 times.) So, if a suspect has a lengthy arrest record, then, in the mind of the officer, the suspect has committed hundreds of crimes, and very likely, committed this one.

  Even if he did not, it will make up for one of the crimes that he committed and did not get caught for. If civil rights-oriented folks read this, it will likely make their heads explode. I'm not saying this is right; I'm just giving some insight into how people think and rationalize their decisions, and remember, cops are still human beings.
- **Weapon involved:** When a weapon is involved in a crime, the officer is much more likely to make an arrest. This goes along with the seriousness of the offense. If a weapon is involved, it is generally a serious offense, and begs police action.
- **Officer-initiated activity:** When a police officer initiates a contact with someone, often he has already decided to take action, or at the very least he has seen something worthy of his attention. What the officer has seen is a probable violation of law. And, because he has witnessed something or has uncovered a crime, he will feel more compelled to make an arrest if one is appropriate.

Also, *many of the calls for service that the police respond to are not crimes*, they are marginally criminal activity at best, public service requests, or disturbing or suspicious activity that just needs to be quickly resolved. So, most of the time, the police are not going to scenes that an arrest would ever be considered. However, when they see criminal activity in front of them, this is the stuff they have been looking for all day, and they are not likely to just let it slide.

System Variables

- **Department size:** Large police departments generally have a higher ratio of officers to supervisors, so there is more autonomy, and officers therefore have more latitude to make their own decisions. Conversely, in a small department, which many have just three officers and a supervisor in the field, the supervisor will likely show up at many calls and contacts that the officers are involved in. Some supervisors tend to take over the calls and make the decisions. Others tend to exert their opinions as to what they think the outcome should be, causing the officer to defer to the supervisor's authority.
- **Alternative resources:** If nonpolice resources are available and sufficient, such as detox centers and mental health facilities, officers are more likely to intervene without making an arrest.

  Example: If an officer encounters a drunk who is passed out on a sidewalk, he usually has no choice but to arrest him and take him to jail to sleep it off. But if a detox center is available, the officer can take the drunk to that location and drop him off without making an arrest.

  Example: If an officer gets a call of a crazy person in the middle of the street, he cannot just warn the person to stop. The activity will likely continue, and the officer is going have to take some action to stop the activity. He could arrest the person for disturbing the peace, but if there is a mental health center available the officer can drop the individual off, and avoid making an arrest.
- **Peer pressure:** The pressure that fellow officers place on each other regarding the level of activity that they produce can have quite an effect on the actions that an officer chooses to take. For instance, if an officer is making a lot of arrests, it may make his peers look bad, so the other officers pressure him to slow it down. Or, an officer is not carrying his fair share of the workload, and officers pressure him to step it up a little.

  Many offenders have been arrested only because the officer felt pressure to make more arrests. Conversely, many offenders have been released because the officer felt pressure to reduce his activity. This concept is called *soldiering*, which was identified in the early years of motivational theories. This concept addresses the fact that *employees will maintain a certain level of activity so as to blend in with the activity of their peers.* Their concern for acceptance into the group is more important than recognition or monetary incentives.

Reducing Discretion

Some critics of law enforcement are not in favor of the level of discretion that police officers have. Critics have made efforts to reduce police discretion by requiring that the police provide guidelines to improve consistency. The problem is, no matter how many guidelines are provided, discretion will always be present in law enforcement.

Police officers work alone, and most instances of discretion cannot be controlled by rules or supervision. Unless there is a supervisor riding with each officer on every shift, it will still be up to the individual officer to make discretionary decisions.

Those arguing for control of discretion say that arbitrary enforcement leads to discrimination. This could certainly be true, and over the years, this has undoubtedly happened, even with the rigorous controls that police agencies use to hire only ethical individuals who make the right decisions for the right reasons.

Those against discretionary control argue that decision making is an important function of the police and it is not practical to eliminate discretion. This is certainly true; no situation that a police officer deals with is identical to the last, so having rules or policies to cover every possible situation is unreasonable and unrealistic.

So, the question becomes, *how much structure and control should be placed on police discretion?* The police are subject to *internal controls*, such as the many policies, procedures, rules, and regulations that they must follow in everything they do. They are also subject to *external controls*, such as police review boards, legal mandates, community policing programs, and case law, such as the exclusionary rule, injunctions, and lawsuits.

But, even with all of these controls, *it all still rests on the individual police officer's willingness to comply.* These officers in the field will always be the ultimate policy makers. The best that the criminal justice system can hope for is that police agencies continue to hire highly ethical individuals, and also take great pains in creating a work environment that perpetuates ethical decisions.

A good example of an external control that has been put in place to reduce police officer discretion is in the area of domestic violence laws. Over many years, the laws related to domestic violence have changed in such a way that places additional responsibilities on and requirements for police officers investigating these cases.

Historically, police officers were reluctant to take action in these types of cases; they felt it was a private family matter, they were dealing with reluctant victims, and there was potential harm to the family if the breadwinner was in jail. The problem with this, however, was that a cycle of abuse would continue without the involvement of the criminal justice system.

To reduce this cycle of violence, laws were changed so that the police were required to make an arrest if there was sufficient evidence (often just the victim's statement) that a crime had occurred. In the past, the police could not make a domestic violence arrest because the crime was a misdemeanor not committed in their presence, and they had to rely on the victim to make a private person's arrest. But with the changes in the law, the police are now allowed to make the arrest, and in fact, are required to.

Pros and Cons of Police Discretion

- **Pro:** All violations of law cannot be enforced. Therefore, police officers must choose to enforce some violations and ignore others. They are expected to do this. Fairness, common sense, and an unbiased mind are important traits for all police officers to possess to ensure that discretion is being exercised properly.
- **Con:** Arbitrary discretion between individual police officers reduces consistency.

  Example: Two individuals are drinking at a bar. Both have the same level of alcohol in their systems when they leave. Subject A is stopped by a police officer who observes driving consistent with being under the influence. Subject B is stopped by a different officer at a different location for the identical driving. The facts of each case are identical, the only difference is the officer making the stop. Subject A is arrested for drunk driving, and Subject B is sent home in a taxi.

  Is it fair that one person gets away with what another is arrested for? No, it is not. But, because of the individual discretion that officers have in conducting their duties, there is nothing to control this from happening. What critics of police discretion wants is some ***meaningful distinction*** when there are differences in these decisions, rather than arbitrary enforcement that leads to inconsistency and a lack of fairness.

  Discretionary authority is a breeding ground for corruption, where police officers potentially could be paid to exercise their discretion. This was a serious problem in the early years of law enforcement, but society can be assured that the vast majority of today's police officers would never even consider such behavior.

Thirty or forty years ago, in some areas of the country, it was not uncommon for a traffic violator to attach a twenty-dollar bill to his license, in hopes of paying his way out of a citation. If someone were to attempt this today, the violator, at the very least would be severely chastised by the officer, and could possibly face arrest for attempted bribery.

It all comes down to the quality of officers that police departments hire and the ability of the organization to maintain an ethical work environment.

Bibliography

Bennett, Wayne W., and Karen M. Hess. *Management and Supervision in Law Enforcement.* Belmont, CA: Thompson Wadsworth, 2004.

Bock, Wally. "Recruitment, New Kids on the Beat." *The Police Chief* (December 1990).

Brown, Gary E. "What You Always Wanted to Know about Assessment Centers but Were Afraid to Ask." *The Police Chief* (June 1978).

Cohen, Stephen L. "Pre-Package vs. Tailor Made: The Assessment Center Debate." *Personnel Journal* (December 1980).

Crank, John P. *Understanding Police Culture*. Cincinnati: Anderson Publishing, 1998.

Delattre, Edwin J. *Character and Cops*. 4th ed. Washington, D.C.: AEI Press, 2002.

Flynn, John T., and Barbara E. Anderson. "The Development of Reliable Oral Interview Procedures for Promotional Candidates." *Journal of Police Science and Administration* (1985).

Fridell, Lorie, Robert Lunney, Drew Diamond, and Bruce Kuba. *Racially Biased Policing: A Principled Response*. Washington, D.C.: Police Executive Research Forum, 2001.

Gaines, Larry K., and Victor E. Kappeler. *Policing in America*. 5th ed. Cincinnati: Anderson Publishing, 2005.

Graham, Gordon. "Civil Liability for Public Sector Organizations." Seminar, 1996.

Gilbert, James N. *Criminal Investigation*. 5th ed. Upper Saddle River, NJ: Prentice Hall, 2001.

Hess, Karen M., and Henry M. Wrobleski. *Police Operations, Theory and Practice*. 3rd ed. Toronto: Wadsworth/Thompson Publishing, 2003.

Holmes, Robert R., and Jerald R. Vaught. "Structured Oral Promotional Examinations." *The Police Chief* (January 1980).

Hunter, Ronald D., Thomas Barker, and Pamela D. Mayhall. *Police–Community Relations and the Administration of Justice*. 6th ed. Upper Saddle River, NJ: Prentice Hall, 2004.

International Association of Chiefs of Police. "Sample Professional Traffic Stop Policy and Procedure." Alexandria, VA: IACP, p. 2.

Joiner, Dennis A. "Assessment Center in the Public Sector: A Practical Approach." *Public Personnel Management Journal* (1984).

Klofas, John, Stan Stojkovic, and David Kalinich. *Criminal Justice Organizations: Administration and Management*. Belmont, CA: Thompson/Wadsworth Publishing, 1990./

Lyman, Michael D. *Criminal Investigation: The Art and the Science*. 2nd ed. Upper Saddle River, NJ: Prentice Hall, 1999.

Lungren, Daniel E. C.O.P.P.S., Community Oriented Policing and Problem Solving: Definitions and Principles. California Department of Justice, Attorney General's Office, 1995.

Murray, Charles, Tetsuro Motoyama, and W. V. Rouse. *The Link Between Crime and the Built Environment: The Current State of Knowledge*. Volume I. Washington, D.C.: U.S. Department of Justice, National Institute of Justice, 1980.

More, Harry W. *Special Topics in Policing*. 2nd ed. Cincinnati: Anderson Publishing, 1998.

More, Harry W., and W. Fred Wegener. *Behavioral Police Management*. New York: Macmillan, 1992.

National Center for Women and Policing. *Equality Denied: The Status of Women in Policing*. Los Angeles: National Center for Women in Policing, 1998.

Nowicki, Ed. "Racial Profiling Problems and Solutions." *Law and Order* (October 2002): 16–18.

Peak, Kenneth J. *Policing America: Methods, Issues, Challenges*. 2nd ed. Upper Saddle River, NJ: Prentice Hall, 1997.

Peak, Kenneth J. *Policing America: Methods, Issues, Challenges*. 4th ed. Upper Saddle River, NJ: Prentice Hall, 2003.

Schott, Richard. G. "The Role of Race in Law Enforcement: Racial Profiling or Legitimate Use?" *FBI Law Enforcement Bulletin* (November 2001): 24–32.

Souryal, Sam S. *Police Organization and Administration*. 2nd ed. Cincinnati: Anderson Publishing, 1995.

Stojkovic, Stan, David Kalinich, and John Klofas. *Criminal Justice Organizations: Administration and Management*. Belmont, CA: Thompson/Wadsworth Publishing, 2003.

Thibault, Edward A., Lawrence M. Lynch, and R. Bruce McBride. *Proactive Police Management*. 6th ed. Upper Saddle River, NJ: Prentice Hall, 2004.

Thurman, Quint C., and Jihong Zhao. *Contemporary Policing: Controversies, Challenges, and Solutions*. Los Angeles, CA: Roxbury Publishing, 2004.

Walker, Samuel, and Charles M. Katz. *The Police in America: An Introduction*. 5th ed. Boston: McGraw-Hill, 2005.

Wallace, Harvey, Cliff Roberson, and Craig Stechler. *Fundamentals of Police Administration*. Upper Saddle River, NJ: Prentice Hall, 1995.

Weston, Paul B., and Kenneth M. Wells. *Criminal Investigation: Basic Perspectives*. 7th ed. Upper Saddle River, NJ: Prentice Hall, 1997.

Whisenand, Paul M., and R. Fred Ferguson. *The Managing of Police Organizations*. 4th ed. Upper Saddle River, NJ: Prentice Hall, 1996.

White, Michael D. *Current Issues and Controversies in Policing*. Boston: Pearson Education, 2007.

Wilson, James Q., and George L. Kelling. "Broken Windows: The Police and Neighborhood Safety." *The Atlantic Monthly* 249 (March 1982): 29–38.

DISCUSSION QUESTIONS

1. As the lead detective in your law enforcement agency, you are aware that several of the banks in your city have been robbed within the last month. Utilizing the SARA model, explain how you would work with the banks to prevent future robberies.
2. Is it important for the members of a law enforcement agency to share similar demographics with the community they serve? Identify advantages and disadvantages of having a diverse police agency.
3. Discuss the evolution of the community policing model. As a police chief, would you implement this model to create relationships between your police officers and the community? Why or why not?
4. List and describe the characteristics that you believe make a great police officer.
5. Describe three sources of stress for police officers. How can this stress impact an officer's ability to do their job?
6. Do you believe that a police subculture exists? Explain whether or not you believe that persons with certain personality traits seek out employment as police officers.
7. In your opinion, what factors should a police officer take into account when deciding whether or not to make an arrest?

THE COURTS

EDITOR'S INTRODUCTION

The U.S. court system is often referred to as the "dual system of courts" because the federal and state systems mirror one another. The federal court system, created with the passage of the Judiciary Act of 1789, called for the creation of one Supreme Court and inferior courts as needed, which led to the creation of federal district and federal appellate courts.

There are 50 independent state court systems as well as separate court systems in Washington, DC, and U.S. territories, each with their own district, appellate, and supreme court. Each court, whether state or federal, has a specific jurisdiction, which means that it has the power to hear cases on particular issues and render verdicts. For example, if a person violates a state law, the state district court has jurisdiction over that case.

In "The Courts," Mia R. Ortiz presents an overview of the U.S. court system. She begins by covering the multiple layers of the 50 independent state court systems, the separate court systems in Washington, DC,and U.S. territories, and the federal court system. Our court system is often referred to as a dual system because the federal and state court processes mirror one another. The concept of *due process*, that every defendant is treated fairly and equally as they move through the judicial process, is also addressed by focusing on certain rights contained within the 4th, 5th, 6th, and 14th Amendments of the U.S. Constitution. Special attention is also given to the creation of specialty courts, which are designed to address specific types of defendants such as those with addiction and mental illness, and those who commit their crimes with a firearm.

In "People and Problems in the Courts," Lawrence F. Travis III provides the reader with the qualifications, roles, and responsibilities of the key decision makers in criminal courts: defense attorneys, prosecutors, and judges. These decision makers are commonly referred to as "the courtroom workgroup" because they work together and develop an understanding of fair and just outcomes in the criminal justice system. A fourth and equally important component of the criminal court system is the jury that determines guilt or innocence, and in many cases, the sentence. This reading concludes with a focus on critical issues such as a defendant receiving a fair trial, plea bargaining, and wrongful convictions.

In "The Goals and Process of Punishment," Lawrence F. Travis III focuses our attention on the last step in the trial process: sentencing the convicted offender. He begins with an exploration of the four main rationalizations for punishing offenders (deterrence, incapacitation, rehabilitation, and retribution). Next comes a discussion of various sentencing strategies, which include probation, determinate and indeterminate sentences, mandatory minimum sentences, intermediate sentences, and three-strike laws. Travis also examines the disparity in sentencing among these options between white and minority defendants. Parole, the mechanism by which an offender is released early from prison, is also discussed.

READING 3.1

THE COURTS

Mia R. Ortiz

BRIEF OUTLINE

A. Introduction
B. Development and Evolution of the Courts
C. Due Process Rights of the Accused
D. A Profile of Criminal Defendants
E. Problem-Solving Courts
F. Courtroom Professionals
G. The Trajectory of the Accused into the Criminal Justice System
H. Summary and Analysis of the American Court System

KEY TERMS

- Bail
- Beyond a Reasonable Doubt
- Exclusionary Rule
- Felony
- Grand Jury
- Miranda Warnings
- Misdemeanor
- Plea Bargaining
- Trial
- Voir Dire

> ***Equal justice under law is not merely a caption on the facade of the Supreme Court building; it is perhaps the most inspiring ideal of our society. It is one of the ends for which our entire legal system exists … it is fundamental that justice should be the same, in substance and availability, without regard to economic status.***
>
> —Lewis Powell Jr., U.S. Supreme Court justice

A. Introduction

The judicial branch of American government is responsible for interpreting laws as they pertain to the Constitution, state, or local laws. The U.S. court system is a multilayered, multi-tiered institution governed and directed by the Constitution, rules of evidence, and the local jurisdiction. Its foundation is based on reviewing and evaluating evidence based on a mandate of justice and fairness. Thus, the decisions made by courts have a direct impact on the accused, the victims, and the community at large. This [reading] provides an overview of the court system, which includes the development and organization of the federal and state court systems, a discussion on the constitutional rights of the accused, a description of the courtroom work group, as well as detail of the trajectory of how criminal cases are processed. Woven into these sections are historical and contemporary court cases as well as discussion on the impact that the U.S. court system has on matters of social justice and ethical concerns among disenfranchised communities.

B. Development and Evolution of the Courts

The initial development of the U.S. court system emerged from the Constitution, specifically through the first acts of Congress under the Judiciary Act of 1789 as part of maintaining checks and balances with the legislative and executive branches of government. Court system began on the principle of federalism, which is the idea of having a central or federal government. Over time, with the emergence of states (and state government), federalism evolved to include the recognition of autonomous state governments and therefore dual court systems: the federal courts and the state courts. Although these systems have for the most part distinct jurisdictions, the court of last resort for both is the Supreme Court of the United States. The description of the federal court system is discussed in the next section.

Federal Court System

District Courts

The structure of the federal court system consists of district courts, appellate courts, and the Supreme Court. The federal district courts consist of 94 judicial districts and the U.S. bankruptcy courts. There is at least one district court in each state as well as in the U.S. territories of American Samoa, Guam, Northern Mariana Islands, Panama, U.S. Virgin Islands, and Puerto Rico. An important question to ask is what cases do the federal courts have jurisdiction over (what types of cases are heard)? The federal court system has jurisdiction over matters that include "the constitutionality of the law, cases involving U.S. laws and treaties, disputes between two or more states, maritime law, and bankruptcy cases" (United States Courts, 2015, nd).

One of the most recent high-profile cases in the federal court system was the matter of the *United States v. Dzhokhar Tsarnaev, 2013.* Tsarnaev was arrested, indicted, and convicted for manufacturing and detonating two pressure cooker bombs near the finish line of the Boston Marathon in 2013, which resulted in the deaths of four people (an act that he did with his deceased brother, Tamerlan Tsarnaev). Additionally, he was convicted of carjacking and killing a university police officer during a shootout. Among many charges, Tsarnaev was charged in the federal system because the bombs were considered a weapon of mass destruction (U.S.C. § 2332a) and the bombing occurred in a place of public use (U.S.C. § 2332), which resulted in malicious destruction of property (U.S.C. § 844).

An important question to raise is why was Tsarnaev charged in federal court instead of the Massachusetts state court? The prosecution can charge a defendant on the federal level if it can be determined that the crime committed impacted interstate commerce. In Tsarnaev's case, the charges of mass destruction and malicious destruction of property had a direct impact on the role of commerce on marathon Monday. Each year, the Boston Marathon attracts millions of runners, and spectators from around the world who rely on the hotels, restaurants, and other businesses that offer special services for marathon participants. The prosecution argued that the bombing significantly interrupted interstate commerce in Boston.

In addition to these offenses, Tsarnaev was also charged with conspiracy (the planning and commission of the bombings). On April 8, 2015, he was found guilty of 30 counts of federal crimes, and on May 15, 2015, the jury recommended death by lethal injection. Tsarnaev's conviction or death sentence will likely be sent to the U.S. Court of Appeals for the First Circuit—the same court where the trial took place—on grounds that he did not have a fair trial (the defendant's request to have the trial outside of Boston for purposes of having a fair jury and trial was denied during pre-trial motions). The First Circuit includes the districts of Maine, Massachusetts, New Hampshire, Puerto Rico, and Rhode Island.

U.S. Courts of Appeals

When cases heard in district courts are appealed, they proceed through one of 12 appellate courts. In 2013 there were nearly 60,000 appeals filed on the appellate level (United States Court of Appeals, 2014). The majority of the cases involve petitions from prisoners to seek sentence reductions or appeals of trial convictions. In criminal cases, the losing party of the initial court matter, known on the appellate level as the appellant, will either present written legal grounds (known as a brief) or engage in oral argument against the appellee (the side arguing to uphold the initial court decision). The briefs or arguments are heard by a panel of appellate judges, and their ruling is final. At the appellate level, it is usually the defendant who challenges the conviction (the prosecution may never appeal an acquittal but may contest the sentence) (Administrative Office of the U.S. Courts, 2015). If one of the litigants is unsatisfied with the judgement of the appellate court or the highest state court, he or she may file a petition to the U.S. Supreme Court for review (known as a writ of certiorari).

One federal court case that proceeded to the appellate court involved Boston attorney Simon Glik, who was arrested in 2007 for videotaping an arrest by police officers in Boston Commons. The police charged Glik with illegal wiretapping, aiding the escape of the prisoner, and disturbing the peace. Although all criminal charges were eventually dropped, Glik sued the city of Boston and the police officers in district court for violating his civil rights. Glik was awarded $170,000 for damages and legal fees. The appellants (the city and the police officers) contested the settlement because the police officers argued that they had *qualified immunity*, in that by their public office status, they could not be held responsible. However, the decision by appellate court judge Kermit Lipez upheld Glik's civil rights; here is an excerpt of his opinion:

> The filming of government officials engaged in their duties in a public place, including police officers performing their responsibilities, fits comfortably within these principles. Gathering information about government officials in a form that can readily be disseminated to others serves a cardinal First Amendment interest in protecting and promoting "the free discussion of governmental affairs" (655 F.3d 78).

The Supreme Court

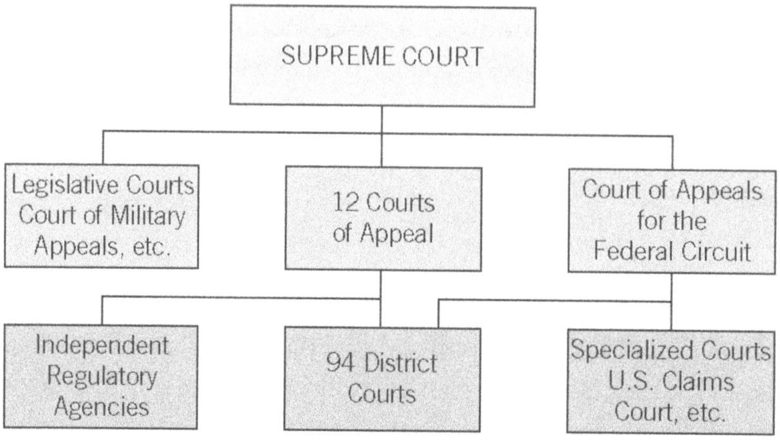

The Supreme Court was created through a provision under Article III of the Constitution. In addition to executing its responsibility of maintaining checks and balances as the head the judiciary branch of government of the United States, the role of the Supreme Court is to operate as the final court for both state and federal jurisdictions and to review cases over concerns of constitutionality. The decisions of all of these matters not only provide a sense of justice in the immediate case, but also provide a precedent (a rule) for decisions in future court cases.

Supreme Court Justices

Currently there are nine Supreme Court justices. Justices are nominated by the president, and then vetted through extensive congressional hearings. Once confirmed by Congress, justices are appointed for life. Although the Supreme Court operates as an independent branch like the executive and legislative branches, presidents typically nominate potential justices with political ideologies that are similar to their own, which may affect court decisions on criminal or civil proceedings in the future. Over the years, the composition of the Supreme Court has changed from solely White men to the inclusion of female and minority justices. In 1967 Thurgood Marshall, an accomplished lawyer who successfully challenged racial segregation in public schools in *Brown v. Board of Education of Topeka* (1954), was appointed as the first African American justice of the Supreme Court. Fourteen years later, Sandra Day O'Connor was the first female justice appointed to the high court. Currently on the bench are three female and one African American justice. With the exception of Justice Ruth Bader Ginsburg (who attended Columbia University's Law School), current justices have graduated from either Harvard or Yale Law Schools.

The State Court System

In most states, the state court system is typically divided into three levels: trial courts, appellate courts, and the court of last resort (typically called supreme courts). It is within the state court system that most of the criminal and civil court cases are processed.

Trial Courts

Trial courts are typically the court where most criminal and civil matters enter after arrest. Depending on the state, trial courts may be further divided into courts of limited or special jurisdiction, where the court only hears certain cases (such as **misdemeanor**, family court, community courts, or other specialized court). Courts of general jurisdiction oversee a variety of criminal and civil matters.

The organization of state court structure varies from state to state. In New York State, the highest court in the state is the Court of Appeals, followed by the Appellate Terms of the Supreme Court, which is followed by Supreme Courts, District Courts, and then City Courts. In the state of North Dakota, the Supreme Court is the highest court, followed by the Temporary Court of Appeals, the District Court, and Municipal Courts. Every state court system is designed to fit the needs of its state jurisdiction.

Court of Appeals

The purpose of the court of appeals is to challenge the ruling of the lower trial court. The court of appeals does not hear new cases, but rather makes rulings as to whether to affirm the lower court's rulings (that is, agree), remand (return to the lower court for retrial), or overturn (reverse the court's decision). Some of the reasons that cases are brought to the state appellate court include the inclusion of inadmissible evidence or testimony (which should have been excluded) or incorrect jury instructions by the judge. The majority of appeals brought by the defendant are rarely successful. In California, only 6 percent of criminal appeals are considered for further appellate action (Judicial Council of California, 2013).

Wrongful Convictions

The greatest miscarriage of justice occurs when a defendant has been wrongfully incarcerated or worse, put to death. In the United States, there have been a number of defendants who have been wrongfully convicted based on misidentification, unreliable testimony, or racial bias. The Innocence Project, an organization that has used DNA evidence to challenge wrongful convictions since the early 1990s, has been pivotal in addressing these injustices. To date, the organization has been successful in exonerating more than 300 wrongfully convicted persons.

State Supreme Court

In the majority of state case matters, the state Supreme Court is the court of last resort. The Supreme Court on the state level, as on the federal level, is composed of the justices who decide the merits of the decisions from the lower and appellate court. Unlike the U.S, Supreme Court, which does hear new cases, the state Supreme Court does not oversee trials. The state Supreme Court will consider cases that were not settled on the appellate level to determine if judicial or other court error in the original court of jurisdiction occurred. There are many notable cases that have been settled on the state Supreme Court level. In California, under *Jones v. Chappell*, the state justices found that chemical elements used in lethal injections were found to be cruel and unusual; this was the impetus toward establishing a moratorium on capital punishment in the state in 2014. In 1783 in the *Commonwealth of Massachusetts v. Nathaniel Jennison*, the court found that slave masters could be held criminally responsible for assaulting runaway slaves in free states.

C. Due Process Rights of the Accused

In the United States defendants are afforded certain rights outlined by the Constitution to ensure that they are treated fairly during the judicial process. Specifically, certain rights (known as due process rights) are outlined within the 4th, 5th, 6th, and 14th Amendments of the Bill of Rights in the Constitution. Due process is the foundation for justice and fairness and is afforded to every defendant who comes before the courts (even for the most egregious of alleged acts or the most notorious of offenders). Moreover, there have been a series of landmark Supreme Court cases that have reaffirmed the significance of these amendments.

Fourth Amendment

Under the Constitution, the Fourth Amendment states the following:

> *The right of the people to be secure in their persons, houses, papers, and effects, against unreasonable searches and seizures, shall not be violated, and no warrants shall issue, but upon probable cause, supported by oath or affirmation, and particularly describing the place to be searched, and the persons or things to be seized.*

Mapp v. Ohio

The right against unlawful search and seizure is invoked prior to arrest and subsequent court involvement and requires law enforcement (in most cases, footnote exceptions) to obtain warrants prior to searching or seizing a defendant's property. However, since such obtained evidence entered into court can affect the liberty of the defendant, it is essential that the evidence be obtained justly as required by the law. One landmark case that tested the constitutionality of search and seizure was *Mapp v. Ohio* (367 U.S. 643). In this case, Cleveland police entered the home of Dollree Mapp without a warrant on a tip that a bomb suspect was in her home. After handcuffing Mapp, the police obtained a gun, communist propaganda, and obscene material in her basement. Mapp was subsequently charged with possession of obscene material. In 1961, in a 6–3 ruling in the Supreme Court, despite the illegal contents that were in the home, the court decided that Mapp's arrest was unlawful because the police failed to enter her home on a valid warrant. This is defined as the *exclusionary rule*, in which evidence that was unlawfully obtained by the police cannot be admitted into evidence against the defendant.

Fifth Amendment

Several important components of the Fifth Amendment are relevant to the criminal justice system. These include the right against self-incrimination and double jeopardy, as well as protection against disclosing privileged communication. In many respects, the Fifth Amendment protections serve as a safeguard against coercive practices that have occurred during police interrogations in which confessions were obtained.

The Right Against Self-Incrimination

The most well-known constitutional right involves what the police are required to say to suspects and detainees at the time of arrest and questioning. These statements, called the ***Miranda warnings***, generally consist of the following:

> You have the right to remain silent. Anything you say can and will be used against you in a court of law. You have the right to speak to an attorney, and to have an

attorney present during any questioning. If you cannot afford a lawyer, one will be provided for you at no cost to you.

The Miranda warnings stem from the landmark Supreme Court case *Miranda v. Arizona* (384 U.S. 436, 1966). In this case, Ernesto Miranda was charged, convicted, and sentenced for rape and kidnapping after confessing to the crime during interrogation, in which he had no attorney, nor was he advised that he could remain silent during questioning. In 1966 the Warren court ruled that the police had violated Fifth Amendment rights due to their neglect of Miranda's rights, and accordingly the conviction was reversed. Additionally, illegally obtained confessions or evidence that has been entered into court can be stricken from consideration in future court actions. The right against self-incrimination extends from any onset of any police involvement. Additionally, Fifth Amendment protects the accused from being required to testify against themselves in court. Should a defendant voluntarily testify, the defendant may invoke his or her Fifth Amendment rights at any time to avoid self-incrimination (that is, "I plead the fifth").

In addition to the Fifth Amendment's protections against self-incrimination, there are also other persons with a direct relationship to the accused who may not be compelled to testify in the effort to incriminate the accused. These persons include spouses, doctors, psychiatrists, the accused's attorney, and clergy.

While *Miranda* has far-reaching implications in the criminal justice system, there are many examples that reflect illegal police practices imposed on suspects. In *Brown v. Mississippi*, police officers whipped and hung defendants in order to obtain a confession to murder. In the case of the Scottsboro Boys, eight young Black men who were accused of raping two White girls were not allowed to consult with an attorney (despite being charged with a capital crime that would lead to a death sentence) and were denied the ability to waive their right to a speedy trial. In fact, the court wanted to try the entire case in and one and a half days. The trial (and subsequent trials) were heard by all-White juries since Alabama had highly discriminatory practices, which prevented African Americans from serving. (For more information on this compelling case, see Carter, 1979.)

The Right Against Double Jeopardy

Another component of the Fifth Amendment is the right against being tried for the same crime twice (also known as double jeopardy). Essentially, a defendant may not be punished for the same conviction twice and may not be retried after an acquittal. Double jeopardy violations do not include grand jury deliberations or mistrial. Additionally, double jeopardy violations do not include criminal cases that are tried at the state and federal level. Because the state and federal courts, in many respects, are separate entities, a defendant may be tried in both courts for the same offense. For example, a person could send child pornography through the mail and be charged with a state offense of possession of child pornography and a federal offense of sending child pornography through the U.S. mail. In addition, double jeopardy has not been violated if the defendant is held to answer in criminal court and is sued in civil court for the same offense. For instance, former football star O. J. Simpson was acquitted of the murder of his ex-wife, Nicole Brown Simpson, and her friend Ronald Goldman but was sued (and was held responsible) in civil court for wrongful death.

Sixth Amendment

Rights of the accused under the Sixth Amendment involve several important matters within court proceedings specifically as it relates to trial. Within the Constitution, the Sixth Amendment states the following:

> In all criminal prosecutions, the accused shall enjoy the right to a speedy and public trial, by an impartial jury of the State and district wherein the crime shall have been committed, which district shall have been previously ascertained by law, and to be informed of the nature and cause of the accusation; to be confronted with the witnesses against him; to have compulsory process for obtaining witnesses in his favor, and to have the Assistance of Counsel for his defence.

There are several fundamental rights that defendants have. First, the defendant has a right to be informed of the criminal charges placed on him or her. This must occur upon arrest and at arraignment when formal charges are filed by the prosecution. Additionally, defendants have the right to view and/or challenge any evidence or testimony against them in court.

Right to an Attorney

The Sixth Amendment affirms that defendants have the right to have an attorney represent them in criminal proceedings regardless of their ability to pay. In *Gideon v. Wainright* (1963), the Supreme Court held that the state of Florida had violated Clarence Gideon's constitutional rights because it had denied Gideon's request to have an attorney represent him in court. As such, the high court overturned Gideon's state conviction (since he was forced to represent himself).

In today's courts the public defender is responsible for providing representation for defendants who are unable to secure their own defense due to their inability to pay. Indigent defense is the most commonly used defense for defendants. According to the Bureau of Justice Statistics, nearly $3 billion were spent for indigent defense in 2012 (Herberman & Kyckelhahn, 2014). Moreover, only 1 in 4 county public defender offices have enough lawyers to properly manage the caseload as set by the National Advisory Commission on Criminal Justice System Standards and Goals (Farole, 2010). In other words, the majority of the country's indigent defense systems are tremendously overwhelmed by growing caseloads

Right to a Jury Trial

Another constitutional right afforded through the Sixth Amendment is the right to a jury trial. Although this is a constitutional right, it is rarely used (only 10 percent of criminal cases go to trial). The majority of defendants will have their matters resolved during a stage within the criminal court process, typically through a practice called **plea bargaining**. Plea bargaining occurs when the prosecution and the defense come to an agreement on the case that will result in the defendant pleading guilty to the agreed upon charges. For attorneys and the courts, there are benefits to this practice: It reduces the volume of cases that go to trial (which can be extremely costly and time consuming); it can also guarantee conviction rates (for district attorneys) and can be a benefit to defense attorneys (particularly indigent defense attorneys with large caseloads). Although there are direct benefits for the court work group, it has been criticized over several concerns. One concern is that defendants may be under pressure to plea bargain, especially if they are currently in custody, with the agreement that they will be able to be released immediately. In some cases, the pains of pretrial detention may be significant enough that defendants may plead guilty to crimes they may not have committed, thus leading to legal, social, and financial consequences that may affect them for the rest of their lives.

Another criticism of plea bargaining relates to the issue of whether the practice circumvents the intentions of the due process rights of the defendants—specifically their right to a jury trial. Though defendants are informed prior to pleading guilty that they are waiving their constitutional rights to a trial and to the right to appeal, the reality is that plea bargaining was never the intention of (nor explicitly stated by) the framers of the Constitution. Due process rights as stated in the Constitution affirm that defendants who are accused of a crime have the right to trial, the right to testify (if they so choose), as well as the right to challenge the evidence and the witnesses against them. Many critics suggest that plea bargaining bypasses this very important legal process (Lynch, 2003, p. 27).

Eighth Amendment

The Eighth Amendment relates to the rights against cruel and unusual punishment and the rights against excessive bail. The Constitution requires that punishment be proportional to the crime for which the defendant was convicted. For example, an individual convicted for a petty, low-level crime should not have the same punishment as someone convicted of murder. A landmark Supreme Court case that tested the cruel and unusual punishment provision included *Furman v. Georgia* (408 U.S. 238), in which a man was sentenced to death for attempted burglary. The Supreme Court struck down this sentence because of the violation to the defendant's constitutional rights.

A Discussion on Bail

While there is no constitutional right to bail, clauses within the Eighth Amendment of the Constitution affirm that when bail is assigned, it must not be excessive. In determining bail, the judge takes the following into consideration as stated in the Eighth Amendment:

> The court takes into consideration several factors: (1) the seriousness of the offense; (2) the Weight of Evidence against the accused; (3) the nature and extent of any ties, such as family or employment, that the accused has to the community where he or she will be prosecuted; (4) the accused's ability to pay a given amount; and (5) the likelihood that the accused will flee the jurisdiction if released.

Absent of capital offenses (such as capital murder) and certain criminal violations (for example, violation of parole, probation, or bench and arrest warrants for failing to appear in court), most defendants will be assigned bail, and in fact, two thirds of defendants will be released on bail prior to trial. Bail refers to the financial or nonfinancial condition of being released from custody. Most courts yield to a bail schedule that has a bail amount assigned for each charge for which the defendant is arrested or arraigned. Bail is divided into two categories: those with financial conditions and those with nonfinancial conditions. Financial conditions include surety bail (defendants pay 10% of the total bail plus secure their release with property collateral); deposit bail (defendants pay 10% of the total bail with the amount refunded at the conclusion of the case); full cash bond (defendants pay the full amount of the bail to the court with the total amount refunded at the conclusion of the case); and property bond (property, usually a home or business, is put up as collateral).

In the 1960s critics argued that financial conditions of bail created significant disparities between affluent and disadvantaged defendants in that those who could not afford bail had to remain detained at pretrial. Further, it was argued that bail bond agents (a for-profit entity) were largely becoming the decision makers in determining release conditions—solely on the basis that the defendant could pay for the bond and thus circumvent the justice system. In 1961 Vera Institute of Justice conducted the Manhattan Bail Project, a research project designed to test whether defendants who were released without paying a financial bail are likely to skip their court appearances (Kohler, 1962). The results showed that fewer than 2% of defendants released without paying a financial condition of bail failed to appear to future court dates. The results of this research proved to be a watershed moment for the bail reform movement and helped inform courts across the country on ways to implement nonfinancial conditions to bail.

In addition to the noted social class disparities that are present in pretrial release decisions, research has also studied the impact that the race of the defendant has on the conditions of bail. Findings show that Black defendants were least likely to be released from the least restrictive pretrial conditions as compared to White defendants (Demuth, 2003; Schlesinger, 2007).

Fourteenth Amendment

The 14th Amendment affords each defendant equal protection the law. This is of particular importance, since there has been an extensive history of the denial of equal justice among defendants from underrepresented communities within the court of law. Specifically, 14th Amendment to the Constitution affirms the following:

> All persons born or naturalized in the United States and subject to the jurisdiction thereof are citizens of the United States and of the State wherein they reside. No State shall make or enforce any law which shall abridge the privileges or immunities of citizens of the United States; nor shall any State deprive any person of life, liberty, or property, without due process of law; nor deny to any person within its jurisdiction the equal protection of the laws.

Loving v. Virginia

In *Loving v. Virginia* (1967), the Supreme Court ruled that laws which banned interracial marriage violated the equal protection clause of the Constitution. The case was brought forward by Richard and Mildred Loving (a White man and a Black woman), who were sentenced to jail for getting married; under Virginia's Racial Integrity Act of 1924, such marriages were deemed illegal. Similarly, in *Brown v. Board of Education* (1954), the Supreme Court determined that school segregation was in fact unequal and therefore violated the equal protection under the law clause of the 14th Amendment.

Consequences of Convictions

Recently, there has been greater discussion about the impact that misdemeanor and violations have on the defendant, the courts, and the community. These convictions bring many consequences for those convicted of lower level crimes. Certain misdemeanor convictions can lead to deportation, denial to hold certain professional licenses, loss of employment, eviction, and required registry into state sex registries. Moreover, police practices such as "broken windows" (where police are required to arrest or issue summons for minor infractions) increase the volume of misdemeanor cases in the court system as well as the cost to prosecute and defend each of these cases.

D. A Profile of Criminal Defendants

Although there is a high volume of cases that are going through the nation's courts, the reality is that the majority of the defendants come from disenfranchised communities. More than a third of the cases that enter the courts are drug related (that is, possession or intent to sell/trafficking). Violent crimes (murder, robbery, and sexual assaults) make up approximately one quarter of the cases, and the remaining cases involve property offenses (that is, burglary, larceny, and auto theft) (Reaves, 2013). Over the course of 2 decades, Black males represent the bulk (45%) of defendants entering the **felony** criminal courts. White defendants reflect a third of the population, and Hispanic defendants represent a fourth. Black males under age 18 represent more than half (55%) of the juvenile population (Reaves, 2013).

Female defendants are less than a quarter of those who enter the court system; this has remained consistent over the past 20 years. Most crimes that female offenders are charged with tend to be lower level offenses or incidents in which they are accessories to violent crimes (such as robbery) (the Cohen & Reaves, 2007). The average age at arrest is currently 32, as compared to 20 years ago, when it was 28. In fact, 1 in 4 defendants are 40 years old or older. This may reflect the revolving door of the criminal justice system in that once a person has been identified through conviction and incarceration, it may be difficult to earn legitimate employment, access to quality housing, and relocating to productive and safer communities; thus, many will return to criminal involvement. Because of the limitations that criminal convictions can have on opportunities for desisting from future criminal behavior, policy stakeholders in the court system have begun to rethink the role of courts and to consider innovative ways in which to address social ills that lead to crime through the use of problem-solving courts.

E. Problem-Solving Courts

Specialized courts are designed to address the defendant's specific criminal, social, or mental health needs more effectively than the traditional criminal court, with the goal of reducing future criminal involvement. Toward the end of the 20th century, there was an emergence of several specialized courts across the country to address specific criminal behaviors and quality of life matters that affect many defendants who come before the court.

Drug Courts

In the past 30 years, the increase in the volume of court cases has largely been attributed to drug-related offenses (for example, possession and distribution). In 1989 the first drug court was enacted in Miami–Dade County, Florida, as a response to the number of drug-related cases that were clogging the criminal courts (National Association of Drug Court Professionals, 2014). Nearly 30 years later, there are close to 3,000 drug courts across the country, with at least one court situated in each state. The purpose of the drug court is to divert defendants away from the traditional criminal court processing so that they may participate in rehabilitation related to their substance abuse. The commitment to the drug court is typically 18 months and requires defendants to attend regularly scheduled meetings where they submit to regular drug testing. Defendants who continually test positive for illicit substances or are charged with new crimes during their drug court involvement may be returned to the regular criminal court processing, where they could be subject to harsher penalties. Participants who successfully complete drug court will have their conviction sealed or the charges dropped entirely. Results from several major studies have concluded that not only are defendants who participate in the drug courts (compared to defendants charged with similar drug charges) more likely to desist from future drug use, they are also less likely to engage in future criminal behavior (Rempel, Green & Kraelstein, 2012).

Domestic Violence Courts

For nearly a decade, domestic violence has accounted for nearly a fifth of all violent crime in the United States (Truman & Morgan, 2014). Domestic violence cases make up a significant portion of criminal court processing. Domestic violence courts have emerged as another problem-solving court to address this issue. In 2009 there were more than 200 domestic violence courts implemented within the United States and 150 that had been developed internationally (Labriola, Bradley, O'Sullivan, Rempel, & Moore, 2009). Although there is variation, domestic violence court revolve around two goals: (a) to provide greater safeguards in securing the victims' safety, which can include access to victims advocate programs internal and external to the courts; and (b) to ensure offenders' accountability in the alleged crime (Labriola et al., 2009). Additionally, there are integrated domestic violence courts that also incorporate family court matters, which include child custody and child protective service matters (Labriola et al., 2009). Leading experts of domestic violence courts are quick to admit that the success of these courts is not tethered to the rates of recidivism, since there have been no results that show that this particular problem-solving court reduces this crime as compared to domestic violence defendants in traditional court setting (Mazur & Aldrich, 2003). However, the major distinction between the two courts is that there are greater supports for victims in the domestic violence court.

Mental Health Courts

According to the National Alliance on Mental Illness, there are 2 million people arrested every year with a serious mental illness with an additional half a million are being treated while incarcerated. The purpose of mental health courts is to engage defendants in participating in treatment. Similar to drug courts, defendants are assigned a case manager, who conducts a psychosocial assessment, and must participate in periodic case meetings in court during their treatment.

Assessment of Problem-Solving Courts

These specialized courts provide many benefits not only to the defendant, but also to the community at large. Such courts provide a new view on the purpose of justice—that is, identifying the quality of life and low-level crimes that can plague a community and a society. In many respects, these courts offer individualized treatment that is distinct from the typical criminal court experience. Moreover, for many the participation in these specialized courts is the first time that defendants have had access to treatment or social services. Although these benefits are significant, critics have argued that there are concerns related to this approach. One concern relates to the fact that in order to receive services (like counseling, rehabilitation, and other social services), a person must be identified in the criminal justice system (arrested, charged, or incarcerated). A second concern is that most defendants have to plead guilty to the offense charged (often through a plea bargaining agreement) in order to be diverted to the specialized court. In addition, such problem-solving courts also call into question the historical purpose of the court system, since judges in these particular courts have dual roles as social worker and dispenser of justice (Neyfakh, 2014).

[...]

G. The Trajectory of the Accused into the Criminal Justice System

Immediately upon arrest, the accused begins the path into the court system. The American court system is a series of many routes that lead to several final outcomes, including acquittal, dismissal, diversion, conviction, and sentencing.

After arrest, the police will send the arrest report to the county district attorney's office for consideration of filing formal charges. The district attorney will dismiss either some or all of the charges. Those charges that will be filed require the defendant to proceed through the next court phase. In some states defendants who have been arrested on felony charges or are involved in high-profile cases will be subject to a **grand jury**. A grand jury is responsible for considering the evidence and/or witnesses to determine if there is sufficient evidence to formally charge (or indict) the defendant.

Arraignment

The next step in the court process after charges have been filed is **arraignment**. Arraignment is the court hearing where the judge informs defendant of the charges as well as his or her constitutional rights to due process. This is also the stage of the process where the defendant enters a plea (guilty or not guilty) to the charges. The court will set the **bail** (either a monetary or nonmonetary guarantee to return for future court dates) and impose protective orders (those that require the defendant to stay away from the victim or location) or other conditions (for example, a curfew or being required to stay away from codefendants who are also charged in this case) on the defendant while the case is being considered in court.

What is the sequence of events in the criminal justice system?

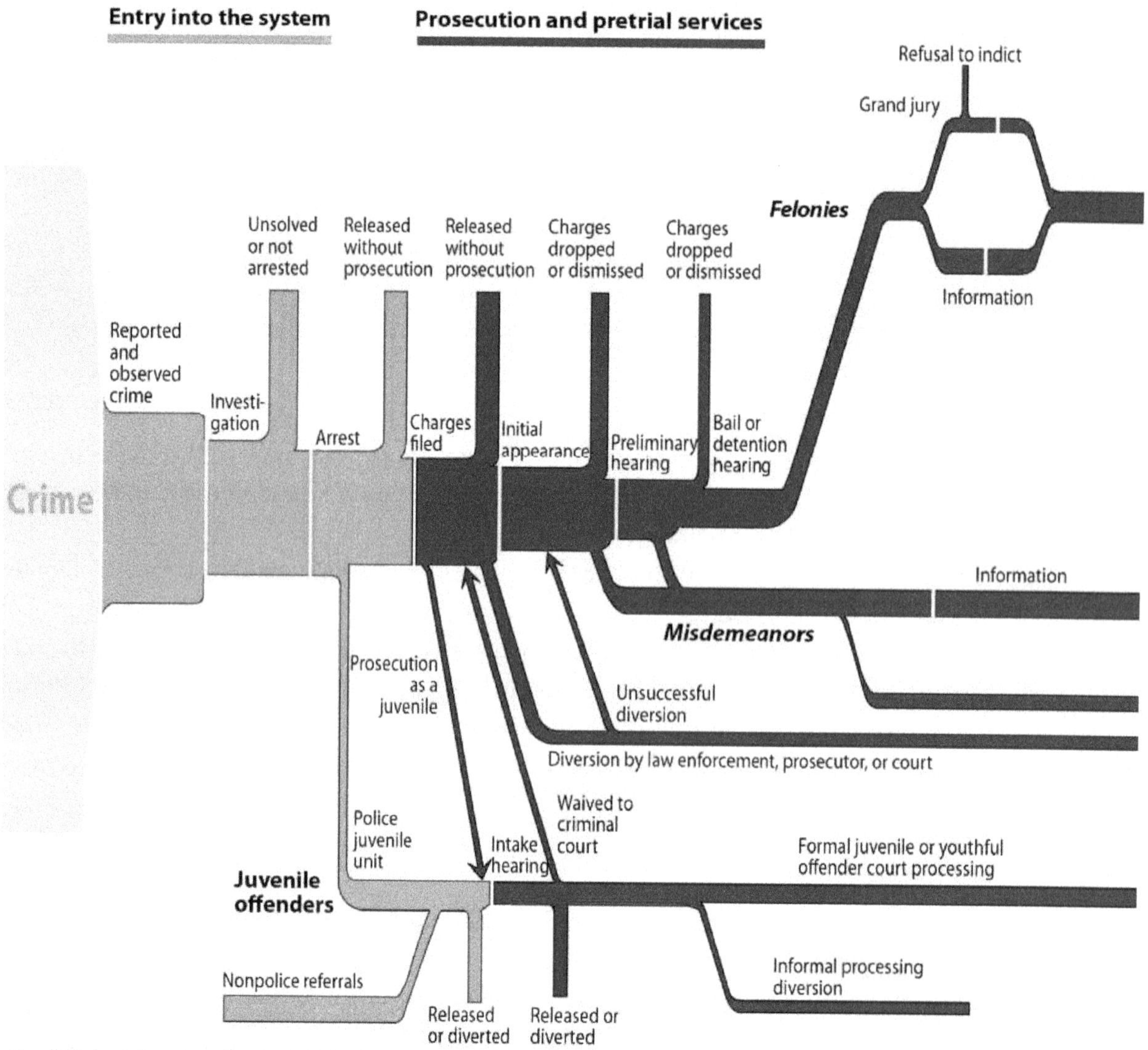

Note: This chart gives a simplified view of caseflow through the criminal justice system. Procedures vary among jurisdictions. The weights of the lines are not intended to show actual size of caseloads.

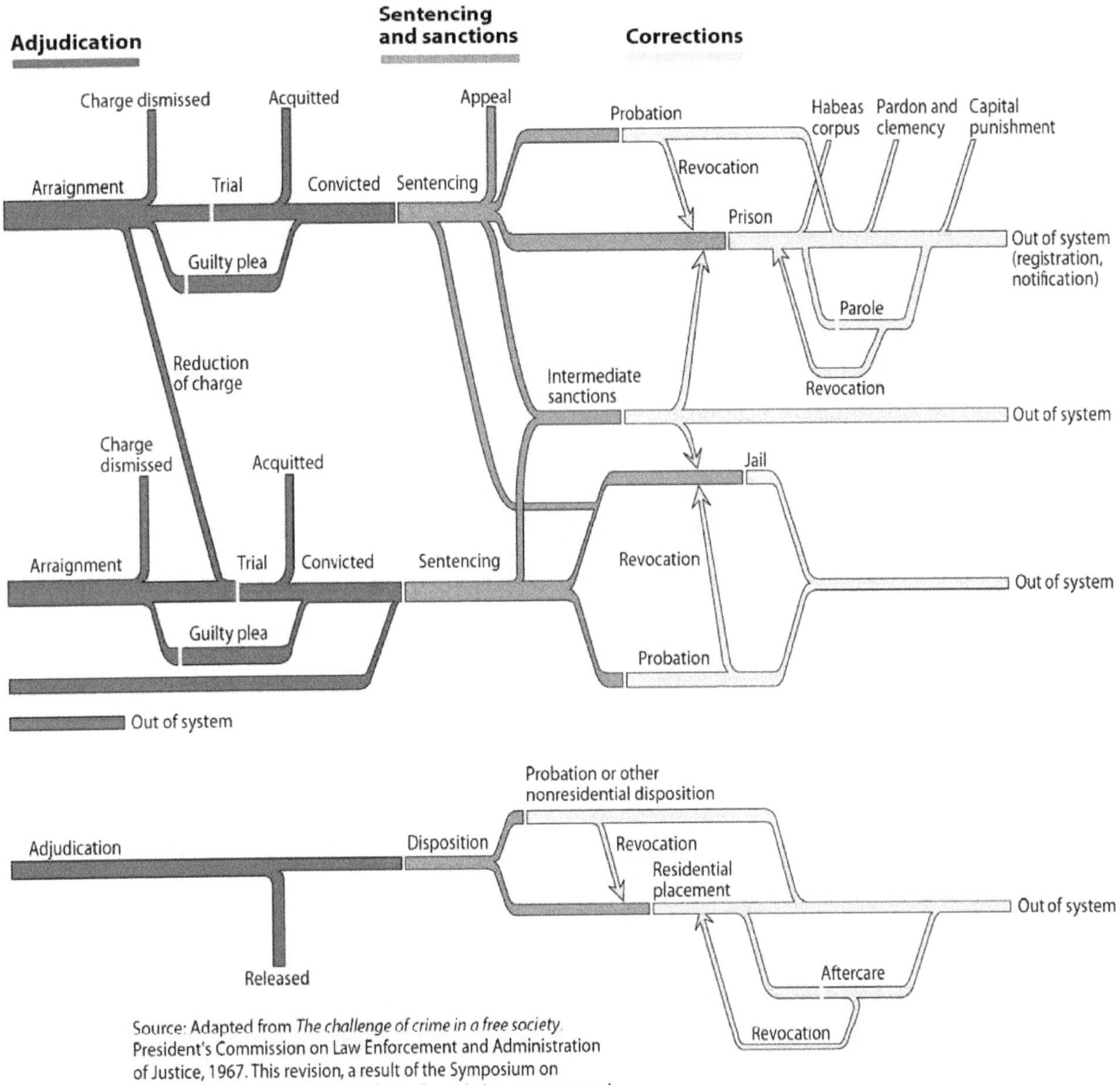

Source: Adapted from *The challenge of crime in a free society*. President's Commission on Law Enforcement and Administration of Justice, 1967. This revision, a result of the Symposium on the 30th Anniversary of the President's Commission, was prepared by the Bureau of Justice Statistics in 1997.

Preliminary Hearings

At the preliminary hearing the district attorney, the defense attorney, and the judge have the opportunity to assess the status of the case to determine if there is a sufficient basis to proceed with a trial. There is no set number of hearings. In the criminal courts, the burden is on the prosecution to bring forth evidence and witnesses against the defendant to establish that there is probable cause (which is a lower standard than beyond a reasonable doubt at trial) that the defendant committed the crimes alleged. In these hearings, the defense attorney is responsible for ensuring that the defendant's' rights are being upheld, specifically in relation to concerns of violations of the Fourth Amendment (unlawfully obtained evidence by the police) and/or Fifth Amendment rights (failure to read rights or unlawful confessions). Reliant on the rules of evidence, the judge's responsibility is to determine what evidence is sufficient to proceed with trial.

Trial

In the instances where the prosecution and the defense cannot agree to resolve the case, the matter will be held for trial. A **trial** is a legal event in which the prosecution is responsible for proving that the defendant was responsible for committing the crime charged. In criminal proceedings, the burden is on the prosecution to prove the case **beyond a reasonable doubt** (a level of certainty that the defendant did in fact commit the crime). In a civil trial, when the case that is tried is about legal responsibility, the legal standard for responsibility is based on the **preponderance of the evidence** (which assumes that more likely than not, the defendant was legally responsible). Trials can consist of two approaches: jury trials (a group of citizens who will determine guilt or innocence) or trial by judge (in which the judge is solely responsible for determining the outcome).

Jury Selection

Although jury service is typically viewed as an inconvenient obligation, it is a civic responsibility (absconders can face fines and possible jail time) and a critical component to the trial stage as well as a constitutional right for the accused. Selecting the jury has tremendous ramifications for both the prosecution and the defense. During jury selection, large pools of potential jurors are vetted based on their background (by completed juror questionnaires as well as attorney oral questions at the time of selection), attitudes on the criminal justice system, and possible allegiances to either the prosecution or the defense. This process (called **voir dire**) allows for judges and attorneys to challenge potential jurors in the effort of having a fair and impartial jury.

Stages Within the Trial

In most trials a typical format is followed. In the criminal court setting, since the burden is on the prosecution, it is always first to present in each stage. In **opening remarks**, the prosecution provides an introduction to the case, an overview of the evidence in the case, and an explanation of why the defendant should be found guilty. This is followed by remarks from the defense, whose role is to cast doubt on the defendant's culpability to commit the alleged offense. During **direct examination**, each side will ask its own witnesses questions related to the case. Additionally, the prosecution and the defense

will have the opportunity to challenge the testimony of the witnesses from the opposite side through **cross-examination**, as well as opportunities to recall past witnesses through **redirect examination**. At the conclusion of the trial, each side will surmise its position to the juror pool through **closing remarks**.

In today's courts the use of technology (namely the use of DNA, fingerprinting, ballistics, and other forms of physical, scientific evidence) has become a significant part of trials and has been further bolstered by popular culture television shows such as *CSI*. However, the inclusion of such physical evidence in terms of determining guilt or innocence serves as a mixed blessing. In one sense, physical evidence can either place the accused at the scene of the crime or eliminate the accused as the suspct (organizations such as the Innocence Project have used DNA evidence as a justification to release the wrongfully convicted from incarceration). However, there is an argument that jurors are becoming too dependent on such evidence to convict. In other words, there is a growing interest among jurors to have scientific certainty rather relying on beyond a reasonable doubt. Such a dependency on certainty may result in acquittals and arguably an injustice.

At each stage of the proceedings, the judge is charged with ruling over objections from the attorneys. During these objections, the judge may either **sustain** the objection (that is, there was an error committed either in the phrasing of a question or in the answer of a witness) or **overrule** the objection (that is, no error has been made and the trial may continue). The judge is also responsible for instructing the jury on the law as well as giving deliberating instructions prior to deliberation.

Verdict

After the jury deliberates, the jury foreperson will deliver the verdict form to the court clerk, who will then read the verdict aloud in court. If the defendant is found not guilty, the defendant's involvement in the criminal portion of the case is over. If the defendant is found guilty, in most cases he or she will be immediately **remanded** (detained) to county jail until sentencing.

H. Summary and Analysis of the American Court System

The American judicial system is, without question, one of the best court systems in the world. Its system and processes have withstood the shifting political identities of presidencies and members of Congress for more than 2 centuries. The institution has been the executor of social change and equality.

Beyond that, it subscribes to an essential mandate in which all accused persons who enter the legal process are entitled to due process and equal treatment under the law. Although this institution serves as a model to other countries around the world, it is certainly not without criticism or limitations.

A criticism to consider is the role of the victim in criminal court proceedings. Typically, the main parties in a criminal case involve the jurisdiction (represented by the prosecution) and the defendant (represented by a defense attorney). Until the past 20 years, victims (with exception to eyewitnesses or subpoenaed testimony) were rarely integral to this process. Victims' rights movements and funds for victims' assistance from the federal government have provided financial assistance for victims. Restorative justice (a system of criminal justice that focuses on the rehabilitation of offenders through reconciliation with victims and the community at large) has been implemented in many courts, but many crime victims still remain disconnected from the court process and feel a sense that their victimization is not taken into account during sentencing. This is a particular concern for survivors of violent crime and survivors of murder victims.

It is also important to recognize that the American judicial system has largely contributed to the largest prison population in the world as a result of draconian and publicly charged sentencing policies such as mandatory minimums, truth in sentencing, three-strikes laws, and harsh sentencing policies for those convicted of drug possession. Not only do these policies increase the state and federal prison rate, they remove the right of the sentencing judge to use discretion in determining a custom punishment.

Connected to the rate of high incarceration is the overrepresentation of minority and economically disenfranchised offenders who proceed through the nation's court system. Although such involvement begins prior to the court process (that is, at arrest), the reality is that poor defendants and defendants of color are more likely to suffer stricter pretrial and bail conditions, remain incarcerated while their case is being processed, and suffer the "pains of incarceration" (that is, employment and family interruption) than their White and/or affluent counterparts. As mentioned earlier in this [reading], the pressure to plea bargain their case remains very high for such defendants, who desire to end the court process quickly regardless of their guilt or innocence. Finally, it is important to consider that the American court system (as with other institutions within the criminal justice system) continues to magnify the growing root problems that exist within our society today, particularly in relation to the lack of access to educational and employment opportunities (especially to those with criminal records), family involvement and reunification, and financial investment in struggling communities. As mentioned in an earlier section, problem-solving courts focus on addressing these root cause issues; however, services are provided to those who are identified in the criminal justice system.

Discussion Questions

1. In your opinion, what group of defendants is most impacted in the criminal justice system—African Americans, women, or economically disenfranchised people?
2. How can victims be better served throughout the court process?
3. What consequences may be associated with the popular culture portrayal of courtroom proceedings?

References

655 F.3d 78

(2014). U.S. Courts of Appeals-Judicial Business 2014. United States Courts. Accessed at: http://www.uscourts.gov/statistics-reports/us-courts-appeals-judicial-business-201

(2015). Administrative Office of the Court of Appeals. United States Courts. Accessed at: http://www.uscourts.gov/about-federal-courts/types-cases/appeals

(2015). United States Courts. *Court Role and Structure. Accessed at: http://www.uscourts.gov/about-federal-courts/court-role-and-structure*

(2014). History, Justice Professionals pursue a vision. National Association of Drug Court Professionals. Accessed at: http://www.nadcp.org/learn/what-are-drug-courts/drug-court-history

(2014). National Center for State Courts. Judicial Selection in the States. Accessed at: Carter, D. T. (1979). *Scottsboro: A tragedy of the American South* (rev. ed.). Baton Rouge: Louisiana State University Press.

Cohen, T. D. & Reaves, B. A. (2007). Pretrial release of felony defendants in state courts (NCJ 214994). Bureau of Justice Statistics. U.S. Department of Justice. Retrieved from: http://www.bjs.gov/content/pub/pdf/prfdsc.pdf

Demuth, S. (2003) Racial and ethnic differences in pretrial release decision and outcomes: a comparison of Latino, Black, and White felony arrestees. Criminology, 41:873–907.

Farole, D. (2010). A national assessment of public defender office caseloads. Bureau of Justice Statistics. Presented at Justice Research and Statistics Association Annual Meeting. Retrieved from http://www.jrsa.org/events/conference/presentations-10/Donald_Farole.pdf

Herberman, E., & Kyckelhahn, T. (2014). State government indigent defense expenditures, FY 2008–2012. Bureau of Justice Statistics. Retrieved from http://www.bjs.gov/content/pub/pdf/sgide0812.pdf

Judicial Council of California. (2013). Court statistics report: Statewide trends 2002–2003 through 2011–2012. Retrieved from http://www.courts.ca.gov/documents/2013-Court-Statistics-Report.pdf

Kohler, S. (1962). Case 29: Vera Institute of Justice: Manhattan Bail Project. Ford Foundation. Retrieved from https://cspcs.sanford.duke.edu/sites/default/files/descriptive/manhattan_bail_project.pdf

Labriola, M., Bradley, S., O'Sullivan, C. S., Rempel, M., & Moore, S. (2009). *A national portrait of domestic violence courts*. New York: Center for Court Innovation.

Lynch, T. (2003). The case against plea bargaining. Regulation. Cato Institute. Retrieved from http://www.cato.org/sites/cato.org/files/serials/files/regulation/2003/10/v26n3-7.pdf

Mazur, R., & Aldrich, L. (2003). What makes a domestic violence court work? Lessons from New York. *Judges' Journal*, American Bar Association. Retrieved from http://www.courtinnovation.org/pdf/what_makes_dvcourt_work.pdf

Neyfakh, L. (2014, March 23). The custom justice of 'problem-solving courts': A new kind of court is reshaping the American legal system—with little oversight. *Boston Globe*. Retrieved from https://www.bostonglobe.com/ideas/2014/03/22/the-custom-justice-problem-solving-courts/PQJLC758Sgw7qQhiefT6MM/story.html

Reaves, B. (2013). Felony defendants in large urban counties, 2009–Statistical Tables. State Court Processing Statistics, Bureau of Justice Statistics. Retrieved from http://www.bjs.gov/index.cfm?ty=pbdetail&iid=4845

Rempel, M., Green, M., & Kralstein, D. (2012). The impact of adult drug courts on crime and incarceration: Findings from a multi-site quasi-experimental design. *Journal of Experimental Criminology, 8*(2), 165–192.

Schlesinger, T. (2005). Racial and ethnic disparity in pretrial criminal processing. *JQ: Justice Quarterly*, 22(2), 170–192.

Truman, J. L., & Morgan, R. E. (2014). Nonfatal domestic violence, 2003–2012 (NCJ 244697). Bureau of Justice Statistics. Retrieved from http://www.bjs.gov/content/pub/pdf/ndv0312.pdf

United States v. Dzhokhar Tsarnaev, 2013 (13-cr-10200)

US Const. amend. IV

US Const. amend. VI

US Const. amend. VIII

US Const. amend. XIV

U.S.C. § 844

U.S.C. § 2332

U.S.C. § 2332a

READING 3.2

PEOPLE AND PROBLEMS IN THE COURTS

Lawerence F. Travis III

IMPORTANT TERMS

assigned counsel
community justice
contract systems
courtroom work group
indigent
innocence projects
jury
jury nullification
Missouri Plan
panel attorneys
peremptory challenges
plea bargaining
priority prosecution
privately retained counsel
pro se defense
prosecutorial case management
public defender
special prosecutor
venire
vertical prosecution
voir dire
wrongful convicton

FOUR SETS OF PEOPLE PLAY MAJOR roles in the court segment of the justice system: (1) defense attorneys, (2) prosecutors, (3) judges, and (4) jurors. These are the people who have a direct effect on decisions in the criminal courts. With the exception of jurors, who are usually typical citizens, all are trained in the law and therefore share a common culture (Glick, 1983:2–3; Holten & Lamar, 1991:115–119). In many ways, prosecutors and defense attorneys are similar, except for the fact that they are adversaries at trial. Very often, judges are recruited from the ranks of prosecutors and (to a lesser extent) defense attorneys. As a result, judges not only share a common training and educational experience, they often share common career paths.

Defense Attorneys

In the field of law, criminal law is not a particularly well-respected specialty (Neubauer, 1984:156). Wice (1978) studied defense attorneys across the country and reported that defense counsel generally were solo practitioners or attorneys working in small offices (with two or three associates). They usually began their private practices late in life, and many obtained their criminal law experience and training in prosecutor's offices. Most were not graduates of the nation's best law schools, and their salaries were generally on the lower end of the earnings scale for the legal profession. As Neubauer (1984:157) reported, "Most lawyers view criminal cases as unsavory." Of the hundreds of thousands of attorneys in the United States, fewer than 50,000 will take criminal cases. The number of criminal law specialists is probably in the vicinity of only 5,000 (Bartollas, Miller & Wice, 1983; Glick, 1983; Neubauer, 1984).

Of those attorneys who routinely do take criminal cases, many do so on a part-time basis to supplement their earnings from a general law practice. Criminal defense services typically are provided by young, inexperienced attorneys, or by older, somewhat less successful attorneys. As Holten and Lamar (1991:124) observe, "The field (criminal defense law) does seem to attract more than its share of marginal practitioners." Among several reasons given to explain the attraction of marginal practitioners is that much of criminal defense work is mundane and uncomplicated. One result of the *Gideon* and *Argersinger* decisions [...] has been an increase in criminal defense work for attorneys. By requiring that defense counsel be appointed for **indigent** (i.e., poor) defendants, these decisions place the burden of paying for defense on the government when the defendant is poor. Nationally the annual cost of providing defense counsel to indigent defendants has been estimated at between 3 and 4 billion dollars.

Traditional defense services were available to a defendant only if he or she could afford to retain the services of an attorney. **Privately retained counsel** is still an option for criminal defendants today, and involves the defendant hiring his or her own attorney, who for a fee then represents the defendant at trial and in all other stages of the court process. For those unable to pay an attorney, however, the effect of the Supreme Court's decisions on the right to counsel has been the development of alternative systems for the provision of defense services. The most common are the creation of a public defender's office and the use of assigned counsel. Box 3.2.1 compares these two systems. About half of all criminal jurisdictions use combinations of indigent defense services (see Box 3.2.2).

Privately retained counsel, public defenders, and assigned counsel comprise the three major methods of securing representation for criminal defendants. A fourth method, **contract systems** (those in which defense services for the poor are secured by contract with a private attorney, the local bar association, or a private law firm), is used in fewer than 10 percent of counties (Harlow, 2000:4). In most states the county is responsible for providing indigent defense services. In the 100 most populous counties, almost 60 percent of indigent defense costs are paid by county governments (DeFrances & Litras, 2000).

In terms of the volume of cases handled, the most common of these forms is the public defender's office (Rubin, 1984:201). Larger jurisdictions (those having the heaviest caseloads) are likely to operate a public defender's office that mirrors the prosecutor's office. In many jurisdictions, the

Box 3.2.1

Characteristics of Public Defender and Assigned Counsel Systems

Summary of public defender system characteristics	
Characteristics	Percent of public defender counties
Affiliation	
County government	38%
State executive agency	25
Judiciary	23
Independent nonprofit organization	8
Other	6
Chief public defenders	
Full-time	78
Part-time	22
Number of full-time staff attorneys	
0	24
1-6	59
7-20	10
21-50+	7
Support staffing	
Secretaries	86
Investigators	58
Administrative assistants	18
Law students	16
Paralegal employees	10
Social workers	9
Fiscal officer	6
Training director	3
Salary ranges	
Full-time chief public defenders	
$6,000-$66,000 (yearly)	
$20,000-30,000 (modal)	

Summary of characteristics of assigned counsel systems	
Characteristics	Percent of assigned counsel counties
Administrative	
Ad hoc (appointments made by individual judges, clerks, public defenders, or others)	75%
Coordinated	25
Lists of available attorneys	
• Compiled on basis of:*	
Lawyers who affirmatively volunteer	43
Inclusion of all lawyers	35
Volunteers who qualify	27
Volunteers who participate in continuing legal education	8
• Categorized according to attorneys' specialization in lists	19
• Established procedures for formal removal	15
Caseload	
Cases distributed among most of the attorneys on the list	44
Average of 1 to 10 cases per assigned counsel	75

* Total exceeds 100% because multiple methods are used.

Source: The Spangenberg Group (1986), National Criminal Defense Systems Study: Final Report *(Washington, DC: U.S. Department of Justice):15, 17.*

Box 3.2.2

Types of Indigent Defense Systems, Percent of Local Jurisdictions Reporting Each Type

Defense System	Percent
Single Systems:	
Public Defender Only	20.8
Assigned Counsel Only	19.3
Contract Attorney Only	7.1
Combined Systems:	
Public Defender and:	
Assigned Counsel	31.0
Contract Attorney	9.6
Both	6.4
Assigned Counsel and:	
Contract Attorney	5.7

Source: C. Harlow (2000), Defense Counsel in Criminal Cases *(Washington, DC: Bureau of Justice Statistics):4.*

public defender is elected and authorized to employ a number of assistant public defenders to serve all indigent defendants. In these systems, the defense attorneys work for the municipality on salary. Young attorneys often seek these positions in order to develop trial experience prior to beginning their own private practices. Some older attorneys, weary of the rigors of private practice, also take positions with the public defender's office. Box 3.2.3 shows the distribution of criminal defense systems by number of counties and size of the populations served. Box 3.2.4 shows the major form of defense system used in each state.

The **assigned counsel** system (often in conjunction with some other form of defense, e.g., a public defender) is used in the majority of criminal jurisdictions, but serves fewer than half of all indigent criminal defendants. In jurisdictions in which criminal caseloads usually are not large enough to justify the expense of developing and operating public defenders' offices, assigned counsel are used. In this system, attorneys voluntarily enter their names to be considered for criminal defense work or, in some places, all members of the local bar are enrolled on the defender's list. As indigents come before the court, the judge appoints an attorney from the list, moving down

Box 3.2.3

Distribution of Indigent [System] Types by Percentage of Counties and Population Served

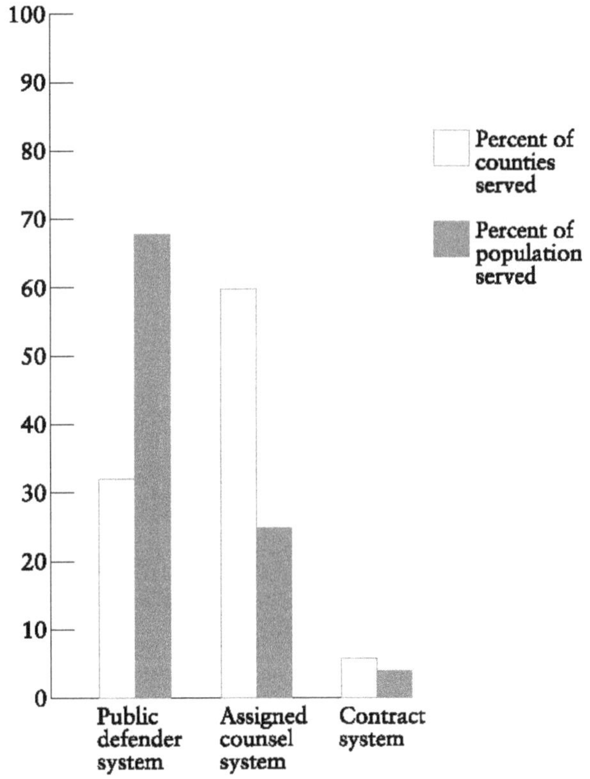

Source: The Spangenberg Group (1986), National Criminal Defense Systems Study: Final Report *(Washington, DC: U.S. Department of Justice):14.*

the list of attorney names as cases are initiated. In this system, the assigned counsel generally is paid a fee based on an hourly rate, but with a maximum. The fee paid generally is less than an attorney would charge a private client (especially when all members of the bar appear on the list). Again, because of the relatively low fees available under this system, only younger, less established attorneys tend to seek out assigned counsel appointments. In the federal system, assigned counsel are referred to as **panel attorneys** because defense counsel are assigned from a list or panel of approved lawyers. Similarly, the "public defender" system in the federal district courts consists of the federal defender organizations, which include both the federal public defender's office and community defender organizations where applicable.

Box 3.2.4

Criminal Defense Systems Most Commonly Used by the States

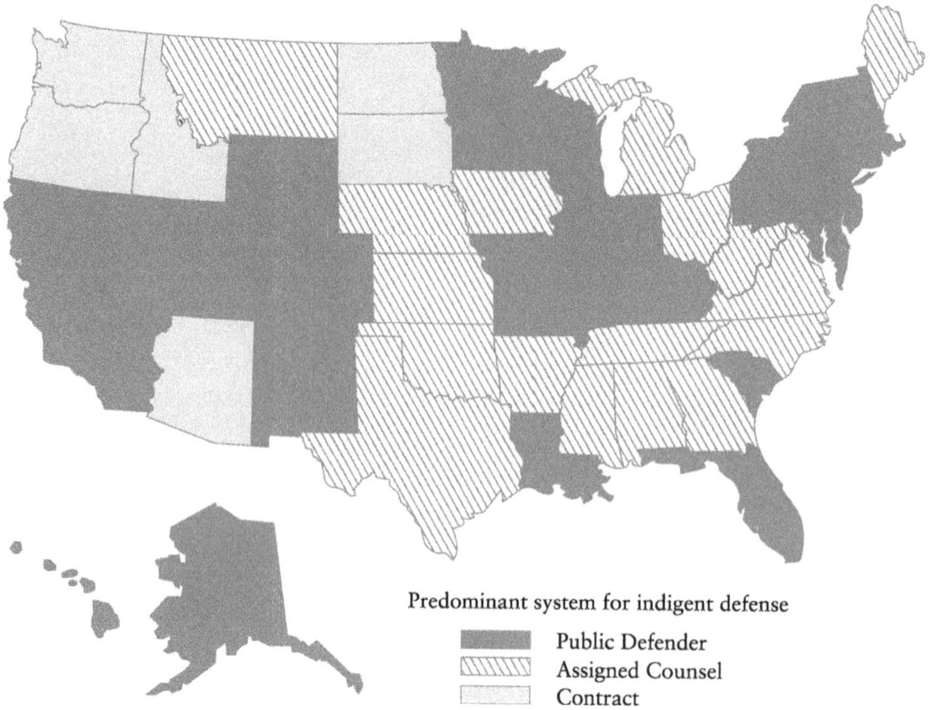

Source: Bureau of Justice Statistics (1988), Report to the Nation on Crime and Justice, *2nd ed. (Washington, DC: U.S. Department of Justice):75.*

There is great variation in the cost of publicly provided defense counsel (The Spangenberg Group, 2007). Costs vary from state to state, within states by county or judicial district, and, often, by type of case. In general, death penalty cases are more expensive than noncapital felonies, which are often more expensive than misdemeanor cases. The American Bar Association reported that the hourly compensation for court-appointed counsel in noncapital cases ranged from a low of $35 per hour for work outside of court in Cook County (Chicago) Illinois to more than $120 per hour for some cases in Texas. The federal rate of compensation was $92 per hour. In fiscal year 2002, the state and federal governments spent more than $3 billion for indigent defense.

There has been some debate regarding which of these systems provides the best defense services to the accused. Traditionally, it has been expected that privately retained counsel, as a result of the clear relationship between who is paying for service and who is receiving service, would provide the best defense. However, analyses comparing privately retained counsel with publicly appointed attorneys have not demonstrated any significant differences in the quality of service provided (Wice & Suwak, 1974). There is some research that indicates that defendants with privately retained counsel may fare better in the judicial process than those with public defenders (Champion, 1989).

Harlow (2000) reported that about 80 percent of defendants in the largest counties were represented by public defenders or assigned counsel, and that about 74 percent of prison inmates had been represented by public defenders or assigned counsel, indicating that type of counsel makes no difference in terms of imprisonment. He reported that just over three-quarters of defendants were convicted regardless of form of representation. Defendants represented by publicly paid defense attorneys were more likely to receive a sentence to jail or prison, but for shorter terms than those represented by privately retained counsel. Box 3.2.5 compares the experiences with defense counsel reported by prison inmates.

A final option for defendants in criminal cases is to defend themselves. Less than 1 percent of felony defendants in the largest counties represented themselves in 1996 (Harlow, 2000:5). Given the adage that "a lawyer who represents himself has a fool for a client," do defendants have the right to make fools of themselves? The U.S. Supreme Court has decided that they do. In *People v. Faretta* (1975), the defendant, Faretta, sought self-representation, but the trial judge denied his request, insisting that Faretta accept the assistance of appointed defense counsel. Faretta appealed, arguing that it was his right to represent himself at trial. The Supreme Court agreed with Faretta that self-representation (***pro se* defense**) is a constitutional right of the defendant. What has not yet been decided, however, is whether a *pro se* defendant who loses in court can appeal the conviction on the basis of incompetent representation.

While relatively rare, *pro se* defenses do occur. Sometimes a defendant feels that no one else can, or will, present the case as well. More often, these defenses occur when the defendant is interested in using the courtroom as a forum for expressing some viewpoint, rather than as a place for settling a criminal case. An article appearing in *Time* (1977) described some of the pitfalls that can upset a *pro se* defense. Among them are cases in which defendants make incriminating statements (e.g., asking a witness how, since the perpetrator was wearing a mask, she could be so sure he was the offender), fail to follow proper procedure, or underestimate the strength of the state's case.

Prosecutors

Unlike defense services, there is no privately retained prosecutor. Rather, prosecutors are usually elected officials whose duty is to provide legal counsel for the state in criminal trials. Only three states (Alaska, Connecticut, and New Jersey) have appointed prosecutors. Depending on the size

Box 3.2.5

State Prison Inmate Reports of Court Experiences by Type of Defense Counsel

	Type of Counsel	
Experience	**Private**	**Public**
Contact with Counsel:		
Within a day of arrest	8.8	26.3%
Within a week of arrest	27.7	33.9
More than a week before trial	32.8	29.6
Within a week of trial	12.6	4.8
At trial	13.6	3.5
None	4.5	1.9
Number of Contacts with Counsel:		
0	4.6%	2.0%
1	24.6	9.6
2-3	44.5	30.6
4-5	13.4	20.7
6 or more	12.9	37.2
Type of Plea:		
Not Guilty	24.3%	31.4%
Guilty	60.6	54.7
No Contest	11.1	10.3
Other	6.7	7.0

Source: C. Harlow (2000), Defense Counsel in Criminal Cases *(Washington, DC: Bureau of Justice Statistics):8.*

of the jurisdiction and the size of its criminal caseload, prosecutors may be either full-time or part-time. Nationally, about 75 percent of chief prosecutors are full-time, and 70 percent of prosecutor's offices also employ at least one full-time assistant prosecutor (Perry, 2006:3). Depending on the size of the prosecutor's office, the prosecutor (frequently called the county attorney, state's attorney or district attorney) may actually serve as a manager, rarely engaging in trial preparation or courtroom appearances. Box 3.2.6 describes the distribution of staff in prosecutor's offices in the United States.

Box 3.2.6

Personnel Categories in Prosecutor's Offices

Position	Percent of Personnel
Chief Prosecutor	3%
Assistant Prosecutor	31
Support Staff	35
Staff Investigators	9
Managers/Supervisors	6
Civil Attorneys	6
Victim Advocates	6
Other	3
Total	100
Estimated total personnel: 78,000	

Source: S. Perry (2006), Prosecutors in State Courts, 2005 *(Washington, DC: Bureau of Justice Statistics):2.*

Prosecutors usually are locally elected for a specified term. In 1990, 97 percent of prosecutors were elected, and the average term was about four years (Dawson, 1992:2). In 2001, the average chief prosecutor had been in office for almost seven years. In the largest jurisdictions, prosecutors work full-time and hire assistants who provide the bulk of legal services of the office. These assistants are salaried employees of the municipality. The overwhelming majority of assistant prosecutor positions are full-time appointments. These positions are most attractive to young attorneys seeking trial experience and to older attorneys who do not wish to engage in private practice or who have not been able to secure a position with a larger law firm. In 2001, almost one-third of prosecutor's offices reported having trouble recruiting or retaining assistant prosecutors, most saying the problem was caused by low salaries (DeFrances, 2002:3).

At the federal level, prosecutorial services are provided by United States Attorneys. United States Attorneys are presidential appointees who are empowered to employ assistants to handle federal criminal cases. In addition, the federal government (as well as some state and municipal governments) sometimes creates an Office of the Special Prosecutor, where an attorney is employed to investigate and prosecute cases arising out of some special circumstance, such as the Watergate investigation during the Nixon administration or the Whitewater investigation during the Clinton administration. A **special prosecutor** is employed when there is concern about possible conflicts of interest, or when a case is so complex that the need to perform the ordinary duties of the prosecutor's office would render it impossible for that office to pursue the case adequately. In the Watergate and Whitewater examples, because the United States Attorneys are appointed by the President, it might be difficult for one of them to investigate criminal allegations against the president.

While similar in many respects, one major difference between the prosecutor's office and the public defender's office is that the prosecutor's office traditionally has been a stepping-stone for political careers. Partly as a result of its elective nature, and partly because the prosecutor can garner considerable media coverage by tackling certain cases (pornography, white-collar crime, child abuse, etc.), the office of prosecutor enables incumbents to prepare for political advancement. An attorney who is interested in a political career as a judge or other elected official often begins in the prosecutor's office (Stumpf, 1988:179-181). Unlike the prosecutor, the public defender generally does not gain voter support, mostly because he or she earns a living by defending the accused (who may be pornographers, child molesters, or other unsavory characters).

Judges

In 2005, there were more than 30,000 judgeships, including appellate courts and courts of limited jurisdiction (Rottman & Strickland, 2006). Judgeships are prestigious positions. To many attorneys, becoming a judge represents the pinnacle of a legal career (Neely, 1983). Compared to the general practice of law, being a judge is more prestigious, more secure, and less stressful. The overwhelming majority of the nation's judges achieve their offices through election. Unfortunately, judicial elections—at least as measured by voter turnout—generally do not provoke much citizen interest. Yet, the selection of judges is important because the characteristics of the judge are often what determine the outcome of a case, more so than does the nature of the case itself (Eisenstein & Jacob, 1977; Jackson, 1974; Levin, 1977).

There are two basic methods by which judges are selected in the United States: election and appointment. In the case of elections, states determine whether judicial races are allowed to be partisan or whether they must be nonpartisan in nature. In elections, judges run for office in much the same way as mayors or state legislators. In states having appointment processes, the governor or state legislature is empowered to appoint judges to office. For years there has been debate about how best to ensure that those selected for judicial positions have the requisite qualifications for the job. Generally, the debate has focused on either the election of judges or on the "Missouri Plan."

In the **Missouri Plan** (so named because it originated in the state of Missouri), a judicial nominating commission rates the qualifications of candidates and identifies qualified candidates or recommends appointment to the governor (Reddick, 2002). The governor appoints someone from the list of qualified/recommended candidates. The appointed judge must then periodically face an uncontested "retention election," in which the sole question before the voters is whether the judge should be retained in office. Should the voters decide to oust the judge, the governor appoints another from a list of qualified candidates. The process is then repeated. Supporters of this system of judicial selection argue that it provides the best of all worlds; that is, the system includes direct voter input in the selection of judges through the retention election, yet it ensures that only qualified candidates become judges and that those judges are at least somewhat insulated from political pressure and isolated from partisan politics. However, the evidence is not clear that this method of choosing judges is better than direct election (Nagel, 1973). Box 3.2.7 describes the methods by which judges are selected in the United States.

Box 3.2.7

Methods of Judicial Selection for Judges of State General Jurisdiction Courts

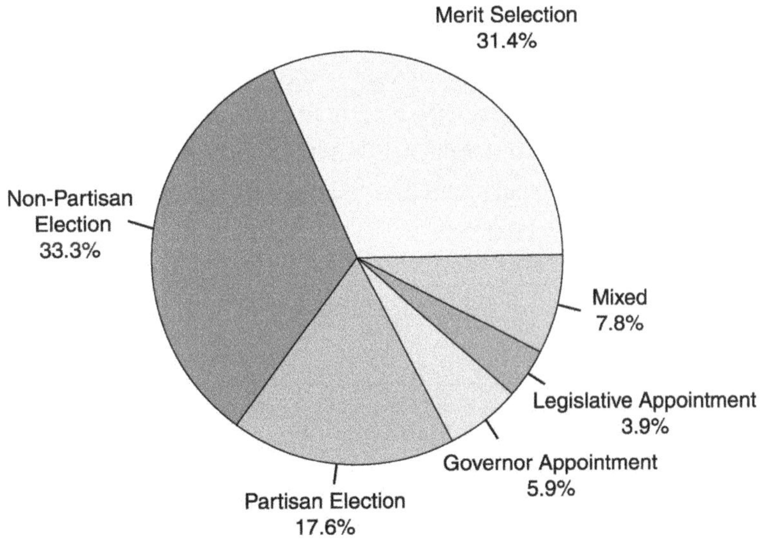

Source: American Judicature Society (2004), Judicial Selection in the States *(Des Moines: American Judicature Society).*

The federal judicial system operates differently in that federal judges are appointed for life terms by the President of the United States. The President generally accepts nominations from the senators of the state in which the district court judge will serve, but he or she is not required to do so. The candidate is then nominated by the President, whose final appointment of the judge is subject to the advice and consent of the Senate. Controversy about the appointment of Supreme Court justices during the Reagan administration illustrated the hazards of Senate confirmation faced by federal judicial nominees.

In the autumn of 1987, then-President Reagan nominated three candidates before he was able to obtain the consent of the Senate. Seeking conservative justices who would be strict constructionists in their interpretation of constitutional issues, the President nominated Judge Robert Bork, followed by Judge Douglas Ginsburg and Judge Anthony M. Kennedy. An active senatorial committee dominated by Democrats closely investigated all three candidates. Judge Bork was found unacceptable on the basis of his record on equal rights issues. Judge Ginsburg removed his name from consideration after acknowledging that he had experimented with marijuana in his youth (*Criminal Justice Newsletter*, 1987). The third nominee, Judge Kennedy, won Senate approval. The controversy surrounding the confirmation hearings on the appointment of Justice Clarence Thomas (President George H.W. Bush's nominee) also illustrates the confirmation process. Justice Thomas was eventually confirmed, despite great controversy regarding charges of sexual harassment.

The principal difference between the federal and state judiciaries is the tenure of judicial office in each. State judges (except those in Rhode Island), no matter how selected, undergo periodic review and face possible removal without impeachment. Judges in Rhode Island, like federal judges, are granted lifetime tenure upon appointment to the bench. Lifetime tenure insulates the judge from improper political or other influence, but it also means that incompetent or corrupt judges cannot easily be removed from office. The removal of a federal judge, for example, can be accomplished only through impeachment.

Jurors

The last important set of decisionmakers in the criminal courts is the jury. The jury is a panel of citizens, selected through the process of **voir dire** (literally, to speak the truth), who are charged with hearing cases and determining guilt or innocence. While rarely used, the criminal trial jury is symbolically important as evidence that the citizenry reigns. The right to a jury trial is provided for in the Constitution of the United States. Regardless of the testimony and other evidence presented at trial, the verdict of the jury is almost totally within its discretion, and it is binding on the court. Only in very rare instances can the defense attorney succeed in convincing the judge to order a directed verdict of acquittal. This occurs when, at the conclusion of presenting its case, the prosecution has failed to provide enough evidence about some important element of the offense. In such cases, the defense counsel requests that charges be dropped because the prosecution has failed to establish its case.

Because of the tremendous discretionary power of the jury, prosecutors and defense attorneys are very careful in the jury selection (*voir dire*) process. Each side is awarded a number of **peremptory challenges**, which allow them to remove otherwise qualified jurors from service. In addition, each side may challenge any number of prospective jurors for cause. Thus, during the selection process, prospective jurors may be asked about how they feel about the defendant, whether they know about the case, and other such questions. Any answer may be cause for a challenge. Peremptory challenges are used by attorneys when they cannot establish a just cause for keeping someone off the jury, yet they believe that the individual will not be receptive to their case.

Both the prosecution and the defense seek to seat jurors whom they believe will support their respective presentations of the case. In many ways, jury selection is the most important part of the trial process (Fried, Kaplan & Klein, 1975). Just as judicial decisions reflect the characteristics of the judge, jury decisions reflect the characteristics of the jury (Kalven & Zeisel, 1966; Simon, 1980). Turner and colleagues (1986) reported that prosecutors and defense attorneys agree, for example, that black jurors are more likely to vote for acquittal, while white jurors are usually in favor of conviction.

Prospective jurors usually are randomly selected from the population within a court's jurisdiction. These prospective jurors form a panel (called the **venire**) from which the attorneys select (through the voir dire process) members who will serve on the jury. Representativeness of the panel of jurors is a thorny issue. In order to ensure that juries reflect the characteristics of the community, courts select prospective juror names from voter registration lists, driver's license records, public utility customer records, city/county directories, tax rolls, and other lists that are likely to include all potential jurors (Rottman & Strickland, 2006). Members of the venire are then randomly sampled from the list. This process, however, frequently fails to produce a representative sample (Fukurai, Butler & Krooth, 1991). Not only do juries frequently lack proportionate representation of minorities, those minorities selected for jury duty tend to come from higher social class standings than might be desired. Thus, jury selection seems to discriminate against minorities in general, and lower-class minorities in particular (Fukurai, 1996). Some persons are exempt from jury duty. The list of exemptions varies from state to state but typically includes certain professions (attorneys, physicians, etc.), public safety and active military members, and those with health problems. Half the states do not identify any exemptions from jury duty, but the judge can choose to dismiss a prospective juror.

During the voir dire process, both prosecution and defense seek to identify possible biases in the potential jurors through their responses to questions. Seltzer, Venuti, and Lopes (1991) reported that nearly 40 percent of jurors were untruthful during the voir dire. Jurors were most likely to lie about whether they or members of their families had been crime victims and whether they knew police officers. While Seltzer, Venuti, and Lopes conclude that juror dishonesty undermines the prospects for a fair trial, their analysis showed no significant differences in the verdicts rendered by truthful and untruthful jurors.

The selection of jury members is important in part because the jury is empowered to decide the ultimate fate of a case. The tradition of English and American law is that the jury can nullify a law by voting to acquit even if the evidence supports conviction. **Jury nullification** occurs when jurors refuse to convict a guilty defendant because of their belief that the law or the government's use of the law in that case is unjust (Simon, 1992). Reviewing the verdict in the Marion Barry trial, Rita Simon argued that the decision to acquit Barry on the felony perjury charges was an example of jury nullification. She suggests that the six African-American jurors refused to convict the defendant because they saw the case as an example of government injustice in which police entrapped the mayor. Controversy about jury nullification has escalated in recent years, especially as crime control policies such as the "war on drugs" are seen to have disproportionate effects on minority group members. The highly publicized murder trial of retired football star O.J. Simpson has been cited by some observers as a case in which the jury ignored the facts and thereby nullified the law (Zatz, 2000). In fact, several jurors believed that the evidence against Simpson had been planted by Los Angeles police. In their view, Simpson had been framed, and the evidence was not believable.

O.J. Simpson, center, clenches his fists in victory after the jury finds him not guilty of the murders of his ex-wife Nicole Brown Simpson and her friend Ronald Goldman. Some observers have cited this case as an example of jury nullification, whereby the jury refuses to convict a guilty defendant because of their belief that the government's use of the law is unjust. Later, a jury in a wrongful-death civil trial found Simpson liable in the deaths of Brown Simpson and Goldman. *Photo credit: AP Photo/Myung Chun.*

Problems in the Criminal Courts

As with every stage of the justice system, the court process is plagued with problems and issues that defy easy resolution. Some have been touched upon earlier in this reading, such as the best mechanism for the provision of defense counsel, the effects of judicial selection, and the process of jury selection. Four additional issues have been identified for further consideration in this section: (1) speedy trial, (2) the role of the press in the trial process, (3) the development of "community courts," and (4) plea bargaining. With severe overcrowding in the nation's jails and hundreds of persons accused of terrorist connections or plans, the right to a speedy trial is again an important practical and constitutional issue. Court delay contributes to jail crowding as defendants wait for hearings and trials. There is also a debate about whether suspects arrested after the September 11, 2001, terrorist attacks and as a result of ongoing anti-terror investigations should be tried in criminal or military courts, and how long the government can hold these persons without trial (Lynch, 2002). The role of the press in trials is also still unresolved. This issue, which was particularly important during the political trials of the student anti-war and civil rights activists in the early 1970s, has resurfaced and again gained prominence with the war on terror. Additional issues involve the role of citizens in the courts and the impact of technology on court operations.

Speedy Trial

The issue embodied in the phrase "speedy trial" is most often thought of as court delay. That is, speedy trial is the solution to the problem of what some perceive as unacceptable delays in the processing of criminal cases from arrest to disposition. The concern over court delay is founded on three related, but different, perspectives (Bureau of Justice Statistics, 1986): (1) there are those who advocate speedy trials for the protection of the rights of the defendant; (2) there are those who see speedy trials as the solution to some of the mistreatment of crime victims by the justice system; and (3) there are those who propose speedy trials as a crime-control strategy.

Lengthy delays between arrest and trial (or between charging and trial) can be to the disadvantage of criminal defendants. Especially in those cases in which the defendant is unable to make bail, denial of a speedy trial amounts to incarceration prior to conviction. By virtue of their inability to obtain pretrial release, defendants awaiting trial for long periods of time are likely to suffer further losses, such as loss of income (if not loss of job), possible loss of residence, separation from family and friends, and, upon conviction, higher rates of incarceration. Thus, at least one group proposes speedy trial as a protected right of the defendant (American Bar Association, 1968). Delays in the prosecution of defendants arrested as terror suspects have raised a number of issues about the right to a speedy trial. An example is the case of José Padilla, an American citizen arrested in Chicago and charged with terrorism. Padilla was arrested as an "enemy combatant" and held for more than two years without being formally charged. In 2004 the U.S. Supreme Court avoided ruling in the case when it noted that Padilla's *habeas corpus* appeal against Defense Secretary Donald Rumsfeld was mistaken and should have been filed against the commander of the military prison in which he was housed (*Rumsfeld v. Padilla*, 2004). While the court has allowed continued detention without trial of foreign combatants, as formal hostilities end, the question of speedy trial rights will come to the fore.

Crime victims frequently are ignored by the justice system. Indeed, the role of the victim in the justice process, if anything, is generally that of witness. The justice system is not designed to alleviate the suffering of crime victims. Lengthy court proceedings, especially those in which the victim is involved as a witness, result in lost work days, mental anguish while awaiting resolution of the case, delays in recouping stolen property, and other costs to the victim. While speedy trials act to the advantage of the accused (especially the innocent accused), it has been suggested that the crime victim has a stake in the early resolution of a criminal case (Walker, 1985:141). In the past two decades, concern for the plight of crime victims has led to the development of victim and witness service programs across the country (Smith & Huff, 1992). Today, the federal office for crime victims lists more than 10,000 programs in its online directory (Office for Victims of Crime, 2008).

Yet another reason for speedy trials is the desire to control crime. Pretrial delays are often blamed for high rates of plea bargaining. Plea bargaining, in turn, is blamed for the lack of deterrent effect of the criminal law. A more quantifiable effect of case processing delays on crime, however, may be the amount of crime committed by criminal defendants who are free on bail and at large in the community. Reaves and Perez (1994:11) reported that 14 percent of felons granted pretrial release were rearrested while awaiting trial. The longer a defendant is at liberty on bail, the greater the likelihood that he or she will commit a new crime while awaiting trial. Speedier trials and convictions (especially those resulting in incarceration) would reduce at least this one aspect of crime (Walker, 1985:53). Finally, the longer the period is between when a crime occurs and when the trial is held, the more difficult it is to secure a conviction. Witnesses sometimes move or die, memories fail, outrage at the offense lessens, and general interest in the case wanes. Indeed, defense attorneys often use delay strategies to win cases; that is, they seek repeated continuances in the hope that witnesses eventually will fail to appear. Box 3.2.8 presents information on case processing time and the right to a speedy trial.

In spite of the relatively widespread support for speedy trials, this is not a reform likely to be easily realized. Speedy trials are not in the best interests of the guilty defendant, nor are they always in the best interests of the prosecutor. Especially when the defendant is incarcerated and awaiting trial, the length of time between arrest and trial serves as an inducement to the defendant to engage in plea bargaining, thereby assuring conviction. Also important is the fact that the general workload of the courts is constantly increasing. A study of American courts revealed that in 2005, fewer than half of all criminal courts were able to close as many cases as were started that

Box 3.2.8

Felony Case Processing Times and Speedy Trial

Average elapsed time from arrest to sentencing by type of offense:

Offense Charged	Elapsed Time in days
All Offenses	184
Murder	412
Rape	261
Other Sexual Assault	270
Robbery	222
Aggravated Assault	188
Other Violent	207
Burglary	161
Larceny	168
Motor Vehicle Theft	99
Fraud	194
Drug Possession	175
Drug Trafficking	130
Weapons Offenses	196
Other offenses	184

Right to a Speedy Trial

A criminal defendant's right to a speedy trial is guaranteed by the Sixth Amendment to the U.S. Constitution: "In all criminal prosecutions, the accused shall enjoy the right to a speedy and public trial...." Determining when this right has been violated, however, is rarely a matter of simple objective fact. In *Barker v. Wingo* (407 U.S. 514, 530–533 (1972)) the Supreme Court spelled out four factors for courts to weigh in determining if a defendant's constitutional right to a speedy trial has been denied. The *length of the delay* is the most important consideration, but it must be judged in light of the *reasons for the delay.* Deliberate attempts to delay by the government weigh heavily in favor of the defendant. Certain reasons, such as the absence of a key witness, are considered valid. The court must also determine *if the defendant asserted his rights to a speedy trial* and *if the delay prejudiced the case against the defendant.*

Source: M. Durose & P. Langan (2004), Felony Sentences in State Courts, 2002 *(Washington, DC: Bureau of Justice Statistics).*

year. That means that the caseload of more than half the criminal courts increased by the end of the year (Schauffler et al., 2006).

The most promising development in reducing delay involves changes in **prosecutorial case management** (Jacoby, Ratledge & Gramckow, 1992). Policies and procedures have been developed to expedite case processing, including moves toward early screening of cases to plan for later processing; assignment of cases to tracks that anticipate trial, plea, diversion, and so on; and continuous monitoring of case progress (Cooper, 1994). Jurisdictions implementing such case management systems have experienced dramatic reductions in case processing time. In general, these changes reflect a recognition of "typical" cases so that prosecutors have better guidance concerning how to proceed and what to expect in a given case. Terry Baumer (2007) reported on an evaluation of an expedited case screening process that provided case reviews "24/7" and resulted in significant reductions in detention time and quicker releases of cases that were going to be discharged. Chaiken and Chaiken (1991) described **priority prosecution** programs in operation in the United States. In these programs, certain types of offenders are selected to receive increased attention to ensure conviction. Rather than treating each case as completely unique, screening classifies cases into types that typically receive different treatments (e.g., diversion, plea bargaining, trial). Based on this, prosecutors can know what to expect in each case and better plan and manage the total caseload.

Nearly two-thirds of prosecutor's offices operated diversion programs or deferred prosecution for first offenders. Prosecutors have also adopted what is known as vertical prosecution for specific types of cases. In large prosecutor's offices, the tradition was to assign different assistant prosecutors to different stages of the court process. Thus, one assistant would handle bail hearings, another charging, yet another arraignment, and so forth. No single prosecutor followed a case from the initial appearance up through sentencing. **Vertical prosecution**, on the other hand, refers to the practice of assigning the responsibility of a case to a single prosecutor who then follows that same case throughout the entire court process. DeFrances, Smith, and van der Does (1996:2) report that more than 40 percent of prosecutor's offices use vertical prosecution for all cases. Some offices use this management technique for specific types of crimes such as sexual assault, drug offenses, homicide, and child abuse. One potential benefit of vertical prosecution is that with specialization, prosecutors develop greater consistency in their handling of cases so that defendants and victims are treated more fairly (Kingsnorth, Mac-Intosh & Wentworth, 1999).

Klemm (1986) reported that case processing time in five cities was more dependent upon the type of plea than on other factors. Thus, defendants who plead not guilty and go to trial experience longer court delays than those who plead guilty. A report from the Bureau of Justice Statistics (1986), based on courts in 12 jurisdictions, echoed Klemm's findings. In addition, Langan and Brown (1997) reported that the time from arrest to sentencing for felony cases differed by type of conviction. While the cases of those convicted at trial took about nine months, cases in which the offender pleaded guilty took only about six months from arrest to sentencing. Moreover, as Feeley (1983) recognized, reforms that aim to promote speedy trials are subject to the desires of the courtroom work group. The judges, prosecutors, and defense attorneys who regularly work in United States courts realize that speedy trials will disrupt their operations and, therefore, generally oppose such reform (even if the opposition is not knowingly and openly voiced). This opposition is usually enough to render the reform ineffective. Case processing delays, in fact, are more likely to be products of this work group and the legal culture of a community than the result of caseload pressures, trial rates, or other factors (Klemm, 1986). In support of this conclusion, a recent comparison of case processing time in nine courts concluded that court "culture" was the most important factor in explaining differences in case processing time (Ostrom & Hanson, 2000). That is, in courts in which judges, prosecutors, and defense counsel understood and shared goals for case-processing time, cases were more quickly resolved. More than types of charges, rates of trial, or other factors, again it was the courtroom workgroup that determined court operations.

The Courtroom Work Group

James Eisenstein and Herbert Jacob (1977) and other observers of the criminal courts have identified what has come to be called the **courtroom work group**. This designation refers to the "regular" players in United Stated criminal courts: judges, prosecutors, and defense attorneys. This group, through close working relationships over time, develops a shared understanding of what are appropriate and inappropriate court procedures and outcomes. The shared norms and definitions among this informal group have real consequences for case outcomes and attempts at court reform. The work group often determines the "going rate" for crimes. For example, what is a suitable penalty for breaking and entering may come to be defined as a six-month jail sentence. Having this shared understanding, all parties are likely to agree to a negotiated plea in which a defendant accused of breaking and entering will be convicted of an offense carrying a six-month jail term (e.g., criminal trespass).

Because all members of the group are responsible for the orderly processing of cases, the development of shared understandings is useful to each of them. Rather than treat every case as unique, it becomes possible to classify cases as typical (i.e., deserving the going rate) or unusual (i.e., requiring alternative processing). Once this informal understanding has been developed, it is exceptionally difficult to change. Myers and Reid (1995) studied efforts to change sentencing outcomes in three Florida county courts. They discovered that sentences imposed on defendants differed across counties, but were quite similar within each county. Thus, they concluded that prosecutors and defense attorneys, as well as judges, were important to efforts to change sentencing. Their research confirms that the courtroom work group is alive and important in those courts.

John Harris and Paul Jesilow (2000) studied the implementation of the three-strikes sentencing law in California. The law was passed as a public initiative, with more than 80 percent of state voters supporting the law. It requires prosecutors to charge defendants who have prior convictions, and it enhances sentences for those who have prior convictions, so that each prior conviction ("strike") results in a longer prison term. It also means that what would be misdemeanor offenses for persons with no prior convictions are sometimes elevated to felonies if the defendant has prior "strikes." In general, Harris and Jesilow found that the effect of the three-strikes law was to destabilize the courtroom work group. The law greatly enhances the importance of the prosecutor's charging decisions (to allege prior strikes), but its popularity with voters prevents prosecutors from avoiding the law in many cases. Harris and Jesilow found some evidence that the work group had already adjusted to reduce the impact of the law, but that new norms for plea negotiations had not yet emerged. They wrote (2000:202): "Despite the obvious need to establish norms within the courtroom workgroup for negotiations concerning strike priors, we find little evidence that such norms will be established in the near future. The situation is clouded further by uncertainty stemming from defendants' willingness to go to trial and by juries' inclination to nullify the law and find defendants not guilty." They suggest that one result of the law is that case outcomes are less predictable, and thus trials are more likely. For this reason, the court process is becoming less efficient, and cases are beginning to backlog. Similar outcomes can be expected whenever efforts are made to treat cases more severely than had been traditional practice.

Free Press and Fair Trial

The circumstance of media coverage compromising the trial process, while relatively rare, is an important concern because it deals with a balance of rights—the right of the defendant to a fair and impartial hearing, and the right of the press to report on operations of the government (or, as might be stated by members of the news media, the public's "right to know"). Press coverage of criminal trials may affect court processes in two significant ways. First, the effects of pretrial publicity may make it difficult, if not impossible, to select a jury that has not been exposed to prejudicial coverage of the case (Brady, 1983). This was the rationale used in the trial of the Los Angeles police officers accused of beating Rodney King. The trial was relocated to a suburban area because the

An artist's drawing shows presiding Judge Steven Taylor urging the jury to steer clear of media accounts of the trial, as courtroom action in the state's murder case against convicted Oklahoma City bombing conspirator Terry Nichols ends for the day on June 8, 2004. Cameras were banned from the Nichols trial. *Photo credit: AP Photo/Pat Lopez.*

defense argued that the officers could not secure a fair trial in Los Angeles. The change of venue (location of trial) for Timothy McVeigh, the individual accused of the bombing of the Oklahoma City Federal Building, was similarly based on a concern that the defendant could not receive a fair trial in the state that was the site of the bombing. Second, in cases in which members of the press are allowed into the courtroom, it is possible that the entire trial will take on a "circus atmosphere." Not only will the behavior of reporters disrupt court proceedings, but the very presence of reporters may alter the behavior of the judge, prosecutor, defendant, jury, and others (Giglio, 1982). Judge Lance Ito was criticized for his failure to control the press in the criminal trial of O.J. Simpson. Despite this concern, there is a cable television network (Court TV) devoted entirely to the legal process, and particularly to the coverage of trials.

Because this issue involves two constitutional guarantees, the right to a fair trial and the right to a free press, the courts generally have adopted a "totality of circumstances" test, wherein they attempt to balance the rights of the media to cover trials against the rights of the state and the accused to proceed in an orderly fashion. The issue becomes important only in those cases that receive the lion's share of media attention—those cases that involve particularly gruesome offenses or are otherwise newsworthy (involving well-known victims or defendants). Ray Surette (1989) concludes that most "media trials" focus on specific types of themes that are typical of entertainment media. These types of trials dominate news coverage of the courts and, Surette argues, distort public understanding and possibly affect future cases. He notes (1989:300): "The significance is that media trials, while publicizing only a single case, probably influence the handling of a large number of defendants, including those who receive no coverage." This influence works in a number of ways, one of which is by sensitizing justice officials to public concern about types of crimes.

It is instructive to compare the American method of handling news media coverage of criminal trials with that of England. In England, the press is strictly forbidden to report on pending criminal cases, under penalty of contempt of court. Once a criminal case has been opened, the British press are banned from commenting on it. Violation of this ban can (and usually does) result in the offending reporter being incarcerated for contempt of court. In the United States, such a ban on reporting would violate the First Amendment's prohibition against "prior restraint" (censoring free speech before it occurs). Rather, United States courts have relied upon posttrial remedies, such as declaring convictions invalid and ordering new trials, as in *Sheppard v. Maxwell* (1966) and *Estes v. Texas* (1965).

The strong American value placed on individual rights, such as free speech, and the nation's commitment to the sovereignty of the citizen prevent us from banning press coverage of trials. The U.S. Supreme Court has ruled that criminal trials must remain public (*Richmond Newspapers, Inc. v. Virginia,* 1980). The other side of the dilemma is the commitment to fairness and a recognition that media coverage of criminal cases can bias juries and result in unfair verdicts. The American solution of posttrial remedies and the British use of prior restraint reflect the different values of the two societies. As Giglio (1982:349) stated, "The British emphasis, therefore, is on justice being done, rather than witnessed." Conversely, the American emphasis is on justice being witnessed, in order to ensure that justice is done.

In practice, much of the problem of balancing the rights to free press and fair trial has been resolved in United States courts through the development of norms of doing business. Occasionally, explicit policies and agreements have been reached among judges, attorneys, and the press. More often, understandings of what constitutes appropriate or inappropriate reporting develop tacitly. The reliance on posttrial remedies for prejudicial media coverage of criminal cases allows the courts and the press to learn from experience and develop policies that will avoid future controversies.

Aside from specific cases, the attention of the media does appear to have effects on the operation of courts. Ray Surette (1999) examined the effect of a well-publicized case on the overall work of courts. Comparing cases processed before and after a highly publicized case of child molestation in a daycare facility, he found that court practices changed in response to the attention. The basic change was that more molestation cases were brought to court. It appeared that one effect of media exposure was to make law enforcement and prosecutors more sensitive to those cases. Prosecutors were less likely to dismiss charges. Of course, this meant that "weaker" cases were brought to trial, and more defendants were acquitted. Other than increasing the number of such cases brought to court, the effects of the publicized case seemed to cancel each other out (more cases, but more acquittals). What is important is that prosecutors (and other justice system actors) do seem to be influenced by the media.

The question of fair trial versus free press is complex because the coverage of criminal cases by the media, although sometimes misleading (for example, by presenting the jury trial as the norm), leads to a better understanding of criminal justice processes for the citizenry. Further, media coverage of criminal cases supports the ultimate accountability of justice system officers to the public. On the other hand, the possible biasing effects of media commentary about criminal cases cannot be denied. In comparing American and British practices, Giglio concluded that one result of freer press coverage of criminal cases in the United States is that American citizens have a better understanding of their system of justice than do citizens of Britain. The inherent difficulty in balancing the good against the bad of media coverage of criminal cases ensures that this issue will remain relevant for some time to come.

The issue of fair trial versus free press has been complicated since the terrorist attacks of September 11, 2001. In response to terrorism, the United States has embarked on a number of practices that raise issues about fair trials. It is not so much media access to trials but rather public access in general. In late 2001, Evan Thomas and Michael Isikoff wrote an article in *Newsweek* entitled "Justice Kept in the Dark." The article examined new policies on the treatment of non-citizen terror suspects, including use of military tribunals for secret trials, holding suspects and witnesses "incognito," and not notifying defendants of the charges against them. While the rights of U.S. citizens are protected, even legal resident aliens could be subjected to secret investigations and trials. The dilemma involves protecting the interests of the defendants in maintaining their freedom while trying to prevent terrorist attacks and not providing terrorists with important information concerning the whereabouts of their personnel.

Community Courts

[...] [W]e discussed the development of specialty courts, including such focused tribunals as drug courts, domestic violence courts, and reentry courts. In combination, these have been called "problem-solving courts" (Casey & Rottman, 2003) because the role of the court has been redefined as that of responding to specific problems such as drug abuse or domestic violence. In a broader way, "community courts" have developed and spread. These are designed to deal with a range of community problems through the application of the criminal law (and less formal adjudication options). The proliferation of community courts has occurred in conjunction with the development of "community prosecution" and the expectation that the prosecutor's office will develop working partnerships with a range of community agencies.

As illustrated in Box 3.2.9, most prosecutor's offices report engaging in at least some community prosecution activities. Community prosecution, according to DeFrances (2002:9), "has been defined by prosecutors as a way to involve the community to solve crime and coordinate their office, law enforcement, local residents, and organizations to improve public safety and quality of life."

Community courts and community prosecution represent an expansion of the role of criminal courts and prosecutors. No longer are prosecutors expected to seek conviction of criminal offenders, or courts expected to simply determine guilt and assign penalties. Rather, prosecutors and judges are to be community advocates and use the resources and power of their offices to solve recurrent community problems. It is not enough to process cases. Community courts and community prosecution seek to address the underlying factors that cause criminal cases to develop. Much like community and problem-solving policing, the philosophy of community courts is that justice system agents must become more proactive in preventing crime and should be more responsive to members of the community in selecting cases for prosecution and court attention (Goldkamp, Irons-Guynn & Weiland, 2003).

John Feinblatt and Greg Berman (2001) note that community courts are designed to produce "community justice." They say (2001:1) community justice "takes many forms, but at its core are partnership and problem solving. **Community justice** is about creating new relationships both within the justice system and with stakeholders in the community, such as residents, merchants, churches, and schools, and testing new and aggressive approaches to public safety rather than merely responding to crime." Among other things, community courts are expected to maintain supervision over offenders and use the criminal sanction to reward treatment progress or punish

Box 3.2.9

Community Activities of Prosecutors, 2005

Type of Activity	Percent of Prosecutors Reporting
Define Office as Community Prosecution	39%
Use Tools Other Than Community Prosecution to Solve Problems	66
Involve Community in Problem Definition	51
Assign Prosecutors to Specific Geographic Location	16
Form Relationships with:	
Police	99
Other Government Agencies	88
Community Associations	70
Private Organizations	56
Regularly Meet with:	
Advocacy Groups	62
School Groups	61
Youth Service Organizations	47
Business Groups	45
Neighborhood Associations	30
Religious Groups	24
Tenant Associations	6

Source: S. Perry (2006), Prosecutors in State Courts, 2005 *(Washington, DC: Bureau of Justice Statistics):9.*

failure. Court or justice services, such as training and employment assistance, should be made available to all members of the community in order to prevent future problems.

One central question that applies to these efforts (and to problem-solving policing as well) is how a proactive stance toward crime prevention may alter the traditional definition of criminal justice. In the past, a reactive criminal justice process responded to persons who had violated the law, but until there was evidence that someone broke the law, the justice system was not authorized to intervene. More proactive stances by criminal justice officials often call for intervention with citizens based on the likelihood that someone who has not yet broken the law may do so in the future. This too is a dilemma that pits individual interests in being free from government intervention against community interests in solving problems and preventing crime.

Plea Bargaining

As shown in Box 3.2.10, the overwhelming majority of criminal convictions come as a result of a negotiated plea of guilty. In a study of the processing of felony cases in New York City, the Vera Institute reported that 98 percent of felony arrests resulted in guilty pleas (Vera Institute, 1977). The Bureau of Justice Statistics (Durose & Langan, 2004) reported that 95 percent of felony convictions resulted from guilty pleas. **Plea bargaining** refers to the process in which the state (through the prosecutor) and the defendant negotiate the terms under which the defendant will enter a plea of guilty. The importance of plea bargaining in the court process cannot be denied. Opinion is divided, however, as to the appropriateness of pleading guilty for considerations (Newman, 1966).

Box 3.2.10

Methods of Conviction of Felons, 2003

Conviction Type:	Percent of Cases
Guilty Plea	95%
Bench Trial	3
Jury Trial	2

Source: M. Durose & P. Langan (2004), Felony Sentences in State Courts, 2003 *(Washington, DC: Bureau of Justice Statistics):8.*

On the one hand, there are those who argue that plea bargaining violates the rights of the accused. Especially in cases in which possible penalties are very severe, or in which the defendant is in jail awaiting trial, the incentives to plead guilty are thought to be too enticing. In most jurisdictions, by pleading guilty, the defendant has waived his or her right not only to a jury trial but also to appeal questions of evidence admissibility. On the other hand, there are those who suggest that plea negotiations are unfair to the state and the victim. These critics argue that plea bargains serve to let the guilty off without sufficient punishment. They contend that negotiated guilty pleas serve to lessen the deterrent effect of the law because offenders are allowed to avoid their due penalties. Further, the idea that justice is open to negotiation is repugnant to the critics of plea bargaining.

Plea negotiations, however, do have some supporters. It has been suggested that the criminal justice system could not possibly provide the number of trials required if every criminal defendant were to demand one. The justice system would collapse under the burden of so many trials. The plea bargain results in a sure conviction of the offender, whereas a jury trial may not, and the defendant who pleads guilty is entitled to a sentence concession as a result of his or her honesty in admitting guilt, his or her demonstration of remorse in pleading guilty, or his or her cooperation with the state (Champion, 1987). Indeed, in *Santobello v. New York* (1966), the U.S. Supreme Court declared that plea bargaining, when properly carried out, is something to be encouraged.

There are several competing views of the reality and purposes of plea bargaining. Some believe that plea bargaining is the effect of better representation of defendants. Malcolm Feeley (1982) argues that plea bargaining is a product of increased adversariness. Prior to the twentieth century and the court reforms that added protections to defendants, trials were perfunctory. Plea bargaining occurs because the defendant now has an advocate, someone who can negotiate for him or her. Others have noted that one desired outcome of plea bargaining is case dispositions that are seen as just or fair (Douglas, 1988; Garafalo, 1991). That is, when the defense and prosecution engage in bargaining, they settle on a case outcome that seems fair. Plea bargaining can thus allow for the individualization of justice.

In an ideal world, perhaps it would be best if every criminal defendant were given a trial and plea bargaining were not allowed. In reality, however, this is unlikely to occur. The caseload-pressure argument, which explains high levels of plea bargaining on the basis of necessity, has not been supported by empirical study (Klemm, 1986; Parnas, 1980). The abolition of plea bargaining in some jurisdictions (Alaska, for example) has not resulted in a tremendous decrease in the number of cases that are concluded as a result of guilty pleas (Call, England & Talarico, 1983; Rubinstein & White, 1979). Thus, not only does it appear that plea bargaining is not associated with limited ability to provide trials, it further appears that plea bargaining is not a practice that can be easily abolished. Similar results were obtained in an analysis of the abolition of plea bargaining in trials within the U.S. Coast Guard.

Whatever else may be said about plea bargaining, it appears to be a functional practice. Again, the concept of a courtroom work group is important. Whether or not pleas of guilty result from formal negotiations between the prosecution and defense, the negotiations will continue, as will the pleas of guilty. Failure to recognize the informal structure of the courthouse—and the professional relationships that exist among the prosecutors, judges, and defense attorneys—leads reformers to believe that plea negotiations are somehow aberrant. Instead, given that the purpose of the court is to resolve disputes, it is only natural that a certain amount of compromise develops among the set of actors that engage in dispute resolution daily. Indeed, the history of plea bargaining indicates that it is a useful and traditional practice (Sanborn, 1986). Plea bargaining is a good example of the effect of people on the justice system. In assessing the operations of the justice process, it is important to remember that the system is comprised of people and operates through people (Champion, 1989).

Additional Issues in the Courts

Earlier in this reading we discussed "community courts." These new courts are expected to increase the involvement of citizens in the court process. For at least the past 100 years, the role of average citizens in the court process has been strictly curtailed. Citizen involvement in the courts has been limited to jury service and service as witnesses. Citizens have often tried to avoid jury duty, and the crime victim was considered important as a witness only. In recent decades, however, there has been an effort to expand the role of citizens in the courts and to increase the voice of victims in court proceedings. The reasons for increasing citizen involvement in the courts are both practical and philosophical.

On the practical side, lack of citizen cooperation hinders the orderly process of court cases. When victims and other witnesses refuse to testify, it is impossible for agents of the justice system to gain convictions of guilty offenders. A perception of increased witness and victim intimidation, especially in relation to crimes associated with gang drug activity, spurred efforts to improve witness and juror protection. Healey (1995) reported that more than 50 percent of prosecutors in large jurisdictions identified victim and witness intimidation as a major problem, while more than 80 percent reported intimidation to be at least a moderate problem. To respond to this problem, the courts have developed a number of responses to victim and witness intimidation, including emergency relocation and support, requests for higher bail or denial of release, increased pretrial and courtroom security, protective custody for victims and witnesses, and community outreach programs seeking to better educate the public and gain the cooperation of community service organizations in assisting victims and witnesses.

The voice of the victim has been amplified in criminal court proceedings throughout the past several decades. Prosecutors often consult with crime victims before accepting a negotiated plea (Dawson, Smith & DeFrances, 1993), and most jurisdictions have provisions for victim input into the sentencing decision. Judges, too, will usually thank citizens who serve on juries and recognize their contribution to the workings of the court. One reason for this concern with citizens' experiences in courts, of course, is that most prosecutors and judges are elected officials and thus need to serve the citizenry. A more important reason, however, is the growing recognition that victims, witnesses, and jurors deserve better treatment than they have traditionally received.

In response to this shift in our thinking about what kinds of consideration are owed to victims, witnesses, and jurors, courts have improved jury selection process, streamlined jury service terms, and improved the physical facilities in which jurors convene. Similar changes have improved conditions for witnesses and victims. In the case of victims, legislation in most states requires the courts (generally the prosecutor's office) to provide services to crime victims. These services include notification about case progress; providing help with and information about restitution, compensation, and victim impact statements; and offering an orientation to the court process. In some jurisdictions, prosecutor's offices are required to provide escort services for victims and witnesses and to assist with referral to community services, the provision of counseling, and the return of property held as evidence (see Box 3.2.11).

A second development affecting the operations of criminal courts consists of the availability of new technologies and the improvement of existing ones. These technological changes include

Box 3.2.11

Victim Services Required of Prosecutor's Offices

Type of Service	Percent of Offices
Notification/Alert	
Notify victim	82%
Notify witness	55%
Orientation/Education	
Victim restitution assistance	60%
Victim compensation procedures	58%
Victim impact statement assistance	55%
Orientation to court procedures	41%
Public education	15%
Escort	
Escort victim	23%
Escort witness	17%
Counseling/Assistance	
Property return	38%
Referral	32%
Personal Advocacy	17%
Counseling	10%
Crisis Intervention	10%

Source: C. DeFrances, S. Smith & L. van der Does (1996), Prosecutors in State Courts, 1994 *(Washington, DC: Bureau of Justice Statistics).*

the increasing use of forensic evidence such as DNA testing, videotape evidence, 911 emergency system audiotapes, polygraph evidence, and expert witness testimony. In some cases, courts have used testimony obtained through remote telephone or video links. Increased computerization of prosecutor's offices and courts also has resulted in increased use of criminal history data in decisionmaking. The majority of prosecutor's offices reported using criminal history data in the charging, bail, plea bargaining, trial, and sentencing stages. While these technological developments often improve the efficiency of court functioning, their use requires the development of staff expertise and expands the jobs of court personnel. Beyond that, the spread of computer literacy and use of computers has generated new forms of crime. Box 3.2.12 reports on the prosecution of "computer crime."

Box 3.2.12

Computer-Related Crimes Reported by Prosecutor's Offices

Type of Offense	Percent Reporting
State Computer Crime Statute	60%
Credit Card Fraud	80
Bank Card Fraud	71
Identify Theft	69
Transmit Child Pornography	67
Computer Forgery	40
Cyberstalking	36
Unauthorized Access	23
Computer Sabotage	5
Theft of Intellectual Property	5
Unauthorized Copying	4
Other	11

Source: S. Perry (2006), Prosecutors in State Courts, 2005 *(Washington, DC: Bureau of Justice Statistics):5.*

These improvements in technology, especially DNA testing and information system technology, have raised new issues about the fairness and accuracy of our courts. Improved evidence and information have increased the recognition of **wrongful conviction**, cases in which innocent persons are convicted of criminal acts. The number of convicted offenders who are later exonerated has increased dramatically in recent years. Samuel Gross and his colleagues (2004) reported that there are more than 40 "innocence projects" in existence in more than 30 states. **Innocence projects** are efforts to investigate claims of innocence maintained by persons convicted of criminal offenses (see http://www.innocenceproject.org). The growth of these projects and the rate of exonerations suggests that many thousands of innocent persons are convicted of crimes each year in the United States (Gross et al., 2004:11). While most of these convictions are for less serious offenses, for which the convicted person serves a relatively short sentence, the likelihood that innocent defendants are convicted of crimes raises questions about the quality of justice. Ron Huff (2002:3) sums up the problem, writing, "Most people can readily understand that convicting an innocent person is unjust, even thought they might express more concern with the guilty who go free. A society that views itself as just and fair simply cannot afford to ignore this problem."

Scandals involving the disclosure of police misconduct that includes fabricating evidence and committing perjury have led to the overturning of convictions of scores of persons in Los Angeles and other cities. Each instance of a wrongful conviction threatens public confidence in fairness and accuracy of the courts. On the other hand, that innocence is ultimately recognized and official misbehavior is eventually punished can be seen as a positive. While not to downplay the seriousness of wrongful conviction, it remains true that exonerations have occurred in only a small percentage of cases. Even counting the thousands of cases in which wrongful convictions might occur, these are in relation to the millions of convictions each year. As perhaps no other issue, the problem of wrongful convictions highlights the tension between due process and crime control. How do we ensure that guilty persons are convicted and punished while preventing the conviction of an innocent person?

Box 3.2.13 provides a table of selected court cases regarding the judicial process.

Box 3.2.13

Selected Court Cases on the Judicial Process

Estes v. Texas 381 U.S. 532 (1965)	New trial ordered because of problems with news media coverage of court case.
Santobello v. New York 404 U.S. 257 (1966)	The plea bargaining process, when properly carried out, is to be encouraged.
Sheppard v. Maxwell 384 U.S. 333 (1966)	Verdict declared invalid because of problems with news media coverage of court case.
People v. Faretta 422 U.S. 806 (1975)	Self-representation (pro se defense) is a constitutional right of the defendant.

The Criminal Courts in the Whole System

Like the police, the criminal courts are a subsystem of the criminal justice system, which itself exists within the whole system of American society. This context can be understood clearly when we consider the fact that those courts that hear criminal cases do so on a part-time basis. Most cases are civil in nature, and criminal cases are a part-time responsibility for the courts. Thus, delay in criminal case processing cannot be easily resolved by merely hiring more court personnel and building more courtrooms, because these changes will have the effect of accelerating both civil and criminal cases.

Donald Black's theory of the sociology of law suggests that as a society becomes more diverse and larger, the use of the law will expand. In the criminal courts, we find that the majority of cases and court personnel are found in a few very large jurisdictions. Moreover, the practice of plea bargaining represents, at some level, a less formal means of social control than trial and conviction. While we see proposals to reduce or eliminate plea bargaining and make formal trials more common, we also see a movement to develop less formal, problem-solving courts. We should not be surprised that the majority of cases are disposed of by plea bargaining. Trials seem to be reserved for those cases in which less formal resolutions are unworkable.

As our thinking about the role of citizens in the courts has changed, the courts themselves have become more sensitive to the needs and desires of victims, witnesses, and jurors. With the advent of community-based justice, we see the development of community courts. As communications technology improves, issues emerge surrounding media coverage, especially television coverage, of courts. The courts themselves adopt, and adapt to, new technologies to improve operations.

The courts are affected by changes in the larger society and, in turn, the courts affect the larger society (Calvi & Coleman, 1989). Many of the conflicts and controversies existing in the courts represent efforts to manage the relationship between the courts and social forces. The role of juries and the selection of judges and prosecutors evidence the United States' commitment to a legal system that is sensitive to our perceptions of what is right and what is wrong. As perceptions change (e.g., drug offenses are seen as more serious than in the past), there is pressure for the courts to change. Yet, we want the courts to be predictable and fair as well as free from improper outside influence. Thus, we want to know what the courts are doing, but we do not want court decisions to be biased by preconceived notions. As with achieving a balance between due process and crime control, the courts must seek a balance between responsiveness to social change and the commitment to impartiality.

Review Questions

1. Identify three ways in which defendants in criminal cases may obtain defense counsel.
2. Summarize the case of *Gideon v. Wainwright* and explain how it relates to *Argersinger v. Hamlin*. [...]

3. Compare criminal defense attorneys with prosecutors. In what ways are their jobs similar?
4. Tell which method of judicial selection you feel is most likely to yield competent judges who are responsive to the public. Explain how the system you select will accomplish this goal.
5. Describe the voir dire process and explain how it allows attorneys to protect the interests of their clients.
6. How can "speedy trial" be expected to reduce strains in other areas of the justice system?
7. The conflict between a free press and a fair trial reflects one of the ideological dilemmas of American criminal justice. Explain this conflict and propose a solution.
8. Take a position on the issue of plea bargaining (i.e., either support or oppose the practice) and give arguments against those who take the opposing position to yours.
9. How do the courts reflect changes in the larger American society?

References

American Bar Association (1968). *Standards Relating to Speedy Trial.* New York: Institute of Judicial Administration.

Bartollas, C., S. Miller & P. Wice (1983). *Participants in American Criminal Justice: The Promise and the Performance.* Englewood Cliffs, NJ: Prentice Hall.

Baumer, T. (2007). "Reducing Lockup Crowding with Expedited Initial Processing of Minor Offenders." *Journal of Criminal Justice* 35(3):273–281.

Brady, J. (1983). "Fair and Impartial Railroad: The Jury, the Media, and Political Trials." *Journal of Criminal Justice* 11(3):241–264.

Bureau of Justice Statistics (1986). *Felony Case-Processing Time.* Washington, DC: U.S. Department of Justice.

Call, J., D. England & S. Talarico (1983). "The Abolition of Plea Bargaining in the Coast Guard." *Journal of Criminal Justice* 11(4):351–358.

Calvi, J. & S. Coleman (1989). *American Law and Legal Systems.* Englewood Cliffs, NJ: Prentice Hall.

Casey, P. &D. Rottman (2003). *Problem-Solving Courts: Models and Trends.* Williamsburg, VA: National Center for State Courts.

Chaiken, M. & J. Chaiken (1991). *Priority Prosecution of High-Rate Dangerous Offenders.* Washing-ton, DC: National Institute of Justice.

Champion, D. (1987). "Felony Offenders, Plea Bargaining, and Probation: A Case of Extra-Legal Exigencies in Sentencing Practices." *Justice Professional* 2(2):1–18.

Champion, D. (1989). "Private Counsels and Public Defenders: A Look at Weak Cases, Prior Records, and Leniency in Plea Bargaining." *Journal of Criminal Justice* 17(4):253–263.

Cooper, C. (1994). *Expedited Drug Case Management.* Washington, DC: Bureau of Justice Assistance.

Criminal Justice Newsletter (1987). "President Cites Crime Issue in Choosing Kennedy for High Court." *Criminal Justice Newsletter* 18(22):4.

Dawson, J. (1992). *Prosecutors in State Courts, 1990.* Washington, DC: U.S. Department of Justice.

Dawson, J., S. Smith & C. DeFrances (1993). *Prosecutors in State Courts, 1992.* Washington, DC: Bureau of Justice Statistics.

DeFrances, C. (2002). *Prosecutors in State Courts, 2001.* Washington, DC: Bureau of Justice Statistics.

DeFrances, C. & M. Litras (2000). *Indigent Defense Services in Large Counties, 1999.* Washington, DC: Bureau of Justice Statistics.

DeFrances, C., S. Smith & L. van der Does (1996). *Prosecutors in State Courts, 1994.* Washington, DC: Bureau of Justice Statistics.

Douglas, R. (1988). "Tolerated Contests? Plea and Sentence in the Victorian Magistrate's Courts." *Journal of Criminal Justice* 16(4):269–290.

Durose, M. & P. Langan (2004). *Felony Sentences in State Courts, 2002.* Washington, DC: Bureau of Justice Statistics.

Eisenstein, J. & H. Jacob (1977). *Felony Justice.* Boston: Little, Brown.

Feeley, M. (1982). "Plea Bargaining and the Structure of the Criminal Process." *Justice System Journal* 7(Winter):338-355.

Feeley, M. (1983). *Court Reform on Trial.* New York: Basic Books.

Feinblatt, J. & G. Berman (2001). *Responding to the Community: Principles for Planning and Creating a Community Court.* Washington, DC: Bureau of Justice Assistance.

Fried, M., K. Kaplan & K. Klein (1975). "Juror Selection: An Analysis of Voir Dire." In R. Simon (ed.), *The Jury System in America.* Beverly Hills, CA: Sage.

Fukurai, H. (1996). "Race, Social Class, and Jury Participation: New Dimensions for Evaluating Discrimination in Jury Service and Jury Selection." *Journal of Criminal Justice* 24(1):71–88.

Fukurai, H., E. Butler & R. Krooth (1991). "Cross-Sectional Jury Representation or Systematic Jury Representation? Simple Random and Cluster Sampling Strategies in Jury Selection." *Journal of Criminal Justice* 19(1):31–48.

Garafalo, J. (1991). "Police, Prosecutors, and Felony Case Attrition." *Journal of Criminal Justice* 19(5):439–449.

Giglio, E. (1982). "Free Press—Fair Trial in Britain and America." *Journal of Criminal Justice* 10(5):341–358.

Glick, H. (1983). *Courts, Politics and Justice.* New York: McGraw-Hill.

Goldkamp, J., C. Irons-Guynn & D. Weiland (2003). *Community Prosecution Strategies.* Washing-ton, DC: National Institute of Justice.

Gross, S., K. Jacoby, D. Matheson, N. Montgomery & S. Patil (2004). *Exonerations in the United States: 1989 through 2003.* Chicago: American Judicature Society.

Harlow, C. (2000). *Defense Counsel in Criminal Cases.* Washington, DC: Bureau of Justice Statistics.

Harris, J. & P. Jesilow (2000). "It's Not the Old Ball Game: Three Strikes and the Courtroom Workgroup." *Justice Quarterly* 17(1):186–203.

Healey, K. (1995). *Victim and Witness Intimidation: New Developments and Emerging Responses.* Washington, DC: National Institute of Justice.

Holten, N.G. & L. Lamar (1991). *The Criminal Courts: Structures, Personnel, and Processes.* New York: McGraw-Hill.

Huff, C.R. (2002). "Wrongful Conviction and Public Policy: The American Society of Criminology Presidential Address." *Criminology* 40(1):1–18.

Jackson, D. (1974). *Judges.* New York: Atheneum.

Jacoby, J., E. Ratledge & H. Gramckow (1992). *Expedited Drug Case Management Programs: Issues for Program Development.* Washington, DC: U.S. Department of Justice.

Kalven, H. & H. Zeisel (1966). *The American Jury.* Boston: Little, Brown.

Klemm, M. (1986). "A Look at Case Processing Time in Five Cities." *Journal of Criminal Justice* 14(1):9–23.

Kingsnorth, R., R. MacIntosh & J. Wentworth (1999). "Sexual Assault: The Role of Prior Relationship and Victim Characteristics in Case Processing." *Justice Quarterly* 16(2):275–302.

Langan, P. & J. Brown (1997). *Felony Sentences in State Courts, 1994.* Washington, DC: Bureau of Justice Statistics.

Levin, M. (1977). *Urban Politics and Criminal Courts.* Chicago: University of Chicago Press.

Lynch, T. (2002). *Breaking the Vicious Cycle: Preserving Our Liberties While Fighting Terrorism.* Washington, DC: CATO Institute.

Myers, L. & S. Reid (1995). "The Importance of County Context in the Measurement of Sentence Disparity: The Search for Routinization." *Journal of Criminal Justice* 23(3):223–241.

Nagel, S. (1973). *Comparing Elected and Appointed Judicial Systems.* Beverly Hills, CA: Sage.

Neely, R. (1983). *Why Courts Don't Work.* New York: McGraw-Hill.

Neubauer, D. (1984). *America's Courts and the Criminal Justice System.* Monterey, CA: Brooks/Cole.

Newman, D. (1966). *Conviction: The Determination of Guilt or Innocence Without Trial.* Boston: Little, Brown.

Office for Victims of Crime (2008). Found at: http://ojp.usdoj.gov/ovc (accessed February 5, 2008).

Ostrom, B. & R. Hanson (2000). *Efficiency, Timeliness, and Quality: A New Perspective From Nine State Criminal Trial Courts.* Washington, DC: National Institute of Justice.

Parnas, R. (1980). "Empirical Data, Tentative Conclusions, and Difficult Questions About Plea Bargaining in Three California Counties." *Federal Probation* 44(2):12.

Perry, S. (2006). *Prosecutors in State Courts, 2005.* Washington, DC: Bureau of Justice Statistics.

Reaves, B. & J. Perez (1994). *Pretrial Release of Felony Defendants, 1992.* Washington, DC: Bureau of Justice Statistics.

Reddick, M. (2002). "Merit Selection: A Review of the Social Scientific Literature." *Dickinson Law Review* 106:729–744.

Rottman, D. & S. Strickland (2006). *State Court Organization 2004.* Washington, DC: Bureau of Justice Statistics.

Rubin, H. (1984). *The Courts: Fulcrum of the Justice System,* 2nd. ed. New York: Random House.

Rubinstein, M.L. & T.J. White (1979). "Plea Bargaining: Can Alaska Live Without It?" *Judicature* 62:266.

Sanborn, J.B. (1986). "A Historical Sketch of Plea Bargaining." *Justice Quarterly* 3(2):111–138.

Seltzer, R., M. Venuti & G. Lopes (1991). "Juror Honesty During the Voir Dire." *Journal of Criminal Justice* 19(5):451–462.

Simon, R. (1980). *The Jury: Its Role in American Society.* Lexington, MA: Lexington Books.

Simon, R. (1992). "Jury Nullification, or Prejudice and Ignorance in the Marion Barry Trial." *Journal of Criminal Justice* 20(3):261–266.

Smith, B. & C.R. Huff (1992). "From Victim to Political Activist: An Empirical Examination of a Statewide Victim's Rights Movement." *Journal of Criminal Justice* 20(3):201–215.

The Spangenberg Group (2003). *State and County Expenditures for Indigent Defense Services in Fiscal Year 2002.* West Newton, MA: The Spangenberg Group, prepared for The American Bar Association Bar Information Program. Found at: http://www.abanet.org/legalservices/sclaid/defender/downloads/2007FelonyCompRatesupdates_nonfelony.pdf, accessed August 12, 2005.

Stumpf, H. (1988). *American Judicial Politics.* New York: Harcourt, Brace, Jovanovich.

Surette, R. (1999). "Media Echoes: Systemic Effects of News Coverage." *Justice Quarterly* 16(3):601–631.

Surette, R. (1989). "Media Trials." *Journal of Criminal Justice* 17(4):293–308.

Thomas, E. & M. Isikoff (2001). "Justice Kept in the Dark." *Newsweek* (Dec. 10, 2001):36–43.

Time (1977). "Fools in Court." (May, 1977):45.

Turner, B., R. Lovell, J. Young & W. Denny (1986). "Race and Peremptory Challenge During Voir Dire: Do Prosecution and Defense Agree?" *Journal of Criminal Justice* 14(1):61–70.

Vera Institute of Justice (1977). *Felony Arrests: Their Prosecution and Disposition in New York City's Courts.* New York: Vera Institute of Justice.

Walker, S. (1985). *Sense and Nonsense About Crime.* Monterey, CA: Brooks/Cole.

Wice, P. (1978). *Criminal Lawyers: An Endangered Species.* Beverly Hills, CA: Sage.

Wice, P. & P. Suwak (1974). "Current Realities of Public Defender Programs." *Criminal Law Bulletin* 10(March):163.

Zatz, M. (2000). "The Convergence of Race, Ethnicity, Gender, and Class on Court Decisionmaking: Looking Toward the 21st Century." In J. Horney (ed.), *Policies, Processes, and Decisions of the Criminal Justice System.* Washington, DC: National Institute of Justice, Criminal Justice 2000, Volume 3:503–552.

Important Cases

Argersinger v. Hamlin, 407 U.S. 25 (1972).

Barker v. Wingo, 407 U.S. 514 (1972).

Estes v. Texas, 381 U.S. 532 (1965).

Gideon v. Wainwright, 372 U.S. 335 (1963).

People v. Faretta, 422 U.S. 806 (1975).

Richmond Newspapers, Inc. v. Virginia, 448 U.S. 555 (1980).

Rumsfeld v. Padilla, 542 U.S. 426 (2004).

Santobello v. New York, 404 U.S. 257 (1966).

Sheppard v. Maxwell, 384 U.S. 333 (1966).

READING 3.3

THE GOALS AND PROCESS OF PUNISHMENT

Lawrence F. Travis III

IMPORTANT TERMS

boot camp
concurrent term
consecutive term
determinate sentencing
deterrence
disparity
false negative
false positive
general deterrence
good time
habitual offender statutes
incapacitation
indeterminate sentencing
intermediate sanctions
just deserts
mandatory minimum sentences
parole eligibility
partial disclosure
presentence investigation (PSI)
presumptive sentencing
rehabilitation
retribution
sentencing
sentencing commissions
specific deterrence
split sentences
three-strikes laws
treatment
"truth in sentencing"

After conviction, the next major decision point in the criminal justice system is sentencing, the decision about punishment. In many ways, the sentencing decision represents the crux of the justice system, for it is at this point that we determine what will be done to, for, with, or about the criminal offender.

Criminal sentences may involve the imposition of fines, community supervision, or incarceration. In some cases, a criminal sentence includes a combination of all of these. Excluding fines and short-term incarceration in a local jail, millions of people each year receive criminal sentences of probation or imprisonment. If we include punishments for all sorts of offenses, including traffic citations, sentences are imposed on more than 15 million people each year. In 2004, more than one million people were convicted of felonies in state courts, only 40 percent of whom were sentenced to prison (Durose & Langan, 2007).

In order to understand how the distinction is drawn between who is incarcerated and who is allowed to remain in the community under supervision, we need to understand the purposes of punishment and the motivations of the people who make the punishment decision. This reading examines these factors.

The Purposes of Punishment

Traditionally, four purposes or justifications for criminal penalties have been advanced: (1) deterrence, (2) incapacitation, (3) treatment (or rehabilitation), and (4) just deserts (or retribution). These theories of punishment answer the question: why punish at all? This is a question the average citizen does not often hear in the context of criminal law. Yet, most of us have heard the expression that "two wrongs do not make a right." Applied to the criminal law, this suggests that imposing a punishment on someone who has broken the law is a "second wrong," which does not make it "right." If I steal your television and am sent to prison for a year because of it, have things turned out right? You are deprived of your television, I am deprived of a year of my life, and all of us pay the costs of trial and imprisonment.

From this point of view, the punishment of crime seems useless, if not wasteful. However, we usually do not think of it this way. Rather, it seems almost automatic that someone who breaks the law will be punished (von Hirsch, 1976). What can justify a system of penalties that can be argued to involve nothing but costs to everyone affected?

Deterrence is a purpose of punishment based on the idea that punishment of the individual offender produces benefits for the future by making the crime less attractive. Deterrence has two parts: **specific deterrence**, in which the object of the deterrent effect is the specific offender, and **general deterrence**, in which the object of the deterrent effect is a wider audience (the general public). According to deterrence theory, punishment is an example of what awaits law violators and serves to educate would-be offenders, so that they will weigh the costs of crime against its benefits (Paternoster, 1987).

With specific deterrence, after I am released from prison, I will think twice before I steal another television because I now know that I will face a year in prison if I steal and am caught. With general deterrence, after seeing what happened to me, you will rethink your plan to replace your missing television by stealing your neighbor's set. In both cases, the punishment serves to prevent future crimes. If society does not punish, there may be no reason for us to obey the law.

Deterrence has a certain intuitive appeal. On the surface, it makes sense that deterrence will "work." Unfortunately, the evidence of its effectiveness is not very clear (Newman, 1983:101-105). Few (if any) criminals believe they will be caught and punished (indeed, if they expected to be caught, they most probably would not commit the offense). While we have used the term "educate," deterrence is really based on fear. Would-be offenders must fear the penalty, and thus we are left with a society in which "proper" behavior is based on fear—a basis that most of us do not favor. Finally, when someone has thought about it and decided not to commit a crime, it is unclear whether the person made the decision based on fear of punishment, fear of public ridicule, fear of eternal damnation, or based on some other factor. Deterrence has strong appeal, but it is difficult to prove. Following a long tradition of research into the workings of deterrence, Gertz and Gould (1995) studied a sample of college students and found that the likelihood of students engaging in crime was affected more by their personal perceptions that the behavior was wrong than by fear of arrest and punishment. Others have studied criminal offenders and found that their decisions about engaging in crime are influenced by their perceptions of being caught and the likely penalty they might receive (Shover, 1996; Wright & Decker, 1994). In a study of 15 active residential burglars, Piquero and Rengert (1999) found that while burglars considered the risk of being caught and punished, the potential pay-off of the burglary was a more important factor in their decision to commit a crime. Nagin and Pogarsky (2001) came to similar conclusions in a study of deterrence in which they found that offender preferences for risk-taking influenced the deterrent effects of punishments. These studies and others (Pogarsky, 2002) suggest that different people view the risk of penalty differently so that it may not be possible to deter all potential offenders with a single penalty.

The theory of deterrence assumes that humans are rational beings guided by a pleasure principle. That is, humans do things that please them and avoid things that hurt them. Further, it holds that we are able to assess the likely effects of our behavior and guide ourselves according to these assessments. As rational beings, we will avoid "bad" behaviors, such as committing crimes, when the behaviors will produce unpleasant results (punishments). Rationality, of course, is difficult to establish. Indeed, many crimes, especially violent offenses among friends and family, are more emotional than rational.

In order for a punishment to deter a would-be offender, two conditions must be met. First, the penalty must be severe enough that the pain of the punishment will outweigh the pleasure of the criminal act. Using an economic example, if the penalty for theft were a $100 fine, it may be severe enough to stop one from stealing $50. Given the opportunity to steal $500, however, the rational person may take the money and pay the fine, keeping a $400 profit. Thus, deterrence depends in part on the severity of punishment.

The second condition is whether the punishment is certain to be imposed. Not only must the punishment be severe enough to outweigh the gain realized by crime, but the likelihood of being punished must be high enough that the offender takes the threat seriously. If the punishment for theft were 10 years in prison, but the chance of being caught and punished were only one in a million, the threat of punishment probably would not deter. Deterrence theory suggests the lower the risk of punishment, the higher the likelihood that a crime will be committed.

Research has indicated that, of these two conditions, certainty of punishment is the more important aspect of deterrence. Given a rational offender, uncertainty of punishment makes deterrence even more troublesome. The offender will assess the likelihood of being caught, and then take steps to reduce the chance of detection before committing an offense. Deterrence may best serve to make offenders more cautious rather than less criminal. In a review of the deterrence literature, Paternoster (1987) suggested that neither certainty nor severity appear to affect the behaviors of deterrence research samples. He warned deterrence researchers to prepare for the possibility that people who commit crimes may not be acting rationally. It may well be that people are not motivated by their perceptions of either the certainty or the severity of punishment. In a study of the specific deterrent effects of punishment for DUI offenses, Kingsnorth, Alvis, and Gavia (1993) suggest that offenders have different perceptions of sanction severity. Thus, a sanction or set of sanctions may not be viewed as very severe by some, or may allow others to minimize the severity of the penalty. For white-collar criminals, whose rational crimes seem particularly suited to deterrence, Benson (1990) suggests that punishments induce feelings of anger and resentment rather than remorse and shame. Thus, the penalty may actually have an anti-deterrent effect. Finally, would-be offenders must perceive that the crime is likely to result in arrest and punishment (Schoepfer, Carmichael & Piquero, 2007).

Incapacitation, like deterrence, suggests that punishment serves to prevent future crime, but not by education or fear. An incapacitative punishment prevents future crimes by the specific offender by removing opportunities for crime. One good reason to imprison a criminal is to ensure that he or she does not have the chance to commit a crime in society again. I cannot steal your television if I am in prison. Probably the most effective incapacitative penalty is capital punishment. Not only do the dead tell no tales, but they also commit no crimes.

The major drawbacks to incapacitation as a justification for criminal punishment are the difficulties in predicting who is likely to commit an offense in the future, and the costs of incapacitating offenders. At the current level of sophistication, it is not possible to identify precisely those persons likely to pose a threat of serious crime in the future (Visher, 1987). The prediction problem is simply too complex.

In any attempt to predict "dangerousness" among a population of criminal offenders (not to mention the general population), one runs a risk of making two types of errors: false positives and false negatives. A **false positive** refers to someone who is predicted to be dangerous (positive on danger), but who turns out not to be a threat (false). A **false negative** refers to someone who is predicted to be safe (negative on danger), but who turns out to be dangerous (false). False positives are incapacitated as if they were dangerous, and thus prison resources are wasted and individual freedoms are needlessly infringed. False negatives are not incapacitated and thus are free to victimize others. Every crime-prediction scheme available makes both types of errors. Under the best of circumstances, the likelihood is that roughly eight false positives will be incapacitated for each truly dangerous offender imprisoned, and that nearly one-half of the dangerous offenders will be classified as posing little danger and released (Wenk, Robison & Smith, 1972). In addition, most predictive models do not account for the possibility that offenders change over time and that their risk of new crime can increase or decrease based on life experiences after a sentence is imposed (LeClair & Guarino-Ghezzi, 1991). Given these limitations, policymakers must decide how much error they are willing to tolerate (Smith & Smith, 1998), balancing concerns about due process (false positives) with concerns about crime control (false negatives).

Largely as a result of the numerous false positives, incapacitation entails a significant increase in prison space (Greenwood, 1982; Van Dine, Conrad & Dinitz, 1979). If we work with the eight-to-one ratio of false positives to "true positives" (actual dangerous offenders), for us to incapacitate 100 more dangerous offenders each year, we also will need to incarcerate 800 more nondangerous offenders. That is, the prison populations increase nine times as fast as the population of dangerous offenders. In order to provide sufficient prison capacity for these larger populations, it would be necessary to build four to six times as many prisons as are currently in operation. Incapacitation is ultimately rational, but a determination of its effectiveness must await the development of accurate prediction devices. Upon reviewing the available evidence about incapacitation, Visher (1987) concluded, "These findings indicate that 'lock 'em up' strategies ... are only slightly more effective against crime than current practice."

Treatment (also called **rehabilitation**) is another rationale based on a reduction of future crime. Unlike deterrence or incapacitation, treatment is concerned with the offender as an individual (Cullen & Gilbert, 1982). Here the punishment imposed is one that fits the individual and is most likely to result in a change in the individual's desire to commit crime. Treatment suggests that individuals commit crimes for a variety of reasons and that the solution to the problem of crime will be achieved through changing individuals so that they will not wish to engage in crime, and by having other options available to them that will allow them to avoid criminality.

As with prediction, the behavioral sciences do not yet have a level of sophistication that allows treatment programs imposed as criminal sentences to be entirely successful. Partly as a result of pragmatic need, the treatment options available for criminal offenders are limited. Generally, offenders receive some type of counseling that is applied to a wide range of offenders. While designed to deal with individuals, the realities of large numbers of offenders and limited treatment resources mean that treatment is applied to groups and tailored (often not very well) to individuals. Adams (1961) reported that such approaches may be very good for some, of no effect for some, and very bad for others. The net result is that, for the total group, the treatment leads to no marked improvement when those for whom the treatment was harmful cancel out those for whom it was beneficial.

Many studies of the effects of treatment have suggested that treatments for criminal offenders generally are not effective (Bailey, 1966; Martinson, 1974). Reviewing the research on correctional treatment, Doris Mackenzie (1997:9-16) noted, "The important issue is not whether something works but what works for whom." Like incapacitation, treatment is eminently plausible, but must await greater sophistication in the design and delivery of services to offenders, as well as in the investment of sufficient resources, before it meets in practice what is expected in theory (Flores et al., 2005).

Despite discouraging results from many attempts at rehabilitation, efforts to treat criminal offenders continue, and may be increasing (Gendreau & Ross, 1987). Many treatment programs show promise of being effective answers to the criminality of specific populations of offenders. Completing a review of the evidence on rehabilitation effectiveness, Gendreau and Ross (1987) argued that we do have successful programs. What is lacking, they contended, is an ability to translate experimental treatments into routine, effective programs for offenders. In contrast, Logan and Gaes (1993) contend that the research continues to show an inability to treat the causes of criminal behavior effectively. Further, they suggest (1993:261) that treatment is not an appropriate goal of punishment.

What appears from the research on treatment effectiveness is that we have not been very sophisticated in our application of treatments. Van Voorhis (1987) suggests that the evidence available shows that some treatments work for some offenders, and that we need to better match treatments with offenders. Gendreau (1996) maintains that we must focus treatments on high-risk offenders. He suggests that one of the reasons why studies of treatment effectiveness show low impact is because we have "wasted" treatment on those who do not need it. Today treatment as a part of sentencing has experienced a resurgence as we seek to prevent future crime (Harland, 1996). Taxman and Piquero (1998) compared treatment and punishment sentences of drunk drivers in Maryland, concluding that treatment approaches seemed more effective at reducing future instances of drunk driving. The problem-solving courts, like drug courts and domestic violence courts, attempt to use the threat or application of criminal sanctions to support treatment programs and ensure that the offender participates in treatment (Casey & Rottman, 2003).

Just deserts (sometimes called **retribution** or desert) is the only justification for criminal punishment that is not "forward-looking." That is, it does not offer a reduction in future crime as the principal justification for the imposition of a punishment. Rather, just deserts is based on the belief that whoever breaks the law "deserves" to be punished. Breaking the law in itself is justification for punishment, whether that punishment reduces, increases, or has no effect on future levels of crime. Essentially, the criminal law is a promise wherein we (the state) promise to punish anyone who violates the law, and in the desert rationale, the promise must be kept.

As a justification for punishment, just deserts places limits on the degree to which someone may be punished. Punishment is expected to be commensurate with (or proportionate to) the severity of the crime committed. For example, public torture and execution of parking violators would deter most of us from parking illegally (if not from driving altogether), and these methods would be acceptable in a purely deterrent system of punishment. In contrast, these extreme forms of punishment for parking violations would be unthinkable in a desert scheme. Further, while a purely deterrent system of punishment does not require that the person being punished be convicted first, the just deserts rationale holds that only convicted offenders should be punished.

Supporters of deterrence often engage in "penalty escalation" because it is easier to alter the severity of punishment than its certainty (Newman, 1983). In this case, the penalty for a given offense—for example, five years imprisonment for theft—is increased (perhaps to 10 years). It is easier to increase penalty severity than to become more efficient at catching and punishing thieves. Further, deterrence rests on an argument that the good of the penalty (in terms of crimes prevented) must outweigh its harm in terms of injury to the punished. It is possible, then, for a deterrent penalty to be imposed on an innocent person, as long as the social good outweighs the individual harm.

Incapacitative penalties also can be argued to have the effect of punishing the innocent. The determination of how severe a penalty should be for incapacitation does not rest on the seriousness of the crime committed but upon a prediction that the offender will commit another crime. Like the queen in *Alice in Wonderland*, proponents of incapacitation invoke the penalty first, and the crime comes later, after the penalty is served. If there in fact is no crime, so much the better.

Treatment penalties assume an "identity of interest" between the state and the offender. The state wants what is best for the offender, that is, to improve his or her chances in life and to reduce the offender's desire to commit crimes. The offender either wants the same thing, or would want it if he or she were competent. Thus, the imposition of a punishment is for the offender's own good. A sanction that seems disproportionate to the seriousness of the offense is not a problem, as long as it is "good" for the offender.

The just deserts justification for punishment is often stated in biblical terms as "an eye for an eye." It fits rather well with our beliefs that, regardless of the reason, those who break the law should be punished (Johnson & Sigler, 1995). The difficulty with desert is that we cannot yet precisely measure levels of crime severity, or of punishment severity (Durham, 1988). Additionally, we are uncomfortable with the idea that punishment can (or should) be imposed simply for the sake of punishment. Retribution is also difficult to achieve in practice. There tends to be widespread disagreement about how much punishment is deserved by those convicted of different kinds of crimes (Griset, 1995). Further, as Nancy Wonders (1996) observed, sentencing is located in the middle of the criminal justice system. Attempts to make sentencing "fair" must contend with both earlier (investigation, arrest, charging) and later (correctional placements, parole release) decisions. Finally, as Myers and Reid (1995) observed, statewide legislation is implemented in different localities, and each of these has its own courtroom work group and definition of appropriate penalties.

These four rationales for the imposition of criminal punishment—deterrence, incapacitation, treatment, and just deserts—have been presented separately and analyzed as if they were required to stand alone. In practice, however, operating sentencing systems are founded on many purposes. It is not unusual, for example, for the sentencing judge to "throw the book" at a defendant for deterrent purposes, while correctional authorities seek to "treat" the offender's problems and rehabilitate him or her, only to have a paroling authority refuse to release the offender because of a fear that the offender will commit a new crime and, therefore, must be incapacitated.

Not only do most sentencing systems expressly serve all four of these functions, but the decisionmakers in those sentencing systems (judges, parole authority members, correctional workers, and administrators) favor different justifications for punishment. To complicate matters even more, these different actors favor different rationales for punishment of different offenders at different points in time. Further, each criminal jurisdiction has its own structure for the determination and implementation of criminal sentences.

Sentencing Structures in the United States

There are substantial differences among the states with regard to how they go about the sentencing of criminals. As the Bureau of Justice Statistics (1984:1) reported:

> It requires more than 200 pages to describe the basic features of the sentencing laws in each state. In addition to the different laws that govern sentencing, there are differences in how specific offenses are defined and classified by the criminal code in each state.

Criminal sentencing has been the topic of a great deal of interest and debate (Clear, 1994; Tonry, 1996; Travis, 2002; Ulmer, 1997; Zalman, 1987). Since 1975, many states have adopted changes in the structures used for criminal sentencing. The result has been the addition of a number of innovative formats for sentencing. If anything, criminal sentencing in the United States has become even more complicated in the past three decades. Michael Tonry (1999:1) observed, "There are now many approaches to sentencing and corrections in this country. Some States have guidelines with parole release, and some without. Some three-strikes states have adopted truth-in-sentencing; some have not. And so on, through the litany of changes in recent decades." Nonetheless, the traditional distinction made between determinate and indeterminate sentencing is useful.

Determinate sentencing structures are those in which each offender knows the exact length and nature of his or her punishment at the time it is imposed. **Indeterminate sentencing** structures are those in which the precise length of the penalty is unknown until some time has passed since the imposition of the penalty. Within each of these classes, there are several types of sentencing structures. Each sentencing structure represents a balance of power among the legislative, judicial, and executive branches of government. The structure of sentencing reflects varying degrees of emphasis on each of the goals of criminal sentencing, and it affects how sentencing is conducted.

Box 3.3.1 depicts sentencing structures found across the United States. The majority of sentencing authority rests with the legislature, which establishes criminal penalties and defines

Box 3.3.1

Basic Sentencing Structures in the United States

The basic difference in sentencing systems is the apportioning of discretion between the judge and parole authorities.	**States employ other sentencing features in conjunction with their basic strategies.**	
Indeterminate sentencing—the judge specifies minimum and maximum sentence lengths. These set upper and lower bounds on the time to be served. The actual release date (and therefore the time actually served) is determined later by parole authorities within those limits.	**Mandatory sentencing**—Law requires the judge to impose a sentence of incarceration, often of specified length, for certain crimes or certain categories of offenders. There is no option of probation or a suspended sentence.	Mandatory sentencing laws are in force in 46 states (all except Maine, Minnesota, Nebraska and Rhode Island) and the District of Columbia. In 25 states, imprisonment is mandatory for certain repeat felony offenders. In 30 states, imprisonment is mandatory if a firearm was involved in the commission of a crime. In 45 states, conviction for certain offenses or classes of offenses leads to mandatory imprisonment, most such offenses are serious, violent crimes, and drug trafficking is included in 18 of the states. Many states have recently made drunk driving an offense for which incarceration is mandated (usually for relatively short periods in a local jail rather than a state prison).
Partially indeterminate sentencing—a variation of indeterminate sentencing in which the judge specifies only the maximum sentence length. An associated minimum sentence automatically is implied but is not within the judge's discretion. The implied minimum may be a fixed time (such as 1 year) for all sentences or a fixed proportion of the maximum.		

(*continued*)

Box 3.3.1

Basic Sentencing Structures in the United States (*Continued*)

In some states the implied minimum is zero; thus, the parole board is empowered to release the prisoner at any time. **Determinate sentencing**—the judge specifies a fixed term of incarceration, which must be served in full (less any "good time" earned in prison). There is no discretionary parole release. **Since 1975 many states have adopted determinate sentencing, but most still use indeterminate sentencing.**	**Presumptive sentencing**—The discretion of a judge who imposes a prison sentence is constrained by a specific sentence length set by law for each offense or class of offense. That sentence must be imposed in all unexceptional cases. In response to mitigating or aggravating circumstances, the judge may shorten or lengthen the sentence within specified boundaries, usually with written justification being required.	Presumptive sentencing is used, at least to some degree, in about 12 states.
In 1976 Maine was the first state to adopt determinate sentencing. The sentencing system is entirely or predominantly determinate in these 10 states: California, Maine, Connecticut, Minnesota, Florida, New Mexico, Illinois, North Carolina, Indiana, Washington	**Sentencing guidelines**—Explicit policies and procedures are specified for deciding on individual sentences. The decision is usually based on the nature of the offense and the offender's criminal record. For example, the prescribed sentence for a certain offense might be probation if the offender has no previous felony convictions, a short term of incarceration if the	Sentencing guidelines came into use in the late 1970s. They are: • used in 13 states and the federal criminal justice system • written into statute in the federal system and in Florida, Louisiana, Maryland, Minnesota, New Jersey, Ohio, Pennsylvania, and Tennessee • used systemwide, but not mandated by law, in Utah

(*continued*)

Box 3.3.1

Basic Sentencing Structures in the United States (*Continued*)

The other states and the District of Columbia use indeterminate sentencing in its various forms. One state, Colorado, after changing to determinate sentencing in 1979 went back to indeterminate sentencing in 1985. The federal justice system had adopted determinate sentencing through a system of sentencing guidelines.	offender has one prior conviction, and progressively longer prison terms if the offender's criminal history is more extensive.	• applied selectively in Massachusetts, Michigan, Rhode Island and Wisconsin • being considered for adoption in other states and the District of Columbia
	Sentence enhancements—In nearly all states, the judge may lengthen the prison term for an offender with prior felony convictions. The lengths of such enhancements and the criteria for imposing them vary among the states.	In some states that group felonies according to their seriousness, the repeat offender may be given a sentence ordinarily imposed for a higher seriousness category. Some states prescribe lengthening the sentences of habitual offenders by specified amounts or imposing a mandatory minimum term that must be served before parole can be considered. In other states the guidelines provide for sentences that reflect the offender's criminal history as well as the seriousness of the offense. Many states prescribe conditions under which parole eligibility is limited or eliminated. For example, a person with three or more prior

(*continued*)

Box 3.3.1

Basic Sentencing Structures in the United States (*Continued*)

	Sources: Surveys conducted for the Bureau of Justice Statistics by the U.S. Bureau of the Census in 1985 and by the Pennsylvania Commission on Crime and Delinquency in 1986.	felony convictions, if convicted of a serious violent offense, might be sentenced to life imprisonment without parole.

Source: Bureau of Justice Statistics (1988), Report to the Nation on Crime and Justice, *2nd ed. (Washington, DC: U.S. Department of Justice):91.*

crimes. There traditionally has been a certain level of sentencing power vested in the executive branch in the form of clemency. The governor of a state or President of the United States can grant pardons, commutations, reprieves, and other forms of mercy. The sentencing power granted to parole authorities and sentencing judges is generally delegated to these offices by the legislature.

In indeterminate sentencing systems, the legislature establishes a range of penalties (minimum to maximum), and the sentencing judge is then authorized to impose a sentence that is not less than the minimum and not more than the maximum. In some cases, the legislature establishes a minimum term and then allows the judge to set a maximum within some absolute outer limit. In other cases, the legislature sets a minimum term that is some fraction of the maximum term decreed by the judge. In any indeterminate sentencing system, a paroling authority is authorized to grant release sometime between the end of the minimum term and the end of the maximum term. Thus, the judge has powers delegated by the legislature, and the paroling authority has power that is limited both by the legislature and by the decision of the judge.

In determinate sentencing systems, the legislature generally reserves most of the sentencing power for itself. In some cases, the legislature actually will determine the sentence to be imposed on persons convicted of a specific offense. Here, the judge and parole authority have no sentencing power. More common is the model in which the legislature describes the expected or normal penalty for an offense, and then allows the sentencing judge to modify it (with reasons given). This is presumptive sentencing; that is, the law establishes what the legislature "presumes" will be the sentence, and then requires the judge to explain any case in which the presumed term length is not imposed. In determinate sentencing systems, the parole authority typically has no sentencing power.

In most cases, the legislature grants the sentencing judge the ability to choose between a sentence of incarceration and one of community supervision. This is considerable sentencing power, even in a system in which the judge's power to determine the length of a prison sentence has been strictly curtailed. The decision as to what decisionmaker receives how much sentencing power reflects a different emphasis on each of the four purposes of criminal sentencing.

Anspach and Monsen (1989) observe that the sentencing process and the achievement of sentencing purposes are complex. In a study of the effects of sentencing reform in Maine, they note that adoption of determinate sentencing alone does not ensure rational sentencing. In abolishing indeterminate sentencing and parole, the legislature in Maine provided sentencing judges with a list of eight purposes of penalties that were themselves contradictory. They conclude that failing to provide a consistent rationale for the imposition of sentences promotes unfair and/or irrational punishments. Thus, while sentencing structures are differently suited to achieving or promoting a specific purpose of punishment, structural reform alone is not enough. The structure of the sentencing process should be coupled with a clear statement about the relative importance of particular sentencing purposes. Similarly, Kramer and Ulmer (1996) found that even within a sentencing structure designed to promote equality in sentencing, judges still imposed different sentences in cases that were similar to each other.

Pamela Griset (2002) examined the development of sentencing policy in Florida over 20 years, as the general sentencing structure in the state moved from essentially indeterminate to determinate sentencing. She observed that sentencing policy is the product of many different decisionmakers, including the legislature, judiciary, and various executive branch officials. With regard to Florida, Griset (2002:299) observed, "Like a dysfunctional family, the three branches of government in different places and at different times, have employed a variety of pathological adaptations in exercising their punishment powers, often resulting in muddled or destructive punishment policy." While one branch might be trying to lengthen terms, another would be seeking to reduce prison terms. One set of decisionmakers might be trying to increase the use of imprisonment while another sought to increase diversion from prison. In short, the shared nature of sentencing power, coupled with the political importance of crime and punishment, often led to inconsistent and contradictory sentencing actions.

Deterrent sentences are best defined and imposed by the legislature, so that it is clear to everyone beforehand that a specific punishment will follow a certain criminal conviction. This is the rationale behind what are known as **mandatory minimum sentences**. In these sentences, the legislature decrees that anyone convicted of a particular offense (say, use of a handgun in the commission of a crime or drunk driving) will be sentenced to a minimum number of days or years of incarceration. The prison sentence is mandatory and is expected to deter offenders. Rottman and Strickland (2006) report that 44 states and the District of Columbia have mandatory minimum prison sentences for offenders convicted of committing at least some felonies while armed with a deadly weapon.

Just deserts, or retributive, sentencing is perhaps best accomplished by granting limited sentencing power to the judge. The legislature sets an expectation or limit on how severe a penalty may be imposed for a particular criminal act, but the judge is expected to "fine tune" the sentence so that the severity of the sentence matches the severity of the offense.

Rehabilitative (treatment) and incapacitative sentences are probably best imposed by granting substantial control in sentencing to the paroling authority. This authority can then determine when the offender is safe for release (that is, cured of criminal tendencies) and can adjust the sentence accordingly. The legislature and sentencing judge are ill-suited to this task because they either do not deal directly with the offender, or their roles occur too early in the process. Both of these rationales require that someone continually monitor the offender for progress.

Alternatively, for the purpose of incapacitation, the legislature can develop **habitual offender statutes** that allow for increased penalties for repeat offenders. One such law is the California "three strikes and you're out" law. This law was enacted as a result of a voter initiative (referendum) and provides for a doubling of the sentence upon a second felony conviction "strike," and a tripling of the sentence (or 25-year term, whichever is longer) on the third "strike" (Harris & Jesilow, 2000). The problem with such laws is that they seek to imprison all offenders meeting the criteria (e.g., a third felony conviction) and thus run the risk of relatively high rates of false positives (Saint-Germain & Calamia, 1996; Turner et al., 1995). Most contemporary **three-strikes laws** increase prison terms for offenders having prior convictions but have been written so that they are applied only to the most violent repeat offenders, reducing their likely impact on overall prison populations (Clark, Austin & Henry, 1997). Kovandzic and his colleagues (2004) assessed the impact of

Children display photos of their father, who is in jail for a term of 25 years to life, during a protest against California's "three strikes" law. California voters and lawmakers approved the three-strikes law amid public furor over the 1993 kidnap and murder of 12-year-old Polly Klaas. *Photo credit: AP Photo/Damian Dovarganes.*

three-strikes laws in 21 states on crime rates. They concluded that there was little reason to believe that such laws resulted in reduced crime rates through either incapacitation or deterrence. In a separate analysis, however, Kovandzic (2001) reported that the habitual offender sentencing provisions of Florida law appear to result in small reductions of crime through incapacitation. The policy question, of course, is whether the increased costs in terms of incarceration are justified by the modest reductions in future crime. In 2005, all but two states had some provision for the sentencing of habitual felony offenders.

Sentencing in the Justice System

Criminal sentencing is the final decision point in the court segment of the criminal justice system (with the possible exception of probation revocation, which is discussed previously). It represents a transitional decision point at which the fate of the offender is determined jointly by correctional and judicial officials. In cases of negotiated pleas of guilty, the prosecutor also plays a large role in determining the sentence (Alschuler, 1978). In noncapital cases in three states (Kentucky, Missouri, and Virginia), the jury sentences those convicted of felonies, and in three more (Arkansas, Indiana, and Texas), the jury recommends a sentence to the judge in felony cases. In these states, however, the judge can alter a jury sentence or recommendation (Rottman & Strickland, 2006).

In capital cases (12 states do not have the death penalty), the jury determines the sentence in 29 states and recommends a sentence to the judge in seven other states. In one state (Nebraska), a panel of judges makes the sentencing decision. In Pennsylvania, the sentence can be decided by either the jury or the judge.

The decision about sentence is bifurcated (Wilkins et al., 1976); that is, it is made in two stages. First, the sentencing judge decides whether to incarcerate the convicted offender. Next, the conditions of sentence are determined. These conditions range from the restrictions and obligations placed upon those who are given probation to the length of term for those incarcerated.

Historically, sentencing judges had a greater voice in setting the conditions of prison confinement for sentenced offenders. The judge used to be able to specify the institution to which an offender would be sent, or to require that the sentence be served "at hard labor." Today, most jurisdictions restrict the judge to setting the term of confinement, and leave to the correctional authorities the discretionary power to establish the place and conditions of confinement.

Especially in indeterminate sentencing systems based on a rehabilitative rationale, the sentencing decision is expected to be based on the results of a **presentence investigation** (PSI) conducted by a probation officer. The PSI report describes the offense and offender, and in many jurisdictions includes a recommendation of sentence from the reporting officer (Czajkoski, 1973). Presentence investigations are common in most felony cases across the nation, thereby involving probation officers in the sentencing decision.

Presentence Investigation

After conviction, the judge generally sets a date for sentencing that is delayed long enough to allow the probation department to conclude a presentence investigation. This investigation includes a detailed assessment of the offense and the offender's criminal and social background. A report on the investigation (the PSI report) is then submitted to the sentencing judge so that it can be relied upon in arriving at an appropriate sentence. In addition to its usefulness at the sentencing stage, the PSI serves many other purposes. It is a basic information source for the correctional programming used in developing probation plans and institutional classification; it provides background data used by parole boards in their decisions; and it serves as a basic resource document for research on correctional authorities, offenders, and corrections (U.S. Division of Probation, 1974).

The typical PSI report includes a face sheet, which contains basic offense and offender demographic information. The textual part of the report generally covers: (1) the offense, that is, it gives the official (police) version and the offender's version of the facts (occasionally the victim's version is also added); (2) the social history of the defendant (describing his or her childhood) and current family, employment, economic, and educational situations; and (3) the prior criminal record of the offender. Much of this information is obtained through interviews with the offender, members of the offender's family, and others who know the offender. The material in the report is not held to the strict evidentiary standards of trial. Michael Weinrath (1999) assessed the accuracy of narrative presentence reports and found that the traditional descriptive report was not an accurate means of predicting whether the offender would successfully complete probation. He urged that we discontinue narrative reports and move to the use of more objective risk assessments for judicial sentencing.

Traditionally, the PSI report did not have to be disclosed to the defendant. In 1949, the U.S. Supreme Court decided the case of *Williams v. New York*, which dealt with the issue of disclosure of the presentence investigation report. Williams had been convicted of capital murder, but the jury had recommended leniency. After reviewing the PSI report, the judge imposed the death penalty. Williams's attorney was not allowed to see the report and verify its accuracy. The Court ruled that there was no constitutional right to review the report. However, in 1977, the Court ruled in *Gardner v. Florida* that when the death penalty is imposed as a result of information contained in a PSI report, the defense has a right to review that report. Therefore, at least in a capital case, the contents of the PSI report must be disclosed to defense counsel.

In jurisdictions where probation officers are allowed to make recommendations to the sentencing judge, sentencing judges have been found to concur with these recommendations in the great majority of cases (Carter & Wilkins, 1967). This is one of the principal reasons why some argue that the defendant should be allowed to review the document. Disclosure of the PSI report, however, is opposed by others, who argue that letting the defendant see the report will cause those interviewed to withhold information, or that disclosure might jeopardize the rehabilitation of the offender, should he or she learn things from the report that would be detrimental to rehabilitative programming.

In many jurisdictions, this issue has been resolved, either through disclosure of the entire report (Dubois, 1981) or, more frequently, through partial disclosure. In **partial disclosure**, the judge either summarizes the facts and the reasons for sentence, allowing the defense to contest any errors, or provides a copy of the body of the report to the defense. In jurisdictions where a copy is provided, there often is a confidential addendum that is not disclosed.

The Sentencing Hearing

There is no constitutional right to a separate hearing for sentencing, but generally a sentencing hearing is held for felony defendants. In most states, there are statutory provisions for sentencing hearings (Rottman et al., 2000). In jurisdictions or cases in which there is no presentence investigation, sentencing typically follows conviction. Although there is not a separate hearing, the defendant is afforded the opportunity to speak on his or her own behalf (usually through counsel), and the state (prosecutor) is asked to comment on sentencing. Sometimes the victim is present and allowed to speak or submit a written statement for consideration at sentencing.

At the point of sentencing, whether or not there is a separate hearing for that purpose, the defendant has the right to counsel. In 1967, in *Mempa v. Rhay*, the U.S. Supreme Court ruled that sentencing was a "critical stage" of the justice system, at which the defendant stands to lose protected rights and interests. The Court held that the offender had the right to be represented at sentencing.

The Parole Hearing

In cases in which the offender is sentenced to incarceration in prison under an indeterminate sentence model, the final sentencing decision is usually rendered by a parole authority. In these cases, the judge imposes a sentence that has a minimum and maximum term, but the actual duration of the penalty is not known. The paroling authority has the power to grant release (that is, limit the duration of confinement) at some point between the end of the minimum term and the end of the maximum term. This decision is usually made by the entire board, or by a panel of board members, after a hearing with the inmate. In Oklahoma, the parole board advises the governor, but it is the governor who holds the authority to grant parole. Only about one-third of the states continue to use parole as the primary means of release for prison inmates. In those states in particular, the parole release decision is an important part of the sentencing process.

Parole eligibility is established by the legislature and defines which types of inmates can be paroled at what points in their sentence. For example, the legislature might require that the offender serve a minimum term before release is authorized. Similarly, the legislature can define certain offenses (or offenders) as ineligible for parole. In cases in which states use the "life without parole" sentence for murder, the legislature has defined murderers as "ineligible" for parole. Given eligibility, the parole authority can grant release to a prison inmate.

At the parole hearing, the paroling authority reviews the criminal and social history of the offender, assesses his or her adjustment to prison, and evaluates the offender's potential for success under parole supervision. The inmate is allowed to speak at this hearing and to present whatever evidence he or she feels is relevant. There is no right to counsel at the parole release hearing. Discretionary release on parole has been criticized for failing to protect the community by releasing dangerous offenders early as well as for violating individual rights through discriminatory decisions. Lawrence Bennett (1995) argues that while these are real problems with traditional parole release systems, the development of guidelines for release decisions and better policies for supervision of parolees can overcome the most serious problems. In contrast, Carolyn Turpin-Petrosino (1999) studied parole in New Jersey and concluded that changes in the law intended to control parole board discretion had no effect on parole decisionmaking. In another study of parole in Nebraska, Jon Proctor (1999) concluded that parole decisions were routine and based primarily on eligibility. He did not find much evidence of discretionary decisionmaking in release determinations. In a study of parole decisions with sex offenders, Huebner and Bynum (2006) report that parole decisions demonstrate effects of both legal and extralegal factors and that protection of public safety is a primary concern.

Conditions of Sentence

Whether the judge chooses probation or incarceration, the second decision in sentencing relates to the conditions of sentence. In cases of probation, the judge retains broad discretionary power to set the conditions of supervision. With incarceration sentences, the power is shared between the legislature and correctional authorities. Box 3.3.2 describes the basic sentences imposed on those convicted of felonies in 2000.

Probation

Probation, as a punishment for criminal behavior, is conditional liberty. The convicted offender is allowed to remain in the community under the supervision of a probation officer, provided that he or she abides by certain conditions of conduct established by the judge. Should the probationer violate the conditions of release, he or she may be taken before the court for a hearing, at which time probation may be revoked and the probationer sentenced to prison.

Box 3.3.2

Types of Felony Sentences Imposed by State Courts, by Offense, 2003

	Percent of Felons Sentenced to Incarceration			
Most serious Conviction offense	**Total**	**Prison**	**Jail**	**Probation**
All offenses	69%	41%	28%	31%
Violent Offenses	77	52	25	23
Murder	95	91	4	5
Sexual Assault	82	59	23	18
Rape	89	67	22	11
Other Sex Assault	78	55	23	22
Robbery	86	71	15	14
Aggravated Assault	71	42	29	29
Other violent	77	42	35	23
Property Offenses	66	38	28	34
Burglary	72	46	26	28
Larceny	67	36	31	33
Motor Vehicle Theft	76	37	39	24
Fraud	59	31	28	41
Drug Offenses	66	39	27	34
Possession	62	34	28	38
Trafficking	68	42	26	32
Weapons Offenses	73	45	28	27
Other Offenses	70	35	35	30

Source: M. Durose & P. Langan (2004), Felony Sentences in State Courts, 2003 *(Washington, DC: Bureau of Justice Statistics):4.*

Probation sentences generally are regarded by offenders and the public as leniency (Gibbs, 1985; Israel & Dawes, 2002; Newman, 1983). Probation may be imposed in a variety of ways. The most common way in which probation is imposed is when a pronounced prison sentence is ordered suspended; that is, when the execution of sentence (the taking of an offender to prison) is suspended. Another very common practice is suspended sentencing, in which the offender is placed on probation before a sentence (prison term) is actually pronounced. A third method entails a direct sentence to probation, in which the sentence is a probation term. However, surprisingly few jurisdictions actually have statutes that specifically recognize and authorize probation as a criminal sentence. Other, less formal mechanisms for probation also may be used, but these more closely mirror "diversion" programs than criminal sentences. That is, there are some jurisdictions in which the conviction will not be entered if the defendant successfully completes the probation term. Spohn, DeLone, and Spears (1998) describe one such practice as a "decision to withhold adjudication" in Miami, Florida.

The offender on probation is supervised by a probation officer who works for the court, but the probationer is responsible to the judge. The judge establishes the conditions of release, including such things as "punish lessons," curfews, partial incarceration, and community service (Parisi, 1980; Umbreit, 1981). Because of the large number of judges, and their individual discretion, probation conditions include a wide variety of restrictions and prescriptions (Jaffe, 1979). [...]

Incarceration

While incarceration will be discussed in greater detail [...], the conditions of a sentence of incarceration involve two dimensions: the type of facility and the length of term. In any jurisdiction with more than one correctional facility, there will be differences in the experience of being imprisoned depending upon where one is incarcerated. Prisons differ in terms of population (hardened, dangerous criminals, or first offenders), type of programs (educational/vocational or industrial), and level of custody (maximum-, medium-, or minimum-security). As an example of the variance in prison experiences, serving three years by working outside on a prison farm for half of the day and attending school for the other half is qualitatively different from spending the same amount of time locked inside a huge maximum-security prison making automobile tags all day.

The decision as to where an offender will serve his or her sentence is sometimes controlled by statute, so that offenders older than a certain age or those convicted of a specified crime must be incarcerated in a maximum-security prison. What the offender will do while incarcerated, and where he or she will be incarcerated, however, are questions that often are left to the discretion of correctional authorities.

The length of sentence is controlled by statutory provisions that define parole eligibility (minimum term) and by the **good time** (reductions in length of prison sentence for good behavior while incarcerated) policies and laws of the jurisdiction. Most states shorten prison terms for good behavior while incarcerated. Rottman and his colleagues (2000) reported that 30 of the 50 states had provisions for the award of sentence reductions for good behavior. In some states, this good time is credited only against the maximum term, that is, by advancing the date of mandatory release. In others, it is counted against the minimum term, that is, by advancing the date of parole eligibility. In still others, it is credited against both the minimum and maximum terms. Thus, the legislature, judge, and parole board all have some power in regard to sentence length, but correctional administrators who award and revoke good time also share in this decision.

Issues in Sentencing

Like the rest of the justice system, sentencing is fraught with questions and unresolved issues. The sentencing process is constantly emerging and evolving, sometimes returning to earlier practices and procedures that previously had been abandoned as inappropriate. Today sentencing is undergoing considerable scrutiny and reform. In the latter part of the nineteenth century, we began to abandon corporal and capital penalties and long, harsh prison terms in favor of rehabilitative strategies including more flexible prison sentences. In the last quarter of the twentieth century, we abandoned rehabilitative, indeterminate sentences in favor of more retributive fixed terms. Today, we are moving away from retributive sentences toward an unclear future.

Four core issues can be identified that allow us to better understand the complex problems of criminal sentencing. Disparity is a central issue today and is the concern at the base of many of the efforts to change criminal sentencing. Corporal and capital punishment have reemerged (perhaps continued) as issues in sentencing. The calculation of prison time and "truth in sentencing" is still a point of contention and, finally, we continue to grapple with the development of intermediate or alternative sanctions.

Disparity

Disparity refers to the unequal treatment of similar offenders at sentencing (Gottfredson, 1979). Most of us would agree that offenders with similar criminal histories who are convicted of the same offense ought to receive similar penalties. When differences in sentences appear among similar offenders, the differences generally are termed disparity. Yet, disparity actually refers to *unwarranted* differences (Gottfredson et al., 1978).

For example, if a jurisdiction follows an incapacitation sentencing rationale and has two first-offender burglars, it would not be disparity if one offender who was determined to pose a great risk of further crime was imprisoned, while the other, thought to pose little risk, was granted probation. Under the concerns of incapacitation, these offenders are not similar. The current debate over disparity hinges, in large measure, on the definition of "similar" (Vining, 1983).

Since 1976, several states and the federal government have enacted legislation that alters their sentencing structures. In large measure, these changes have been aimed at increasing equity (reducing disparity) in criminal sentences (Anspach & Monsen, 1989; Goodstein & Hepburn, 1983; LaGoy, Hussey & Kramer, 1978; Ulmer, 1997; von Hirsch & Hanrahan, 1979). Several states have implemented presumptive or determinate sentencing to ensure that similarly situated offenders receive similar sanctions. The results of these reforms are now being studied; the evaluation of their success is unclear (Griswold, 1987).

One type of determinate sentencing that states and the federal government have adopted in hopes of controlling disparity and ensuring more certainty in punishment is based on the use of sentencing guidelines. Sentencing guidelines identify the factors that judges should consider in sentencing and give an indication of what would be an acceptable penalty for each of many different types of cases. The federal government adopted a sentencing guideline system in November 1987 (*Criminal Justice Newsletter*, 1987). By 2005, 18 states also had developed sentencing guidelines. As shown in Box 3.3.3, in five jurisdictions, the guidelines are mandatory; in seven, they are voluntary. In the remaining jurisdictions, the guidelines are advisory, in that the judge may deviate from the guidelines. Most jurisdictions use decision matrices in which offense seriousness and risk or prior criminal record are used to determine appropriate sentences. A few use other types of guidelines in which general principles guide the sentencing judge in selecting an appropriate punishment (Griffin & Katz, 2002).

Box 3.3.3

Sentencing Guidelines in 2005

Guideline Type:	Number of States	Percent
None	32	64%
Voluntary	7	14
Advisory	6	12
Mandatory	5	10

Source: D. Rottman & S. Strickland (2006), State Court Organization, 2005 *(Washington, DC: Bureau of Justice Statistics):254–259.*

The individual whims of justice system officials (judges, parole board members, etc.) that come out in the exercise of discretionary authority have been identified as the culprit for sentencing disparity. This concern is driven in large measure by perceptions that sentencing decisions reflect ethnic and sex discrimination more so than differences in crimes and risk of new crimes (Crew, 1991; Spohn, 2000; Spohn & Cederblom, 1991). To combat the disparity in decisions, reformers have moved to give legislatures tighter control over sentencing power by more closely defining sentences and the factors to be relied upon in determining punishments (Bureau of Justice Assistance, 1996). The effects of reform are unclear, and may involve changes in the rates at which people are incarcerated, the types of crimes for which offenders are imprisoned, and the lengths of terms (Tonry, 1999). Twenty-three states and the District of Columbia have created **sentencing commissions**, formal bodies assigned to assess and oversee criminal sentencing and recommend reforms.

In the Spring of 2004, the U.S. Supreme Court decided the case of *Blakely v. Washington* (2004). With the sentencing guidelines of the State of Washington, the judge is allowed to increase a prison term if the judge finds that the offense or offender represent an aggravated or more serious case than normal. The Supreme Court ruled that relying only on a judicial determination of facts in this instance violates a Constitutional right to have facts determined by the jury. It is still unclear what might be the full effects of this decision. While some commentators feared the decision spelled the end to sentencing guidelines, a more cautious and restrained assessment of the decision suggests that sentencing guidelines, especially in most state systems, can survive constitutional challenge (Skove, 2004). The next year the Court decided *United States v. Booker* (2005), in which it ruled that while federal judges must consider the federal sentencing guidelines, they are allowed to alter sentences for other factors.

Kathleen Daly and Rebecca Bordt (1995) reviewed available data on sentencing, looking for differences in punishment related to the sex of the defendant. They found that women were generally given less severe sentences than men. Daly and Bordt suggest that these differences are partly explained by differences in the types of offenses and prior records of men and women, but also probably reflect the justice system's recognition of the sex differences that exist in society. Cassia Spohn (1994) has reported similar persistent differences in the sentencing of blacks as compared to whites. Black defendants generally receive more severe sentences than whites, but again the picture is complicated by differences in rates of conviction for certain types of offenses and in prior criminal records of whites and blacks (Pratt, 1998). It may be that these differences in offenses and criminal records explain some of the differences in sentencing, yet it is also likely that criminal sentencing reflects the disadvantaged status of minority group members in American society (Zatz, 2000). Steffensmeier and Demuth (2001) found that sentences in Pennsylvania were harshest for Hispanic defendants and least harsh for white defendants, indicating that minority status, whether racial or ethnic, appears to be associated with sentencing outcomes. Gainey, Steen, and Engen (2005) found that offender characteristics such as sex, race, and the decision to go to trial versus enter a guilty plea explained the use of alternatives to incarceration with drug offenders. Griffin and Wooldredge (2006) reported that the adoption of sentencing guidelines in Ohio had mixed effects on the sentencing of female offenders, but that females might benefit from some "chivalrous" treatment in sentencing. In the end, the research indicates that the problems of sentencing disparity are complex and may not be easily solved.

Corporal and Capital Punishment

In America, from colonial times through the early part of the nineteenth century, most punishments for serious offenses involved physical pain, such as branding, maiming, flogging, and death. In recent history, we have abandoned those forms of punishment in favor of the more humane alternative of incarceration. Yet, more recently, there has been a rebirth of support for physical punishment (Foucault, 1977; Newman, 1978, 1983). The death penalty is back. In 1991, 14 inmates were executed and nearly 2,500 inmates were on death row in the United States. In 2005, 60 inmates were executed, and nearly 3,300 inmates were on death row. Between 1977 and 2001, there were 1,004 executions in 34 states and the federal system (Snell, 2006). The types of offenses for which the death penalty may be imposed are described in Box 3.3.4, while Box 3.3.5 describes the offenders who were on death rows around the country in 2005.

Flogging or whipping as a sanction for offenses was finally abandoned in this country in the 1970s, when the state of Delaware removed the whipping post from its penitentiary. In a review of case law through the year 2000, Maddan and Hallahan (2002) conclude that is possible that corporal punishment, in the form of whipping, could be revived in the United States. The constitutionality of corporal and capital punishment is always subject to question. The U.S. Supreme Court has not ruled the death penalty to be cruel and unusual punishment or to be otherwise unconstitutional. Moreover, in the 1976 case of *Gregg v. Georgia*, the Court held that the death penalty, per se, is not unconstitutional. Earlier, in *Furman v. Georgia* (1972), the Court focused on the procedures by which the death penalty was imposed. Having found the existing procedures too vague and unstructured, the Court did not address the issue of the death penalty itself. The *Gregg* decision was the first of several in which revised procedures for imposing the death penalty were reviewed by the Court. Given an acceptable procedure (jury recommendation based on a presentation of aggravating and mitigating factors identified in the statute), the Court also addressed the constitutionality of the death penalty itself.

Some support the death penalty as an incapacitative sanction, saying that murderers pose too great a risk to society. Vito and Wilson (1988) addressed this issue and found that most prisoners in their sample who were sentenced to death were not particularly dangerous. Less than 25 percent of death row inmates who were released committed new crimes, and none committed a new homicide. Others suggest that an alternative to capital punishment is to impose life sentences without possibility of parole (Cheatwood, 1988). The debate over capital punishment continues. The public, it appears, specifically supports capital punishment, and generally is in favor of harsher criminal sanctions (Flanagan, 1987). Public opinion surveys reveal that more than three-quarters

Box 3.3.4

Capital Offenses, by State, 2005

Alabama. Intentional murder with 18 aggravating factors (Ala. Stat. Ann. 13A-5-40(a)(1)-(18)).

Arizona.* First-degree murder accompanied by at least 1 of 14 aggravating factors (A.R.S. § 13-703(F)).

Arkansas.* Capital murder (Ark. Code Ann. 5-10-101) with a finding of at least 1 of 10 aggravating circumstances; treason.

California.* First-degree murder with special circumstances; train wrecking; treason; perjury causing execution.

Colorado.* First-degree murder with at least 1 of 17 aggravating factors; treason.

Connecticut.* Capital felony with 8 forms of aggravated homicide (C.G.S. 53a-54b).

Delaware.* First-degree murder with aggravating circumstances.

Florida.* First-degree murder; felony murder; capital drug trafficking; capital sexual battery.

Georgia.* Murder; kidnapping with bodily injury or ransom when the victim dies; aircraft hijacking; treason.

Idaho.* First-degree murder with aggravating factors; aggravated kidnapping; perjury resulting in death.

Illinois.* First-degree murder with 1 of 21 aggravating circumstances.

Indiana.* Murder with 16 aggravating circumstances (IC 35-50-2-9).

Kansas.* Capital murder with 8 aggravating circumstances (KSA 21-3439).

Kentucky.* Murder with aggravating factors; kidnapping with aggravating factors (KRS 32.025).

Louisiana.* First-degree murder; aggravated rape of victim under age 12; treason (La. R.S. 14:30, 14:42, and 14:113).

Maryland.* First-degree murder, either premeditated or during the commission of a felony, provided that certain death eligibility requirements are satisfied.

Mississippi. Capital murder (97-3-19(2) MCA); aircraft piracy (97-25-55(1) MCA).

Missouri.* First-degree murder (565.020 RSMO 2000).

Montana. Capital murder with 1 of 9 aggravating circumstances (46-18-303 MCA); capital sexual assault (45-5-503 MCA).

Nebraska.* First-degree murder with a finding of at least 1 statutorily-defined aggravating circumstance.

(continued)

Box 3.3.4

Capital Offenses, by State, 2005 (*Continued*)

Nevada.* First-degree murder with at least 1of 15 aggravating circumstances (NRS 200.030, 200.033, 200.035).

New Hampshire. Six categories of capital murder (RSA 630:1, RSA 630:5).

New Jersey. Murder by one's own conduct, by solicitation, committed in furtherance of a narcotics conspiracy, or during commission of a crime of terrorism (NJSA 2C:11-3c).

New Mexico.* First-degree murder with at least 1 of 7 statutorily-defined aggravating circumstances (Section 30-2-1 A, NMSA).

New York.* First-degree murder with 1 of 13 aggravating factors (NY Penal Law §125.27).

North Carolina.* First-degree murder (NCGS §14-17).

Ohio.* Aggravated murder with at least 1 of 10 aggravating circumstances (O.R.C. secs. 2903.01, 2929.02, and 2929.04).

Oklahoma. First-degree murder in conjunction with a finding of at least 1 of 8 statutorily-defined aggravating circumstances.

Oregon. Aggravated murder (ORS 163.095).

Pennsylvania. First-degree murder with 18 aggravating circumstances.

South Carolina.* Murder with 1 of 11 aggravating circumstances (§ 16-3-20(C)(a)).

South Dakota.* First-degree murder with 1 of 10 aggravating circumstances; aggravated kidnapping.

Tennessee.* First-degree murder with 1 of 15 aggravating circumstances (Tenn. Code Ann. § 39-13-204).

Texas. Criminal homicide with 1 of 9 aggravating circumstances (TX Penal Code 19.03).

Utah.* Aggravated murder (76-5-202, Utah Code Annotated).

Virginia.* First-degree murder with 1 of 13 aggravating circumstances (VA Code § 18.2-31).

Washington.* Aggravated first-degree murder.

Wyoming. First-degree murder.

**As of December 31, 2005, 27 States excluded mentally retarded persons from capital sentencing: Arizona, Arkansas, California, Colorado, Connecticut, Delaware, Florida, Georgia, Idaho, Illinois, Indiana, Kansas, Kentucky, Louisiana, Maryland, Missouri, Nebraska, Nevada, New Mexico, New York, North Carolina, Ohio, South Dakota, Tennessee, Utah, Virginia, and Washington. Mental retardation is a mitigating factor in South Carolina.*

Source: T. Snell (2006), Capital Punishment, 2005 *(Washington, DC: Bureau of Justice Statistics):2.*

Box 3.3.5

Characteristics of the Death Row Population, December 31, 2005

Total Number Under Sentence of Death	3,254
Male	98.4%
Female	1.6
White	55.5%
Black	42.2
Other	2.4
Hispanic	12.7%
Non-Hispanic	87.3
Education:	
Less than 8th Grade	14.3%
9th –11th Grade	36.9
High School/GED	39.6
Any College	9.2
Median	11th Grade
Married	22.2%
Divorced/Separated	20.5
Widowed	2.9
Never Married	54.4

Source: T. Snell (2006), Capital Punishment, 2005 (Washington, DC: Bureau of Justice Statistics):6.

of those polled support capital punishment in general. However, general support for the death penalty does not translate into support for capital punishment in specific cases (Vito & Keil, 1998). Durham, Elrod, and Kinkade (1996) presented respondents with examples of specific cases and found that people make distinctions between different kinds of murders and murderers so that the general agreement on support for the death penalty in the abstract translates into different sentencing recommendations in particular cases.

Those supporting corporal punishment argue that physical pain, properly administered, is less destructive, less costly, and more effective than lengthy incarceration (Newman, 1983). Those who are opposed to corporal punishment suggest that such penalties will continue to be considered cruel and unusual and, therefore, unconstitutional. If the issue were raised in the U.S. Supreme Court, it is not clear how the Court would decide the question. A principal rationale in support of corporal punishment is that our current practices are not effective in controlling crime, and that our prisons and jails are too crowded to accommodate many more prisoners. Added to this is the reasoning that as death is allowed as a penalty for crime, penalties less than death should also not be considered too severe.

To date no state has reinstituted corporal punishment, but there are continuing calls for physical punishments, including "chain gang" service. Among intermediate penalties are programs of community service in which convicted offenders are required to perform some labor, often physical, as part of their sentence. It is difficult to predict how the system will respond to suggestions for a return to corporal punishment. On the one hand, it could be seen as a practical alternative to incarceration for those convicted of serious offenses for which probation seems too lenient. On the other hand, it is entirely likely that, if accepted, corporal punishment would be added to current penalties, resulting in sentences to prison with corporal punishment, or bodily punishment as a condition of probation. Whatever the result, the resurgence of this once-discredited response to criminality illustrates the intractable nature of the issues involved in sentencing.

The importance of pain as a component of criminal punishments, however, has regained prominence. Todd Clear (1994) has written about how the imposition of harm (pain) for harm has become a central component of contemporary sentencing and correctional practice. The renewed emphasis on the imposition of physical suffering on criminal offenders is illustrated by the popularity of **boot camp** or "shock incarceration" programs in prisons (Lutze, 1998). By 1996 there were more than 50 boot camp programs operating in 32 states (Bourque, Han & Hill, 1996:7). As seen in Box 3.3.6, these programs include a heavy emphasis on physical training and manual labor. The programs are expected to be more physically demanding than traditional imprisonment, and are of shorter duration than most prison sentences. In essence, the increase in physical pain involved in the boot camp experience balances a shorter length of confinement. While we may not adopt electric shock or return to flogging offenders, the spread of "boot camps" indicates that we are not opposed to using some forms of corporal sanctions.

Using Time as a Penalty: Truth in Sentencing

We already have seen how provisions for good time affect sentencing decisions by adding correctional administrators to the list of officials who exercise authority in sentencing decisions. What is not as clear is the complexity of using time as a penalty. Although the death penalty can be used

Box 3.3.6

Program Elements of Boot Camp Programs Reported by Correctional Administrators

Program Element	Percentage of Programs
Physical Training	100%
Physical Labor	100%
Drill/Ceremony	100%
Alcohol Treatment	100%
Drug Treatment	100%
Substance Abuse Education	100%
Basic Education	96%
Vocational Education	46%

Source: E. Cowles, T. Castellano & L. Gransky (1995), "Boot Camp" Drug Treatment and Aftercare Interventions: An Evaluation Review (Washington, DC: National Institute of Justice):6.

for heinous murders, the basic limitation on criminal penalties in the United States is time. While conditions of confinement vary, for the individual offender the length of term is critical. How long an offender serves is dependent on several factors, each of which has importance for the severity of punishment and the operation of correctional institutions.

Prison time is typically measured in days, although sentences are generally imposed in months and years. Most states with provisions for good-time award reductions of sentence on a "per days served" basis. Good time is expected to be an incentive to encourage inmates to obey prison rules. James Emshoff and William Davidson (1987) recognized that sentence reductions may affect inmate behavior, but contended that other factors are at least as important. A typical model awards one day of good time for every two served, so that after serving 20 days, 10 days are added to complete the month. A six-year sentence is then reduced to four years (one-third reduction). In some states, good time is awarded on a sliding scale so the longer the sentence, or the longer the term served, the more good-time days received. Thus, an inmate could earn 10 days for every 30 for the first three years, and 15 days for every 30 for the next three years, and so on, "sliding" up the scale of good-time award. To this sentence may be added "meritorious" good time, earned by the inmate for special accomplishments such as exceptional industry, donating blood, and the like. Reductions for good behavior, then, can be substantial.

Whatever the reductions for good behavior, there are other time calculations that are questionable. For an offender unable to secure pretrial release on bail, what part of his or her pretrial time counts as time served? The time spent in jail after conviction but before going to prison generally counts toward a prison sentence. The decision whether to count the time spent in jail prior to conviction is generally left to the discretion of the judge or correctional authorities. Thus, an offender who is in jail for six months prior to conviction and three months after conviction, prior to transport to the prison, may be granted nine months off his or her sentence, and generally must be granted three months. A question remains, however, as to whether the offender also should be granted good time for time served before going to prison. Generally, good time is not awarded for time spent in jail.

A final consideration is the ability of the judge to impose terms for multiple convictions to run either consecutively or concurrently. A **consecutive term** is one in which each sentence must be served in order, one following the other. A **concurrent term** is one in which all the sentences run at the same time. Two five-year terms imposed consecutively total 10 years; the same terms imposed concurrently total five years.

The unresolved problem in the calculation of prison time is that the imposed sentence generally is not the same as the actual term served, as can be seen in Box 3.3.7. Von Hirsch and Hanrahan (1979) suggest that one of the major difficulties faced in sentencing reform is that we do not sentence offenders in "real time." The public sees the sentence imposed as being the maximum term ordered by the judge, without reference to good time or to the fact that concurrent terms are imposed frequently. Thus, if an offender sentenced to three concurrent five-year terms is released in two years, the public may begin to believe that the law does not mean what it says. The Bureau of Justice Statistics (Durose & Langan, 2003) estimates that

Box 3.3.7

Estimated Percentage of Sentence to be Served in State Prison by Conviction Offense

Conviction Offense	Mean Sentence	Time to be Served	Percent of Sentence
All Offenses	53 mo.	27 mo.	51%
Violent Offenses	84 mo.	52 mo.	6%
Property Offenses	41 mo.	20 mo.	49%
Drug Offenses	48 mo.	20 mo.	43%
Weapon Offenses	38 mo.	24 mo.	63%
Other Offenses	39 mo.	19 mo.	50%

Source: M. Durose & P. Langan (2004), Felony Sentences in State Courts, 2003 *(Washington, DC: Bureau of Justice Statistics):5.*

felons sentenced to prison in state courts in 2000 will serve only 55 percent of their sentences before being released.

Concern about the gap between the length of sentence imposed by the court and that actually served by convicted offenders spurred a call for "truth in sentencing." In 1995, Congress passed legislation calling for states to develop **"truth in sentencing"** so that those convicted of violent offenses will serve at least 85 percent of the term they receive. Federal aid is available to states that adopt such truth-in-sentencing laws, and many states have changed or are considering a change in their sentencing laws to achieve more truthful sentences. Thus far, the solutions sought by the states involve reserving prison space for those convicted of violent crimes by reducing the rate of imprisonment and length of terms for nonviolent offenders. Of course, one solution to the problem would be the imposition of prison sentences in "real time." However, most legislators are unwilling to admit to the public that violent offenders, on average, will serve a little more than four years instead of the 10 years to which they are sentenced.

As a result, the impact of truth in sentencing is likely to be the diversion of repeat, nonviolent offenders to community sanctions such as probation, and a substantial lengthening of terms served by violent offenders. The effects of these changes on both community corrections and prison populations are difficult to estimate. It is clear, however, that truth-in-sentencing as currently envisioned will change both prison and community corrections populations. Ditton and Wilson (1999) reviewed the impact of truth-in-sentencing laws through 1998, noting that offenders sentenced under the new laws will not be released for many years and thus it is too early to tell the full effects of the reform. Box 3.3.8 summarizes their findings. Durose and Langan (2007:3) report that "the average time served in prison for a violent felony remained relatively stable between 1994 and 2004."

Box 3.3.8

The "Truth in Sentencing" Reform

Highlights

Three decades of sentencing reform—1970s through 1990s

- *Indeterminate sentencing:* Common in the early 1970s, parole boards have the authority to release offenders from prison.
- *Determinate sentencing:* States introduced fixed prison terms which could be reduced by good-time or earned-time credits.

(*continued*)

Box 3.3.8

The "Truth in Sentencing" Reform (*Continued*)

- *Mandatory minimum sentences:* States added statutes requiring offenders to be sentenced to a specified amount of prison time.
- *Truth in sentencing:* First enacted in 1984, TIS laws require offenders to serve a substantial portion of their prison sentence. Parole eligibility and good-time credits are restricted or eliminated.
- Violent offenders released from prison in 1996 were sentenced to serve an average of 85 months in prison. Prior to release they served about half of their prison sentence or 45 months.
- Under truth-in-sentencing laws requiring 85% of the sentence, violent offenders would serve an average of 88 months in prison based on the average sentence for violent offenders admitted to prison in 1996.
- Nearly 7 in 10 State prison admissions for a violent offense in 1997 were in States requiring offenders to serve at least 85% of their sentence.
- By 1998, States and the District of Columbia met the Federal Truth-in-Sentencing Incentive Grant Program eligibility criteria. Eleven States adopted truth-in-sentencing laws in 1995, 1 year after the 1994 Crime Act.

Discrepancy between sentence and time served

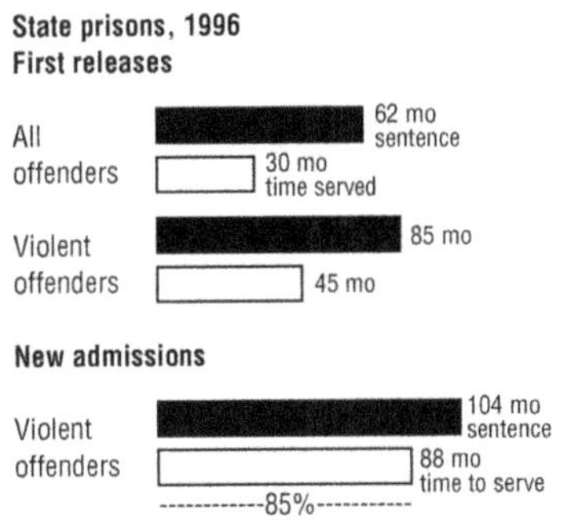

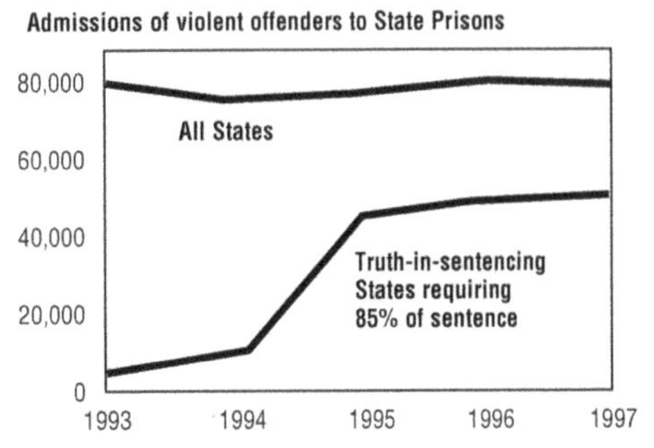

Source: P. Ditton & D. Wilson (1999), Truth in Sentencing in State Prisons *(Washington, DC: Bureau of Justice Statistics):1.*

Intermediate Sanctions

Throughout the past decade there has been increasing interest in the development and implementation of **intermediate sanctions** for crime or punishments that fall somewhere between imprisonment and traditional probation. Historically, sentencing judges have been given a choice between community supervision and confinement in prison or jail as the primary sanctions for crime. Especially as the numbers of people convicted of crime have increased, and prison and jail populations have exceeded the capacity of institutions, these choices have been seen as inadequate. In 1985, Pierre DuPont called for the development of a meaningful continuum of sanctions ranging from no restriction to maximum-security incarceration. This call has been echoed by others (Klein, 1997; Morris & Tonry, 1990; Petersilia, 1987).

In response to the perceived need for a wider variety of sanctions, a number of innovative practices have emerged. These include various combinations of incarceration and community supervision dispositions. Specific forms of these sanctions will be discussed in more detail [...], but a brief listing is in order. Sanctions combining incarceration with supervision have emerged, including shock probation, shock parole, placement in community residential facilities, home incarceration, and **split sentences** (sentences combining a period of incarceration with a period of probation supervision) (Petersilia, Lurigio & Byrne, 1992). So too, penalties have been developed that make the experience of community supervision more severe. These include day reporting, intensive supervision, electronic monitoring, and community service orders.

The growth of these penalties blurs the traditional distinction between incarceration and community supervision. Prison boot camps involve a short, intense incarceration. The offender goes to prison, but for a much shorter period. Observers note that these sanctions allow gradations in punishment along a continuum (Holsinger & Latessa, 1999; McCarthy, 1987; Schwartz & Travis, 1996). Thus, penalties can escalate from traditional probation supervision through intensive supervision to day reporting (offenders report to the probation office daily). If more restrictive punishments are desired, the offender could be placed under house arrest (restricted to his or her home), sent to a residential facility (halfway house), or sent to prison. As Box 3.3.9 shows, judges often impose multiple penalties on convicted offenders.

Recalling our discussion of sentencing disparity, the development of a range of punishments is potentially troublesome. If sentencing decisions were suspected of being based on prejudice when only a few choices were available, the provision of more choices increases the chances of disparate treatment. The more things that can be done to punish an offender, the greater the discretion of sentencing decisionmakers. Conversely, the relative degree of disparity may be reduced. Rather than a simple "either/or" issue of incarceration, disparate sentences may be closer in degree of restrictiveness. The difference between intensive supervision and day reporting is not as great as that between probation and prison.

Box 3.3.9

Additional Penalties Imposed on Felons by Conviction Offense, 2003

	Percent of felons with an additional penalty of:				
Most serious Conviction offense	**Fine**	**Restitution**	**Treatment**	**Community Service**	**Other**
All offenses	25%	12%	3%	4%	7%
Violent Offenses	23%	11%	3%	3%	6%
Murder	17	7	1	1	1
Sexual Assault	22	10	4	2	7
Rape	21	10	4	1	6
Other Sex Assault	23	10	3	2	8
Robbery	13	10	1	2	4
Aggravated Assault	27	11	3	3	7
Other violent	26	12	2	4	9
Property Offenses	24%	21%	2%	4%	6%
Burglary	23	20	2	4	5
Larceny	21	19	1	5	7
Motor Vehicle Theft	22	19	2	3	11
Fraud	28	24	2	5	8
Drug Offenses	27%	6%	6%	4%	7%
Possession	25	3	11	5	11
Trafficking	27	8	2	3	5
Weapons Offenses	18%	4%	2%	4%	6%
Other Offenses	29%	10%	3%	4%	8%

Source: M. Durose & P. Langan (2004), Felony Sentences in State Courts, 2003 *(Washington, DC: Bureau of Justice Statistics):10.*

See Box 3.3.10 for a table of selected court cases on sentencing.

Box 3.3.10

Selected Court Cases on Sentencing

Williams v. New York 377 U.S. 241 (1949)	There is no constitutional right to review a presentence investigation (PSI) report. See later controlling case, *Gardner v. Florida* (1977).
Mempa v. Rhay 389 U.S. 128 (1967)	An offender has the right to representation by counsel at the point of sentencing.
Furman v. Georgia 408 U.S. 238 (1972)	Current procedures for imposing the death penalty violate the equal protection clause of the Fourteenth Amendment and the prohibition against cruel and unusual punishment.
Gardner v. Florida 430 U.S. 349 (1977)	Death penalty statutes that contain sufficient safeguards against arbitrary and capricious imposition are constitutional.
Gregg v. Georgia 428 U.S. 153 (1976)	When the death penalty is imposed as a result of information contained in a presentence investigation (PSI) report, the defense has a right to review that report.

Source: Portions of this table were adapted from R.V. del Carmen, S.E. Ritter & B.A. Witt (2005), Briefs of Leading Cases in Corrections, *4th ed. (Newark, NJ: LexisNexis Matthew Bender).*

Due Process, Crime Control, and Sentencing in the Whole System

The sentencing decision links the court subsystem to the correctional subsystem of the justice process. Sentencing decisions reflect the demands and stresses placed on corrections, and indicate how the justice process reacts to social change. For example, with the emergence of drug abuse as a serious criminal problem, the sentencing of those convicted of drug-related offenses has changed. Many more drug offenders are sentenced to prison than in the past, and their sentences to prison are longer than before. Thus, as society has come to see drug offenders as more serious criminals, the increased seriousness has been reflected in more severe sentences. These sentences have changed the composition of correctional (especially prison) populations (Barnes & Kingsnorth, 1996; Beck, 1997; Kraska, 1992).

Further, as the corrections subsystem has struggled with crowding, the sentencing decisions of criminal courts have changed. The imposition of probation sentences for felons increased

A Maricopa County female chain gang in traditional black and white striped uniforms is pictured cleaning up trash in Phoenix, Arizona, in April 1997. Convicted criminals laboring by the roadside, linked together with shackles and chains, are no longer ghosts of Southern-style justice, as chain gangs make a comeback across the United States. *Photo credit: AP Photo/Eric Drotter.*

(Champion, 1988; Petersilia et al., 1985). Judges are using jail sentences as sanctions for those convicted of felonies (McCarthy, 1989). Moreover, the actual length of sentence served by convicted offenders has frequently been reduced by correctional decisionmakers (Farnsworth, Golden & Tester, 1991). The interplay between corrections and sentencing that is driven by prison and jail crowding illustrates the systemic nature of the justice process.

Remember too, that one of the primary motivations for reform of criminal sentencing and the development of alternative sanctions is a desire for fairness. Thus, not only do we seek punitive and incapacitative alternatives to prison for crime control reasons, we seek equitable sanctions for diverse individuals. The sentencing decision is the point at which the full weight of state power can be brought to bear on the individual. The challenge for sentencing is to achieve crime control goals while respecting the rights of the individual offender. Yet, available evidence suggests that criminal sentences reflect differences in sex, race, and age (Spohn, 2000; Steffensmeier, Kramer & Ulmer, 1995). If we seek equal treatment of persons at sentencing, it is likely that we will first have to develop equal treatment of persons in the broader society.

Perhaps the major obstacle to reforming criminal sentencing in the United States lies not in sentencing's considerable complexity of operation and calculation, but more in the lack of effort among our citizens to achieve understanding of the sentencing process. In order to achieve a rational and workable system of sentencing, it may first be necessary to be more open and honest about the meaning of criminal sentences—and more consistent in our purposes served by criminal sanctions.

Review Questions

1. Identify the four traditional purposes of criminal penalties.
2. What types of errors are involved in the prediction of dangerousness at sentencing?
3. Distinguish between determinate and indeterminate criminal sentencing structures.
4. What is the presentence investigation, and what purposes does it serve?
5. What is the sentencing hearing, and what takes place at one?
6. Identify two principal types of sanctions imposed on serious criminal offenders.
7. What is meant by sentencing disparity?
8. Besides sentencing disparity, identify two other current issues in criminal sentencing.

References

Adams, S. (1961). *Effectiveness of Interview Therapy with Older Youth Authority Wards: An Interim Evaluation of the PICO Project.* Sacramento, CA: California Youth Authority.

Alschuler, A.W. (1978). "Sentencing Reform and Prosecutorial Power: A Critique of Recent Proposals for 'Fixed' and 'Presumptive' Sentencing." In *Determinate Sentencing: Reform or Regression?* Washington, DC: U.S. Government Printing Office, 59–88.

Anspach, D. & S. Monsen (1989). "Determinate Sentencing, Formal Rationality, and Khadi Justice in Maine: An Application of Weber's Typology." *Journal of Criminal Justice* 17(6):471–485.

Bailey, W. (1966). "Correctional Outcome: An Evaluation of 100 Reports." *Journal of Criminal Law, Criminology & Police Science* 57:153–160.

Barnes, C. & R. Kingsnorth (1996). "Race, Drug, and Criminal Sentencing: Hidden Effects of the Criminal Law." *Journal of Criminal Justice* 24(1):39–55.

Beck, A. (1997). "Growth, Change, and Stability in the U.S. Prison Population, 1980–1995." *Corrections Management Quarterly* 1(2):1–14.

Bennett, L. (1995). "In Defense of Parole—Is It Worth the Effort?" *Perspectives* 19(3):14–17.

Benson, M. (1990). "Emotions and Adjudication: Status Degradation among White-Collar Criminals." *Justice Quarterly* 7(3):515–528.

[Bourque, B., M. Han & S. Hill (1996). *A National Survey of Aftercare Provisions for Boot Camp Graduates.* Washington, DC: National Institute of Justice.

Bureau of Justice Assistance (1996). *National Assessment of Structured Sentencing.* Washington, DC: Bureau of Justice Assistance.]

Bureau of Justice Statistics (1984). *Sentencing Practices in 13 States.* Washington, DC: U.S. Department of Justice.

Carter, R.M. & L.T. Wilkins (1967). "Some Factors in Sentencing Policy." *Journal of Criminal Law, Criminology & Police Science* 58:503.

Casey, P. & D. Rottman (2003). *Problem-Solving Courts: Models and Trends.* Williamsburg, VA: National Center for State Courts.

Champion, D. (1988). "Felony Plea Bargaining and Probation: A Growing Judicial and Prosecutorial Dilemma." *Journal of Criminal Justice* 16(4):291–301.

Cheatwood, D. (1988). "The Life-Without-Parole Sanction: Its Current Status and a Research Agenda." *Crime & Delinquency* 34(1):43–59.

Clark, J., J. Austin & D. Henry (1997). *"Three Strikes and You're Out": A Review of State Legislation.* Washington, DC: National Institute of Justice.

Clear, T. (1994). *Harm in American Penology: Offenders, Victims, and Their Communities.* Albany, NY: SUNY Press.

Crew, B. K., (1991). "Sex Differences in Criminal Sentencing: Chivalry or Patriarchy?" *Justice Quarterly* 8(1):59–83.

Criminal Justice Newsletter (1987). "Despite Warnings of 'Chaos,' No Delay on Sentencing Reforms." *Criminal Justice Newsletter* 18(21):1, November 2, 1987.

Cullen, F.T. & K.E. Gilbert (1982). *Reaffirming Rehabilitation.* Cincinnati: Anderson.

Czajkoski, E.H. (1973). "Exposing the Quasi-Judicial Role of the Probation Officer." *Federal Probation* 37:9.

Daly, K. & R. Bordt (1995). "Sex Effects and Sentencing: An Analysis of the Statistical Literature." *Justice Quarterly* 12(1):141–175.

Ditton, P. & D. Wilson (1999). *Truth in Sentencing in State Prisons.* Washington, DC: Bureau of Justice Statistics.

Dubois, P.L. (1981). "Disclosure of Presentence Reports in the United States District Courts." *Federal Probation* 45(1):3–9.

DuPont, P. (1985). *Expanding Sentencing Options: A Governor's Perspective.* Washington, DC: U.S. Department of Justice.

Durose, M. & P. Langan (2007). *Felony Sentences in State Courts, 2004.* Washington, DC: Bureau of Justice Statistics

Durose, M. & P. Langan (2004). *Felony Sentences in State Courts, 2002.* Washington, DC: Bureau of Justice Statistics

Durose, M. & P. Langan (2003). *Felony Sentences in State Courts, 2000.* Washington, DC: Bureau of Justice Statistics.

Durham, A.M. (1988). "Crime Seriousness and Punitive Severity: An Assessment of Social Attitudes." *Justice Quarterly* 5(1):131–153.

Durham, A., H. Elrod & P. Kinkade (1996). "Public Support for the Death Penalty: Beyond Gallup." *Justice Quarterly* 13(4):705–736.

Emshoff, J.G. & W.S. Davidson (1987). "The Effect of 'Good Time' Credit on Inmate Behavior: A Quasi-Experiment." *Criminal Justice and Behavior* 14(3):335–351.

Farnsworth, M., J. Golden & K. Tester (1991). "Felony Court Processing in an Urban County: Coping with a Limited Capacity to Punish." *Journal of Criminal Justice* 19(5):421–438.

Flanagan, T.J. (1987). "Change and Influence in Popular Criminology: Public Attributions of Crime Causation." *Journal of Criminal Justice* 15(3):231–243.

Flores, A., A. Russell, E. Latessa & L. Travis (2005). "Evidence of Professionalism or Quackery: Measuring Practitioner Awareness of Risk/Need Factors and Effective Treatment Strategies." *Federal Probation* 69(2):9–14.

Foucault, M. (1977). *Discipline and Punish.* New York: Pantheon.

Gainey, R., S. Steen & R. Engen (2005). "Exercising Options: An Assessment of the Use of Alternative Sanctions for Drug Offenders." *Justice Quarterly* 22(4):488–520.

Gendreau, P. (1996). "The Principles of Effective Interventions with Offenders." In A. Harland (ed.), *Choosing Correctional Options that Work: Defining the Demand and Evaluating the Supply.* Thousand Oaks, CA: Sage.

Gendreau, P. & R. Ross (1987). "Revivification of Rehabilitation: Evidence from the 1980s." *Justice Quarterly* 4(3):349–407.

Gertz, M. & L. Gould (1995). "Fear of Punishment and the Willingness to Engage in Criminal Behavior: A Research Note." *Journal of Criminal Justice* 23(4):377–384.

Gibbs, J.J. (1985). "Clients' Views of Community Corrections." In L.F. Travis III (ed.), *Probation, Parole, and Community Corrections.* Prospect Heights, IL: Waveland.

Goodstein, L. & J. Hepburn (1983). *Determinate Sentencing and Imprisonment.* Cincinnati: Anderson.

Gottfredson, D.M., C.A. Cosgrove, L.T. Wilkins, J. Wallerstein & C. Rauh (1978). *Classification for Parole Decision Policy.* Washington, DC: U.S. Government Printing Office.

Gottfredson, M.R. (1979). "Parole Guidelines and the Reduction of Sentencing Disparity: A Preliminary Study." *Journal of Research in Crime and Delinquency* 16(2):218–231.

Greenwood, P. (1982). *Selective Incapacitation.* Santa Monica, CA: RAND.

Griffin, B. & L. Katz (2002). "Sentencing Consistency: Basic Principles Instead of Numerical Grids: The Ohio Plan." *Case Western Reserve Law Review* 53(1):1–75.

Griffin, T. & J. Wooldredge (2006). "Sex-Based Disparities in Felony Dispositions Before and After Sentencing Reform in Ohio." *Criminology* 44(4):893–923.

Griset, P. (1995). "Determinate Sentencing and Agenda Building: A Case Study of the Failure of a Reform." *Journal of Criminal Justice* 23(4):349–362.

Griset, P. (2002). "New Sentencing Laws Follow Old Patterns: A Florida Case Study." *Journal of Criminal Justice* 30(4):287–301.

Griswold, D. B. (1987). "Deviation from Sentencing Guidelines: The Issue of Unwarranted Disparity." *Journal of Criminal Justice* 15(4):317–329.

Harland, A. (ed.) (1996). *Choosing Correctional Options That Work: Defining the Demand and Evaluating the Supply.* Thousand Oaks, CA: Sage.

Harris, J. & P. Jesilow (2000). "It's Not the Old Ball Game: Three Strikes and the Courtroom Workgroup." *Justice Quarterly* 17(1):185–203.

Holsinger, A. & E. Latessa (1999). "An Empirical Evaluation of a Sanction Continuum: Pathways Through the Juvenile Justice System." *Journal of Criminal Justice* 27(2):155–172.

Huebner, B. & T. Bynum (2006). "An Analysis of Parole Decision Making Using a Sample of Sex Offender: A Focal Concerns Perspective." *Criminology* 44(4):961–992.

Israel, M. & J. Dawes (2002). "'Something From Nothing': Shifting Credibility in Community Correctional Programmes in Australia." *Criminal Justice* 2(1):5–25.

Jaffe, H.J. (1979). "Probation with a Flair: A Look at Some Out-of-the Ordinary Conditions." *Federal Probation* 43(1):25–36.

Johnson, I. & R. Sigler (1995). "Community Attitudes: A Study of Definitions and Punishment of Spouse Abusers and Child Abusers." *Journal of Criminal Justice* 23(5):477–487.

Kingsnorth, R., L. Alvis & G. Gavia (1993). "Specific Deterrence and the DUI Offender: The Impact of a Decade of Reform." *Justice Quarterly* 10(2):265–288.

Klein, A.R. (1997). *Alternative Sentencing, Intermediate Sanctions and Probation*, 2nd ed. Cincinnati: Anderson.

Kovandzic, T. (2001). "The Impact of Florida's Habitual Offender Law on Crime." *Criminology* 39(1):179–204.

Kovandzic, T., J. Sloan & L. Vieraitis (2004). "'Striking Out' as Crime Reduction Policy: The Impact of 'Three Strikes' Laws on Crime Rates in U.S. Cities." *Justice Quarterly* 21(2):207–239.

Kramer, J. & J. Ulmer (1996). "Sentencing Disparity and Departures from Guidelines." *Justice Quarterly* 13(1):81–106.

Kraska, P. (1992). "The Processing of Drug Arrestees: Questioning the Assumption of an Ambivalent Reaction." *Journal of Criminal Justice* 20(6):517–525.

LaGoy, S.P., F.A. Hussey & J.H. Kramer (1978). "A Comparative Assessment of Determinate Sentencing in the Four Pioneer States." *Crime & Delinquency* 24:385–400.

LeClair, D. & S. Guarino-Ghezzi (1991). "Does Incapacitation Guarantee Public Safety: Lessons from Massachusetts' Furlough and Prerelease Programs." *Justice Quarterly* 8(1):9–36.

Logan, C. & G. Gaes (1993). "Meta-analysis and the Rehabilitation of Punishment." *Justice Quarterly* 10(2):245–263.

Lutze, F. (1998). "Are Shock Incarceration Programs More Rehabilitative Than Traditional Prisons? A Survey of Inmates." *Justice Quarterly* 15(3):547–566.

Mackenzie, D. (1997). "Criminal Justice and Crime Prevention." In L. Sherman, D. Gottfredson, J. Eck, P. Reuter & S. Bushway (eds.), *Preventing Crime: What Works, What Doesn't, What's Promising.* Washington, DC: U.S. Department of Justice, 9-1-9-76.

Maddan, S. & W. Hallahan (2002). "Corporal Punishment in the 21st Century: An Examination of Supreme Court Decisions in the 1990s to Predict the Reemergence of Flagellance." *Journal of Crime and Justice* 25(2):97–120.

Martinson, R.M. (1974). "What Works?" *The Public Interest* (Spring):22.

McCarthy, B. (1989). "The Use of Jail Confinement in the Disposition of Felony Arrests." *Journal of Criminal Justice* 17(4):241–251.

McCarthy, B. (ed.) (1987). *Intermediate Punishments.* Monsey, NY: Criminal Justice Press.

Morris, N. & M. Tonry (1990). *Between Prison and Probation: Intermediate Punishments in a Rational Sentencing System.* Oxford: Oxford University Press.

Myers, L. & S. Reid (1995). "The Importance of County Context in the Measurement of Sentence Disparity: The Search for Routinization." *Journal of Criminal Justice* 23(3):223–241.

Nagin, D. & G. Pogarsky (2001). "Integrating Celerity, Impulsivity, and Extralegal Sanction Threats Into a Model of General Deterrence: Theory and Evidence." *Criminology* 39(4):865–892.

Newman, G.R. (1978). *The Punishment Response.* Philadelphia: J.B. Lippincott.

Newman, G.R. (1983). *Just and Painful.* New York: Macmillan.

Parisi, N. (1980). "Combining Incarceration and Probation." *Federal Probation* 44(2):3–12.

Paternoster, R. (1987). "The Deterrent Effect of the Perceived Certainty and Severity of Punishment: A Review of the Evidence and Issues." *Justice Quarterly* 4(2):173–217.

Petersilia, J. (1987). *Expanding Options for Criminal Sentencing.* Santa Monica, CA: RAND.

Petersilia, J., A. Lurigio & J. Byrne (1992). "Introduction: The Emergence of Intermediate Sanctions." In J. Byrne, A. Lurigio & J. Petersilia (eds.), *Smart Sentencing: The Emergence of Intermediate Sanctions.* Beverly Hills, CA: Sage, 1992, ix–xv.

Petersilia, J., S. Turner, J. Kahan & J. Peterson (1985). *Granting Felons Probation: Public Risks and Alternatives.* Santa Monica, CA: RAND.

Piquero, A. & G. Rengert (1999). "Studying Deterrence with Active Residential Burglars." *Justice Quarterly* 16(2):451–471.

Pogarsky, G. (2002). "Identifying 'Deterrable' Offenders: Implications for Research on Deterrence." *Justice Quarterly* 19(3):343–369.

Pratt, T. (1998). "Race and Sentencing: A Meta-Analysis of Conflicting Empirical Research Results." *Journal of Criminal Justice* 26(6):513–523.

Proctor, J. (1999). "The 'New Parole': An Analysis of Parole Board Decision Making as a Function of Eligibility." *Journal of Crime and Justice* 22(2):193–217.

Rottman, D. & S. Strickland (2006). *State Court Organization, 2005.* Washington, DC: Bureau of Justice Statistics.

Rottman, D., C. Flango, M. Cantrell, R. Hansen & N. LaFountain (2000). *State Court Organization, 1998.* Washington, DC: Bureau of Justice Statistics.

Saint-Germain, M. & R. Calamia (1996). "Three Strikes and You're In: A Streams and Windows Model of Incremental Policy Change." *Journal of Criminal Justice* 24(1):57–70.

Schoepfer, A., S. Carmichael & N. Piquero (2007). "Do Perceptions of Punishment Vary Between White-Collar and Street Crimes?" *Journal of Criminal Justice* 35(2):151–163.

Schwartz, M. & L. Travis (1996). *Corrections: An Issues Approach,* 4th ed. Cincinnati: Anderson.

Shover, N. (1996). *Great Pretenders: Pursuits and Careers of Persistent Thieves.* Boulder: Westview.

Skove, A. (2004). Blakely v. Washington: *Implications for State Courts.* Williamsburg, VA: National Center for State Courts.

Smith, W. & D. Smith (1998). "The Consequences of Error: Recidivism Prediction and Civil-Libertarian Ratios." *Journal of Criminal Justice* 26(6):481–502.

Snell, T. (2006). *Capital Punishment, 2005.* Washington, DC: Bureau of Justice Statistics.

Spohn, C. (2000). "Thirty Years of Sentencing Reform: The Quest for a Racially Neutral Sentencing Process." In J. Horney (ed.), *Policies, Processes, and Decisions of the Criminal Justice System.* Washington, DC: National Institute of Justice, Criminal Justice 2000, Volume 3:427–501.

Spohn, C. (1994). "Crime and the Social Control of Blacks: Offender/Victim Race and the Sentencing of Violent Offenders." In G. Bridges & M. Myers (eds.), *Inequality, Crime, and Social Policy.* Boulder, CO: Westview.

Spohn, C. & J. Cederblom (1991). "Race and Disparities in Sentencing: A Test of the Liberation Hypothesis." *Justice Quarterly* 8(3):305–327.

Spohn, C., M. DeLone & J. Spears (1998). "Race/Ethnicity, Gender and Sentence Severity in Dade County, Florida: An Examination of the Decision to Withhold Adjudication." *Journal of Crime and Justice* 21(2):111–138.

Steffensmeier, D. & S. Demuth (2001). "Ethnicity and Judges' Sentencing Decisions: Hispanic-Black-White Comparisons." *Criminology* 39(1):145–178.

Steffensmeier, D., J. Kramer & J. Ulmer (1995). "Age Differences in Sentencing." *Justice Quarterly* 12(3):583–601.

Taxman, F. & A. Piquero (1998). "On Preventing Drunk Driving Recidivism: An Examination of Rehabilitation and Punishment Approaches." *Journal of Criminal Justice* 26(2):129–143.

Tonry, M. (1999). "The Fragmentation of Sentencing and Corrections in America." In *Sentencing and Corrections Issues for the 21st Century* (September). Washington, DC: National Institute of Justice.

Tonry, M. (1996). *Sentencing Matters.* New York: Oxford University Press.

Travis, L.F., III (2002). "Criminal Sentencing: Honesty, Prediction, Discrimination, and Ethics." In M. Braswell, B. McCarthy & B. McCarthy (eds.), *Justice, Crime, and Ethics,* 4th ed. Cincinnati: Anderson, 2002:175–187.

Turner, M., J. Sundt, B. Applegate & F. Cullen (1995). "'Three Strikes and You're Out' Legislation: A National Assessment." *Federal Probation* 59(3):16–35.

Turpin-Petrosino, C. (1999). Are Limiting Enactments Effective? An Experimental Test of Decision Making in a Presumptive Parole State." *Journal of Criminal Justice* 27(4):321–332.

Ulmer, J. (1997). *Social Worlds of Sentencing: Court Communities Under Sentencing Guidelines.* Albany, NY: SUNY Press.

Umbreit, M.S. (1981). "Community Service Sentencing: Jail Alternative or Added Sanction?" *Federal Probation* 45(3):3–14.

U.S. Division of Probation (1974). "The Selective Presentence Investigation Report." *Federal Probation* 38(4):52–53.

Van Dine, S., J.P. Conrad & S. Dinitz (1979). "The Incapacitation of the Chronic Thug." *Journal of Criminal Law and Criminology* 65:535.

Van Voorhis, P. (1987). "Correctional Effectiveness: The High Cost of Ignoring Success." *Federal Probation* 51(1):56–62.

Vining, A.R. (1983). "Developing Aggregate Measures of Disparity." *Criminology* 21(2):233–252.

Visher, C. (1987). "Incapacitation and Crime Control: Does a 'Lock 'Em Up' Strategy Reduce Crime?" *Justice Quarterly* 4(4):513–543.

Vito, G. & T. Keil (1998). "Elements of Support for Capital Punishment: An Examination of Changing Attitudes." *Journal of Crime and Justice* 21(2):17–36.

Vito, G.F. & D.G. Wilson (1988). "Back from the Dead: Tracking the Progress of Kentucky's Furman Commuted Death Row Population." *Justice Quarterly* 5(1):101–111.

von Hirsch, A. (1976). *Doing Justice.* New York: Hill & Wang.

von Hirsch, A. & K.J. Hanrahan (1979). *The Question of Parole.* Cambridge, MA: Ballinger.

Weinrath, M. (1999). "Are New Directions Warranted for the Presentence Report? An Empirical Assessment of Its Predictive Utility in the Adult Court System." *Journal of Crime and Justice* 22(1):113–129.

Wenk, E.A., J.O. Robison & G.W. Smith (1972). "Can Violence be Predicted?" *Crime & Delinquency* 18(3):393–402.

Wilkins, L.T., J.M. Kress, D. Gottfredson, J.C. Calpin & A. Gelman (1976). *Sentencing Guidelines: Structuring Judicial Discretion.* Albany, NY: Criminal Justice Research Center.

Wright, R. & S. Decker (1994). *Burglars on the Job: Streetlife and Residential Break-Ins.* Boston: Northeastern University Press.

Wonders, N. (1996). "Determinate Sentencing: A Feminist and Postmodern Story." *Justice Quarterly* 13(4):611–648.

Zalman, M. (1987). "Sentencing in a Free Society: The Failure of the President's Crime Commission to Influence Sentencing Policy." *Justice Quarterly* 4(4):545–569.

Zatz, M. (2000). "The Convergence of Race, Ethnicity, Gender, and Class on Court Decisionmaking: Looking Toward the 21st Century." In J. Horney (ed.), *Policies, Processes, and Decisions of the Criminal Justice System.* Washington, DC: National Institute of Justice, Criminal Justice 2000, Volume 3:503–552.

Important Cases

Blakely v. Washington, 542 U.S.296 (2004).

Furman v. Georgia, 408 U.S. 238 (1972).

Gardner v. Florida, 430 U.S. 349 (1977).

Gregg v. Georgia, 428 U.S. 153 (1976).
Mempa v. Rhay, 389 U.S. 128 (1967).
United States v. Booker, 543 U.S. 220 (2005).
Williams v. New York, 377 U.S. 241 (1949).

DISCUSSION QUESTIONS

1. What innovative practices can be implemented to increase the diversity of jury pools?
2. Is the criminal justice system the best way to help those with drug and alcohol addiction?
3. Describe whether or not you believe that the U.S. Supreme Court rulings in *Miranda v. Arizona* and *Mapp v. Ohio* make a police officer's ability to gather evidence of a crime more difficult.
4. There is evidence to suggest that indigent defendants are more likely to be convicted because they cannot afford to hire a private attorney. What suggestions can be made to improve the public defender system in the United States?
5. Which purpose of or justification for punishment should be the basis of our criminal justice system? Why? Provide an example of how a punishment can meet two of the purposes of punishment at the same time.
6. How do you define sentence disparity? What mechanisms would you put in place to reduce sentence disparity in our criminal justice system?

CORRECTIONS

EDITOR'S INTRODUCTION

Although we often think of "corrections" in terms of jails and prisons, the term refers more broadly to the sets of informal and formal systems used to punish people for nonconforming behavior. The readings in this unit explain that theories, purposes, and techniques of punishment have changed over the centuries. These shifts can be understood as a transition from punishment based more on retributive justice to deterrence and rehabilitation in more contemporary times. How punishment "looks" and "feels" at different points throughout history is connected to leading theories of human behavior and motivation. The "get tough on crime" approaches more characteristic of the U.S. criminal justice system in the 1980s and 1990s are reflective of such shifts. Perceptions that crime was out of control due to sharp increases in predatory criminals roaming American streets resulted in a sharp movement away from rehabilitation approaches characteristic of the 1970s to deterrence-oriented approaches in recent decades. For institutional (e.g., jails and prisons) corrections to be effective, there must be close linkages between all aspects of these institutions, including how they are designed, staffed, and managed in ways that best ensure they accomplish their core missions.

In "The History of American Corrections: Where Did We Come From?," John T. Whitehead, Mark Jones, and Michael C. Braswell apply a historical lens to better understand our contemporary system of corrections. Ideas related to punishment looked different over the centuries and even millennia, shifting in response to changing goals of punishment and theories that helped explained criminality. While long-term incarceration was rarely used historically, it has become more commonplace as cultures have shifted away from retribution as the primary goal of punishment to a focus on rehabilitation and ultimately control.

The next reading, "Institutional Corrections," by Carolyn Petrosino, goes over how the United States has experienced a decades-long growth in incarceration rates that started in the 1980s and continued through much of the early 21st century. Petrosino confronts explanations for this growth and reminds the reader that liberals and conservatives offer different accounts of this reality. This growth, however, is explained in large part by a "get tough on crime" mentality that began to dominate criminal justice policy in the early to mid-1980s. The impact of this trend is explained through the lens of marginalized groups, including women and racial minorities. The author challenges us to consider the important ethical questions connected to these trends.

In the last reading, "Prisoners and Prison Life," by John T. Whitehead, Mark Jones, and Michael C. Braswell, the authors remind us that all types of incarceration represent a significant manifestation of governmental power. Correctional institutions are separate and distinct types of institutions that have few comparisons. Jails and prisons result in a consequential deprivation of liberties such as basic freedom, access to goods and services, access to relationships, and security. The authors describe the impacts of prisonization as well as special topics related to correctional environments, including long-term prisoners, death row, and the impacts of institutional victimization.

READING 4.1

THE HISTORY OF AMERICAN CORRECTIONS: WHERE DID WE COME FROM?

John T. Whitehead, Mark Jones, and Michael C. Braswell

[READING] OUTLINE

1. Introduction
2. Corrections in the Prehistoric Era
3. Correctional Practices in Ancient Societies
4. The Middle Ages
5. English Corrections During the Enlightenment
6. Corrections in the United States
7. The Birth of the Penitentiary
8. Prisons in the Industrial Era
9. The Indeterminate Sentence and Parole
10. Corrections in the Progressive Era
11. The "Big House" Era
12. Rehabilitation: The "Anything Works" Era
13. Deinstitutionalization and "Nothing Works"
14. Corrections in the "Get Tough" Era
15. Conclusion

WHAT YOU NEED TO KNOW

- Ancient societies used some of the correctional practices found in modern America. For example, the Mesopotamians had a type of jail, and ancient Greece and Israel used capital punishment.
- Colonial Americans used shaming punishments such as branding, the ducking stool, and the stocks.
- The Quakers were very influential in the development of American corrections, especially the penitentiary.
- The Quakers used the separate system while New York State used the Auburn or congregate system, but both systems emphasized many similar features.

- The indeterminate sentence and parole have their roots in Australian and Irish corrections.
- The Progressive Era influenced the development of probation and at least the idea of treatment. It was at this point that science began to influence how we view criminals and how they should be punished or treated.
- After World War II, rehabilitation, at least in theory, guided the operation of prisons, especially in California.
- In the 1960s and 1970s, attacks on rehabilitation emanated from both political conservatives and liberals. Even the Quakers participated in criticisms of rehabilitation.
- Concerns over rehabilitation led to a punitive or "get tough" era in correctional policy and practice.

Introduction

The dilemma of how to treat those who violate the prescribed rules of a society or community is as old as settled life itself. The question of whether a community should assist or punish an offender is just as old. This [reading] briefly examines the history of humankind's efforts at dealing with those who break rules and laws. Specifically, the development of American corrections is traced to its roots in previous time periods in America, as well as antecedents in Western Europe, and to several ancient civilizations that influenced Western thought, political philosophy, and penal practices. The focus is on the evolution and history of Western penal systems. Although penal practices in nonWestern societies are worthwhile topics of study, they did not influence American penal practices to the degree that European penal systems did.

[...]

The Middle Ages

As the Roman Empire's influence began to crumble, the administration of criminal justice increasingly came under the influence of the Christian church and small Germanic kingdoms. Although imprisonment as a long-term punishment was seldom used, the seeds of the penitentiary were born during the Middle Ages. In most of Europe, criminals were still subjected to physical punishments, and some were given economic sanctions. In some cases, trial by ordeal, in which an accused would be required to undergo a procedure that supposedly would determine guilt or innocence through divine intervention, would act as both a trial and a form of punishment. If one did not survive the ordeal, the issue of further punishment was moot.

The seeds of the penitentiary planted during the Middle Ages focused on punishments administered by church authorities. Most of these medieval church-based punishments were administered against members of the clergy—priests, nuns, and monks. A holding area in the church or the monastery would be set aside to isolate—and, in some cases, physically punish—the offending clergy member. The physical punishment might involve being placed in stocks for several hours or being whipped with a rod.[1]

The idea behind these punishments was to coerce the offending member of the clergy to make penitence through the punishment and isolation of the prison experience. Toward the beginning of the Middle Ages, this ecclesiastical or church-based punishment was used only against the clergy. The idea of long-term punishment through isolation and coerced penitence survived, though, and carried over to the secular realm. By the end of the medieval period, around 1550, long-term imprisonment as a means of punishment was becoming more common throughout Europe.

The medieval European idea of long-term punishment was short by today's standards, with several months to a year considered long-term. Medieval prisons, including English "gaols," from which the word "jail" is derived, were not equipped to handle prisoners for longer periods. There were few, if any, mechanisms for long-term punishment of criminals. So many offenses were punishable by death that long-term imprisonment was not even considered, and many offenders were banished from their community for life as a long-term punishment. Jail conditions were usually so horrific that many prisoners died if incarcerated for a lengthy period. Many personal amenities, including blankets, clothing, and sometimes even decent food, were given only to those who paid the jailer, or for those who had friends or relatives to provide for them. As a result, jail conditions were particularly brutal for the poor.

English Corrections During the Enlightenment

During the latter part of the Middle Ages and the early Industrial Era, England and other European powers began expanding their world presence by exploring or invading "new worlds." England also experienced substantial social unrest and increasing crime because of rapid population increases in its cities, particularly in London. English government officials sought ways to rid the streets of petty criminals—serious criminals were usually executed—and make money in the process.

One of the more original correctional measures taken in the late eighteenth century to relieve crowding was the use of hulks, or dilapidated ships anchored off English ports, to detain offenders. The hulks, sometimes referred to as "hell holds" or "floating hells," were notoriously inhospitable, filthy, and disease-ridden. They offered nothing in the way of rehabilitation. The hulks were merely temporary warehouses, an alternative to nothing. The conditions in the hulks prompted John Howard, the sheriff of Bedfordshire, to write *The State of the Prisons* in 1777. Howard's criticisms of hulk conditions encouraged the British Parliament to pass legislation providing for the building of more safe, secure, and sanitary prisons on land.[2]

The use of hulks continued for a number of years, but the promise of material riches in North America generated another innovative idea for disposing of England's criminal element. Private business interests stepped forward to offer transportation to the American colonies. Those who transported debtors and criminals often received a fee from government officials in England and a fee from commercial interests in the colonies. By no means were the majority of American immigrants in the seventeenth and eighteenth centuries released from English prisons, but thousands of petty criminals and debtors were sent to the American colonies during that time. The American Revolution brought a halt to importation of English prisoners to the United States.[3]

Corrections in the United States

The village-style, communal life of colonial America did not lend itself to extensive use of institutional incarceration. Resources and expertise for erecting jails or prison facilities were for the most part nonexistent. A few jails were used as short-term housing facilities for those awaiting trial or imposition of sentence. Some offenders served short jail terms, but one reason jails were not used as frequently as in later times was due to economics. Even today, jails and prisons are a financial drain on society. It is expensive to feed and house prisoners. Another economic motive has been connected to the scarce use of prisons and jails. Incarcerated inmates could not contribute to the community's economy because they were not able to work. If a small town in colonial America had incarcerated its citizens on a frequent basis, very few of these inmates (most of whom would have been men) would have been able to work and feed their families.

The most common Colonial Era–sanction for crimes was the same as that of today: the fine. Though the fine was the most commonly administered sanction in colonial America, that era's hallmark was the public punishment.[4] Such punishments are the stuff of legend—in folklore, history, film, and literature. Thus, most punishments were precursors not to institutional corrections but to community-based corrections.

The primary purpose of Colonial Era–punishments was to shame and embarrass the offender. It was hoped that shaming would have both a punitive and rehabilitative effect. The offender would be so embarrassed by being publicly punished that he or she would be repentant, in the religious sense, and sin no more. The use of the terms "repentant" and "sin" is not an attempt at cryptic sarcasm. Among most colonials of European ancestry, the most common explanation for committing crime was religious in nature. According to them, all people were born sinners and, unless aided by a strong faith in God, were bound to fall astray and break the laws and community mores of the town.

Colonial Americans did not lack creativity when it came to administering public punishments. Nathaniel Hawthorne's *The Scarlet Letter* was a fictionalized account of one such punishment. In the novel, the protagonist, Hester Prynne, bore a child out of wedlock. While such behavior is not criminal in today's society, it was treated very seriously in many colonial communities. The woman would be required to have the letter "A" (for adultery) sewn on her garment and would be required to wear the garment in public for a specified length of time.

Other behaviors brought punishments similar to the "scarlet letter." Sometimes offenders were branded with a hot iron rather than being required to wear a sewn letter on their garments. Offenders might be branded with the letter "V" for vagrant or vagabond, "D" for drunkard, or other letters that denoted their crime.

The ducking stool was another punishment designed to shame the offender. It was usually used against women who were slanderers, chronic gossips, or general busybodies. The offender would be strapped into a chair, taken down to the river, and dropped into the water several times in public view. Such a punishment was designed to embarrass the offender's husband, in hopes that the husband would do more to control his wife's behavior.[5]

The stocks were used for a variety of offenses. Offenders were required to spend varying periods of time—anywhere from several hours to several days, depending upon the infraction—usually in full public view with their hands and head in the stocks. Very often the offender was allowed nothing but bread and water, and townspeople were not discouraged from verbally and even physically abusing the offender as they walked the streets of the town.

The brank, or "scold's bridle," was a painful punishment that was primarily used against women who committed verbal offenses such as excessive gossiping, slander, or being disrespectful to men (be it a husband or local leader). William Andrews described the brank as:

> ... an iron framework, which was placed on the head, enclosing it in a kind of cage; it had in front a plate of iron, which, either sharpened or covered with spikes, was so situated as to be placed in the mouth of the victim, and if she attempted to move her tongue in any way whatever, it was certain to be shockingly injured. With the brank on her head she was conducted through the streets, led by a chain, held by one of the town's officials, an object of contempt, and subjected to the jeers of the crowd and often left to their mercy.[6]

Did shaming punishments work? It is difficult to say. First, it is difficult to define or measure, let alone evaluate, whether a punishment "works." For shaming punishments to accomplish their intended effect, several factors must be present. First, an offender must be capable of feeling shamed. Some children in elementary school are ashamed to have their name put on the chalkboard for misbehaving, while other children snicker at this "punishment." In the same vein, being publicly branded as a criminal did not then, and does not now, embarrass all offenders.

Second, in order for shaming to have its desired effect, a community must mutually agree that certain behaviors are indeed shameful, as many colonial villages did. As the populations in American towns and cities grew larger and more diverse in culture, mores, lifestyles, and religious beliefs, there was less agreement on which behaviors were right and which were wrong. In recent decades, some jurisdictions have enacted "scarlet letter" punishments, such as requiring child sex offenders to have their picture posted on an Internet web page and requiring convicted drunk drivers to post a bumper sticker on their car indicating they have been convicted of drunk driving. Some offenders would be embarrassed by these requirements, but some would not. This might depend in part on the values possessed by that offender's peer group and family. If an offender comes from a family in which a criminal conviction is not a badge of shame or from a peer group where a criminal conviction is a badge of courage, that type of shame is absent.

Third, the offender who was supposed to be shamed and shunned sometimes became a martyr. The scorn would be heaped on those who decreed or administered the punishment. For example, Hawthorne took a sympathetic view of Hester Prynne in *The Scarlet Letter*. Many other punishments also engendered sympathy rather than hostility toward the offender.

Similar sympathetic attitudes existed toward some offenders in America's early years. Eventually, many Americans became disenchanted with public punishments and sought alternatives to the frequent use of capital punishment. The increased urbanization of American society, the growing belief that criminal behavior was associated with an evil urban environment as well as a sinful nature, and the revulsion against public punishment all generated efforts designed at reforming rather than simply humiliating the criminal.

The final question about the efficacy of public punishments does not pertain to whether it "works" in terms of recidivism or public outrage. The U.S. Supreme Court has used the phrase "evolving standard of decency" in deciding whether certain punishments are Constitutional. The physically torturous punishments described here do not seem compatible with contemporary standards of decency.

If fines and public punishments were not effective in stopping the undesired behavior, or if the offense was severe, the individual may have been banished. This was often a death sentence in itself because the likelihood of surviving in the wilderness or reaching another settlement before dying of starvation, exposure, or other dangers was slim. The offender was often branded or otherwise given a physical marking to warn other settlements of his or her criminality. If the offender returned or refused to leave, then hanging was used as a last resort for the community to protect itself. Thus, imprisonment, as such, was used only until some other form of punishment was carried out, or until the individual (or his or her relatives) paid the fine imposed.[7]

The Birth of the Penitentiary

In the 1700s, the cities along the eastern seaboard experienced a host of problems associated with urban growth. "Red light" districts emerged, and droves of immigrants and citizens descended upon the cities, burdening charity services and creating a population of vagrants and minor thieves. Because the older forms of punishment, which depended on public humiliation, did not work on this transient, heterogeneous city population, new forms of social control were necessary. The congregate care facility was born of the need to control and provide services to larger numbers of people.[8] Orphanages were used to house orphaned or abandoned youngsters; hospitals were created to house the sick and infirm; mental institutions were opened to take care of those who had previously been cared for by families or tolerated by communities; and workhouses or poorhouses were used to control and house those who had no work or means of making a living.

Soon the population of poorhouses or workhouses overlapped with those in jails, and eventually the jail was utilized not merely as a holding facility but also as a type of punishment. Because poor people would never be able to pay a fine (certainly not as long as they were being held), keeping them incarcerated became the punishment itself. There was little difference between the fate of the street person who ended up in a workhouse and that of the one who ended up in a jail. Houses of correction, an institutional model found in England, recognized this overlap and operated under the assumption that poor people must be taught a trade and "corrected" from their life of idleness.[9] In effect, this practice made it a crime to be poor, with the punishment being incarceration and forced labor. If the individual proved pliable and learned quickly, he or she could earn release and utilize the learned trade to become a productive citizen.

To a great degree, the origin of the penitentiary has religious roots. Correctional reformers wanted to make less use of publicly degrading punishments that did little to alter offenders' behavior. They sought to provide an environment in which offenders could, in solitude, make penitence with God. This would be done by coerced Bible study and religious instruction. It is ironic that penitentiaries are viewed today as centers of human degradation and violence. The original intention behind the penitentiary's creation held much higher promise.

If one state deserves credit (or blame) for the birth of the American penitentiary, it would be Pennsylvania. In 1682, thanks in large measure to the efforts of William Penn, a new penal code, commonly called "Penn's Code," was established in Pennsylvania. It provided for bail eligibility for all prisoners, free food and lodging for prisoners (historically, prisoners had been expected to pay a fee for their food and accommodations), and the provision of jails to replace pillories and stocks.[10]

Quakers (such as William Penn), whose numbers in early American history were greater in Pennsylvania than in other states, had a strong hand in creating the penitentiary, though they did not actually create American prisons on their own. In fact, New-Gate Prison, an underground prison was opened in an abandoned copper mine in Simsbury (now East Granby), Connecticut, in 1773. The prison was used to detain conventional criminals as well as to detain Loyalists (those who opposed American independence from Great Britain) during the Revolutionary War.

In Pennsylvania, Quaker ideals contributed to the move to make penal institutions a humane alternative to public, corporal punishments, and in some cases, to capital punishment. Sentiment against public and corporal punishments had been building since the late 1600s. It culminated in the conversion of Philadelphia's Walnut Street Jail in 1790 to America's "first true correctional institution."[11] Benjamin Rush—a signer of the Declaration of Independence—and others instituted innovations that were designed to change the jail from a place of incapacitation to one where reformation might occur.[12] At least a rudimentary system of classification was imposed; women and men were separated, as were children from adults and the sick from the well. In addition, those who were believed to be capable of reformation were separated from those who were perceived to be hardened criminals.

Some attempt was made to have those incarcerated inside the Walnut Street Jail work at some craft. With these changes, jails took a giant step toward the institution we now call a prison or a penitentiary. The Walnut Street Jail was designed to keep inmates busy through manual labor. Walnut Street was also supposed to require that prisoners work and live in solitude, away from the unhealthy influence of other prisoners. It was also designed to classify inmates, segregating inmates by gender, age, and type of offense. Walnut Street officials hoped to keep women away from men, children away from adults, and minor offenders away from serious offenders. Contact with the outside was nonexistent or kept to a minimum. The only influence on the offender was the Bible and a religious guide as an aid in finding salvation. After a due period of "penitence," the individual was to emerge a new person.[13] The transformation of a holding facility to one where correction was encouraged and expected was accompanied by an unbounded optimism about what such facilities might be able to do. Clergy members, politicians, and educators all believed that the institution was the perfect place to instill the characteristics of sobriety, regularity, and piety in the wayward inmates found within.

As with many penal experiments, the staff at Walnut Street found that reality got in the way of high expectations. Cells quickly became overcrowded, so the ideal of solitude was dashed, as was the ideal of segregating offenders. There was not enough work that could be done under secure environments, a problem that plagues corrections even today. After several years, the idealism of those who transformed the Walnut Street Jail deteriorated as a result of management problems such as overcrowding and corruption.

Despite its shortcomings, the Walnut Street Jail was viewed as a humane alternative to corporal and public punishments, which had fallen out of favor with a large sector of the public. The Walnut Street experiment gave rise to other correctional innovations, most notably the founding of the modern penitentiary.

The 1820s: Eastern vs. Auburn

The next significant developments in American prison history were the opening of Eastern State Penitentiary at Cherry Hill, Pennsylvania, in 1821, and the opening of Auburn Prison in Auburn, New York, in 1829. Alexis de Tocqueville made the prisons at Cherry Hill, Auburn, and Walnut Street one of the "subjects of inquiry" of his famous treatise on American democracy.[14] The method of discipline and administration used at Eastern came to be known as the "Pennsylvania system," and Auburn became associated with the term "congregate system." Under the Pennsylvania model, each inmate lived in a separate cell with a separate exercise yard. Clergy members visited inmates and attempted to help them attain a spiritual awakening or rebirth. Handcrafts were performed inside the cell. Complete and absolute separation from all other influences was enforced (or at least that was the intent). In actuality, though, inmates developed an ingenious method of communicating with each other through a code of tapping noises over the plumbing pipes.

The primary hallmarks of both the Pennsylvania and Auburn systems were total solitary confinement and religious instruction. Prisoners were confined to their cells for 23 hours a day, with one hour allowed for exercise. Inmates were allowed no contact with each other. The congregate system at Auburn was also characterized by confinement to individual cells. Unlike the Pennsylvania system, however, inmates were allowed to work and eat together, but were not allowed to speak to each other. Smaller cells could be built because the inmate did nothing but sleep in them. Instead of individual handcrafts, industrial manufacturing could be brought into the prison, and inmates could work on assembly-line projects. This was touted as a way for prisons to become profitable institutions for the state, rather than ones that drained public resources.

The two models of this new form of punishment were presented for public scrutiny and adoption. The Pennsylvania (or Philadelphia or Eastern or separate system) model and the New York (or Auburn or congregate care) model were compared and contrasted, becoming the topic of editorials, debates, and public speeches. Some Europeans even came to see the two prisons, seeing them as much a part of the American experience for tourists as the buffalo, "wild" Indians, and the transcontinental railroad.[15]

Both systems incorporated religious instruction into their programming. The only reading material most inmates had access to was a Bible. The thinking was that inmates, left alone with themselves and a Bible, and an occasional visit from a member of the clergy, would see the error of their ways, make penitence (hence the word "penitentiary"), and sin no more after leaving the institution.

Samuel Walker points out that although the systems differed somewhat in their operation, both reflected a new belief about the causes of criminal behavior.[16] Crime, which in the past was believed to be the result of inborn sin, was now believed to be the result of bad external influences. With that in mind, prisons were placed in remote areas in the hope that a pristine rural environment would help cleanse inmates of the evil influence of the big cities. This same thinking pervaded

English corrections. In *The Fatal Shore*, the classic account of the Australian penal colonies, Robert Hughes wrote that nature is the unaltered fingerprint of its Creator, and that its monotony and solitude serve as a moral text for human betterment.[17]

Religious thinking was still pervasive in the institution, but religion came to be seen as linked with the cure for crime, not the cause of it. With both models, influences from the outside and other criminals were felt to be detrimental to the inmate's progress toward correction and therefore no visitation or outside reading material could be brought in. In addition, the silent system was enforced in both models, meaning that inmates were harshly punished for speaking to each other.[18]

The penitentiary was only part of a larger movement toward institutionalizing Americans that lived on the margins of society. Mental hospitals and orphanages sprang up around the country as well. The ascendancy of President Andrew Jackson and his egalitarian ideas signaled American attempts to help (and isolate) those who could not fit into mainstream society. The institution was seen as the method for dealing with these people. David Rothman writes that the idea of the institution, or the "asylum," was almost utopian in its outlook because hopes were so high for what these institutions could accomplish.[19]

Although the penitentiary was created with noble intentions of assisting convicted criminals, it did not live up to its promise. Religious beliefs, no matter how lofty, could not be force-fed on nineteenth-century penitentiary inmates any more successfully than with anyone else, even in a humane peaceful environment. The penitentiary did not provide an atmosphere conducive to fostering religious ideals of love, repentance, and forgiveness. Most inmates left the penitentiary embittered rather than rehabilitated. Isolation, which was designed to be a healthy mental influence, instead resulted in increased mental illness among the inmates. Despite its shortcomings, the penitentiary was copied by other nations. It is still the preferred method of punishment for serious crimes in the United States and most other countries around the world.

Prisons in the Industrial Era

The end of the Civil War created a huge labor vacuum in the American South. Because slavery had officially become outlawed, southern business interests (especially agricultural interests) turned to an alternative labor supply. Inmate labor had been a staple in northeastern penitentiaries. The factory models of inmate labor at prisons in Pennsylvania, New York, and Massachusetts mirrored the economic base of the region. An important source of revenue in the northeast was the factory. The main industry in the antebellum south was farming, which relied heavily on slave labor. The South, which had relied on slave labor to support farming before the Civil War, now turned to prison inmates to replace slaves.

BOX 4.1.1

The Eastern and Auburn Systems: Comparison and Contrast

Similarities	Differences	
	Eastern System	**Auburn System**
Strong belief in rehabilitation	Called the "separate" system	Called the "congregate" system
Belief in establishing strict routine, regimen, and military model as important to rehabilitation	Prisoners worked, ate, and slept in total confinement, and only saw selected visitors	Prisoners slept alone in their own cell. Prisoners worked and ate together, but were prohibited from speaking or exchanging glances
Believed that prison should fill the void left by inadequate or improper influence from family, church, school, or community	Saw itself as "purist" in terms of rehabilitation, and viewed Auburn as incomplete and inconsistent with rehabilitative ideals.	Stated that the "pure isolation of Pennsylvania was impractical and believed it drove prisoners insane

Aubum

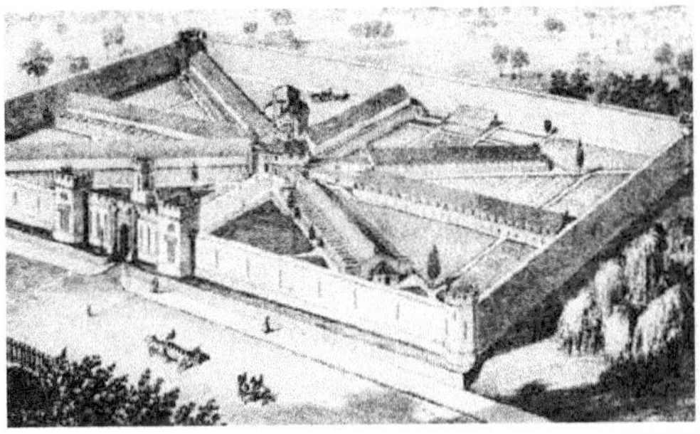

Eastern

Enterprising law enforcement and court officials were quick to supply convict labor. Under the "convict lease" system, a business interest or farmer would lease an inmate's labor from the state for a fee, or sometimes for free, in order to save the cost of feeding and housing the prisoner. Under the "state account" system, prisoners built or manufactured goods that would be sold by the state.[20]

These systems often led to outrageous abuses. States that leased the inmates took an "out of sight, out of mind" attitude. As long as the inmates were not costing the state any money or, better yet, if they generated revenue for the state, their care and welfare was of no concern. Likewise, private business interests were largely unconcerned with assisting prisoners or preparing them for life after prison. Making money, rather than looking forward to an inmate's behavior after release, assumed primary importance. Some landowners worked the prisoners 12 to 14 hours a day, gave them barely enough to eat, and provided them with inadequate clothing. Many prisoners died or became sick and injured. Periodic media coverage of the terrible conditions under which these prisoners lived spurred some oversight and change, but the system continued on into the 1940s.[21]

The Indeterminate Sentence and Parole

American parole was essentially imported from the British. After the American Revolution, England was no longer able to send debtors and those in trouble with the law to America. Instead, the British established penal colonies in and near Australia. One of the penal colonies was located at Norfolk Island, several hundred miles from the Australian coast.

As with the entire Australian penal experiment, the prison at Nor-folk was beset with numerous problems, including inmate disruptions. In 1840, the British sent Alexander Maconochie to Norfolk to supervise the prisoners. Maconochie brought with him the idea that prisons should help to reform the criminal, punishing him or her (most were men but there were some females) for the past, but also training him or her for the future. Toward that end, he established an indeterminate sentence, in which the amount of time an inmate served depended partly upon his or her behavior while in prison.[22]

Maconochie established a gradual release system, by which inmates worked to earn "marks" for good behavior, which, if obtained, would grant them increasing amounts of freedom within the prison, and culminate in their release. This release method was referred to as the "ticket-of-leave" system, and it was usually 12 to 18 months in duration. If at any time during the ticket-of-leave period the prison received bad reports about the inmate, the offender could be returned to serve the remainder of his or her sentence in prison. The ticket-of-leave system had been established in 1834, six years before Maconochie's arrival at Norfolk. Maconochie refined the system, establishing a five-step release process: (1) strict custody, (2) labor in work gangs, (3) freedom in certain places on Norfolk, (4) conditional release (ticket of leave), and (5) complete freedom.[23]

Like many would-be penal reformers throughout both English and American history, Maconochie was criticized and eventually relieved of his position in 1844 for "coddling" inmates. Upon his return to Great Britain, Maconochie did not relent in advocating penal reform. His ideas were popular with other penologists, including a fellow Englishman named Walter Crofton. Crofton received an appointment as superintendent of prisons in Ireland, which at the time was under the dominion of the British.

Crofton established a system similar to the one used by Maconochie at Norfolk. Inmates who gained conditional freedom, or ticket of leave, were supervised by a police official if they lived in a rural area. A civilian employee, a close approximation to the modern parole officer, supervised those who lived in urban areas.

Crofton's "Irish system" gained widespread attention in the Western world, including the United States. Zebulon Brockway, at the 1870 Cincinnati Congress of Penitentiary and Reformatory Discipline, advocated the Irish system in a speech titled "The Ideal of a True Prison System for a State." The necessary ingredient for Brockway's system was the indeterminate sentence. The thinking was that a prisoner's fate should be left in part up to the prisoner. The debate over the value of indeterminate sentencing persists to the present day, though it has fallen from favor in recent years.[24] Brockway espoused ideals of classification, earning levels of liberty, education, and training for amenable offenders. The idea that an offender should be the "master of his own fate" was an important principle of the meeting. Release should be earned, not given as a matter of course. Brockway had the chance to implement his ideas in the building and opening of Elmira Reformatory in Elmira, New York, in 1876.[25]

This institution was built for young offenders who could benefit from a strict regime of disciplined living and education. Staffed largely by ex-military personnel, the institutional program had a decidedly militaristic emphasis. Staff were given military ranks, uniforms were used, and inmates were led in marching formations. Inmates also had the opportunity to learn to read and write and study for some vocations. Discipline was harsh. Although Brockway believed in prisoners earning liberties, he was known for inflicting severe punishments as well.[26]

The reformatory model was often used as the pattern for newly built institutions for women. The first completely separate women's prison was built in 1873 near Indianapolis, Indiana, and followed a more custodial model, but several other states that built prisons for women in the late 1800s and early 1900s utilized a reformatory model instead. These institutions were usually staffed by women and built in rural areas where female inmates could work outdoors, a much needed reform from the cramped and unsanitary conditions that were present when they were housed in facilities for men. Together in a single room, women in prisons for men were usually ignored—and without programs, recreation, or attention, except for sexual exploitation.[27]

Corrections in the Progressive Era

The period from 1890 to 1920 is often referred to as the Progressive Era. It was a time of great social change in the United States. Linked with increasing socialism in Europe and the United States, many attempts at social reform were begun during the Progressive Era. Conservation and environmentalist advocates made great strides during this period. Antitrust legislation, designed to control the abuses of big business, also emerged at this time.

Organized labor gained strength during the progressive era. Many professional organizations were established during this time period. The National Prison Association, which was founded in the 1870s, became increasingly active during the Progressive Era. The National Probation Association was founded in 1907. The Mutual Welfare League, an early attempt at inmate self-governance, was created during the Progressive Era. The League was established at Sing Sing prison in New York with the approval of Warden Thomas Mott Osborne. The League succeeded initially, but problems at Sing Sing continued, and negative publicity about the attempt at inmate self-governance led to Osborne's resignation.[28] According to Samuel Walker, despite its failure, the League's significance is that it recognized the existence and legitimacy of a distinct inmate subculture, which had been ignored or suppressed for most of America's penological history. Most previous correctional administrators refused to acknowledge that inmates had their own communities within institutions. Inmate leaders, whether they were formally selected or merely informally acknowledged by other inmates, did exist in prisons. Many corrections professionals thought then (and many still do) that to acknowledge a power structure and leadership hierarchy among inmates is "giving in." In order to maintain absolute power over inmates, corrections practitioners should treat all inmates alike and not give deference to inmate wishes to deal with staff on an official basis. Osborne disagreed, and so did George Beto, who directed the Texas prison system from 1961 to 1972. Beto appointed seasoned inmates as "building tenders" to help maintain order in Texas prisons. His philosophy was that if prison officials did not choose inmate leaders, the inmates would instead.[29]

It was during the Progressive Era that the term "criminal justice system" began to emerge. The criminal justice system came under more intense scrutiny from the academic profession than it had in years past. Those who worked in criminal justice professions, including correctional wardens, came to view themselves as professionals, rather than just employees.

During the Progressive Era, the scientific method emerged as the answer to human problems. Phrenology and biological approaches to explaining crime reached their peak during this era, especially in Europe, though their influence was felt in the United States. Cesare Lombroso, an Italian prison physician, published his beliefs that criminals could be identified by physical traits.[30]

Although Lombroso's work did not have a major impact on prison officials, his work was part and parcel of the idea that medical science held the answers to dealing with criminals. It was during the period from the turn of the twentieth century to the early 1940s that the eugenics movement made headway into American mental hospitals and prisons. Eugenics is the study of methods of protecting and improving the quality of the human race by selective breeding. The thinking was that many criminals were morally or mentally defective from birth or as a result of their genetic makeup. The key to stop the breeding of such criminal types was sterilization, sometimes referred to at the time as asexualization. Indiana passed the first sterilization law in 1907. All institutions that housed "confirmed criminals, idiots, rapists and imbeciles" were required to have two surgeons on staff.[31] If in the opinion of a board of medical managers and prison personnel an inmate's mental or moral condition placed him or her beyond any affordable help, the prisoner would undergo sterilization.

Several states, including Virginia, followed suit with similar laws. Virginia's sterilization laws were upheld by the U.S. Supreme Court in the 1927 case of *Buck v. Bell*. Carrie Buck was a patient at Virginia's Colony for Epileptics and Feeble Minded at Lynchburg. She had been diagnosed as having a mental age of nine. The institutional physician, Albert Priddy, recommended that Buck be sterilized in accordance with Virginia's law, which allowed for the sterilization of certain convicted criminals and mental patients. During the judicial proceedings that would decide Buck's fate, she and the rest of her family were referred to as a group of "shiftless, ignorant and worthless class of anti-social whites."[32] Supreme Court Justice Oliver Wendell Holmes Jr. wrote the majority opinion upholding Virginia's sterilization law. Writing that "three generations of imbeciles are enough," Holmes went on to state that "cutting the Fallopian tubes" was the equivalent to vaccination. Buck was sterilized in 1927.[33]

Sterilization proliferated through the 1920s and 1930s. Ethnic minorities and the poor were frequent targets of eugenics. News of atrocities performed in the name of creating a master race in Nazi Germany eventually made its way to the United States. America was fighting to eliminate Nazism, and the eugenics movement had a Nazi flavor to it.

Amidst the American war effort against Germany, the U.S. Supreme Court dealt a blow to sterilization efforts in the 1942 case of *Skinner v. Oklahoma*. Justice William Douglas declared that marriage and procreation were basic civil rights, and that placing the power to sterilize in evil or reckless hands could cause races or types that are inimical to the dominant group to wither and disappear.[34] This signaled the end of most sterilization for a time. However, even today, some courts and correctional practitioners have called for chemical castration as the only viable solution for dealing with repeat sexual offenders.

Although the ideal of individualized treatment was popular, the reality was somewhat different in most states. California was the exception. This state led the way in individualized treatment for prison inmates and parole supervision and produced the first parole supervision manual. Still, parole supervision was minimal. Jonathan Simon states that few California jurisdictions had resources adequate to the task of individualized parole case management until the 1950s, a time by which all states had adopted parole and probation systems.[35]

BOX 4.1.2

A Correctional History Timeline

900-1400 BCE	The Mosaic Law is written.
451 BCE	The Twelve Tables, Rome's earliest laws, are written.
400 BCE	Athenian law prescribes stoning, compulsory suicide, and exclusion from social communication as punishment for crimes.
1066	William the Conqueror builds the Tower of London to house enemies of the Crown.
1166	The Assize of Clarendon authorizes the construction of English jails.
1180	Henry II orders jails for every English county.
1200	One of France's early prisons is built, the Chatelet.
1470	The use of French prisons increases under Louis XI. The Bastille begins housing prisoners.
1500	Galley servitude increases in France, Italy, and Spain.
1556	The first English prison is constructed at Bridewell.
1615	James I introduces forced transportation as punishment.
1679	The first American prison opens in Nantucket, Massachusetts.
1773	Chaplains and surgeons begin visiting English jails.
1775	Transportation of English prisoners to America ends.
1779	The Penitentiary Act calls for solitary confinement, religious instruction, work, and uniforms in English prisons.
1787	Transportation of English convicts to Australia begins.
1787	The Society for Alleviating the Misery of Public Prisons is founded in Philadelphia.
1790	The Walnut Street Jail is opened in Philadelphia.
1796	New York's first prison opens in Greenwich Village.
1811	Maryland State Penitentiary opens, one of the first "big house" prisons.
1815	Striped clothing is used by prisoners.
1816	Auburn Prison in New York opens.
1825	Ossining (Sing Sing) Prison in New York opens.
1829	Eastern Penitentiary opens in Philadelphia.

(continued)

BOX 4.1.2

A Correctional History Timeline (*Continued*)

1840	Alexander Maconochie begins parole experiments on Norfolk Island near Australia.
1841	John Augustus begins his probation work.
1847	The first American boys reformatory opens in Westborough, Massachusetts.
1850	Parole becomes part of French law.
1853	The English Penal Servitude Act provides for remission of sentences.
1854	The prison marks system begins in Ireland.
1869	English shipment of prisoners to Australia ends.
1870	The Cincinnati Congress convenes, includes first members of the National Prison Association.
1871	*Ruffin v. Commonwealth*—Supreme Court ruling perpetuates "slave of the state" doctrine.
1876	Elmira Reformatory opens in New York.
1878	Edward Savage of Boston becomes America's first paid probation officer.
1895	The first federal penitentiary opens at Fort Leavenworth, Kansas.
1899	The first American prison toilets are installed, in Maryland.
1910	First federal parole law signed.
1929	Federal Bureau of Prisons is set up.
1934	Alcatraz opens in California.
1944	In *Coffin v Reichard,* the "slave of the state" doctrine is overturned.
1964	*Cooperv. Pate* holds that prisoners may sue correctional officials for violation of constitutional rights.
1971	Attica prison riot results in 43 deaths.
1980	New Mexico prison riot results in 33 inmate deaths.
1982	Georgia establishes intensive probation.
1983	Inspired by a "Spiderman" comic strip and the New Mexico prison riot, New Mexico uses electronic monitoring.

(*continued*)

BOX 4.1.2

A Correctional History Timeline (*Continued*)

1983	The Special Alternative Incarceration Unit opens in Georgia, triggering similar "boot camp" prison implementation in other states.
1985	Marion County, Kentucky, opens a private prison.
1992	The Wolds Prison becomes England's first private prison.
1995	Corrections commissioner Ron Jones brings back chain gangs in Alabama.
2006	The adult correctional population grew to nearly 7.2 million offenders under supervision.

Sources: Sam Houston State University. "Chronology of Criminal Justice History"; Newbold, G. (1999). "A Chronology of Correctional History." Journal of Criminal Justice Education *10(1):87–100;* Walker, S. (1998). Popular Justice. *New York: Oxford University Press; Friedman, L.M. (1993).* Crime and Punishment in American History. *New York: Basic Books.*

The "Big House" Era

Robert Johnson calls the early 1900s through the 1950s the era of the "big house."[36] One of the most famous prison movies of this era was *The Big House*, which was released in 1930. Prisons during this era enjoyed some improvements in conditions, but virtually no public interest was directed at them throughout both World Wars (1917–1918 and 1941–1945). Not until a rash of prison riots in the 1950s did public interest awaken. In the meantime, prisons proceeded to function largely outside of public scrutiny; some were run humanely, some were places of shocking cruelty. According to Johnson, "big houses" were "a world populated by people seemingly more dead than alive, shuffling where they once marched, heading nowhere slowly…."[37]

Examples of "big house" prisons included Leavenworth (Kansas), which primarily functioned as a military prison; Alcatraz, San Quentin, and Folsom, all located in California; Sing Sing and Attica in New York; Eastern (Pennsylvania); the Georgia State Prison in Reidsville; Stateville (Illinois); and Jackson (Michigan). All of these facilities, and those like them, were either built, renovated, or expanded during the "big house" era. The "big house" prison still conjures up the image of the stereotypical prison in the eyes of the public.

Rehabilitation: The "Anything Works" Era

The end of World War II brought a renewed sense of optimism in America. Americans believed that because they had conquered the Axis war machines, their ability to solve any problem was practically unlimited. There was a particularly strong belief that American wealth, industrial might, and scientific advancements in technology held the solutions to social problems, including crime. The positivist ideal that criminal behavior could be "cured" through scientific means greatly influenced American corrections throughout the 1950s and 1960s.

It was a time of great experimentation and innovation in the treatment of all forms of deviant or variant behavior. Radical interventions such as electroshock therapy and frontal lobotomies were fairly common methods of dealing with the mentally ill—or with criminals who were thought to be mentally ill. Recall that although sterilization had been used on habitual criminals and mental patients for several decades, Nazi abuses of the practice during World War II turned American opinion against it.

Eventually, more benign forms of intervention became common methods of assisting criminals in institutions and in the community. Religious programs, the bulwark of nineteenth-century penitentiaries, lost significance. Prisons began hiring more counseling staff. Educational, vocational, and substance abuse programs proliferated. Though security had always been the primary focus of the prison, prisons (particularly those in the northeastern United States) gradually began to place more emphasis on secular forms of rehabilitation.

In the 1950s, the disciplines of sociology, psychology, and psychiatry began to influence prison programming. Counselors (sometimes called prison sociologists) were employed to diagnose and classify the inmates according to their problems and security risk. In many states, inmates started their prison term in "classification centers" where they took a multitude of educational, aptitude, and interest tests and medical examinations to determine their needs, aptitudes, and interests.[38] The test results were then used to send the inmate to the appropriate prison, tag him or her with the appropriate custody level (based on violence and escape risk), and assign him or her to the appropriate mix of educational, vocational, and treatment programs.

By the 1960s, some prisons, most notably in California, were fully engaged in offering a wide array of programs. In addition to basic and advanced education, a prisoner might partake in group therapy, transactional analysis, or behavior modification; even transcendental meditation and yoga were offered in some prisons. The "big house" was replaced by the "correctional institution." Psychology replaced religion as the reform agent.[39]

It should be noted that even at the apex of the rehabilitative era, not all prisons displayed the same commitment to reform. For every Vienna, Illinois, there was a Tucker prison farm. Vienna was a federal institution known as the "prison without walls" because the enriched program offerings, including college classes, were available to townspeople as well as inmates. On the other hand, Tucker prison farm was the notorious Arkansas prison farm where inmates were brutalized with the "Tucker telephone," an electrical apparatus that transmitted electric shocks to the inmates' genitals and body parts. The litany of horrors that occurred at this prison farm (and the Cummins farm close by) was the impetus for the federal district court overturning the hands-off doctrine that had insulated prison authorities from court scrutiny for years. The federal court, shocked at the conditions under which prisoners lived, held that if the state chose to run a prison system, then it must run it in a way that met basic Constitutional protections.[40]

Deinstitutionalization and "Nothing Works"

During the 1960s, public opinion once again began to shift. The 1960s witnessed a tremendous proliferation in the amount of crime reported.[41] The 1960s was also a time of tremendous social upheaval in the United States. Civil rights concerns, opposition to American military involvement in Vietnam, the increase in illegal drug use by young people, and a general unease about the safety of walking the streets of American cities were among the problems that contributed to an anti-rehabilitation mindset within the public. Attitudes toward rehabilitation began to sour for other reasons as well. Rehabilitation programs, the indeterminate sentence, and correctional institutions in general came under attack from a number of sources.

BOX 4.1.3

Inmate Lawsuits in American History

The question of what legal rights prison inmates are entitled to is hotly debated by inmates, groups devoted to inmate rights, and civil libertarians on one side, with correctional administrators and state governments frequently on the other side. Most of the legal battles have been fought in the federal courts, and the Supreme Court of the United States has intervened on several occasions in the area of prisoner rights. Until relatively recently, inmates did not fare well in court actions against their keepers. In *Ruffin v. Commonwealth* (1871), the Court ruled that inmates are virtual slaves of the state and have few if any civil rights. Bear in mind that in 1871 the word "slavery" did not have the negative stigma that it does today. Slavery had only been abolished a few years prior. A state that had no objection to enslaving its citizenry would have little objection to treating inmates as slaves.

The situation changed little until the 1960s and 1970s. The civil rights movement, a more liberal public attitude coward treatment of inmates, and the interventionist philosophy

(continued)

BOX 4.1.3

Inmate Lawsuits in American History (*Continued*)

held by some federal judges and members of the U.S. Supreme Court during Earl Warren's and Warren Burger's tenures as Chief Justice, led to many changes in prisons. In 1971, a federal court ruled in *Holt v. Sarver* that the entire Arkansas prison system violated the Eighth Amendment ban on cruel and unusual punishment. Similar rulings followed in Texas, Georgia, and other states. Federally appointed monitors controlled many prisons, especially in the South.

No area seemed off-limits to the courts when it came to inmate lawsuits. Lawsuits filed by inmates proliferated during the 1970s. The Supreme Court ruled in the areas of confinement conditions, access to legal information and counsel, damages against staff members who hurt inmates, due process during disciplinary hearings, racial segregation, use of force by staff, mail privileges, medical care, communication with the press, and freedom of religion. Although inmates lost many more lawsuits than they won, the perception that courts were allowing inmates to run the prisons became widespread.

An anti-prisoner-rights backlash has ensued since the 1980s. Some of the trends that generated inmate litigation in the 1960s, 1970s, and early 1980s reversed themselves in the mid-1980s and 1990s. The U.S. Supreme Court, under the leadership of William Rehnquist, favored a more hands-off doctrine than the Warren and Burger Courts. Federal judges appointed by Presidents Reagan and Bush took a similar hands-off approach to inmate litigation. Public opinion shifted away from sympathy toward inmates.

Nevertheless, the impact of judicial intervention in prisons is still evident today. Prisons are much more humane institutions than they were prior to the 1970s. Staffs are more properly trained, inmates receive better medical care, and institutions and work conditions are more secure and safe than before. Though judicial intervention did not alleviate many of the problems in prisons, and some have argued that courts did more harm than good, it did make a lasting impact.

Sources: Holt v. Sarver, *309 F. Supp. 362 (ED Ark. 1970);* Ruffin v. Commonwealth, *62 Va. (21 Gratt.) 790 (1871).*

One source of discontentment with prisons lay in a growing antagonism toward institutions in general as an avenue for solving social problems. During the 1960s and 1970s, the feeling grew that institutional life was counterproductive in trying to deal with individual problems. Orphanages became increasingly unpopular with the public, thus greater efforts were devoted toward placing children in foster care. The mental hospital also became an increasingly unpopular institution; many mental patients were released and mainstreamed into the communities where they lived.

Likewise, prisons came to be viewed as counterproductive toward reforming criminal behavior. Prisons were viewed as breeding grounds or schools for criminals. The view was that prisons increase one's propensity to be bitter at society and therefore increase one's propensity to commit crime. The answer, as with the mental patients and orphaned or abandoned children, was to try to address the criminal's problems in the community rather than behind prison walls.

A second attack of sorts came from the White House. In 1964, President Lyndon Johnson, fulfilling an election promise to deal with crime, established a Commission to conduct a comprehensive study of crime and the administration of criminal justice in the United States. The result of the Commission's efforts was *The Challenge of Crime in a Free Society*, which was released in 1967. One suggestion made by the Commission was that more use be made of community-based sanctions such as probation and parole, with less reliance on the prison institution. The Commission's feelings mirrored the popular sentiment that prisons were not succeeding at rehabilitating criminals and therefore were not reducing crime.[42]

A third attack on rehabilitation efforts of the time came from a seemingly unlikely source: the Quakers. The Quakers had been advocating penal reform and rehabilitation efforts since the eighteenth century. In fact, the Quakers were very instrumental in the establishment of early American penitentiaries. However, in a 1971 report titled *Struggle for Justice*, the Quakers stated that prisons were failing to rehabilitate inmates. They further charged that the indeterminate sentence, one of the hallmarks of rehabilitation efforts and a necessary ingredient to a parole system, was being abused and manipulated by many prison and parole officials. The indeterminate sentence was merely being used as a tactic to coerce institutional conformity, not as an effective rehabilitation tool.[43]

A fourth element or event in the battle against prison rehabilitation occurred in 1971 at Attica prison in New York. On September 9, 1971, more than 1,300 inmates at Attica rioted and took 40 hostages. The inmates, including both whites and African Americans, issued a list of demands contained in a manifesto titled "To the People of America." They demanded better treatment and listed 15 specific demands, including more religious freedom, sensitivity to religious dietary demands, and better educational programs. The inmates were making many of the same demands that were being made in successful inmate litigation actions across the country.

Over the next four days, the siege continued. Attempts by Tom Wicker of the *New York Times*, Black Panther leader Bobby Seale, and defense attorney William Kunstler to mediate the situation proved fruitless. On September 13, Governor Nelson Rockefeller ordered that the prison be retaken. Prison guards and state police, who appeared to be inadequately trained in riot control, stormed the prison. In the ensuing nine minutes of mayhem, 29 inmates were killed, as were 10 of the hostages; four more people died later.[44]

The carnage was captured on film, and the clear message sent forth was that penal rehabilitation efforts in New York were a monumental failure. Though such a conclusion may have been shortsighted and further study would reveal that some assistance efforts did help some inmates, the visual image of the Attica riot carried much greater weight than anecdotal success stories or dry research studies. The tragedy at Attica was ironic because New York had been a pioneer in prison rehabilitation for well over a century. Since the establishment of the Auburn prison, and since Zebulon Brockway's rehabilitation efforts at Elmira in the nineteenth century, New York had prided itself on its penal rehabilitation efforts.

To make matters worse, a fifth attack on prison rehabilitation came from a research report commissioned by the New York Department of Corrections in the early 1970s. Robert Martinson and a team of researchers were hired to review several rehabilitation programs around the country. They reviewed programs in prison-based and community-based programs. Martinson's report gave a gloomy picture of rehabilitative efforts, especially those that were prison-based.[45] To avoid embarrassment, New York blocked release of the report. When court action on the part of inmates forced the release of Martinson's report in 1974, the phrase "nothing works" became the rallying cry of those who had long opposed prison rehabilitation, and of others who had recently become disenchanted with rehabilitation efforts.

Martinson's stinging indictment of rehabilitation efforts, however, was partly due to his bitterness toward New York officials who had quashed the release of his findings. Moreover, Martinson did not actually state that nothing worked. He was more optimistic about community-based rehabilitation efforts than about those based in prisons. After the initial release of the report and the anti-rehabilitation backlash it generated, Martinson backtracked, stating that the initial report was overly pessimistic about rehabilitation.[46] But the damage had already been done. Martinson's findings were the justification for dismantling many prison rehabilitation programs. The impact of the Martinson report is still evident today. Correctional officials often become nervous when evaluators and researchers use the phrase "what works" in research reports or journal articles.

Though gradual, perhaps the most significant development was a fear among many Americans that the social order had broken down and that an increase in crime was the result of that breakdown. One supposed remedy was a restoration of "law and order" to the streets and a sentiment that criminals should stop being "coddled" in prison and on probation and should start being punished. This sentiment, along with concern about the war in Vietnam, helped Richard Nixon in his successful 1968 presidential campaign. Nixon ran for office on a tough law-and-order campaign pledge. Ironically, Nixon would be forced to resign from office in 1974 because of crimes committed under his leadership.

In the 1970s, a number of events conspired to drive the rehabilitative ethic out of the rhetoric and mission of prisons. The Attica riot in 1971 brought the inside of the prison to the American public. The drama of prisoners holding knives to the throats of hostages played out in living rooms across the nation and did exactly the opposite of what the organizers of the riot intended. Instead of leading to better programs and treatment, and the right to be "treated like men," the public, which had been reasonably supportive of prison programming, turned away. It was hard to reconcile the prisoner wielding a machete and other crudely lethal weapons, with one who needed understanding and educational programs.

Another blow to the rehabilitative mission was the Martinson Report of 1974.[47] This report, paid for and then suppressed by the New York Department of Correction, was a meta-analysis and evaluation of more than 200 prison and correctional programs across the country. Its "sound-byte" result? Nothing worked. Actually, the findings were a little more complicated. Martinson attempted in later years to modify his original harsh stance, but the damage had been done. Politicians interested in reducing the budget bottom line and/or wanting to appear "tough on crime" promoted the ethic of punishment first, and treatment not at all. Some academics also offered their support, promoting a philosophical justification for retribution and even managing to transform the attempt to correct into a moral wrong. Politicians and others continued to argue against rehabilitation, calling it "coddling" inmates, well into the late 1980s and 1990s, but the rehabilitative era was already gasping for air in the late 1970s and comatose by the mid-1980s.

Corrections in the "Get Tough" Era

The movement away from rehabilitation impacted sentencing and penal practices. Among the academicians who recognized and discussed this shift were Andrew von Hirsch, Malcolm Feeley, and Jonathan Simon. Andrew von Hirsch advocated a "just deserts" model of sentencing and penal practice rather than one based on rehabilitation. Like many corrections professionals, von Hirsch has not advocated a total abandonment of offender assistance, nor has he advocated undignified treatment of offenders.[47] Feeley and Simon, in "The New Penology," recognize a shift toward an "insurance-based" model of penology. Under this conceptual model, the emphasis is on neither rehabilitation nor punishment but on accurate prediction, identification, and profiling of criminals. Under the new penology, corrections merely serves as a warehousing, or "waste management" apparatus, for criminals—especially those from the lower economic class.[48]

Todd Clear has stated that America is in the midst of a "penal harm" movement. Believers in "penal harm" advocate tough prison conditions designed to make inmates as miserable as possible. The rationale is partly based on specific deterrence and partly on retribution. If prison conditions are poor enough, inmates will not want to commit the crimes that bring them to prison. At the same time, the public exacts a matter of revenge on criminals. The penal harm idea places little if any emphasis on rehabilitation services, recreation programs, or anything designed to make the inmates' lives more pleasant.[49]

The 1980s witnessed numerous innovations in corrections, but one thing that did not disappear was the reliance on prison as the primary method of dealing with serious lawbreakers. Despite the continued reliance on prisons, corrections agencies across the country (especially in states that incarcerated large numbers of its populations) did at least attempt to devise some alternatives to incarceration. Georgia, which led the nation in the percentage of citizens in prison, pioneered many of these efforts. Other states, including Oklahoma, California, and New Jersey, devised programs designed to divert people from prison. Intensive probation, which had been tried and abandoned in some states two decades prior, was reborn in several states. Electronic monitoring, which had been developed on an experimental basis in the 1960s, soon followed. The boot camp prison was used in Georgia and Oklahoma. Halfway houses, under a variety of names, expanded.

Although these programs received much attention from the media as well as corrections professionals, they served very few offenders. The vast majority of criminal offenders continued to be punished by fines (for minor offenses such as traffic crimes), regular probation (for serious misdemeanors and minor felonies), and prison (for serious felonies). Although the penitentiary had been unheard of as a means of punishment early in America's history, by the 1980s Americans could conceive of no way to deal with serious crimes other than prisons, which have become increasingly expensive to build, staff, operate, and maintain.

In the 1980s, prison administrators struggled with a massive influx of offenders. Incarceration rates soared, prisons met and exceeded their maximum capacity levels, state-sentenced prisoners were held back in jails awaiting space, and then jails filled to capacity and beyond. Prisoners were housed in cafeterias, gyms, tents, and even in ships (harking back to the old barges used in the harbor of London during the 1700s). State legislatures increased prison budgets—doubling, tripling, and then quadrupling the amounts allocated for departments of correction. States went on building binges to meet the ever-expanding numbers. In the frantic attempt to find beds, programs were purely a luxury item. Classification efforts continued, but the decision where to send an inmate depended on space available, not program needs. Thus, the cycle was repeated. Ideals of reform and optimistic beliefs that institutions could change lives were strangled by overcrowding and other problems that drained resources. Once again, punishment became the only promise.

> Some web sites are devoted in whole or in part to the historical aspects of corrections. One is maintained by the New York Correction History Society, www.correctionhistory.org. Some state corrections departments' web sites include brief histories of corrections in that state. The Library of Congress web site, www.loc.gov, includes digital images of prisons and prisoners at various points in American history.

Conclusion

One lesson to be learned from history is that the rhetoric of correctional policy and reform often does not mesh with reality. Politicians and correctional reformers frequently make either well-intentioned or self-serving promises about improving society by changing prisons. Most correctional reforms throughout American history have been aimed at either rehabilitating the criminal or ensuring that crime will be reduced through correctional practices. Although American corrections can claim some successes, the truth is that many correctional practices have done neither. A contemporary example is found in the case of Sheriff Joseph M. Arpaio of Maricopa County, Arizona. Sheriff Arpaio's tough, "no frills" administration of the Maricopa County Jail has earned him the nickname "America's toughest sheriff." Although many people around the country applaud his approach to jail administration, demonstrating a connection between the methods Sheriff Arpaio uses to run the jail and a reduction in crime is difficult. Historically, ruthless jail and prison administration has led to little more than riotous institutions and high recidivism. While get-tough rhetoric associated with corrections can claim little success, liberal-minded rehabilitation attempts cannot claim a large degree of success either. High-minded ideals of improving society through institutional rehabilitation often fail to meet expectations.

Many attempts at prison reform have unintended consequences. The penitentiary, which was originally designed with high religious ideals of repentance, forgiveness, and brotherly love, is now associated with human depravity and cruelty. Rehabilitation, which was designed to assist offenders, has been attacked as either hopeless naiveté put into practice, or as merely another guise for exercising social control over inmate populations.

Another lesson learned from history is that the level of civilization in a society is reflected by the conditions of its prisons. Societies both past and present that are viewed by many Americans as barbarous typically maintain inhumane prisons in which inmates have few civil rights. How will history judge the United States? Despite its shortcomings, American penal efforts, when compared to those of many other countries, may be viewed favorably. Prisoners have more civil rights in American prisons than in many other countries, and prison conditions are much more humane in America than in many other countries. The challenge for the twenty-first century is maintaining a proper balance between the well-being of inmates (i.e., rehabilitation) and ensuring that imprisonment is unpleasant enough to act as a deterrent to crime.

One mistake common to correctional administration is the attempt to shut out outside involvement in the administration of jails and prisons. Many people both inside and outside institutional walls wrongly assume that what goes on inside the prison has no relation to the community and that what goes on in the community has no effect on prisons. The civil rights protests in the streets during the 1960s and similar calls for civil rights in prisons during that time period are evidence that the "out of sight, out of mind" way of thinking about prisons is shortsighted. Just as advocates of community policing emphasize that law enforcement can best succeed with the support of the public, so should correctional administrators and policymakers realize that correctional programming, both institutional and community-based, must have public support to succeed.

[...] [T]he most recent history of corrections is marked by conflicting trends. On the one hand, practices such as mandatory sentencing, three-strikes laws, and life-without-parole sentences are part of the punitive or get-tough trend that has been part of correctional policymaking for the past three decades. However, some penologists argue that effectively administered correctional interventions can make a positive impact on recidivism.[50] [...]

Ethics Focus: What is Barbaric?

History offers examples of practices that were considered acceptable and even praiseworthy at one time but are now considered either barbaric or simply antiquated. One example is the use of punishments like the stocks, where offenders were put on public display to both punish them and deter others from such offenses.

Are we doing anything in the twenty-first century that you think will eventually be considered barbaric or, at best, antiquated? For example, do you think that one day people might consider lethal injection barbaric? Will the idea of locking people up in prisons ever turn into a practice that will appear cruel and unusual or just terribly old-fashioned, or, conversely, will the future provide a primary means of punishment that is so harsh that imprisonment will seem quaint by comparison? What do you think? Discuss.

At the Movies

Frankie and Johnny, 1991.
An ex-con works as a cook in a diner as he tries to readjust to live on the outside after spending years in prison. The support he receives from the diner's owner and staff helps him through the transition.

Brubaker, 1980.
Based upon true events, a new Corrections Commissioner goes undercover as an inmate to see for himself what is really going on in the state prison.

Discussion Questions

1. In what ways has corrections changed since the days of ancient civilizations? Compared to other civilizations, are Americans doing a better or worse job at sanctioning lawbreakers?
2. Compare the corrections systems of the Israelites, the ancient Greeks, and the ancient Romans. List some strengths and weaknesses of those systems.
3. Did America move in the right direction during the deinstitutionalizaton movement? Why or why not?
4. In view of the history of corrections, is the get-tough approach to dealing with offenders proper or misguided? Explain.
5. Describe the differences between the Pennsylvania (separate) system and the New York (congregate) system of prisons.
6. When viewing the history of correctional rehabilitation efforts, do you think those who said "nothing works" were correct? Explain.
7. Some say to ignore history is to be condemned to repeat its mistakes. Do you notice any current practices that seem to ignore the lessons of history?

Further Reading

Morris, N., and D.J. Rothman (1997). *The Oxford History of the Prison: The Practice of Punishment in Western Society.* New York: Oxford University Press.

Walker, S. (1997). *Popular Justice: A History of American Criminal Justice,* 2nd ed. New York: Oxford University Press.

Notes

1. Peters, 1995.
2. Senna and Siegel, 1998.
3. The English government began an even more adventurous project with unwanted petty criminals after the American Revolution. England began shipping convicts to Australia, effectively using the continent and some of its outlying areas as giant penal colonies. This gargantuan penal experiment is chronicled in Robert Hughes's *The Fatal Shore.*
4. Friedman, 1993.
5. Andrews, 1991.
6. Andrews, 1991, 39.
7. Barnes and Teeters, 1951.

8. Rothman, 1971/1990.
9. Durham, 1994.
10. Walker, 1998.
11. Walker, 1998.
12. Durham, 1994; Garland, 1990.
13. Johnson, 1997; Durham, 1994.
14. Beaumont and deTocqueville, 1994, 381.
15. Barnes and Teeters, 1951.
16. Walker, 1998.
17. Hughes, 1986.
18. Conley, 1992.
19. Rothman, 1990.
20. Walker, 1998.
21. Barnes and Teeters, 1951.
22. Walker, 1998.
23. Hughes, 1986.
24. Friedman, 1993.
25. Reichel, 1997, 80–81; Walker, 1980.
26. Sullivan, 1990.
27. Sullivan, 1990.
28. Rotman, 1995.
29. Crouch and Marquart, 1989.
30. Lombroso-Ferrero, 1994.
31. Friedman, 1993, 335.
32. Friedman, 1993, 337.
33. Friedman, 1993, 337.
34. Friedman, 1993, 338.
35. Simon, 1993.
36. Johnson, 1997.
37. Johnson, 1997.
38. Johnson, 1997, 37.
39. Johnson, 1997, 41.
40. Spencer, 1997.
41. It is still unclear whether crime dramatically increased in the 1960s or whether methods of measuring crime improved. The Uniform Crime Reports, started in the 1930s, were largely ignored by most local law enforcement agencies. Many did not bother to keep track of the amount of crime in their jurisdiction. The FBI received increasing participation during the 1960s, which may have accounted for the increase in crime.

42. President's Commission on Law Enforcement and the Administration of Justice, 1967.
43. American Friends Service Committee, 1971.
44. Walker, 1998.
45. Martinson, 1974.
46. Martinson, 1979.
47. von Hirsch, 1976.
48. Feeley and Simon, 1992.
49. Clear, 1994.
50. See Lipsey and Cullen, 2007.

References

Albert, E.M., T.C. Denise and S.P. Peterfreund (1988). *Great Traditions in Ethics,* 6th ed. Belmont, CA: Wadsworth.

American Friends Service Committee (1971). *Struggle for Justice: A Report on Crime and Punishment in America.* New York: Hill and Wang.

Andrews, W. (1991). *Old Time Punishments.* New York: Dorset.

Barnes, H.E., and N.K. Teeters (1951). *New Horizons in Criminology,* 2nd ed. New York: Prentice Hall.

Beaumont, G., and A. Tocqueville (1994). "On the Penitentiary System in the United States and Its Application in France." In J.E. Jacoby (ed.), *Classics of Criminology,* 2nd ed., 372–386. Prospect Heights, IL: Waveland.

Clear, T.R. (1994). *Harm in American Penology.* Albany, NY: SUNY.

Conley, J. (1992). "The Historical Relationship among Punishment, Incarceration and Corrections." In S. Stojkovic and R. Lovell (eds.), *Corrections: An Introduction,* 33–65. Cincinnati: Anderson.

Crouch, B.M., and J.W. Marquart (1989). *An Appeal to Justice.* Austin, TX: University of Texas.

Drapkin, I. (1989). *Crime and Punishment in the Ancient World.* Lexington, MA: Lexington.

Durham, A. (1994). *Crisis and Reform: Current Issues in American Punishment.* Boston: Little, Brown.

Feeley, M.M., and J. Simon (1992). "The New Penology: Notes on the Emerging Strategy of Corrections and Its Implications." *Criminology* 30:449–474.

Freidman, L.M. (1993). *Crime and Punishment in American History.* New York: Basic.

Garland, D. (1990). *Punishment and Modern Society: A Study in Social Theory.* Chicago: University of Chicago Press.

Hughes, R. (1986). *The Fatal Shore: The Epic of Australia's Founding.* New York: Vintage.

Johnson, R. (1997). "Race, Gender, and the American Prison: Historical Observations." In J. Pollock (ed.), *Prisons: Today and Tomorrow,* 26–51. Gaithersburg, MD: Aspen.

Lipsey, M.W., and F.T. Cullen (2007). "The Effectiveness of Correctional Rehabilitation" A Review of Systematic Reviews." *Annual Review of Law and Social Sciences* 3: 297–320.

Lombroso-Ferrero, G. (1994). "Criminal Man." In J.J. Jacoby (ed.), *Classics of Criminology,* 2nd ed., 116–131. Prospect Heights, IL: Waveland.

Martinson, R. (1979). "Symposium on Sentencing: Part II." *Hofstra Law Review* 7:243–258.

Martinson, R. (1974). "What Works? Questions and Answers about Prison Reform." *The Public Interest* 35:22–54.

Peters, E.M. (1995). "Prison Before the Prison: The Ancient and Medieval Worlds." In N. Morris and D.J. Rothman (eds.), *The Oxford History of the Prison*, 3–47. New York: Oxford University.

Pollock, J. (1997). "Rehabilitation Revisited." In J. Pollock (ed.), *Prison: Today and Tomorrow*, pp. 158–208. Gaithersburg, MD: Aspen.

President's Commission on Law Enforcement and the Administration of Justice (1967). *The Challenge of Crime in a Free Society*. Washington, DC: U.S. Government Printing Office.

Reichel, P. (1997). *Corrections*. Minneapolis: West.

Rothman, D.J. (1990). *The Discovery of the Asylum: Social Order and Disorder in the New Republic*. Boston: Little, Brown.

Rotman, E. (1995). "The Failure of Reform: United States, 1865–1965." In N. Morris and D.J. Rothman (eds.), *The Oxford History of the Prison*, 169–198. New York: Oxford University.

Senna, J.J., and L.J. Siegel (1998). *Essentials of Criminal Justice*. Belmont, CA: West/Wadsworth.

Simon, J. (1993). *Poor Discipline: Parole and the Social Control of the Underclass, 1890–1990*. Chicago: University of Chicago.

Souryal, S.S. (1998). *Ethics in Criminal Justice: In Search of the Truth*, 4th ed. Newark, NJ: LexisNexis Matthew Bender.

Spencer, D. (1997). "The Classification of Inmates." In J. Pollock (ed.), *Prison: Today and Tomorrow*, 84–115. Gaithersburg, MD: Aspen.

Stone, W. (1997). "Industry, Agriculture and Education." In J. Pollock (ed.), *Prison: Today and Tomorrow*, 116–157. Gaithersburg, MD: Aspen.

Sullivan, L. (1990). *The Prison Reform Movement: Forlorn Hope*. Boston: Twayne.

von Hirsch, A. (1976). *Doing Justice: The Choice of Punishments*. New York: Hill and Wang.

Walker, S. (1998). *Popular Justice: A History of American Criminal Justice*, 2nd ed. New York: Oxford University.

Walker, S. (1980). *Popular Justice: A History of American Criminal Justice*. New York: Oxford University Press.

Court Cases

Buck v. Bell, 274 U.S. 200 (1927).

Coffin v. Reichard, 143 F.2d 443 (1944).

Cooper v. Pate, 378 U.S. 546 (1964).

Holt v. Sarver, 309 F. Supp. 362 (E.D. Ark. 1970).

Ruffin v. Commonwealth, 62 Va. (21 Gratt) 790 (1871).

Skinner v. Oklahoma, 316 U.S. 535(1942).

READING 4.2

INSTITUTIONAL CORRECTIONS

Carolyn Petrosino

[READING] OUTLINE

KEY TERMS

- Big house
- Community model
- Convict lease system
- New York (congregate) system
- New penology
- Pennsylvania (separate) system
- Security levels
- Supermax facility

A. Introduction

The primary mission of the correctional component of the criminal justice system is to carry out the sentences received by convicted offenders. Sentences can range from probation to short-term jail sentences and fines to lengthy terms of imprisonment, and even the death penalty. Accordingly, there are several different corrections agencies that oversee this objective. Since most convicted offenders are under probation supervision, (more than 50%),[1] probation offices are involved with the bulk of offenders.

However, institutional corrections refers to those facilities designed to detain or imprison offenders who are either awaiting court actions or who have been convicted and sentenced to jail or state or federal prison. Offenders who receive a sentence of up to one year or less typically serve time in a local county jail; longer sentences are typically served in a state prison unless stated otherwise. Those convicted of federal crimes serve time in the federal correctional system, known as the Federal Bureau of Prisons. There are approximately 1,800 state and federal correctional facilities in the United States. Local jails and county facilities outnumber prisons, at approximately 3,100.

Institutional corrections receives a good deal of notoriety due to the startling fact that the United States imprisons more people than any other nation. The Bureau of Justice Statistics reports that as of December 31, 2013, there were 2.2 million people locked up in jails, state, and federal prisons.[2] It is difficult to fully comprehend the meaning of this statistic until it is compared to the incarceration rate of other nations. The International Centre for Prison Studies reports the following data[3] in Table 4.2.1.

TABLE 4.2.1 Incarceration Rate by Nation

Country	**Incarceration rate**
United States	2,217,000
China	1,657,812
Russian Federation	667,546
Brazil	607,730
India	411,992
United Kingdom (England and Wales)	85,743
France	66,761
Germany	61,872
Canada	37,864
United Kingdom (Northern Ireland)	1,715

Why are the numbers as large as they are in the United States? During the 1970s crime in the United States increased significantly. Much has been written about the causes of this rise; some of the major explanations include: the criminal justice system is too soft on criminals and thus does not deter crime; drug trafficking is a growing problem which feeds addictions; and there is simply more opportunities for crime. Conservatives and liberals, both displeased with the justice system but for different reasons, agreed that changes were necessary. The result was the popularity of determinant sentencing policies that would cause more people to be incarcerated for longer periods. Determinant sentencing not only substantially decreased judicial discretion, it also limited the discretion of parole authorities. By definition, determinant sentences are designated by a fixed term that is only reducible by earned "good" time (credit given for good behavior) and time already served before sentencing. Thus, the time of parole release is not subject to the discretion of parole authorities. Examples of determinant sentences include Truth in Sentencing, mandatory sentences for drug possession and or firearms, and Three-Strikes laws. The frequent use of these and other determinant sentencing models helped to exponentially grow the incarceration rate and a corresponding increase in the number of prisons in the United States. Some have referred to this expansion period as the onset of the "prison-industrial complex," which emerged from a "confluence of special interests"[4] comprising political and economic entities. The term *prison-industrial complex* suggests that there were business and profit interests intertwined with the government's crime policy, which incentivized the buildup of prisons throughout the United States for economic gain rather than to effectively addressing crime.

B. The Role of Institutional Corrections in the Criminal Justice System

Jails

Jails play a vital role in institutional corrections. Recall that most crime is primarily defined by jurisdiction and that in every state there are at least two levels of criminal law enforced within the state (that is, state and local). Individuals who violate local laws and are sentenced to terms of 1 year or less will serve their time in the local jail as stated earlier. According to the American Jail Association, there are about 3,100 jails in the United States.[5] Lockups are not the same as a jail. The former is a temporary holding area that is commonly located in and controlled by the local police department, whereas jails are correctional facilities where jail (not state prison) sentences are served. Jails are usually managed and staffed by county sheriff departments or other county correctional personnel. In addition to housing individuals serving shorter sentences, jails provide other functions. Persons who are awaiting various court actions such as bail, arraignment, trial, sentencing, or other hearings are frequently held in jail. Parolees who are arrested and are pending a parole revocation hearing are also held in jail. All of these needs are critical and are integral to the function of the criminal justice system. It is estimated that jails hold 5% of the 2.2 million persons incarcerated.

Cook County Jail in Chicago, Illinois, is reported to be the largest jail in the United States.[6] In 2012 it had an average daily population of more than 9,400.[7] It has an operating budget of $226 million and a staff of 3,800.[8] Besides housing pretrial and sentenced persons, this jail offers an array of offender programs that include an electronic monitoring program, a day reporting center, a prerelease center, a vocational rehabilitative impact center, the women's justice program, and the female furlough program. Of course the average jail has far fewer offenders to house, as well as fewer program options.

Prisons

Prisons are correctional facilities that are designed to hold offenders who are sentenced to terms of incarceration that exceed a year. The number of these prisoners increased from 2012 to 2013[9]. Most states have several prisons to house state prison inmates (see Table 4.2.2). Even though the public may view prisons as places for dangerous criminals, just a little over half of state prison inmates are there for violent crimes. Federal prisons are located in various locations in the United States and are not found in each of the 50 states.

TABLE 4.2.2 Number of prisons by state*

Alabama	15
Arizona	10
California	25
Colorado	23
Delaware	4
Florida	48
Maine	6
Massachusetts	12
Mississippi	14
Texas	50
Vermont	7
Wyoming	3

**State prisons are also referred to as correctional facilities.*
(Source: Adapted from List of U.S. State Prisons. Available at: ***https://en.wikipedia.org/wiki/List_of_United_States_state_prisons****).*

Privatize Facilities and Accountability

What are private prisons? Charles H. Logan defines private prisons as "a place of confinement that is privately owned, operated, or managed under contract by the government," (pg. 292).[10] Private prisons held 8% of the total U.S. prison population at the end of 2013 (Bureau of Justice Statistics, 2014b). There is a good deal of controversy surrounding the use of private facilities. What issues of concern come to your mind? One of the most worrisome aspects is that private prisons are for profit. The corporations that own them have an interest in financial gain from running these facilities. Today there are approximately 18 corporations involved in the business of guarding offenders in private facilities. Where do their profits come from? Housing more inmates? Hiring correctional personnel for lower salaries and benefits? Limiting institutional programs such as health care services and educational/vocational or drug treatment programs? What are the possible consequences from these inadequacies? Other areas of concern include state monitoring and the manner of accountability to government authorities. Finally, is the public safer when offenders are housed in private prisons?

[...]

D. Mass Incarceration

The United States has the dubious distinction of having the highest incarceration rate in the world.[11] It has 751 people in prison or jail for every 100,000 in population. Russia, as a modern industrialized nation, is second, with 627 per 100,000. (China has numbers higher than Russia, but mingled in reported numbers are persons in administrative detention who are held for "reeducation."). The Netherlands' rate is 458 per 100,000.[12] The incarceration rate of other modern nations is much lower: England, 151 per 100,000; Germany, 88 per 100,000; and Japan, 63 per 100,000.[13] The United States has less than 5% of the world's population but almost 25% of the world's prisoners.

Various sociopolitical forces and crime policies facilitated the high level of incarceration found in the United States (see Table 4.2.3). An informative research paper issued by the Sentencing Project identifies factors that have driven incarceration. The most important one is the "get tough on crime" approaches, which utilize harsher sentencing policies. This punitive approach emerged from a number of developments that became apparent during the 1960s and 1970s, as mentioned earlier. Crime increased rather dramatically in the mid- to late 1960s and into the 1970s (see Table 4.2.4). Because the 1970s saw a turn away from rehabilitation efforts in corrections, as well

TABLE 4.2.3 Table of correctional populations by year in the United States[14]

Year	Correctional population
1910	68,735
1930	120,496
1940	165,585
1950	178,128
1960	226,344
1970	198,831
1980	302,377
1990*	745,000[15]
2000*	1,391,261[16]
2010*	1,605,127[17]

(Source: Bureau of Justice Statistics, December 1986.)

TABLE 4.2.4 U.S. crime rates

Year	Total number of reported crimes
1960	3,384,200
1968	6,720,200
1970	8,098,000
1978	11,209,000
1980	13,408,300
1988	13,923,100
1990	14,475,600
1998	12,475,634

(Source: U.S. Crime Rates 1960–2013. Available at: http://www.disastercenter.com/crime/uscrime.htm. Accessed on July 20, 2015.)

as discretionary decision making by criminal justice professionals, policy makers embraced the idea of determinant punishment—lengthy sentences as the means to deal with the problem of crime. The appearance of crack cocaine in the 1980s and the devastating ease of addiction caused a moral panic that stimulated a strong response. Furthermore, crime had become politicized. As a topic, crime was elevated from a local problem to a national concern as interpreted by political candidates vying for national office. Policing strategies were also modified to respond to increased crime. Broken windows policing was introduced in the 1980s. It required police to focus on low-level crimes in an effort to stop the deteriorating neighborhood conditions that invite more serious crime. Additional sentencing models (that is, truth in sentencing, mandatory sentences for drug offenses, three-strikes laws, and so on) caused *more* people to go to jail for *longer* periods of time.

The U.S. incarceration rate was created by policies that were intended to do just that: imprison more offenders for longer periods of time. Perhaps many would view this outcome as evidence of an effective crime policy. But there are additional effects that may not be considered so positive. There is significant racial disparity evident in the effort to forge mass incarceration. The typical inmate is a young African American or Hispanic male with little consistent work history and limited education. According to Austin and Irwin as cited in Pratt (2009), the incarceration rate of minority men is "two to six times higher than Whites"[18] (p. 3). Many of the crimes that are punishable by stiff penalties are those that are primarily committed by poor urban dwellers.

The number of women in prison increased by 646% between 1980 and 2010 and of the 2.2 million persons incarcerated in the United States, 205,000 of them are women.[19] Although their numbers are extremely low, women are incarcerated at a faster rate (1.5 times more) than are men. Oklahoma incarcerates more women per capita than any other state, at 130 per 100,000; and Maine reports the lowest rate (21 per 100,000).

The average incarcerated female is a 20- to 30-year-old African American who also has children, a poor education, minimal work experience, a substance abuse background, and a history of being physically and/or sexually abused.[20] Unlike the typical male criminal, women are often involved as accomplices to a boyfriend or husband who is involved in a criminal lifestyle. Their crimes often involve drug offenses, low-level property crime, prostitution, and other public order crimes, as well as domestic violence–related crimes.

A fact less known is that women enter the U.S. correctional system with more health issues than their male counterparts. Poverty alone brings its own set of health risks. These women often suffer from poor nutrition, hypertension, diabetes, and poor dental and gynecological health. Moreover, mental health problems are more pronounced among incarcerated women. "In 2005, 73% of women in state prisons had mental health problems, compared to 55% of men in state prisons."[21] The challenge for correctional administrators is to provide adequate health care for all inmates but to be particularly aware that incarcerated women are less healthy than nonincarcerated women and have greater and different needs from that of incarcerated men.

E. Questions of Ethics in Corrections

Criminal Justice students who are learning more about institutional corrections and corrections in general, will discover many moral issues that are encountered by corrections personnel. An initial area confronting policymakers and the public is whether it is morally acceptable to spend millions of dollars to incarcerate offenders to the detriment of other public services that rely on tax dollars. For example, it has been reported that up to 75% of imprisonment spending occurs at the state level where dollars are drawn from the general fund—the source for many other public services including health care and education. With prison costs rising dramatically since 1970, what is the effect on the ability of state governments to sufficiently address other public needs? A 2012 report published by California Common Sense announced the following key findings:

- **Corrections' growing slice of the State budget, High Education's shrinking slice.** As California's Department of Correction's share of the State General Fund budget increased steadily through most of the last three decades, higher education's share declined consistently.
- **Corrections inmate population explosion driving higher costs.** Over the last 30 years, the number of people California incarcerates grew more than eight times faster than the general population. Our calculations show that 55% of the increase in the cost of the state prison system between 1980 and 2012 ... can be traced to this rapid growth.

- **Annual salary increases for prison guards, stagnant faculty salaries over last decade.** Whereas prison guard salaries are subject to periods of sustained salary increases, faculty salaries have seen only weak growth over the years, falling in real terms over the past decade.[22]

These findings should not come as a surprise, but it is important for the public to be aware of the repercussions for vigorously pursuing mass incarceration. Of course, the experience of California will be unlike most other states, but perhaps it does serve as the proverbial canary in the coal mine for other states. The greater moral question is whether it is right to not fully fund higher education or public education for the sake of incarcerating thousands.

Another issue involves how accessible prisons are for the family and friends of the incarcerated. We stated earlier that the typical inmate is a Black or Hispanic young man who is from an economically distressed urban community. We also know that strong family ties and connection with one's community are conditions that support reintegration. Yet many prisons are located in hubs that are located far from the social support systems of many inmates. In Florence, Colorado, there is 1 prisoner for every 3 citizens. The county of Fremont, where Florence is located, has 13 prisons,[23] many of which house inmates from states other than Colorado in order to ease overcrowding elsewhere. However, even if inmates are housed in a prison within their own state, they have no control over where they will be sent, which affects the ability for family to visit. If classification committees are able to keep inmates close to the communities where their family reside, would that not be helpful to all parties?

Another example of a moral dilemma involves the use of private prisons. Is it appropriate for the state to contract the supervision, management, and care of convicted persons to private corporations? Private prisons began to appear in the 1980s but caught steam in the 1990s after the Clinton administration restricted the federal workforce budget. It was the Justice Department and the Federal Bureau of Prisons that initially contracted private prisons for detaining illegal immigrants[24] and other categories of prisoners.

Private prisons are provided funds for each prisoner they house. It is clear that it is in the best interest of these facilities to maintain a high number of prisoners. If the administrators of these prisons have a say over how well or how poorly an inmate is adjusting, it is possible that their motivation could include *delaying* release by easily writing up charges. According to Global Research, Corrections Corporation of America (CCA) inmates housed in New Mexico lost "good behavior time" at a rate 8 times higher than those in conventional state prisons. Private prisons benefit from overcrowded state prisons that seek relief by contracting their services. Thus, there is a business interest in mass incarceration. Just as any group seeks to influence policy, private corporations utilize lobbyists to influence legislators. A recent report stated:

> The three main companies have contributed $835,514 to federal candidates and over $6 million to state politicians. They have also spent hundreds of thousands of dollars on direct lobbying efforts. CCA has spent over $900,000 on federal lobbying and GEO spent anywhere from $120,000 to $199,992 in Florida alone during a short three-month span this year.[25]

The final example of a moral issue that we will offer concerns the use of supermax prisons. There is no doubt that secure facilities are needed to keep dangerous individuals away from anyone that they could possible hurt. But is segregation along with isolation the only means to gain safety? As far back as the 1990s, 34 states operated supermax prisons.[26]

As mentioned earlier, inmates held in supermax facilities are in almost total isolation. What are the psychological effects from this condition? We know from history, specifically the Pennsylvania model, that isolation produced destabilization of some offenders. Should we expect any different outcome today? Not enough research has been done in this area. The supermax facility is a black box of sorts in which too little, if anything, is fully understood regarding the impact of this experience. Is this morally right, despite the nature of the inmates subjected to this environment?

F. Conclusion

Institutional corrections has and will continue to be instrumental to the criminal justice system. As long as individuals commit crime and pose too high a risk to serve their sentences in the community, there will be a need for institutional corrections. We have more than 200 years of recorded observations of institutional corrections in the United States. Much has been learned, but clearly there is a long way to go. Some pivotal questions that must be answered include: What should be the primary purpose of corrections? How do we best go about achieving and maintaining it? How do we stay clear of political distractions and pressures and maintain a commitment to the purpose of corrections? Finally, how do correctional agents see the nobility and value in their tasks, maintain their humanity, and remain the utmost professionals in their work? You are students today, but you are also future leaders in criminal justice and corrections. How will you improve corrections in the United States?

Discussion Questions

1. We have seen our correctional system focus on rehabilitation and then on punishment. Which do you think is most effect in responding to crime? Why?

2. Female criminality differs in nature from male criminality. Should men and women therefore be punished differently as a result?
3. How can the correctional system mitigate racial disparities in jails and prisons?

References

American Jail Association. (n.d.) Statistics of note. Retrieved from https://members.aja.org/About/StatisticsOfNote.aspx

Anand, P. (2012). Winners and losers: Corrections and higher education in California. California Common Sense. Retrieved from http://cacs.org/research/winners-and-losers-corrections-and-higher-education-in-california

Austin, J., & Irwin, J. (2012). *It's about time: America's imprisonment binge* (4th ed.). Belmont, CA: Wadsworth.

Avilucea, I. (2015, March 30). Mercer inmate suing county claims sexual assault routinely ignored. *Trentonian*. Retrieved from http://www.trentonian.com/general-news/20150330/mercer-inmate-suing-county-claims-sexual-assault-routinely-ignored

Bureau of Justice Statistics. (1992). Correctional populations in the U.S., 1990. Retrieved from http://www.bjs.gov/content/pub/pdf/cpus90.pdf

Bureau of Justice Statistics. (2010). Correctional populations in the U.S., 2009. Retrieved from http://bjs.gov/content/pub/pdf/cpus09.pdf

Bureau of Justice Statistics. (2011). Correctional populations in the U.S., 2010. Retrieved from http://www.bjs.gov/content/pub/pdf/cpus10.pdf

Bureau of Justice Statistics. (2014a). Correctional populations in the United States, 2013. Retrieved from http://www.bjs.gov/content/pub/pdf/cpus13.pdf

Bureau of Justice Statistics. (2014b). Prisoners in 2013. Retrieved from http://www.bjs.gov/content/pub/pdf/p13.pdf

Bureau of Justice Statistics. (2014c). Survey of sexual violence in adult correctional facilities, 2009–11-statistical tables. Retrieved from http://www.bjs.gov/content/pub/pdf/ssvacf0911st.pdf

Cahalan, M. W. (1986). Historical corrections statistics in the United States, 1850–1987. NCJ-102529, Bureau of Justice Statistics. Retrieved fromhttp://www.bjs.gov/content/pub/pdf/hcsus5084.pdf

Ford, M. (2015, June 8). America's largest mental hospital is a jail. *Atlantic*. Retrieved from http://www.theatlantic.com/politics/archive/2015/06/americas-largest-mental-hospital-is-a-jail/395012

Global Research. (2014). The prison industry in the United States: Big business or a new form of slavery? Retrieved from http://www.globalresearch.ca/the-prison-industry-in-the-united-states-big-business-or-a-new-form-of-slavery/8289

Hallinan, J. T. (2003). *Going up the river.* New York: Random House.

International Centre for Prison Studies. (n.d.a). Highest to lowest prison population total. Retrieved from http://www.prisonstudies.org/highest-to-lowest/prison-population-total?field_region_taxonomy_tid=All&=Apply

International Centre for Prison Studies (n.d.b). *World prison population list* (10th ed.). Retrieved from http://www.prisonstudies.org/sites/default/files/resources/downloads/wppl_10.pdf

Johnson, R. (2002). *Hard time*. Belmont, CA: Wadsworth/Thomson Learning.

Krisberg, B., Marchionna, S., & Hartney, C. (2015). *American corrections: Concepts and controversies* Thousand Oaks, CA: Sage.

Kurki, L., & Morris, N. (2001). The purposes, practices and problems of supermax prisons. *Crime and Justice, 28*, 385–424.

Liptak, A. (2008, April 23). U.S. prison population dwarfs that of other nations. *New York Times*. Retrieved from http://www.nytimes.com/2008/04/23/world/americas/23iht-23prison.12253738.html?pagewanted=all&_r=0

List of U.S. State Prisons. (2010). Retrieved from https://en.wikipedia.org/wiki/List_of_United_States_state_prisons

Mancini, M. J. (1996). *One dies, get another: Convict leasing in the American South, 1866–1928*. Columbia: University of South Carolina Press.

McShane, M. D. (1996). Chain gangs. In M. D. McShane & F. P. Williams (Eds.), *Encyclopedia of American prisons* (pp. 117–144). London: Taylor & Francis.

Moser, W. (2013, April 1. Cook County Jail is America's biggest. *Chicago Magazine*. Retrieved from http://www.chicagomag.com/Chicago-Magazine/The-312/April-2013/Cook-County-Jail-Americas-Biggest-Jail-By-the-Numbers

Olson, D. E. (2013). An examination of admissions, discharges and the population of the Cook County Jail, 2012. Retrieved from http://works.bepress.com/cgi/viewcontent.cgi?article=1016&context=david_e_olson

Pratt, T. C. (2009). *Addicted to incarceration*. Thousand Oaks, CA: Sage.

Sanchez, A. (2011, June 23). Private prisons spend millions on lobbying to put more people in jail. *ThinkProgress*. Retrieved from http://thinkprogress.org/justice/2011/06/23/251363/cca-geogroup-prison-industry

Schlosser, E. (1998, December). The prison-industrial complex. *Atlantic*. Retrieved from http://www.theatlantic.com/magazine/archive/1998/12/the-prison-industrial-complex/304669

Sentencing Project (2012). Incarcerated women. Retrieved from http://www.sentencingproject.org/doc/publications/cc_incarcerated_women_factsheet_sep24sp.pdf

United States Crime Rates 1960–2013. (n.d.). Disaster Center. Retrieved from http://www.disaster-center.com/crime/uscrime.htm

US Department of Justice (2014). Correctional Populations in the United States, 2013. Bureau of Justice Statistics. Retrieved from http://www.bjs.gov/content/pub/pdf/cpus13.pdf

Vyas, A. G. (1991). Book Review: Logan, C. H. (1990). *Private prisons: Cons and pros*. New York: Oxford University Press. *Social Forces, 70*, 1. Pg. 292.

Notes

1. Bureau of Justice Statistics, 2014a.
2. U.S. Department of Justice, 2014.
3. International Centre for Prison Studies, n.d.a.
4. Schlosser, 1998.
5. American Jail Association, n.d.
6. Ford, 2015.
7. Moser, 2013.
8. Olson, 2013.
9. Bureau of Justice Statistics, 2014b.
10. as cited in Vyas, 1991.
11. Austin & Irwin, 2012.
12. International Centre for Prison Studies, n.d.b.
13. Liptak, 2008.
14. Cahalan, 1986.
15. Bureau of Justice Statistics, 1992.
16. Bureau of Justice Statistics, 2010.
17. Bureau of Justice Statistics, 2011.
18. Pratt, 2009.
19. Sentencing Project, 2012.
20. Krisberg, Marchionna, & Hartney, 2015.
21. Krisberg, Marchionna, & Hartney, 2015, p. 293.
22. Anand, 2012.
23. Hallinan, 2003.
24. Global Research, 2014.
25. Sanchez, 2011.
26. Kurki & Morris, 2001.

READING 4.3

PRISONERS AND PRISONER LIFE

John T. Whitehead, Mark Jones, and Michael C. Braswell

[READING] OUTLINE

1. Introduction
2. The Prison Population
3. Prison Adjustment
4. Deprivations of Prison Life
5. Long-Term Inmates
6. Prison Victimization
7. Supermax Prisons
8. Death Row
9. Offender Needs
10. Race in Prison
11. Women in Prison
12. Spiritual Adjustment in Prison
13. Conclusion

What You Need to Know

- More than one-half (52%) of the prisoners in state prisons are in prison for a violent offense, approximately 20 percent are in for a property offense, and another one-fifth are in for a drug offense. More than one-half of federal prisoners are in prison for a drug offense, and less than 10 percent are in for a violent offense.
- All prisoners suffer the deprivations of imprisonment, including loss of freedom, loss of autonomy, and reduced possessions. Some prisoners suffer even more by being sexually victimized in prison.
- At yearend 2006, more than 3,000 offenders were on death row. The year 2006 saw 66 executions, 19 fewer than in 2000.

- Prisoners have problems with both substance abuse and mental illness. Approximately one-half of all prisoners are drug-dependent or have substance abuse problems. The 2004 Survey of Inmates indicated that 56 percent of state inmates, 45 percent of federal prisoners, and 64 percent of jail inmates had a mental health problem.
- Although the percentage of black prisoners has declined, blacks still make up more than 40 percent of state prisoners. Racial tension continues to be a problem in prisons.
- Women make up a little more than 7 percent of prisoners. Women are less violent than men, and their prisons have less violence than men's prisons.

Introduction

[...] [R]eformers like the Quakers thought that prisons would be quiet places where offenders could reflect on their lives as they spent their days praying and working. They thought that prisons would be like monasteries where prisoners would reform. Later prison leaders were not as clearly religious as the Quakers, but they still believed in rehabilitation. In fact, rehabilitation continued as a stated goal of prison life well into the twentieth century. In the last 20 years, however, prisons have emphasized punishment, deterrence, and incapacitation.

Whatever the particular prison philosophy of the day, prisoners adjust and cope. They manage to live their days inside prison walls or fences in ways that allow them to complete their sentences. This [reading] will examine how prisoners cope with the deprivations of prison such as loss of freedom and loss of possessions and security. We will look at long-term inmates and supermax prisons. We will review what is known about victimization in prison, including sexual victimization and victimization by guards. In addition, we will consider some special issues such as death row, women in prison [...], and racial adjustment. We will also discuss some of the problems of probationers and parolees, such as the abuse of alcohol and other drugs.

The Prison Population

At the end of 2006, prisons were bursting at the seams, with 1,570,891 prisoners under federal or state jurisdiction, an increase of 2.8 percent over the number in 2005. The prison population was 93 percent male and 7 percent female. Of state prisoners, it is estimated that 35 percent were white, 38 percent black, 21 percent Hispanic or Latino, 4 percent "other," and 3 percent of two or more races.[1]

In 2004, more than one-half (52%) of the prisoners in state prisons were in prison for a violent offense (murder, manslaughter, rape, other sexual assault, robbery, assault, or other violent crime).[2] One-fifth (21%) were in prison for a property offense (burglary, larceny, motor vehicle theft, fraud, or other property offense), 20 percent were in for a drug offense, and 7 percent were in for a public order offense.[3]

In 2006, the largest group (53%) of federal prisoners were in prison for a drug offense. Less than 10 percent (9.4 %) of federal prisoners were incarcerated for a violent offense. These figures represent a major change compared to 1985, when 28 percent of federal prisoners were in prison for a violent offense, and only 34 percent were incarcerated for a drug offense.[4]

An important concern is the differential incarceration rates for whites and blacks. For males, whites have an incarceration rate of 487 per 100,000 in the population, but blacks have a rate of more than 3,000 per 100,000 in the population, and Hispanics/Latinos have a rate of more than 1,200 per 100,000 in the population. In other words, about one in every 33 black men in the country was a sentenced prisoner in 2006, compared to one in every 205 white men.[5]

As the prison population was increasing, the crime rate was decreasing. For example, the violent crime rate decreased 22.5 percent from 1997 to 2006 and 4.2 percent from 2002 to 2006. (Note: The violent crime rate did increase by 1 percent from 2005 to 2006).[6] Some criminologists argue that this crime drop was at least partially the result of putting more offenders in prison. In other words, some claim a deterrent and incapacitative impact of putting more offenders in prison. Others, however, argue that the crime drop was due to other factors.

> For further statistics on prisons and prisoners, go to www.ojp.usdoj.gov/bjs and look for *Prisoners in 2006*. A more up-to-date report on prison statistics may be available, as this report is issued every year by the Bureau of Justice Statistics.

Are We Imprisoning the Wrong Offenders?

A number of prison critics argue that prisons contain too many offenders who do not need to be incarcerated. These critics argue that we are using too many scarce prison beds for either property offenders or drug offenders. Austin and Irwin, for example, did an ethnographic study of 154 males sentenced to prison in Washington, Nevada, and Illinois. Their interviews with these male offenders led them to conclude that a little more than one-half of the persons being admitted to prison are actually being admitted for petty crimes. These are "crimes with no aggravating features—that is, no significant amount of money, no injury, or any other feature that would cause ordinary citizens to view the crime as particularly serious."[7] Austin and Irwin argue that some crimes generally considered "serious" may not be as serious as they appear. They note a particular robber, for example, who robbed convenience stores with a BB gun tucked in his belt. He showed the gun in his belt to the clerk but did not take it out of his belt or point it at the clerk.

Austin and Irwin are probably correct that not every criminal labeled "dangerous" by offense type is as dangerous or threatening as the name of the offense implies. It seems, however, that these critics may have gone a bit too far. Even if a robber uses only a BB gun and keeps it tucked in his belt, that scenario is filled with the potential for violence. Surely some convenience store clerks would interpret a gun—real, BB, or even toy—as threatening. One possible response is for the clerk to pull a gun from under the counter and shoot the robber. Thus, to dismiss such a robbery situation as not serious or violent is potentially misleading.

It is also noteworthy that approximately 11 percent of the offenders admitted to state prisons each year were convicted of burglary.[8] Although prison critics may label burglary as a "property" crime, many average citizens regard this crime as more serious than other property crimes such as shoplifting. Burglary involves trespass into one's personal space (one's home) and also involves a very real potential for violence. Either the burglar or the victim may have a weapon at hand and resort to using it. Indicating the seriousness with which some people regard burglary is the criminal law allowance in at least one state of deadly force against burglary.[9] Moreover, many burglars are looking for guns.[10] Clearly, there is some probability that stolen guns will be fenced or otherwise transferred to other criminals directly engaged in violent crime. Therefore, while Austin and Irwin may be correct that some "violent" crimes are not as threatening as claimed, it is also correct that some crimes labeled "property" or "nonviolent" crimes may be more threatening than claimed.

Much stronger is the evidence that U.S. prisons, especially federal prisons, house more drug offenders than necessary. Changes in federal sentencing policies have resulted in a dramatic increase in the percentage of federal prisoners convicted of drug crimes. When the costs of incarceration continue to increase, it is imperative to question the wisdom of incarcerating such a high percentage of drug offenders.

Prison Adjustment

Some people claim that prisons today are too easy or comfortable for prisoners. Such objections often follow stories of prisoners being able to watch cable television, attend a concert, or participate in a sports event (such as a baseball game against a team from another prison). In one presidential campaign, for instance, candidate and magazine publisher Malcomb "Steve" Forbes criticized a Connecticut women's prison for being "plush" because it had "airy courtyards," a shuffleboard court, and oak bunk beds (instead of less expensive metal frame beds).[11]

Others contend that prison is too harsh. Some of these critics point to prisons in other countries where sentences are much shorter in length and where housing units resemble college dormitories more than the cell bars and prison walls that many have in mind when they think of a "prison."

Both types of charges may ignore prison reality. Prison life involves many discomforts and problems that the "too soft" critics often forget or do not consider. On the other hand, the "too harsh" critics may not be aware of the adjustments prisoners create to make their lives as comfortable as possible.

Deprivations of Prison Life

Gresham Sykes[12] provides a useful starting point in discussing prison conditions with a list of deprivations that all prisoners experience. The first such deprivation is the deprivation of liberty. Prisoners are deprived of their liberty or freedom. They are locked up and confined. Such confinement may be total: 24-hour lockup in solitary confinement or in a new supermaximum facility. Alternatively, it may be minimal: a federal prisoner may be in a prison camp that has dormitories rather than cells and a painted white line rather than a wall or a fence around the institution. In either case, however, the prisoner is expected to stay within a certain area and may not travel about as a free citizen.

One aspect of confinement that many people forget is that confinement often translates into few visitors. If a prisoner is locked up even 100 miles from home, distance alone may make visits by relatives quite difficult. The prisoner's family may simply not have transportation to the prison.

A second deprivation is that of goods and services. Prisoners are limited in their access to possessions and services. One aspect of this deprivation that is ignored by many critics is that Americans define themselves to a great extent by their possessions. Most are concerned about their clothes, cars, residences, and the "stuff" (as the late comedian George Carlin would say) possessed within their homes and cars. Americans live in a materialistic society and tend to

BOX 4.3.1

Deprivations of Prison Life

- Deprivation of Liberty/Freedom
- Deprivation of Goods and Services
- Deprivation of Autonomy
- Deprivation of Heterosexual Contact
- Deprivation of Security

Source: Sykes, G. (1958). The Society of Captives: A Study of a Maximum Security Prison. *Princeton, NJ: Princeton University Press.*

value having increasingly more and better-quality possessions (e.g., one may be proud of having a late-model car or designer blue jeans or a particular brand of shoes rather than a $15 pair of shoes from a discount store). Prisoners are issued a uniform with no permission for individualizing differences and are allowed only certain things—a few books, magazines, and pictures for their cells. Even necessities may be in short supply. One prison, for example, allowed inmates only two rolls of toilet paper per week (they were able to get more only if they had the money to buy it).

A third deprivation is that of autonomy. Free persons can make all sorts of everyday choices—when to get up, when to go to bed, when to eat, what to eat, when to schedule activities, and when to take some time to relax. Prisoners are regimented. They are told when to get up, when to eat, when to work, when to recreate, and when to go to bed. Their choices are minimal. Sykes contends that part of this regimentation is intended to treat prisoners like children. Adults choose; children are directed. So the message to prisoners is that they are like children who need to be told what to do and when to do it.

A fourth deprivation is that of sexual contact and expression—at least legitimate heterosexual contact. Adults on the outside can engage in sexual activity essentially when and where they choose. Except in rare circumstances, prisoners are forbidden heterosexual contact, let alone intercourse. Prisons are usually same-gender facilities with little or no opposite-sex presence. One exception is conjugal visitation, such as an overnight visitation program at San Quentin in California for prisoners who are legally married. Interestingly, women partners who are not legally married feel discriminated against.[13] (For a discussion of coed prisons, see Box 4.3.2.)

Some homosexual sex does occur in prisons. One study of federal prisoners reported that 12 percent of all federal inmates reported participation in homosexual sexual activity in their current prison. The percentage was higher for those inmates in penitentiaries, as opposed to less secure facilities such as camps.[14] Such homosexual activity, however, is contrary to prison rules and regulations. What is sometimes forgotten is that humans define themselves to a considerable extent by contact with the opposite sex. As anyone who has attended an all-male or all-female college can confirm, the absence of one gender from an environment can lead to behaviors that would not occur when both genders are present.

A fifth deprivation is deprivation of security. Prisons are not always safe places. Many of the offenders are violent; some are disturbed. Many prisoners note that the worst thing about prison is the company they are forced to keep. For example, a recent study of three Ohio prisons showed that about 25 percent of the inmates studied were victimized by either assault or theft during the six months prior to their interviews. Adding robbery, simple assault, and property damage to the definition of victimization increased the victimization percentage to almost one-half (48%).[15] Official statistics showed that in 1997 there were 4,095 inmate assaults on other inmates—1,860 in New York, 1,499 in Texas, and 394 in Ohio.[16]

BOX 4.3.2

Coed Prisons

One suggestion to improve prisons is to offer more coed facilities. Smykla, for example, contends that single-sex imprisonment "exacerbates the sexual abnormality of offenders by fostering development of homosexual and often violent subcultures, ignores the fact that much criminal behavior stems, directly or indirectly, from the absence of healthy relationships with the opposite sex, or the inability to explore problems of sexual identification, impedes postrelease adjustment, engenders continued criminality, and caricaturizes traditional sex-role stereotypes" (Smykla and Houston, 1999:204). Houston, on the other hand, argues that women often do better in segregated environments where they do not fall under the sway of negative male influence and where they may enter programs that are geared to their special needs rather than to male needs. Houston argues that in coed prisons women often enter programs dictated by their walk partner (the term for relationships in such prisons) rather than their own needs. In addition, coed prisons often result in pregnancies and abortions (Smykla and Houston, 1999:215). One woman prisoner noted that she developed some relationships with male inmates at a coed prison that were harmful to her adjustment and rehabilitation (Parker-Jimenez, 1997).

What do you think? Should we attempt to have more coed prisons? Is the debate over coed prisons similar to the debate over single-gender colleges versus coed colleges? How so?

Outside of prison, given adequate resources, one can avoid living in a violent section of a city or town. Prisoners, though, must live in their assigned cells, and their neighbors may be undesirable. (A later section of this [reading] will examine prison victimization in greater detail.)

Guenther has added to Sykes's list of deprivations.[17] One addition is pain involving visits, even visits by spouses. Guenther notes that fellow prisoners or guards can be very callous about such visits, using the occasion to suggest to a prisoner that his wife is free and can be seeing a lover while the prisoner is counting the years until release. Related to this, letters to prisoners from family members are not always pleasant and uplifting. Letters can remind a prisoner of problems back home when he or she has no way to help resolve those problems due to being miles away and unable to intervene. A letter can even include negative comments such as a son expressing anger at his father for things his father (the prisoner) did or failed to do.

Still another problem in prison life is holiday time such as Thanksgiving and Christmas. Guenther notes that prisoners tend to watch television during the holiday season just like the rest of us.[18] Programs and commercials remind the prisoner that he or she is locked up during a time of year when most people are busy planning parties and family gatherings that celebrate the occasion. In plain terms, the prisoner is exposed to a media barrage of images of family togetherness while he or she might experience only a few holiday cards or some canned turkey on Thanksgiving and Christmas. Time passes slowly in prison, and this sense is exacerbated during holidays. In view of this, the Angola prison in Louisiana has volunteers that come in over the holidays to help prevent suicide attempts.

Most prisoners experience these problems or deprivations. This makes it difficult to say that prisons are "country clubs" and are too soft. Even if a prisoner has access to some amenities that might seem luxurious, such as a jogging track or a tennis court, the deprivations of freedom, autonomy, possessions, heterosexual sex, and security are constant reminders that one is being punished for a crime. One prisoner remarked, for example, that even though the dining hall at her federal prison looked more like a popular restaurant chain than a prison cafeteria, it only covered up the repressive atmosphere that was very much the daily reality.[19]

On the other hand, some writers contend that prisons are not as negative as others claim. In a study of the federal prison at Lompoc, California, anthropologist Mark Fleisher notes that many inmates do not see prison as very intimidating or unpleasant:

> Lompoc inmates claim that doing time isn't punishment. They hasten to add that when they're released to the street the high risk of returning to federal or state prison by committing new crimes will not prevent them from doing so. For these high-risk criminals, crime is a way of life and going to prison isn't a burden.... Many inmates say, too, that daily life in Lompoc, and in other prisons where they have done time, is easier, less frustrating, and more secure than life on the street. For many of them, in fact, prison has become their preferred lifestyle....[20]

One problem with this assessment is that it may be out of date. Recent changes in prisons (e.g., cutbacks in opportunities for education) have made the prison experience more negative.[21] The assessment also ignores the negative environments that many prisoners come from and return to after release. A major reason some prisoners say prison is not so bad is that their home environments are problematic. Therefore, their assessment of the prison environment is made in reference to the environment in which they were living, not in comparison to a desirable home environment. If these prisoners had grown up in more positive environments, they probably would not rate prison so highly. More importantly, if they had grown up in more positive surroundings, they might not have become criminals.

One danger in labeling prisons as "not that bad" or as "comfortable" is that such labels can make it easier to build more prisons and to send more offenders to prison. If prison is not so terrible, then there will be less reluctance on the part of prosecutors and judges to send offenders to prison. Perhaps the most accurate way to assess prison environments is to note that they are varied. Some are negative with high rates of victimization. Some, especially federal minimum-security facilities, are probably not that different from many college environments. Some prisons may be "luxurious" or even be places where heroin or other drugs are available to prisoners, but such prisons are often deviant cases in which the administration has lost control of the facility.[22] Many more are in between the extremes.

One of the most detailed and rigorous studies of a prison environment concluded that prison is often a place where not much happens. Prisoners endure the prison environment and come out roughly the same persons they were when they entered. To emphasize this point, the study authors called prison "the deep freeze."[23] The good news about the "deep freeze" nature of prisons is that most prisoners do not come out worse than they entered. The bad news is that most prisoners had either inadequate or maladaptive coping skills when they entered prison. Rather than improving those skills, prison has little or no impact: the offenders come out with the same inadequate or maladaptive skills. This is a major reason for the discouraging recidivism statistics. The released prisoner is no better prepared to avoid crime on release than he or she was on the day he or she entered the facility.

Another prison expert notes that often prisoners try to find niches in prison.[24] Niches are places or situations that provide something that a particular prisoner may be seeking. For example, a prisoner who believes he is weak might seek confinement in a segregated cellblock with 24-hour lockdown so that he feels safe. He wants security and does not want to defend himself against assaults. Other prisoners, though, need more social interaction and would hate such total confinement.

For example, *The New Yorker* magazine once printed a New York state prisoner's diary that shows how the prisoner created such a niche for himself.[25] This prisoner preferred privacy and security and took steps to achieve those goals as much as possible. He managed to get coffee and donuts and other food supplies from a friend in the kitchen so he could eat in his cell instead of in the cafeteria. He managed to get a job with another inmate in the clothing office for inmates being released or going to court. Besides their official chores, their responsibilities apparently centered on making themselves coffee, listening to the radio, and chatting about everyday topics. At night, he would either go to a Jaycees (Junior Chamber of Commerce) meeting or work on art (glass pictures) in his cell, as well as fixing himself an evening meal or snack. In this fashion, he was able to avoid most other inmates and achieve relative privacy and security in an unsafe world.

Carroll offers a more systematic account.[26] He notes that on a typical morning in Rhode Island's largest prison, about 400 inmates out of approximately 700 are working and that about 150 are in educational or therapy programs. Many of these programs are run by private vendors who contract with the state to provide the programs. Minimum-security inmates may be working outside the prison in either public or nonprofit agencies. Rhode Island allows these agencies to purchase inmate labor at $3.00 per hour. Maximum-security inmates are most likely to be idle, as they cannot go outside the prison to work, and security issues may prevent them from going to work or programs inside the prison. (For further discussion of prison labor, see Box 4.3.3.)

In recent years, some states have tried to make prison even more painful. In response to criticisms that prisons are too soft, many prisons have opted to curtail amenities. Thus, some prisons have cut back on such amenities as exercise equipment and cable television. One concern in response is that some helpful amenities, such as college courses, are being eliminated. To discontinue college courses is to take away a major chance for the inmate to improve himself or herself. This lessens

BOX 4.3.3

Prison Labor

Prison labor has a long history, including the infamous road gangs of the South after the Civil War. In one sense, Southern prison camps were an extension of slavery after it had been outlawed.

The ideal of prison labor is a job in which the inmate is involved in activity that contributes to the welfare of the prison or the community. The labor can be service-oriented or product-oriented. Prisoners can make license plates, furniture, and other goods, or do such things as take hotel or airline reservations for national companies.

As has been the case throughout the history of prison labor, a major objection to the practice is its possible effect of taking jobs away from free-world citizens. A privately operated prison in Texas, for example, recently opened a circuit board assembly operation in its prison. The private company running the circuit board operation got a brand new facility for which it pays rent of only $1 per year. It pays its workers minimum wage. The company closed its free-world plant and moved the entire operation to the prison, laying off 150 workers (Erlich, 1997).

Do you think any prison industry should be allowed to exist if it takes jobs away from law-abiding citizens? One problem is that you could argue that every prison job takes a job away from someone outside prison. For example, although the manufacture of license plates has been a long-standing prison industry, it could be set up outside prisons and create jobs for law-abiding citizens. Instead of using prisoners to clean up prisons, outside cleaning companies could be paid to come in and clean up prisons just like they clean other sorts of buildings in the outside world. So do we run prison industries that give prisoners something to do and perhaps a chance to learn responsibility and other positive work habits, or do we keep all prisoners idle? Where do we draw the line of what jobs are appropriate for prisoners and which are not?

the chances of success once released from prison. Another legitimate concern is that amenities reduce the frustration in prison and lessen the odds of violence and riots in prison. A female prisoner noted that exercise equipment helped her to both "pass the time" and to relieve stress.[27] This is important for staff and inmate safety. If "frills" reduce the chances of injury to staff and inmates, they may well be worth the price of some critics calling the prison too soft.

Long-Term Inmates

Long-term inmates can and do perceive prison quite differently than short-term prisoners. Long-term prisoners are more concerned about privacy and stability than are younger, short-term prisoners. All inmates must cope with the loss of relationships with family and friends, but long-term inmates face the additional problem of complete cut-off of relationships. If a prisoner is going to serve only two years, he or she expects to re-establish relationships upon release. A 20-year or life stay makes it likely that many relationships will never be re-established. Likewise, young, short-term prisoners do not have to establish friendships in prison. They can pass time until they are released back to their friends in the community. Long-term prisoners have less in common with younger prisoners, so they may not want to establish ties with them. Establishing relationships with fellow long-term prisoners can be difficult because transfers and releases can end any friendships built.[28]

Program planning for long-term inmates, especially those with extremely long sentences or life sentences, can be very difficult:

> They have too much time to fill, too remote a future, and too little hope. How many correspondence courses can a man take, how many vocational programs can he complete? And what is the point of it all, when the time for learning is indefinite, and the time to apply learning is limited? And ... how can one learn among noisy young inmates playfully filling in a few painless days in a brief interlude of captivity?[29]

Toch offers the suggestion that prisons consider career planning for long-term inmates.[30] By this, he means that prisons take into account the fact that long-term inmates will be in prisons for periods long enough to plan a career. Rather than just teach an inmate how to repair a car and become an auto mechanic, for example, teach him or her how to become first an auto repair instructor's helper and then an auto repair instructor. If an inmate is going to be in prison for a long time, it does not make sense to treat him or her as if he or she is going to be released tomorrow. This career planning and training helps the inmate as well as helping the prison in its service delivery to all inmates.

Prison Victimization

The previous section on prison adjustment discussed the deprivations that prisoners experience, including the deprivation of security. As noted in that section, 25 to almost 50 percent of prisoners report assault, theft, robbery, or property damage in the previous six months of their incarceration. Clearly, prison is a dangerous place. Sexual victimization and victimization by guards are two issues that deserve special attention.

Sexual Victimization

Scientific studies of sexual victimization have been hindered due to the sensitive nature of the subject. Men, especially, are not very forthcoming about their sexual victimization in prison. Many men would rather lie or say nothing about a victimization experience in confinement.

In an early study of sexual victimization in New York, Lockwood found that 28 percent of male inmates had been targets of sexual aggression at least once while in custody. Only one inmate, however, stated that he had been sexually assaulted.[31] In a study of 330 federal male inmates, Nacci and Kane reported that only one inmate had been "raped" (sodomized) in a federal prison. Defining being "targeted" as being forced (or someone had attempted to force them) into performing sexual acts against one's will, they found that only 2 percent of the respondents had been targets of sexual aggression in a federal prison, but that 9 percent had been targets in either a federal or a state prison taken together.[32] In line with Lockwood's study, however, 29 percent of the inmates reported having been "propositioned' for sex.[33] In still another study, of 101 prisoners in Delaware, again only one inmate reported having been raped during his lifetime incarceration history, but five inmates reported that others had attempted to rape them in prison. Respondents reported that they thought the incidence of rape had decreased in prison because of greater guard vigilance and because of fear of contracting HIV/AIDS.[34]

One indication that more than one male prisoner was in fact a victim of sexual victimization in the studies just noted is the recent investigation of Human Rights Watch.[35] Human Rights Watch reported numerous cases of such sexual violence behind bars based on court cases, prison records, and testimony from family members.

In a more recent study, Struckman-Johnson and Struckman-Johnson studied both male and female victimization, thus offering the first direct male-female comparisons. These researchers found that about 20 percent of both genders reported sexual victimization and that, in worst-case incidents, men were much more likely to report that the perpetrator of sexual violence against them was another inmate (72%). Women, however, reported that staff were the perpetrators in 41 percent of the worst-case incidents, and inmates were perpetrators in less than one-half (47%) of the worst-case incidents. Moreover, higher percentages of males answered that their worst-case incident resulted in "oral, vaginal, or anal sex" compared to women (70%

of the men, compared to 29% of the women). Finally, more than one-half of the male prisoners reported an incident classified as rape compared to less than one-third (28%) of the women. The research indicated that women are often concerned about inappropriate touching as well as more serious acts of sexual victimization and that staff are often perceived as problematic in women's prisons.[36]

For further statistics on sexual victimization in prison, go to www.ojp.usdoj.gov/bjs and find the Bureau of Justice Statistics report titled *Sexual Victimization in State and Federal Prisons Reported by Inmates, 2007*. You can find, for example, the 10 prisons with the highest victimization prevalence and the six prisons with the lowest prevalence.

Prior research has indicated a number of correlates of male victimization. Specifically, victimization is related to the following characteristics: young, small size, physically weak, white, homosexual, first offender, having so-called "feminine characteristics" such as hair or voice tone, lack of assertiveness or aggression, shyness, lacking "street smarts," or a record that includes a sexual offense against a minor.[37]

The seriousness of the problem was highlighted by the Prison Rape Elimination Act, enacted in 2003. This Act has prompted a federally sponsored investigation into the issue, including the first national survey of prison inmates concerning sexual victimization. This survey found that 2.1 percent of prisoners reported an incident involving another inmate, 2.9 percent reported an incident involving staff, and 0.5 percent reported having been sexually victimized by both other inmates and staff. While the overall prevalence of sexual victimization was approximately 4.5 percent, some prisons had rates as high as 13 to 15 percent.[38]

Based on the sensitive nature of this topic and the difficulty of conducting research about it, we will never have a completely accurate picture of the extent of sexual victimization in prison. It is clear, however, that some victimization does occur and that prison authorities need to take steps to prevent as much victimization as possible.

Victimization by Guards

The victimization of prisoners by guards is covered in depth [...]. Here we simply note that it is a problem of prison life.[39] Jerome Washington was a prisoner in the state of New York. His prison stories recount several guard actions against prisoners that could be considered forms of victimization. For example, on one New Year's Eve night, a 21-year-old prisoner was gang-raped in the bathhouse while a guard smoked a cigarette and "took his time responding to the screams that [were] soon gagged away with a bar of prison soap."[40] On one occasion, a prisoner befriended a pigeon, and a guard responded by killing the bird and cutting out the head, heart, wings, and legs. When the prisoner complained to the guard captain, the captain threatened the prisoner with 30 days in the hole (solitary confinement) for violating the rule against pets. Still another prisoner was allegedly beaten to death. When the prison doctor refused to sign the death certificate, a prison official had to drive 25 miles to find a doctor who would sign a death certificate attesting that the prisoner had hanged himself. These stories, although not proven true, suggest that guards do engage in behaviors that range from insensitive to inhumane and that on some occasions they escape accountability for such actions.

AP Photo/via St. Louis Post Dispatch, HO

This video image shows a prisoner with a broken ankle apparently being dragged from his cell at a detention facility in Texas. Missouri prisoners housed in rented cells as part of a lease agreement with Texas made claims of abuse, sparking an investigation into possible civil rights violations.

As noted above, Struckman-Johnson and Struckman-Johnson found that 20 percent of Midwestern women prisoners reported being sexually victimized and that staff were the perpetrators in 41 percent of the worst-case victimizations.[41] Similarly, Rathbone's research on women prisoners in Massachusetts found that guards frequently victimized women prisoners or pressured them into so-called consensual sex.[42]

It is difficult to obtain accurate data. Guard victimization of prisoners is criminal, and guards are reluctant to divulge such information. Prisoners, especially women prisoners, may be so afraid and powerless that they are reluctant to report any victimization. It is safe to conclude that victimization occurs at some times in some prisons. The complete extent of such victimization will never be known exactly.

Summary on Prison Life and Victimization

We have now looked at the conditions of daily life in prison and at the special problems of prisoner victimization by fellow prisoners and guards. One must remember that prisons vary. Some are relatively problem-free, some are problem-ridden, and some are in between these extremes. With this qualification in mind, a key question persists: What do prisoners (many of whom have committed horrible crimes and thus may not deserve much) deserve from society while they are in prison?

One prison expert, John Conrad, argues that the "undeserving" deserve safety, lawfulness, industriousness, and hope.[43] Safety and lawfulness go together. If the inmates and guards are following the laws and rules, there will be a minimum of assaults and other victimizations in prison. Conrad defines industriousness as "a full day of work at jobs that are worth doing and [getting] paid accordingly."[44] By hope, he means that the prisoners have some confidence that things can get better. Educational and vocational programs allow prisoners such a sense of hope.

To those who would argue that even these four factors are too much, Conrad contends that denying safety, lawfulness, industriousness, and hope will have disastrous consequences:

> If there is only a system in which prisoners are interchangeable units, that system will degenerate into pernicious anarchy in which terror imposes its own values. No criminal is so undeserving as to deserve consignment to such a condition. I have seen such prisons.... The society that maintains them deserves what it gets.[45]

Supermax Prisons

A recent development in prisons is the supermax (or maxi-maxi or administrative segregation) facility. Intended for the "worst of the worst" offenders, these prisons are designed for prisoners who have broken the rules in a regular prison (perhaps by assaulting other prisoners or guards). These prisons are designed to maximize security and surveillance. Guard booths are constructed so that visual and auditory monitoring of every cell is easy. Prisoners may be fed through a slot in the door, forbidden to speak with other prisoners or to have pictures of family members in their cells, or kept in their cells 23 hours a day and allowed out only into an exercise "cage" where they have a few square yards to walk. Two examples of supermax prisons are Pelican Bay in California and the Federal Penitentiary at Marion, Illinois. A recent estimate put the number of prisoners in these facilities at approximately 25,000 inmates.[46]

One disturbing element of supermax prisons is the sensory deprivation experienced by prisoners. This deprivation was considered so severe in Indiana that it sparked an inquiry from Amnesty International, a class action lawsuit by the Indiana Civil Liberties Union, and a 37-day hunger protest from the prisoners.[47]

Psychological research indicates that sensory deprivation leads to increased symptoms of psychological trauma and disturbance. Nine of 10 supermax prisoners reported anxiety compared to 4.5 persons out of 10 in the general population. Eighty-four percent of supermax prisoners reported lethargy, and 77 percent reported depression, compared to 17 percent and 23.5 percent, respectively, for populations outside prison.[48] In Colorado, testing revealed that prisons with administrative segregation had a disproportionately high rate of prisoners with mental health needs and more prisoners with personality disorders.[49] On the other hand, some inmates do actually volunteer for supermax confinement due to fear of injury, a desire to be alone rather than share a cell, or as a way to get out of a work assignment.[50]

Another problem is that inmates may not receive appropriate mental health services. In Pelican Bay, for example, in 1990, one master's degree-level psychologist was responsible for the care of 3,500 prisoners. Prisoners needing psychiatric treatment were literally bussed to another prison (Vacaville) and back if they needed more than the counselor could provide at Pelican Bay.[51]

Prison officials argue that prisoners in supermax facilities have proven how difficult they are to manage in a traditional prison and that their rule violations in traditional settings justify the drastic measures in the supermax prisons.

There is little empirical evidence proving that supermax prisons are effective. A study of the opening of supermax prisons in three states did not find any reduction in the levels of inmate-on-inmate violence in those jurisdictions.[52] In addition, some correctional officers report greater job dissatisfaction where no interaction is allowed with inmates.

Death Row

At the end of 2006, 3,228 offenders were on death row, 17 fewer than at yearend 2005. The year 2006 saw 66 executions, 19 fewer than in 2000. California led the nation with 656 death row inmates, followed by Texas (391), Florida (374), and Pennsylvania (219).[53] [...]

After interviewing 35 men on Alabama's death row, Johnson concluded that life on death row often involved two "deaths": the death from the execution itself and the extra "death" of living on death row.[54] The prisoner's time on death row is marked by anticipation of death in the electric chair (which was the method of execution in Alabama at the time of the study) and by a dulling, meaningless routine. At the time of the research, death row inmates spent most of their time in their cells and had little to do but read, listen to the radio, and chat with the men in adjoining cells. Thus,

> For further statistics on the death penalty, go to the web site of the Death Penalty Information Center to find their Death Penalty Fact Sheet at www.deathpenaltyinfo.org.

> Many condemned prisoners lead palpably empty lives. They feel isolated and lonely. Visits are scarce or nonexistent. Exercise provides little relief, and may become, instead a burdensome departure from inactivity. Alone and uncared for, some condemned prisoners are consumed by apathy, emerging as stuporous, inert figures who do little more than survive each day.[55]

Further, Johnson contends that guards create death anxiety by such means as taking every newly arrived inmate on a tour of the execution chamber and taunting them whenever the electric chair needs to be tested.

The aptly titled book *Welcome to Hell*[56] contains letters of death row prisoners documenting problems such as noise, vermin, annoying fellow prisoners, unappetizing and insect-laden meals, deprivation of privacy and human contact, and lack of cleansers to clean one's cell.

However, there are some indications that death row is not always as stupefying as Johnson found in Alabama. In some states, death row prisoners work just like other prisoners. For example, Tennessee death row inmates entered data into computers for a state agency and Texas death row inmates were employed in prison industries just like other inmates. One Texas inmate was even able to sell his artwork over the Internet. As the book and movie *Dead Man Walking* showed, Louisiana allows its death row prisoners to meet with spiritual advisors, such as Sister Helen Prejean, who can help the inmate prepare spiritually for death.[57] Going even further, Missouri has "mainstreamed" death-eligible prisoners, that is, mixed them in with the general prison population.[58]

There are conflicting pieces of information. While Johnson's study of one death row paints a disturbing picture of mind-deadening inactivity and guard behavior that approaches psychological torture and a collection of inmate letters details numerous problems, it nevertheless appears that some prisons' inmates are working and appear to be treated humanely. Research is needed to obtain a more complete picture of the current status of death rows across the nation.

Offender Needs

Offenders are multi-problem individuals. It is likely that many street criminals will have such problems as below-average intelligence, less than a high school education, a history of alcohol and other drug abuse, few (if any) job skills, and a lack of family attachments. In addition, a number of offenders have children for whom they are legally responsible, mental or emotional difficulties, and/or a history of abuse in their childhoods. The approximately one-half of prisoners that are African-American face the problems that confront all blacks in the United States: prejudice and discrimination. Whether on probation or in prison, the typical offender has one or more of these needs.

Alcohol-Drug History

Offenders often have alcohol and other drug problems. The 2004 Survey of Inmates in State and Federal Correctional Facilities showed that more than one-half (56%) of state prisoners had used illegal drugs in the month before their offense, one-third (32%) had used an illegal drug at the time of their offense, and more than one-half (53%) were dependent on or were abusing drugs. The percentages for federal prisoners were just slightly lower. Fifty percent of federal prisoners had used illegal drugs in the month before their offense, 22 percent used illegal drugs at the time of their offense, 26 percent used alcohol at the time of their offense, and 45 percent reported being drug-dependent or that they were abusing drugs.[59] After admission to prison, more than 40 percent of prisoners who used drugs in the month before their offense had participated in drug treatment or programs.[60] (For information on the drug problems of probationers, see a later section of this [reading].)

In their study of armed robbers in St. Louis, Wright and Decker noted that two-thirds (40 of 59) of their respondents who told them what they did with their money used the money for gambling or alcohol or other drugs. The researchers concluded that giving robbers money would not end their need to steal but instead would just "set off a round of drinking and drug taking that would plunge them deeper into financial desperation and thereby *increase* their lawbreaking" (emphasis in original).[61]

Mental Health Needs

The 2004 Survey of Inmates shows that 56 percent of state inmates, 45 percent of federal prisoners, and 64 percent of jail inmates had a mental health problem. These percentages were higher for women than for men. For example, approximately three-quarters of female inmates in state prisons and jails had mental health problems.[62] More than one-third of state prisoners and one in six jail inmates with a mental problem had received treatment after admission.[63] (See Box 4.3.4 for information about the related problem of prisoner suicide. [...])

Educational attainment was also a problem. Forty percent of state prisoners and more than one-fourth (26.5%) of federal prisoners had not finished high school. About another one-fourth of prisoners had a General Equivalency Diploma (GED) instead of a regular high school diploma.[64]

Prison Responses to Prisoner Needs

[...] [O]ne, one current trend in corrections is punitiveness. Part of this punitive trend is an unwillingness to address prisoner needs. For example, programs offering college courses and degrees to inmates are now considered by many to be "coddling." Counseling programs are considered unnecessary "frills." All that is considered necessary is a punishment regime. There are many people who consider Angola State Penitentiary in Louisiana to be an ideal prison because it sends most of its prisoners to work in agricultural fields that are actually part of the prison complex.

Prisons like Angola do keep prisoners busy. In that sense, they are probably better than prisons that do little to combat idleness. In fact, it could even be argued that legitimate labor such as farm labor at Angola is more humane than forced idleness that does nothing to uplift the human spirit and encourages such negative outcomes as boredom, depression, and even riots.

BOX 4.3.4

Suicide in Prison

According to the most recent available data, 168 inmates in state prisons and 314 jail inmates nationwide committed suicide in 2002. Both numbers are about the same as the numbers for 2001. Suicides accounted for 5.8 percent of state prison inmate deaths, and almost one-third of local jail inmate deaths (Mumola, 2005).

When standardized to comparable proportions according to gender, age, and race in the whole United States, the prison suicide rate, 14 suicides per 100,000 inmates, is lower than the resident population rate of 18 suicides per 100,000 United States residents. Even after standardization, however, the jail suicide rate—47 suicides per every 100,000 jail inmates—is considerably higher than the national resident rate (again, 18 suicides per 100,000 residents) (Mumola, 2005).

Risk factors include alcohol and other drug problems, a history of previous suicide or self-injury attempts, and previous self-injury in custody. Hanging at night is the frequent mode, with slightly disproportionate numbers taking place on weekends and in the early phases of custody. "The most common emotion in suicides is hopelessness or helplessness, intense anguish, or 'ennui'" (Liebling, 1999:297–298).

Liebling argues that it is helpful to distinguish three distinct profiles of suicides in prison: life or long-sentence prisoners, psychiatrically ill prisoners, and poor copers. Each group has its own motivation and features. Poor copers constitute the highest proportion of prison suicides, accounting for about 30 to 45 percent of prison suicides. In general, though, prison suicide attempters had important coping problems. Many felt less able to pass time in their cells and thus were especially vulnerable to committing suicide (Liebling, 1999).

Suggested interventions include transfer to a shared cell, courses on coping and problem-solving skills, and psychological support. Prisoner support in the form of listener schemes or "buddy" schemes has been used in both Great Britain and the United States (Liebling, 1999).

A problem with the contemporary trend toward eliminating amenities and so-called frills is that farm labor or its equivalent does little or nothing to deal with the real needs that offenders have. When a man leaves Angola, he may know something about farming sugar cane, which could possibly help him get a job and stay out of crime, but more than likely, he will go back to an urban environment (in Louisiana, this would be in New Orleans or Baton Rouge) where there will be no opportunity to farm. Without an adequate education or vocational skills appropriate for his urban home environment, and without treatment for any substance abuse problems he might have, the prisoner will be much more likely to recidivate. Even a factory job in prison may not provide much in the way of vocational training. The job might be available in prison because the wages are extremely low—below prevailing market rates—and if the prison labor were not available the manufacturer would probably take the operation to a third-world country for a similar below-market wage rate.[65]

Offering substance abuse treatment, college courses, or job training programs in prison may seem to make prison too soft because such programs detract from the punitive character of prisons. Perhaps it is reasonable to say that prisoners can get into treatment or college courses or vocational programs after prison. However, a critical opportunity may be missed by taking such an approach. Offering substance abuse treatment and educational and vocational programs in prison may be "coddling" society more than the inmates. It may help inmates to avoid criminal activity after release, thereby insulating society from such criminal activity.

Lack of treatment could also translate into a constitutional violation. California's lack of mental health treatment, for example, occasioned Magistrate-Judge John F. Moulds of the Eastern District of California court to describe the system as inflicting cruel and unusual punishment, contrary to the Eighth Amendment. For example, a report found that California prison over-relied on medication and did not use proper monitoring of such medications.[66]

Race in Prison

Until about 30 years ago, blacks were a minority in America's prisons. Whites dominated the prisons numerically and in terms of power. From then until the year 2000, there was a dramatic increase in the number of blacks in prison, and then a decline among black prisoners between 2000 and 2006. Overall, African Americans, male and female, make up approximately 40 percent of the prisoner population (41.6%) under state jurisdiction, and Hispanic or Latino persons make up approximately 20 percent.[67]

There has been little research on the interaction of black inmates and white inmates in prisons today, and most of the research that does exist is dated. Despite the lack of current studies, it is obvious that racial tension is a key aspect of current prison life.

One of the basic issues concerning race in prison is the perception that the criminal justice system discriminates unfairly in law enforcement and sentencing, resulting in the disproportionate number of blacks in prison. One writer argues that the "war on crime" is simply a disguise for a war on his race:

> It's respectable to tar and feather criminals, to advocate locking them up and throwing away the key. It's not racist to be against crime, even though the archetypical criminal in the media and the public imagination almost always wears "Willie" Horton's [a black criminal's] face. Gradually, "urban" and "ghetto" have become code words for terrible places where only blacks reside. Prison is rapidly being re-classified in the same segregated fashion.[68]

Criminologists debate the extent to which race unfairly enters in as a factor in arrest, prosecution, and sentencing decisions. Many African-American prisoners conclude that racism is a prominent factor and, as a result, come to prison with resentment. That resentment affects their daily interactions with both prisoners and guards. Prison officials must deal with this issue every day.

Women in Prison

Women still represent only a small percentage—approximately 7.2 percent—of the prison population, but their numbers have been increasing.[69] In 1980, women made up 4.1 percent of the prison population and in 1990 made up 5.7 percent.[70] The many important differences between women's and men's prisons are addressed fully in [...]. Here we simply note a few important points about women in prison.

First, there are fewer women's prisons than men's prisons. There may be only one or two women's prisons in a state, and because of this, women prisoners may have to serve their sentences at greater distances from their homes than males who have more prisons available to them. This may make it difficult for women prisoners to have visitors as frequently as they would like.

Women are typically less violent and aggressive than men, and thus their prisons provide more of a sense of security than do men's prisons and female prisoners can be less fearful of assaults than male prisoners. However, women's prisons can include minor violence[71] and sexual abuse of prisoners by guards [...], and they may be more nitpicking in rule enforcement. Society still has somewhat of a double standard for behavior. Women are expected to be more obedient and docile than men. What might pass in a men's prison as normal behavior might be cited as a rule violation in a women's prison. Guards will cite women for improper language or jostling, behaviors ignored by guards in male prisons.

Women's prisons may look more appealing than men's prisons. The cells or dormitory areas often look less like stark cellblocks than men's. However, also stemming from societal notions about appropriate gender roles, educational and vocational programs in women's prisons are often more limited. Cosmetology and food service might be the main vocational training programs in a women's prison whereas such options as auto mechanics and television repair might be available for male prisoners. Part of the problem with women's prisons is that the smaller number of prisoners means that less money is allocated for women's prisons, including training programs, than for men's prisons.

As we can see, there is a mixture of elements that makes women's prisons better than men's prisons in some respects and worse in others. They have less serious violence and probably look better to the uninformed eye, but they can also be rather harsh in terms of strict rule enforcement based on societal expectations of gender-appropriate behavior. A woman prisoner may not fear a physical assault but she may well fear a guard citing her for a rule violation for what many would consider relatively harmless language or behavior. Few programs exist for the myriad of problems facing women, such as unemployment or underemployment, drug addiction, unresolved issues relating to childhood sexual and physical abuse, and difficulties associated with being a mother in prison.

Spiritual Adjustment in Prison

If spiritual adjustment is mentioned in connection with prison life, usually this refers to the provision of chaplains and official religious services. Traditional religious services and chaplains are helpful for prisoners as they attempt to adjust to the pains of imprisonment and as they try to change their lives while inside in preparation for release. A relatively recent development is faith-based programming and even some faith-based prisons, including two in Florida.

Faith-based prison initiatives are based on the premise that religion can be a powerful force for change. The hope is that offering faith-based programs to prisoners will help them to re-orient their lives to positive values and goals. Recall that [...] America's prisons were founded by religious people such as the Quakers who wanted to reform criminals with religion.

Research is being conducted on the effectiveness of contemporary faith-based programs. One problem with the research is that prisoners who volunteer for such programs are motivated individuals, so any evaluation of a program must take into account the positive motivation of such prisoners and distinguish any effect of the program from the effect of having motivated subjects. A related point is that faith-based programs need to be compared to nonreligious programs that are high-quality programs. Because a great deal of effort appears to be going into faith-based programs, it would be unfair to compare them to mediocre or less substantial nonreligious programs.

Some critics worry that faith-based initiatives may divert resources from traditional, non-faith-based programs such as educational and vocational programs. These critics caution that many prisoners have significant problems that need to be addressed. There is even concern that some states want to reduce the number of state-paid chaplains and replace them with faith-based volunteers.[72]

Another issue is providing access to all religions, not just Christianity. Perhaps more important than providing access to all religions, however, is providing access to the spiritual in whatever guise the prisoner may pursue it. Jean Harris, notorious for killing Dr. Herman Tarnower (the creator of the "Scarsdale Diet") served 12 years in New York's Bedford Hills Correctional Facility for women. She found meaning by reading Viktor Frankl's account of his suffering in a Nazi concentration camp and was inspired by his decision during the Holocaust that "he, and not they, would decide how he would react to what they did to him."[73] Such a simple thing as reading helped Harris come to grips with her life behind bars. Just as prisons need to offer education and vocational training programs, there should be opportunities for prisoners to do what they can do to make their lives as meaningful as possible despite the fact of their incarceration.

> Go to www.humankindness.org to learn more about the Human Kindness Foundation, the Prison Ashram Project, and the writings of Bo Lozoff.

Bo Lozoff has been doing prison ministry work for about a quarter of a century. He teaches prisoners how to meditate and do other spiritual practices including spiritual reading. He is eclectic and uses the sacred texts and teachers of Christianity, Judaism, Hinduism, Islam, Buddhism, and other religions to help prisoners develop the spiritual dimension of their lives. In addition to going to prisons, he also prints a newsletter and has written several books that he offers to prisoners at no charge.

Some prisons offer life skills programs such as moral reconation therapy, a cognitive-behavioral treatment for offenders that is intended to raise moral reasoning.[74] Offering such programs is one possible approach. For many inmates, however, it may not be a particular program that awakens in them the desire to find deeper meaning in their lives; it may simply be a guard or prison counselor who takes an interest in them and shows by his or her actions that there can be meaning in the inmate's life. To paraphrase one prison authority, the example of one guard or counselor who shows by example that he or she is in touch with a deeper dimension of life and that he or she cares for the prisoners encountered every day may be worth more than any life skills program costing hundreds of thousands of dollars.[75] (For more about religion in prison, see Box 4.3.5.)

BOX 4.3.5

Some Findings on Faith-Based Prison Programs

Research on the ability of faith-based programs to reduce recidivism has produced some interesting results. Five studies that all promoted Christianity as a way to reduce recidivism failed to do so. However, a program that involved prison chaplains and faith-based volunteers connecting high-risk sex offenders with a community support group of faith-based persons who wanted to help offenders did reduce recidivism by about one-third. A possible inference from this is that the effective program used the principles of effective correctional treatment such as focusing on criminogenic needs (O'Connor, Duncan, and Quillard, 2006), while the other programs did not use those principles. A second point is that faith-based programs may be more effective in helping prisoners cope with the many losses (deprivations) of prison life and thereby help them to counteract the dehumanizing tendencies of prisons than in reducing recidivism (Clear et al., 2000). A third lesson is that perhaps the government's concern for reducing recidivism, while completely legitimate, is quite distinct from religion's interest in saving one's soul. As Hewitt argues, "Rebirth is only the start of learning about grace and how faith may work in one's life. Although the inmate has accepted forgiveness and begins to walk down the path of change, it could be years before there is sufficient clarity in his or her salvation to notice measurable change in behaviour [such as reduced recidivism]" (Hewitt, 2006: 554). Both faith-based programming and research on such programs are still relatively new. Current research should be reporting additional findings in the next few years.

What do you think? Is it essential that faith-based programs reduce recidivism? Or is it enough that we think that faith-based programs are affecting prisoners spiritually and that it may take years for that spiritual change to show results?

Sources: O'Connor, T.P., J. Duncan, and F. Quillard (2006). "Criminology and Religion: The Shape of an Authentic Dialogue." Criminology & Public Policy *5:559-570. Clear, T.R., P.L. Hardy-man, B. Stout, K. Lucken, and H.R. Dammer (2000). "The Value of Religion in Prison: An Inmate Perspective."* Journal of Contemporary Criminal Justice *16: 53–74. Hewitt, J.D. (2006). "Having Faith in Faith-Based Prison Programs."* Criminology & Public Policy *5:551–558.*

Conclusion

This [reading] has looked at prisoners and prison life. We have seen that some criticize prison life for being too soft while others argue that it is too harsh. The current trend is to remove some of the amenities of prison life and return prisons to more Spartan circumstances. Prison victimization was also discussed, including both sexual assaults and victimization of prisoners by guards. Often those who criticize prisons for being too soft neglect to consider the problems of prison adjustment. The issues of death row prisoners, race in prison, supermax prisons, and women in prison were examined. The issues covered in this [reading] show that prison life is difficult in many ways and can have long-term effects on prisoners. Those effects continue in other areas, especially on the release experience.

[...] [W]e will devote additional attention to women prisoners, correctional officers, juvenile correctional interventions, special populations, and the administration and management of correctional institutions. [...]

Ethics Focus: How Far Should We Go in Protecting Inmates from Each Other?

Consider the following situation:

You are a correctional officer at a maximum-security prison. Recently, an inmate who was considered a bully and sexual predator was raped in the cellblock shower by four other inmates. The victim had himself participated in several previous sexual assaults on younger or weaker inmates. You heard about this assault through the prison grapevine and had confirmed that it had taken place through some reliable sources. The victim had not come forward and more than likely would not. Some of the other officers had indicated that if anyone ever deserved such an assault, it was the inmate in question. In addition, an investigation would require a lot of paperwork and a lot of your time.

What should you do?

At the Movies

The Farm: Life Inside Angola Prison, 1998.
This is a documentary about Angola, the Louisiana State Penitentiary. One highlight of this film is the segment that filmed an actual parole hearing that indicates to everyone except the three parole board members hearing the case that the prisoner requesting parole did not in fact commit the rape for which he was convicted.

The Shawshank Redemption, 1994.
This movie is about a wrongly imprisoned prisoner and a corrupt warden and how both get justice in the end.

Discussion Questions

1. A friend learns you are taking this corrections course and studying prisons. She remarks that "those prisoners have it made and should be put to work more and suffer more for the crimes they committed." Keeping Sykes's deprivations of prison life in mind and noting statistics on sexual victimization, how would you respond?
2. Discuss victimization in prison. How and to what extent do prisoners victimize other prisoners? How do guards victimize prisoners?
3. What is life like on death row? What would a humane death row look like?
4. What do prisoners deserve? Even though offenders may have injured others, what does society owe prisoners?
5. Imagine you are the commissioner of corrections in a state that has only one prison for males. What would your prison be like? What amenities would you provide for prisoners? What would a typical day's schedule be like? Justify your ideal prison.
6. How far should society go to help parolees or prisoners who have completed their sentences? When a prisoner leaves prison, what does society owe that offender as he or she tries to readjust to life outside of prison?

Further Reading

Bergner, D. (1998). *God of the Rodeo: The Quest for Redemption in Louisiana's Prison*. New York: Ballantine Books.

Carceral, K.C. (2006). *Prison, Inc.: A Convict Exposes Life Inside a Private Prison*. New York: New York University Press.

Lozoff, B. (1985). *We're All Doing Time: A Guide for Getting Free*. Durham, NC: Human Kindness Foundation.

Ross, J.I., and S.C. Richards (2002). *Behind Bars: Surviving Prison*. Indianapolis: Alpha.

Notes

1. Sabol, Couture, and Harrison, 2007. For periodically updated statistics, consult the Bureau of Justice Statistics, available at http://www.ojp/usdoj.gov/bjs/
2. Sabol, Couture, and Harrison, 2007.
3. Sabol, Couture, and Harrison, 2007.
4. Sabol, Couture, and Harrison, 2007.
5. Sabol, Couture, and Harrison, 2007.

6. FBI, Uniform Crime Reports, Crime in the United States, 2006.
7. Austin and Irwin, 2001, 26.
8. Austin and Irwin, 2001.
9. See, e.g., Alabama Code, 13A-3-23.
10. Wright and Decker, 1994.
11. Forbes, 1994.
12. Sykes, 1958.
13. Comfort et al., 2005.
14. Nacci and Kane, 1983.
15. Wooldredge, 1998.
16. U.S. Department of Justice, 1998.
17. Guenther, 1978.
18. Guenther, 1978.
19. Parker-Jimenez, 1997.
20. Fleisher, 1989, 131.
21. Austin and Irwin, 2001.
22. Carroll, 1998.
23. Zamble and Porporino, 1988.
24. Toch, 1977.
25. Sheehan, 1977.
26. Carroll, 1998.
27. Parker-Jimenez, 1997.
28. Flanagan, 1995.
29. Toch, 1995, 246.
30. Toch, 1995.
31. Lockwood, 1980.
32. Nacci and Kane, 1983.
33. Nacci and Kane, 1983.
34. Saum et al., 1995.
35. Human Rights Watch, 2001.
36. Struckman-Johnson and Struckman-Johnson, 2006.
37. Human Rights Watch, 2001.
38. Beck and Harrison, 2007.
39. Marquart, 1986.
40. Washington, 1994, 72.
41. Struckman-Johnson and Struckman-Johnson, 2006.
42. Rathbone, 2006.
43. Conrad, 1982.

44. Conrad, 1982.
45. Conrad, 1982, 329.
46. Pizzaro and Narag, 2008.
47. Larson, 1993.
48. Haney, 2003.
49. O'Keefe, 2008.
50. Pizzaro and Narag, 2008.
51. Specter, 1994.
52. Pizzaro and Narag, 2008.
53. *Capital Punishment, 2006*—Statistical Tables. Available at http://www.ojp.usdoj.gov.
54. Johnson, 1998.
55. Johnson, 1998.
56. Arriens, 1997.
57. Prejean, 1993.
58. Cunningham et al., 2005.
59. Mumola and Karberg, 2006.
60. Mumola and Karberg, 2006.
61. Wright and Decker, 1997, 59-60.
62. James and Glaze, 2006.
63. James and Glaze, 2006.
64. Harlow, 2003.
65. Erlich, 1997.
66. Specter, 1994.
67. Sabol, Couture, and Harrison, 2007.
68. Wideman, 1995, 503.
69. Sabol, Couture, and Harrison, 2007
70. Beck et al., 2000.
71. Bottoms, 1999.
72. O'Connor et al., 2006.
73. Anderson, 1995.
74. Finn, 1998.
75. Lozoff and Braswell, 1989.

References

Alabama Code, 13A-3-23.

Anderson, G.M. (1995). "Women and Criminal Justice: An Interview with Jean Harris." *America* 172 (March 18, 1995):10–17.

Arriens, J. (ed.) (1997). *Welcome to Hell: Letters and Writings from Death Row*. Boston: Northeastern University Press.

Austin, J., and J. Irwin (2001). *It's About Time: America's Imprisonment Binge*, 3rd ed. Belmont, CA: Wadsworth.

Beck, A.J., T.P. Bonczar, P.M. Ditton, D.K. Gilliard, L.E. Glaze, C.W. Harlow, C.J. Mumola, T.L. Snell, J.J. Stephan, and J.W. Wilson (2000). "Correctional Populations in the United States, 1997." *Bureau of Justice Statistics Bulletin*. Washington, DC: U.S. Government Printing Office.

Beck, A.J., and P.M. Harrison (2007). "Sexual Victimization in State and Federal Prisons Reported by Inmates, 2007." *Bureau of Justice Statistics Bulletin*. Washington, DC: U.S. Government Printing Office.

Bottoms, A.E. (1999). "Interpersonal Violence and Social Order in Prisons." In M. Tonry and J. Petersilia (eds.), *Prisons*, 205–281. Chicago: University of Chicago Press.

Capital Punishment, 2006—Statistical Tables. Available at http://www.ojp.usdoj.gov

Carroll, L. (1998). *Lawful Order: A Case Study of Correctional Crisis and Reform*. New York: Garland.

Comfort, M., O. Grinstead, K. McCartney, P. Bourgois, and K. Knight (2005). "'You Can't Do Nothing in this Damn Place": Sex and Intimacy among Couples with an Incarcerated Male Partner." *Journal of Sex Research* 42(1):3–12.

Conrad, J.P. (1982). "What Do the Undeserving Deserve?" In R. Johnson and H. Toch (eds.), *The Pains of Imprisonment*, 313–330. Beverly Hills: Sage.

Cunningham, M.D., T.J. Reidy, and J.R. Sorensen (2005). "Is Death Row Obsolete: A Decade of Mainstreaming Death-Sentenced Inmates in Missouri." *Behavioral Sciences and the Law* 23:307–320.

Erlich, R. (1997). "Inmate Labor May Not Be Beneficial." In C.P. Cozic (ed.), *America's Prisons: Opposing Viewpoints*, 102–110. San Diego: Greenhaven Press.

Federal Bureau of Investigation (FBI) (2007). *Uniform Crime Reports, Crime in the United States, 2006*. Available at www.fbi.gov/ucr/cius2006/

Finn, P. (1998). "The Delaware Department of Correction Life Skills Program." *Bureau of Justice Statistics Bulletin*. Washington, DC: U.S. Government Printing Office.

Flanagan, T.J. (1995). "Correctional Policy and the Long-Term Prisoner." In *Long-Term Imprisonment: Policy, Science, and Correctional Practice*, 249–257. T.J. Flanagan (ed.), Thousand Oaks, CA: Sage.

Fleisher, M.S. (1989). *Warehousing Violence*. Newbury Park, CA: Sage.

Forbes, S. (1994). "Can You Believe This?" *Forbes* 154 (3):21.

Guenther, A. (1978). "The Impact of Confinement." In N. Johnston and L.D. Savitz (eds.), *Justice and Corrections*, 596–603. New York: John Wiley & Sons.

Haney, C. (2003). "Mental Health Issues in Long-Term Solitary and 'Supermax' Confinement." *Crime & Delinquency* 49:124–156.

Harlow, C.W. (2003). "Education and Correctional Populations." *Bureau of Justice Statistics Special Report*. Washington, DC: U.S. Government Printing Office.

Human Rights Watch (2001). "No Escape: Male Rape in U.S. Prisons." Available at http://www.hrw.org/reports/2001/prison/report4.html

James, D.J., and L.E. Glaze (2006). "Mental Health Problems of Prison and Jail Inmates." *Bureau of Justice Statistics Special Report*. Washington, DC: U.S. Government Printing Office.

Johnson, R. (1989). *Condemned to Die: Life under Sentence of Death*. Prospect Height, IL: Waveland.

Larson, J.K. (1993). "Society Behind Bars: Race, Rights and Religion." *The Christian Century* 110 (32):1123.

Liebling, A. (1999). "Prison Suicide and Prisoner Coping." In M. Tonry and J. Petersilia (eds.), *Prisons*, 283–359. Chicago: University of Chicago Press.

Lockwood, D. (1980). *Prison Sexual Violence*. New York: Elsevier.

Lozoff, B., and M. Braswell (1989). *Inner Corrections: Finding Peace and Peace Making*. Cincinnati: Anderson.

Maguire, K., and A.L. Pastore (eds.) (1999). *Sourcebook of Criminal Justice Statistics 1998*. Washington, DC: U.S. Department of Justice.

Maitland, A.S., and R.D. Sluder (1996). "Victimization in Prisons: A Study of Factors Related to the General Well-Being of Youthful Inmates." *Federal Probation* 60 (2):24–31.

Marquart, J.W. (1986). "Prison Guards and the Use of Physical Coercion as a Mechanism of Prisoner Control." *Criminology* 24:347–366.

Mumola, C.J. (1999). "Substance Abuse and Treatment, State and Federal Prisoners, 1997." *Bureau of Justice Statistics Special Report*. Washington, DC: U.S. Government Printing Office.

Mumola, C.J. (2005). "Suicide and Homicide in State Prisons and Local Jails." *Bureau of Justice Statistics Bulletin*. Washington, DC: U.S. Government Printing Office.

Mumola, C.J., and J.C. Karberg (2006). "Drug Use and Dependence, State and Federal Prisoners, 2004." *Bureau of Justice Statistics Bulletin*. Washington, DC: U.S. Government Printing Office.

Nacci, P.L., and T.R. Kane (1983). "The Incidence of Sex and Sexual Aggression in Federal Prisons." *Federal Probation* 47 (4):31–36.

O'Connor, T.P., J. Duncan, and R. Quillard (2006). "Criminology and Religion: The Shape of an Authentic Dialogue." *Criminology & Public Policy* 5:559–570.

O'Keefe, M.L. (2008). "Administrative Segregation From Within: A Corrections Perspective." *The Prison Journal* 88:123–143.

Parker-Jimenez, J. (1997). "An Offender's Experience with the Criminal Justice System." *Federal Probation* 61 (1):47–52.

Pizzaro, J.M., and R.E. Narag (2008). "Supermax Prisons: What We Know, What We Do Not Know, and Where We Are Going." *The Prison Journal* 88:23–42.

Prejean, H. (1993). *Dead Man Walking: An Eyewitness Account of the Death Penalty in the United States*. New York: Vintage Books.

Rathbone, C. (2006). *A World Apart: Women, Prison, and Life Behind Bars.* New York: Random House Trade Paperbacks.

Sabol, W.J, H. Couture, and P.M. Harrison (2007). "Prisoners in 2006." *Bureau of Justice Statistics Bulletin*. Washington, DC: U.S. Government Printing Office.

Saum, C.A., H.L. Surratt, J.A. Inciardi, and J. Bennett (1995). "Sex in Prison: Exploring the Myths and Realities." *The Prison Journal* 75:413–430.

Sheehan, S. (1977). "Annals of Crime." *The New Yorker*, October 31, 1977:48–55.

Smykla, J.O., and J. Houston (1999). "Coed Prison: Should We Try It (Again)?" In C.B. Fields (ed.), *Controversial Issues in Corrections*, 203–218. Boston: Allyn & Bacon.

Snell, T.L., and L.M. Maruschak (2002). "Capital Punishment 2001." *Bureau of Justice Statistics Bulletin*. Washington, DC: U.S. Government Printing Office.

Specter, D. (1994). "Cruel and Unusual Punishment of the Mentally Ill in California's Prisons: A Case Study of a Class Action Suit." *Social Justice* 21:109–117.

Struckman-Johnson, C., and D. Struckman-Johnson (2006). "A Comparison of Sexual Coercion Experiences Reported by Men and Women in Prison," *Journal of Interpersonal Violence* 21:1591–1615.

Sykes, G. (1958). *The Society of Captives: A Study of a Maximum Security Prison.* Princeton, NJ: Princeton University Press.

Toch, H. (1995). "The Long-Term Inmate as a Long-Term Problem." In T.J. Flanagan (ed.), *Long-Term Imprisonment: Policy, Science, and Correctional Practice*, 245–248. Thousand Oaks, CA: Sage.

Toch. H. (1977). *Living in Prison: The Ecology of Survival.* New York: Free Press.

U.S. Department of Justice (1998). *State Efforts to Manage Violent Long-Term Offenders*. Washington, DC: U.S. Department of Justice.

Washington, J. (1994). *Iron House: Stories from the Yard.* New York: Random House.

Wideman, J.E. (1995). "Doing Time, Marking Race (Incarceration and Racism)." *The Nation*, October 30, 1995, 503.

Wooldredge, J.D. (1998). "Inmate Lifestyles and Opportunities for Victimization." *Journal of Research in Crime and Delinquency* 35:480–502.

Wright, R.T., and S.H. Decker (1997). *Armed Robbers in Action: Stickups and Street Culture*. Boston: Northeastern University Press.

Wright, R.T., and S.H. Decker (1994). *Burglars on the Job: Streetlife and Residential Break-Ins*. Boston: Northeastern University Press.

Zamble, E., and F.J. Porporino (1988). *Coping, Behavior, and Adaptation in Prison Inmates*. New York: Springer-Verlag.

DISCUSSION QUESTIONS

1. The Progressive Era was consequential to our understanding of punishment. Describe the ways in which punishment was reimagined as a consequence of the Progressive Era, and the factors that supported this reimagination.

2. The 1990s are often described as an era of "mass incarceration" in the American criminal justice system. Describe why this time period is referred to in this way. Identify the shifts in American culture and crime that pushed American penal strategies in this direction.
3. Adjusting to prison life is an expectedly difficult processes, particularly for those with no prior experience navigating the word of institutional corrections. Identify and describe the factors associated with prison and jail settings that make acclamation to prison life so challenging.

Ingram Content Group UK Ltd.
Milton Keynes UK
UKHW030055150623
423482UK00007B/185

9 781793 539021